LITERACY IN TRADITIONAL SOCIETIES

LITERACY IN TRADITIONAL SOCIETIES

EDITED BY

JACK GOODY

CAMBRIDGE
AT THE UNIVERSITY PRESS
1968

Published by the Syndics of the Cambridge University Press
Bentley House, 200 Euston Road, London N.W. 1
American Branch: 32 East 57th Street, New York, N.Y. 10022

Library of Congress Catalogue Card Number: 69-10427

Standard Book Number: 521 07345 6

Printed in Great Britain
at the University Printing House, Cambridge
(Brooke Crutchley, University Printer)

TO M.I.F., M.J.C.H. AND I.P.W.

CONTENTS

ACKNOWLEDGEMENTS

I am indebted to the editor of *Comparative Studies in Society and History* for permission to reprint the paper by Watt and myself (pp. 27–68), which first appeared in vol. v, no. 3 (April 1963), pp. 304–45; and also to the editor of the *Bijdragen Tot de Taal-, Land- en Volkenkunde* for permission to reprint the paper by M. Meggitt first published in vol. CXXIII (April 1967), pp. 71–82.

INTRODUCTION

by JACK GOODY

THE TECHNOLOGY OF THE INTELLECT

Considering the importance of writing over the past 5,000 years, and the profound effects it has on the lives of each and all, surprisingly little attention has been given to the way in which it has influenced the social life of mankind. Studies of writing tend to be histories of the development of scripts, while literary scholars concentrate upon the content rather than the implications of communicative acts. And while post-war interest has directed attention to the influence of changing communications on society, most writers have been concerned with later developments such as printing, radio and television.[1]

It is especially surprising that so little interest in literacy—and the means of communication generally—has been shown by social scientists. Those working in 'advanced' societies have taken the existence of writing for granted and have therefore tended to overlook its enabling effects on, for example, the organization of dispersed parties, sects and kin. On the other hand, social anthropologists have thought of their discipline as being primarily concerned with 'preliterate', 'primitive', or 'tribal' societies and have generally looked upon writing (where it existed) simply as an 'intrusive' element. But even where writers are specifically investigating the differences between 'simple' and 'advanced' societies, peoples, mentalities, etc., they have neglected to examine the implications of the very feature which is so often used to define the range of societies with which they claim to be dealing, namely, the presence or absence of writing.

The importance of writing lies in its creating a new medium of communication between men. Its essential service is to objectify speech, to provide language with a material correlative, a set of visible signs. In this material form speech can be transmitted over space and preserved over time; what people say and think can be rescued from the transitoriness of oral communication.

[1] See in particular the somewhat extravagant work by Marshall McLuhan, formerly of Toronto, which elaborates on themes developed also at Toronto by Innis (see p. 56 n. 1) and later by E. A. Havelock (whose *Preface to Plato* appeared in 1963) and others; an appraisal of the work of Innis, McLuhan and the Toronto school has recently been made by Carey (1967) and by Compton (*New American Review*, no. 2, New American Library, New York, 1968, pp. 77–94). The work of Innis and Havelock influenced the paper that Watt and I wrote (pp. 27 ff. below), but our more concrete interest in the subject arose from the wartime deprivation of written matter we experienced in different parts of the world and our sojourn amongst non-literate, illiterate or semi-literate peoples.

The range of human intercourse can now be greatly extended both in time and in space. The potentialities of this new instrument of communication can affect the gamut of human activity, political, economic, legal and religious. In the administrative sphere, complex bureaucratic organizations are directly dependent upon writing for the organization of their activities, especially financial. It provides a reliable method for transmitting information between the centre and the periphery, and hence mitigates the fissive tendencies of large empires.[1] While censuses and taxes feature in non-literate states such as Ashanti and Dahomey, and the use of tallies and counters is widely attested, the efficiency of these operations is greatly increased by the use of simple literate techniques. So, too, in the organization of long-distance trade and of estate agriculture: it is writing that assists the calculation of the profit and the loss.

In the sphere of religion, it is significant that the religions of conversion, the excluding religions, are all religions of the book. In the non-literate societies of Africa, at any rate, magico-religious activity is singularly eclectic in that shrines and cults move easily from place to place. The literate religions, with their fixed point of reference, their special modes of supernatural communication, are less tolerant of change. When this occurs, it tends to do so in sudden shifts, through the rise of heresies or 'movements of reform' that often take the shape of a return to the book—or to its 'true' interpretation.

But if literate religions are in some ways less flexible, they are also more universalistic and in this sense more 'ethical'. The very fact that they represent systems to which other men and nations can, indeed should, be converted means that their prescriptions for right-doing cannot be set in too particularistic a mould. In other words, the myths they recount, the rites they perform, the rules they promote need have no specific relationship with any particular social structure with which they are associated and in some respects (as with the preferred marriage to the father's brother's daughter that so often accompanies the introduction of Islam) may significantly change the social organization of the converted. At the same time, the congregation of worshippers extends outside the clan, tribe or nation and, at least in Christianity and Islam, becomes a quasi-kingroup, all the members of which are 'brothers'.[2] The existence of this 'brotherhood' tends in turn to weaken the strength of primary kinship ties, as Christ himself insisted when he said, 'For whosoever shall do the will of

[1] I have not elaborated upon the specific uses of literacy because they are considered in a more concrete form in the work of the contributors. Both Gough and Bloch refer to writing in relation to the organization of the state.

[2] In the recent civil war in Nigeria (1967), General Gowon denied that this was a battle of Muslims against Christians. 'If it was,' he said, 'I would be fighting on the other side.'

God, the same is my brother, and my sister, and mother' (Mark iii. 35). And, again, 'I am come to set a man at variance against his father...' (Matthew x. 35). Thus literate religions tend to be more 'salvationist'; they place greater emphasis on individual paths to righteousness. Though this difference is one of degree, it does link up with the 'individualizing' tendency of a literate technology and an elaborate division of labour that is discussed later (p. 62).

The legal implications of literacy are closely tied up with the features of politics and religion already mentioned. A universalistic legal system provides a framework within which commerce can develop, and at the same time a mode of settling disputes within the multi-ethnic communities that trading tends to produce.[1]

These are some of the uses of writing that affect social organization. But writing is not a monolithic entity, an undifferentiated skill; its potentialities depend upon the kind of system that obtains in any particular society.

In the first place, there are variations in the materials used which have important implications. The administrative possibilities of paper are greater than those of stone or baked clay. More importantly, there are very significant differences in the graphic form. The greater the use that is made of the phonetic principle, the more flexible the system of signs. With the coming of the alphabet, speech itself can be transcribed. Its simplicity allows a large proportion of the society to master the technique. Demotic literacy becomes possible. And the fundamental implications of this were suggested in the earlier paper, reprinted in this volume, in which Watt and I considered the special case of classical Greece, where alphabetic literacy first emerged, and in which we tried to relate certain aspects of the Greek achievement to this breakthrough in technology.

The discussion of the role of literacy in Greece owes much to E. A. Havelock, and our comments require some qualification in the light of his more recent work. In the *Preface to Plato* (1963: ix) he calls into question 'the whole assumption that early Greek thought was occupied with metaphysics at all, or was capable of using a vocabulary suitable for such a purpose'. He points out that we know the thoughts of early Greek thinkers only from sources already influenced by Aristotle (Cherniss 1935; McDiarmid 1953). The Pre-Socratics themselves were living in a period still adjusting to the conditions of a possible future literacy and wrote in the formulaic style characteristic of oral composition (Parry 1930; Lord 1960). They were 'essentially oral thinkers, prophets of the concrete linked by habit to the past, and to forms of expression which were also forms of

[1] See Wilks' essay for a discussion of this point.

experience' (Havelock: x). It was only by the time of Plato that the language had changed sufficiently to express new ideas, which he sees generated by changes in the technology of the intellect, or what he calls 'the technology of preserved communication' (Havelock: xi)—more simply, communications technology.

I stress this point in order to make it clear that our original argument was not phrased in terms of technological determinism; it attempted to review the liberating effects of changes in this technology. The article should perhaps have been entitled the 'implications' rather than the 'consequences' of literacy, but it seemed unnecessary to insist (more than we did) that other factors could militate against the realization of its potentiality for change. In the study of behaviour there are few, if any, 'sufficient causes'; we are interested in the potentialities of literate communication.

Many problems arise out of the suggestions we made concerning the functions of literacy, and some of these are raised by the studies that follow. The most general is one that affects a large number of societies, in Asia and elsewhere, that were the recipients, though not the inventors, of alphabetic literacy. The Semitic alphabet diffused widely over the world, throughout the Eurasian continent up to the borders of China, in parts of the Pacific, through circum-Saharan Africa and down the east coast to Madagascar. But nowhere was the impact as radical as it had been in classical Greece. Indeed the kind of situation which so often arose elsewhere seems more akin to the 'restricted literacy' that characterized pre-alphabetic scripts (see below, p. 36). In other words, the potentialities of the medium were not exploited to anything like the same extent.

The reasons behind this situation are many, and not easy to unravel. But one way of tackling the problem is to explore the 'ethnography' of literacy in 'traditional' or pre-industrial societies, to analyse in detail the uses made of writing in a particular social setting, to approach the question from the standpoint not so much of the library scholar but of the fieldworker with experience of the concrete context of written communication. This is what we have tried to do in the essays that follow.

Such an attempt seemed desirable on a number of grounds. Sociologists, we noted, have generally taken their field of study to be the advanced literate societies, while social anthropologists have mainly concentrated upon 'simple' structures, the 'elementary forms' of religion or kinship, 'premonetary economics', 'primitive', 'exotic', 'unsophisticated', 'practical' or preliterate societies. But, at least during the past 2,000 years, the vast majority of the peoples of the world (most of Eurasia and much of Africa) have lived in neither kind of situation, but in cultures which were influenced in some degree by the circulation of the written word, by the presence of groups or individuals who could read and write. They lived on the margins of literacy, though this is a fact that many observers have tended to ignore. Yet, if our assumptions about the role of writing and literacy were even partially right, then the societies of south-east Asia or the western Sudan require an analytic treatment different from that given to an Australian tribe. Let me put the point in a more direct way. In the study of the Dogon 'cosmology', the 'zodiacal' system takes on a somewhat different picture when one recalls that they live within a short distance of the Islamic centre of Mopti, and within some 150 miles of Timbuktu, the home of the medieval 'University' of Sankore (Dubois 1897); that some at least of the inhabitants claim descent from the 'Mande', a people who include many of the main transmitters of Islamic learning in west Africa; and that part at least of this learning consisted of the complicated compendia of magical squares, charms, etc. compiled in north Africa by Al-Būnī and others in the fourteenth century; and that these compendia were themselves based upon a Middle-Eastern tradition that influenced the Jewish Cabala, Eastern astrology and European magic. We cannot expect to find the same close fit between religion and society that sociologists often perceive in non-literate cultures when the reference point is not some locally derived myth subject to the homeostatic processes of the oral tradition but a virtually indestructible document belonging to one of the great world (i.e. literate) religions.

It is clear that even if one's attention is centred only upon village life, there are large areas of the world where the fact of writing and the existence of the book have to be taken into account, even in discussing 'traditional' societies. It is also clear that, for the study of institutions which have been profoundly influenced by writing (and of these religion is perhaps the most important), the village community is a legitimate isolate only in a limited sense. To suppose that one can study Burmese Buddhism in the same framework as one studies Australian totemism is to commit an intellectual solecism. In a literate world religion (and significantly the qualifiers are synonymous) the network of 'primitive classifications' cannot possibly have the same correspondence with other aspects of the social structure as they have in a small-scale hunting community. In terms of social groups, what 'fits' in Rangoon is hardly likely to fit in rural Ceylon; if a fit does emerge (outside the mind of the observer), then it is clearly relevant to generalized human experience rather than to particular social structures, and there will no doubt be a large number of alternative forms of behaviour that would be equally appropriate; for the concept of 'fit' to be of any serious interest, it must also be possible to demonstrate its absence and the alternatives (Merton 1957; Nagel 1961).

THE ARTICULATED VILLAGE

Part of what I have been saying in these last few paragraphs appears as a central theme in the writings of Redfield and his pupils at Chicago. In a retrospective account of this work Redfield explains how the shift of attention from the tribes of North America to the settled agriculturalists further south involved a change in perspective, a movement away from the analysis of isolated cultures and the study of complete social structures.

In his account of a Yucatan village of Chan Kom, Redfield (1934: 1) described 'the mode of life in a peasant village...These villages are small communities of illiterate agriculturalists, carrying on a homogeneous culture transmitted by oral tradition.' But they are 'politically and economically dependent upon the towns and cities of modern literate civilization' in terms of which the peasants 'in part define their position'.

Redfield made some attempt to see the village in terms of what he called a folk-urban continuum but this phrase was meant in an analytic rather than an existential sense. He did not free himself from the need to insist upon homogeneity, which is looked upon as one of the keynotes of the little community. In a series of lectures given in 1953, Redfield defined this community by its distinctiveness, its smallness, its self-sufficiency and its homogeneity. 'Activities and states of mind are much alike for all persons in corresponding sex and age positions; and the career of one generation repeats that of the preceding. So understood, homogeneous is equivalent to "slow-changing"' (1955: 4).

One result of the insistence on homogeneity emerges in his references to literacy. For, 'illiterate' though his peasants may have been in Maya[1] (it is not clear who was ever literate in that language), even when he was first there 26 per cent of those over eighteen were 'literate' in Spanish. This meant, at least, that the central government could transmit its orders indirectly. And it also permitted the circulation of two kinds of books, both connected with religion, namely, Catholic prayers and the Church

[1] Only the priesthood appears to have been literate in pre-conquest times. Mayan hieroglyphic writing is almost exclusively ritual and calendrical in content. The astronomical calculations of the inscriptions (which relate almost exclusively to the passage of time) are thought by Thompson to be divinatory in kind (1950: 63). The three surviving codices are also priestly books concerned with divination and astrology (23, 65). Indeed the activities of the Mayan high priests centred around their writings rather than around sacrifices, which they attended only at the principal feasts. They compiled their works and taught their sciences, which, a near-contemporary Spaniard relates, concerned 'the computation of the years, months, days, the festivals and ceremonies, the administration of the sacraments, the fateful days and seasons, their method of divination and their prophecies, events and the cures for diseases, their antiquities and how to read and write with the letters and characters with which they wrote, and [to make] drawings which illustrate the meaning of the writings' (Bishop Landa, *Relación de las cosas de Yucatán*, *c.* 1566, quoted by Morley 1946: 171).

calendars used in naming ceremonies. It is only possible to reconcile these statements with others to the effect that Chan Kom was 'a world of oral and face-to-face communication' and 'without books' (Redfield 1934: 6, 11) by assuming that the author was trying to describe an earlier phase of a long-term historical process, where the urban elements (including books) were seen as recent intrusions into the homogeneous culture of this peasant world. Certainly there is a surprising lack of fit between the reality and the model.

Another result of the move into Latin America was the search for 'general and comprehensive patterns of thought in the minds of these Indians' (Redfield 1955: 23). The peasant village was different from the tribe, but it displayed the self-same features upon which tribal sociologists had insisted, a culture, comprehensive patterns of thought, illiteracy, homogeneity and self-sufficiency.

Middle America brought certain modifications in approach; India pushed the process yet a stage further. In 1965, a year after the appearance of *The Little Community*, Redfield wrote, 'In that book I thought of small communities as independent of things outside them. In the present chapters there is a very preliminary exploration of one kind of dependent community, that of peasants...' (1965: vi). The change came about through the work of Barnes in Norway and of Singer, Marriott, Lewis and others in India. Redfield now saw these communities as ones 'where the local culture is continually replenished by contact with products of intellectual...social strata; the local (or little) community is culturally heteronomous—dependent on norms coming to it from without, from the great community' (Singer 1959: x).

The soggy language of sociological discourse sometimes obscures what Redfield wants to say and the proliferation of phrases like 'the social organization [or 'structure'] of tradition' do little to clarify the issues at stake. The concept of a little community is not so much an abstraction as a distraction and has led to a dialogue of little moment. Reconsidering his contentions, Obeyesekere attempts to show, in the Sinhalese context, that 'cultures are integrated' and 'peasant cultures are wholes' (not halves). He appears to do this by deriving local Buddhism from local factors—'there is good ideological reason for giving the Buddha a presidential status in the pantheon', which he sees as a 'structural unity'; and the trend of his remarks is illustrated by the assertion that the little community or peasant society 'is after all the focus of anthropological enquiry' (Obeyesekere 1963: 143, 146). Leaving aside the confusion caused by the idea of 'a culture' and the problems of deciding when a culture is not integrated, a structure not unified, the question is not where scholars pass their time but whether such a frame of reference is adequate for the analysis of any part of a complex field of social relationships that clearly extend beyond the village. To this any observer who is not mesmerized by the concept of culture must answer negatively. The point was made by Dumont and Pocock in their general discussion of village studies (1957); it is made more specifically by Ames in his own account of Sinhalese religion. This, he writes, 'is Buddhist-dominated rather than specific to any village because the monkhood, which is nationwide rather than village-centred, is the dominant status group in the religious system' (Ames 1963–64: 21). He rejects the same village fallacy of anthropologists working in the Eurasian field that Skinner criticizes in his work on Chinese markets. 'Anthropological work on Chinese society, by focusing attention almost exclusively on the village, has with few exceptions distorted the reality of rural social structure.' But, even for Skinner, the approach in terms of boundary-maintaining 'communities' or 'traditions' presents an analytical problem. For he goes on to argue that the important culture-bearing unit is rather an 'intermediate social structure', the standard market *community*—'the locus in the Chinese case of Redfield's "little tradition"...Insofar as the Chinese peasant can be said to live in a self-contained world, that world is not the village but the standard marketing community' (Skinner 1964: 32). While this could be so for an individual's range of physical movement (though clearly trade and government provide many an exception), the Chinese countryman (whether peasant, gentry or bureaucrat) clearly did not live in a self-contained universe; for with the possibility of written communication (not to speak of the more overt influence of national government and institutions), the physical community no longer limits the field of socio-cultural interaction.[1]

But the work of Redfield's students does demonstrate a concern with the interaction between town and village, for example, in Miner's study of *The Primitive City of Timbuctu* (1953) and especially in the work of Singer (1959), Marriott (1955) and others on Indian society. Here, too, there is an implicit rejection of the myth of a village world that encapsulates Indian culture. Country and town are seen as part of an inclusive field of socio-cultural activity, even if the full implications are somewhat dulled by analysing this social field only in terms of the interaction between the great and the little communities, with the great tradition providing an umbrella overall.

There is still overmuch concern with the quasi-metaphysical problem

[1] Freedman has done much to redress the balance of the earlier village-centred studies of the Malinowskian tradition by taking a regional view. He writes: 'Chinese civilization was agrarian, but its rural society was not uniformly peasant.' Since one out of every ten village families (in Kwangtung) was that of a merchant or official, 'the countryside was far from being a homogeneous peasant sector of Chinese society' (1966: 76).

of wholes and parts.[1] For Redfield peasant societies are part societies. But in Islamic or Hindu societies, what is the 'whole'? In all except the simplest structures, the boundaries of a field of social action differ for the various activities in which a man engages; the norms and interests that guide his action can be only inadequately described in terms of 'a culture' when in one context a man behaves 'as' a Muslim or Hindu, in another 'as' a trader, in another 'as' a member of a particular caste or patronymic group.[2]

This kind of situation, where the social fields of individuals or groups have no single socio-cultural frontier, is common not only among peasant societies, as I understand the term,[3] but also in many of the centralized societies of pre-colonial Africa; it exists, for example, wherever markets are found. Indeed, it is the market that Redfield, like others, seizes upon as the institution that 'pulls out from the compact social relations of self-contained primitive communities some part of men's doings and puts people into fields of economic activity that are increasingly independent of the rest of what goes on in the local life' (Redfield 1956: 46). In his north Indian study, Lewis (1955; 1958) emphasized, as others have done, the extra-village ties based upon caste, kinship and marriage: 'Rampur, like other villages in North India, is fundamentally a part of a larger inter-village network based upon kinship ties' (1958: 313). Marriott, on the other hand, stresses the religious aspects of the continuous process of communication between a little, local tradition and the greater traditions that have their place 'partly inside and partly outside the village' (1955: 218). But too little attention is paid to the nature of this system of communication, to the fact that peasants—in Redfield's sense of 'the rural dimension of old civilizations' (1955: 29)—belong to societies that possessed the important technology of writing, that all the 'world religions' are literate religions (although the writing down of the Rig Vedas was late), that a significant aspect of what is inside the village (in terms of the 'great tradition') consists of books and their interpreters.

That such a fact should be of primary importance to a society is the argument pursued in the paper by Watt and myself which follows this introduction. The implications for the study of such societies are hinted at in Redfield's final work. 'If we enter a village within a civilization we see at once that the culture there has been flowing into it from teachers who

[1] E.g. Singer 1959: xi; Marriott 1955: 209 (little communities are characterized by 'the paradox of isolability within nonisolability', though the author realizes that the holism of the community approach is inadequate); Redfield 1955.

[2] 'as' requires some more clumsy periphrasis if it is to indicate what is involved. While the concept of 'a culture' seems to me to have little value, the concept of 'culture' as learned behaviour does have a limited utility.

[3] For a discussion of African 'peasants', see Fallers 1961.

never saw that village, who did their work in intellectual circles perhaps far away in space and time' (1956: 70).

Indeed the process of 'sanskritization', so important a feature of recent discussions of Indian culture, is itself linked inextricably with the extension of literate activity in the shape of a legal code and holy scriptures (Staal 1962–63). As Mayne remarked, Hindu Law has 'the oldest pedigree of any known system of jurisprudence, and even now it shows no signs of decrepitude. At this day it governs races of men, extending from Cashmere to Cape Comorin, *who agree about nothing else except their submission to it*' (1892: ix, my italics).

It follows that the analysis of social action in the structural-functional framework used by tribal sociologists in their studies of societies outside the range of literacy can hardly be adequate here without important modifications. Significantly enough, the original proponents of the functionalist approach (Malinowski and Radcliffe-Brown) worked on small islands, under conditions which their students have often tried to duplicate in their search for bounded, isolated and 'primitive' communities in the major continental areas of the world.

For the study of those vast areas where world religions are part of the social horizon, the limitations of this approach are obvious. Indeed it would seem hardly necessary to make the point if we were not at a juncture in intellectual life where concepts and approaches originally developed with specific reference to preliterate societies are being increasingly employed in the study of literate culture. Durkheim's work on primitive classification is being applied to societies within the orbit of the major civilizations. The polarities and oppositions of *la pensée sauvage* turn up in ancient Greece, and tools developed in the study of the narratives of American societies are applied to the Oedipus story, the Book of Genesis and even contemporary literature, with little sense of the basic incongruity involved.

Polarities of some sort are of course present in all societies; their significance, however, varies widely. Aristotle describes one Pythagorean theory in the following terms:

Others of this same school say that there are ten principles, which they arrange in twin columns, namely:

limit	unlimited
odd	even
one	plurality
right	left
male	female
at rest	moving
straight	crooked

light	darkness
good	bad
square	oblong

...How these principles may be brought into line with the causes we have mentioned is not clearly explained by them [quoted Guthrie 1962: I, 245].

It is clear that a table of correspondences of the Pythagorean kind is more limited in its meaning for Greek society than for a non-literate one. While the constituent elements may be relatively fixed, the table as a whole is inevitably a very partial representation of 'Greek culture', not even accepted by all the brotherhood and certainly rejected by Aristotle; this was especially true of the numerical identifications, in which, writes Guthrie, the Pythagoreans 'were highly arbitrary and inconsistent' (1962: I, 277). In any social context such a set of identifications may be more or less partial, more or less individual, more or less arbitrary, more or less inconsistent.

The introduction to a book of this kind is not the place to pursue this line of argument to its logical conclusion. But before too readily applying to literate societies concepts developed in another setting, we should first examine some of the uses and functions of literacy, the kind of difference that this radical change in the technology of the intellect has upon a society and its members.

RESTRICTED LITERACY

The factors that restrict the full development of literacy are many. As in other fields, social restrictions continue despite the release from technological limitations. What specific factors prevent the realization of the full potentialities of literacy?

First, there is the tendency to secrecy, to restrict the circulation of books. In West Africa, such secrecy even gathers round the Qur'ān itself, increasing its magical efficacy as well as the power of its custodians. The magical books of medieval Europe acquired a similar character. Many of the ceremonial texts of Egypt and Mesopotamia 'were not intended to be read by human eyes', for they were essentially communications between man and god, not man and man (Oppenheim 1964: 234). The same secrecy characterized the activities of Pythagoras and his followers, in whose work the magical, numerological elements are considerable (Guthrie 1962: I, 150 ff.). One contemporary commentator remarked that for them 'not everything was to be divulged to all men'; there was a 'feeling against open discussion of Pythagorean doctrine', a commitment to *arcana* and, it was said, a five-year rule of silence on initiates to the brotherhood. But in these respects Pythagoras scarcely typifies the Greek reaction to the growth of learning.

Such restrictive practices tend to arise wherever people have an interest in maintaining a monopoly of the sources of their power. Of the Bāroṭs of Gujarat, a caste of genealogists that spread over the whole of north India, Srinivas wrote: '[They are] extremely secretive about their books, and...are suspicious of people who want to know what is in them. The Bāroṭs are used to parting with information recorded in their books only to their patrons, and not to outsiders. They fear that they may be driven out of business by unscrupulous rivals' (Srinivas 1959: 41).

It is not only these specialized castes who have an interest in preserving their monopoly. The study of Vēda itself, enjoined by the lawbooks, is limited to the twice-born, that is, members of the higher castes, but for the past two thousand years has usually been restricted to Brahmans (Ingalls 1959: 3). In discussing the transmission of learning in India, Ghurye recounts how the founder of the Navadvipa school, Vasudeva Sarvabhauma, when he had completed his study of the Upanishads at Banaras, went to Mithila for further studies under Paushadhara Misra. This teacher had in his possession the only manuscript of the foremost work on logic, the 'Chintamani' by Gangesa. 'He imposed a condition on his students that they were not to transcribe any copy of the work in order that the Mithila college may retain its monopoly...' However Vasudeva committed the whole to memory and then went to start a new school 'which outrivalled Mithila college as a centre of learning' (Ghurye 1950: 24–5).

But in India oral transmission was employed not only to preserve a literate monopoly, but also because of its archaic (and to some extent intrinsic) values. Just as the Muslims of West Africa prefer a handwritten to a printed Qur'ān, so in India the most sacred words continued to be transmitted by oral (i.e. the original) means for a long time after literacy was available as a 'technique of preserved communication'. For while writing was widely used for certain purposes by the reign of the Buddhist king Asoka (274–237 B.C.), the most important elements of the Hindu corpus, the Rig Vedas, were not written down until the eighth or ninth century A.D. Many of the same features of restricted literacy are found there that appear in the Islamic world of the western Sudan—the family schools, the long years of textual learning (between 12 and 24 years of age), the persistence of oral modes of instruction (Ghurye 1950: 2, 12). In early post-alphabetic times, Indian scholars had the same sort of doubts about writing as Plato. A verse in the Paniniyasiksha declares that a person who knows not the meaning and one who reads what is written are regarded as the lowest of readers and reciters. The Narada Smrti saw listening to the contents of a book as a hindrance to knowledge and discouraged book-learning. 'The knowledge that is acquired from books and not received from a teacher does not shine in a deliberative assembly, i.e. is not operative and fruitful' (Ghurye 1950: 20). Elsewhere the book that has not been memorized is compared to wealth in the possession of others—all of which, Ghurye (1950: 21) claims, points to the 'adverse nature of the atmosphere for writing and gathering books'. Great emphasis was placed upon *memoriter*, and the learned tradition was principally maintained by an unbroken succession of teachers. As in Islamic tradition, it was customary to keep and repeat the names of teachers of a school of learning, providing the kind of 'genealogy of learning' that Wilks describes for the Dyula of West Africa (below, p. 162). The importance of teachers was inversely related to the use made of the storage capabilities of books; every teacher was himself a 'living library'.

An illustration of the desire to channel access to books through an authorized teacher—a combination of the literate and oral modes that is apparent in the *guru* system and is so often a feature of religious literacy —was encountered during our stay in the western Gonja town of Bole in 1965. A man from the Jebagtay section, who always wore a tattered gown and wandered aimlessly through the market-place, was said to have become sick because he had read certain parts of the Qur'ān without taking the necessary precautions. 'If you read secretly without performing these you will become mad' (E. N. Goody, field notes, 3849). Even a literate needs to be guided through the learning to be won from books; an independent approach to the written word is fraught with mystical dangers.

The *guru* tradition is characteristic of situations of restricted literacy, where the role of the teacher as the mediator of knowledge is given pre-eminent importance. He adds personal charisma to book-learning, in a combination of oral and literate modes of communication. The position of the *guru* is clearly bolstered by the fact that it is religious tradition he is imparting, and one that encourages a partial withdrawal from (or at least a special attitude to) mundane affairs. 'Truth' requires a mediator, a contemplative treatment, and an internalization through the memory, modes of learning that are more appropriate perhaps to the mystical than the empirical approach.[1]

There was, of course, more than one Brahman tradition of learning in India. There was the Vēdic tradition, largely oral; there was the esoteric

[1] While the methods of the *guru* are usually associated with a religious tradition, they spill over into secular fields. A sociology student from a mid-western college wrote of her Indian professor in the following words: 'We used to sit in silence for twenty minutes. It is, among other things, a tremendously authoritarian procedure, and one that systematically exempts itself from the empirical validation of propositions. Final appeal is to a mystically "right" answer which is known only to the guru.'

tradition of the tantras[1] and much of the Vedānta, and there was the sastric tradition of analysis and exegesis. The latter was essentially an urban tradition, which taught grammar, rhetoric, poetry, logic and philosophy, but it still required 'a formidable amount of memorizing'. Consequently learning was oriented in a traditionalist direction, even among the intellectuals who were more adept at commentary than at creation (Ingalls 1959: 5, 6). And, as recent observers have noted, the emphasis on rote learning continued in the new universities established in the nineteenth century (McDonald 1965–6: 459).

This mode of teaching fails to take full advantage of the potentialities of 'preserved communication'. Books serve as a mnemonic and have themselves to be committed to memory before they are considered as 'read'. Consequently, initial instruction places more emphasis on the repetition of content than the acquisition of skill. Under these conditions book-learning takes on an inflexibility that is the antithesis of the spirit of enquiry which literacy has elsewhere fostered.

We are dealing here partly with oral residues in a literate culture, the kind of culture lag that occurred when 'early type-designers laboriously cut punches for the myriad ligatures which had been a godsend to scribes but were only encumbrances in typography' (Ong 1965: 146). The examples are many of the skeuomorphism of new media; it affected the whole educational system of Europe in the Middle Ages. 'In accord with the rhetorical outlook, students were virtually never taught objective description or reportorial narration...Rhetoric, despite its deep involvement in the written medium, retained its earlier, expressly oral contours intact: normally it included as one of its five parts *pronunciatio* or delivery—which meant oral delivery—as well as memory' (Ong 1965: 147). Such forms of education are characteristic of many pre-industrial societies, where literacy is seen as an aid to oral communication.

Such a situation is most likely to arise where there is a strong association between writing and religion. For then it is learning the Word of God (or of his prophets) or the proper order of service that takes central place. The skill is subordinate to the content and that in turn subordinate to the demands of orthodoxy. The exclusive religions not only attempt to exclude the circulation of 'heretical' thoughts but offer a set of relatively fixed

[1] The *tantras* were books which contained the metaphysical and mystical doctrine of certain sects, and represent a revision of Vēdic doctrine. 'Though they are not positively hostile to the Veda, they propound that the precepts of the Veda are too difficult for our age, and that, for this reason, an easier cult and an easier doctrine have been revealed in them. Moreover, these sacred books are accessible, not only to the higher castes, but to Sudras and women too. On the other hand, it is true that they contain Secret Doctrines which can only be obtained from a teacher (*guru*) after a ceremonial initiation...and which must not be communicated to any uninitiated person' (Winternitz 1927: I, 587).

answers to a range of important problems. Greece and Rome were unique in keeping literacy largely secular, in rejecting (at least in their more creative phases) the attractions of an exclusive cult and in avoiding the inhibiting effects of religious literacy that dominated the culture of western Europe until the advent of the printing press.

In an interesting comparison of Brahmans and Shamans in a Himalayan village, Berreman contrasts the religiously innovating Shamans with the traditionalist Brahmans. 'A good Brahmin is a conservative, learned man who performs his prescribed duties with accuracy. The Brahmin is, almost by definition, a cultural and social conservative' (Berreman 1963–64: 61). Berreman rightly links this difference to the relative status position of the individuals involved. But, in addition, the conservative behaviour of Brahmans reflects the fact that they are working to fixed texts, preserved communications, although these are oral as well as written.

This conservative function of writing in relation to magico-religious activity emerges early on in the history of writing. Mesopotamian legal codes, Oppenheim notes, represent aspirations rather than codifications, having the 'aim of bringing the law into line with changed social, economic, or political conditions...But the writing down of sacred lore was undertaken 'to "freeze" a tradition, not to adapt and adjust it to reality' (Oppenheim 1964: 231, 232).

These features of restricted literacy are vividly illustrated in Tibet. The country had an alphabetic system of writing, knowledge of which varied greatly from district to district. Everywhere its main purpose seems to have been religious; literacy came with the Buddhist monks. 'The principal reason for learning to read', writes Ekvall, 'is a religious one—the desire to read the many prayers, charms, and sermons of the Buddhist scriptures and religious manuals' (1964: 125). Reading is taught by monks; instructional material is religious in content; the turning of pages is an essential part of the most effective ritual observance; possession of books is a matter of status; in sum, literate activity is a means to grace, a method of achieving virtue and eventual liberation because it opens the way to the learning of new prayers. 'The illiterate cannot use a book in his praying, except to hold it in his hands and raise it to his forehead to "rub off the blessing" as he intones the syllable *OHm*. The literate, on the other hand, derives greater benefit by being able to scan the lines and turn the pages, for such activity is also part of verbalization. He visualizes the meanings in their written form and holds them in his mind. Such comprehension constitutes an added degree of observance' (Ekvall 1964: 125).

While possibly half the male population can read, their reading is largely religious and largely receptive. In this theocratic society literate techniques shared the fate of the wheel. Rotary motion was combined with the power of the printed or written word in the shape of the prayer wheel, a specifically Tibetan invention but one that may have originated in the 'revolving library' of China, which was invented 'to enable illiterates to gain the merit that comes from reading the scriptures'. But though rotary motion was employed for religious ends, it was never adapted to the transport of men or goods. 'The devotion of the principle of the wheel to the uses and practices of religion appears to have inhibited the Tibetans from using it for mundane purposes' (Ekvall 1964: 121). This is not entirely true of writing, which had administrative uses. But under Buddhism it was mainly an instrument of propaganda and worship; the three hallowed practices of reciting, writing (or printing) and reading the word (*CHos*) became ends in themselves. Books were carried unopened in procession and used to line the tomb of a grand lama. Throughout Tibet monks would sit along the banks of streams 'printing pages of charms and formulas on the surface of the water' (Ekvall 1964: 114), striving only to make as many impressions as possible as they slapped down the woodcut blocks. Tibet demonstrates the epitome of grapholatry.

In certain ways writing encouraged the growth of magico-religious activity. The priest was the man of learning, the literate, the intellectual, in control of natural as well as supernatural communication. Nor do only the higher levels of religious activity utilize the book, for it would be wrong to think of literacy as sweeping away the more magical elements of ritual and belief. What was formerly oral now gets set down in writing and just as religious myths become crystallized in the words of the Holy Book, so too magical formulae become perpetuated in the spae-books, grimoires and numerological treatises that spread throughout the literate world. I do not mean here to assert any radical dichotomy between 'religion' and 'magic'. But in the shadow of the fixed and established Books of God that form the core of world religions, another category of text has circulated, one that dealt in magic formulae and numerical squares, in providing specific solutions for particular problems, a potion to win a mistress, a spell to bring back a runaway servant.

This tradition of magical texts goes back to the beginnings of writing itself, stemming as it does from the Mesopotamian world where writing itself developed. The extensive manipulation of letters and numbers is made possible only by writing. The series of transformations of God's name is essentially a literate technique. The magical squares that were the subject of so many Muslim texts have the same general origin, although they probably come from India or China. Indeed the development of mathematics is often associated with the use of number magic; it has been plausibly maintained that the 'Pythagorean' theorem concerning the square on the hypotenuse was discovered in the course of such numerological experimentation (Allman 1911). The theorem is now recognized to be older than Pythagoras, much of whose mathematics has an eastern origin (Guthrie 1962: 217). But the interpenetration of mathematics and magic in the school is well attested; Dodds, for example, sees Pythagoreanism partly as 'a development of shamanism and partly as a development of number mysticism and the speculations about cosmic harmony' (1951: 167). The world of nature was for them constructed on a mathematical plan; things were generated from numbers—an idea to whose mystical overtones Aristotle objected. From our standpoint, we note the 'magical' nature of a good deal of the treatment of numbers, but also the fact that much of the Greek mathematical achievement had to do with the generation of geometrical figures from numbers, a process that was assisted by the practice of representing numbers 'in visible form, by rows of dots, letters or pebbles arranged in regular patterns' (Guthrie 1962: 242, 256). Many of these mathematical achievements, as in the case of Mesopotamia, were not related to alphabetic writing (as algebra is) but they depended upon graphic representation, which completely transformed the possibilities for numerical manipulation.

Magical texts of this kind often gain part of their power by a genealogy that derives from the Holy Book and the early history of man. According to the Samaritans, for example, all magical teaching stemmed from one book, the Book of Signs, that Adam brought with him from Paradise to enable him to have power over the elements and invisible things. The Jewish *Sefer Raziel* makes similar claims, as well as tracing its origin from Solomon, the son of David, as did so many works of this kind in Europe. The same tradition found its way into the Qur'ān: 'And to Solomon we taught the use of blowing winds...and we subjected to him some of the evil ones, who dived for him, and did other things besides.' For the Arabs, it was the Jews and Africans who were the great magicians: the Jews and Romans looked upon the Christians as the *mathematici* and later Christians derived much of their magical lore from Jewish and Arab sources. For all this knowledge was secret knowledge, which was yet more powerful if it came from outsiders, especially ones whose lineage led them back to the supernatural sources of power.

The Book of Magic flourished in situations of restricted literacy partly because its interpretation was a specialized task. But writing also permitted the construction of more elaborate schemes as well as the greater manipulation of letters, words and numbers. As in logic and grammar, words and sentences could be dissected and the parts reassembled in different ways.

Numbers, too, could be laid out in tables, essentially a graphic concept, and their qualities subjected to visual inspection. Both together could be drawn into new and esoteric relationships by means of elaborate tables of correspondences.

An example of such an Islamic table is given in Table 2. As Doutté remarks, 'the dominant idea behind this jadwal is that there exists a precise correspondence between the different elements' (1909: 161) and it is the nature of this link that gives the square so great a significance in human affairs; it is not simply a classificatory device but has operative power for the solution of problems. The numerical squares, each line of which adds up to the same total, have a similar significance, on the Pythagorean principle that numbers hold the key to the operation of the world. The simple 9-cell table, adding up to 15, is shown in Table 1; Doutté illustrates a 16-cell table which has power to cure the sterility of women (1909: 914).

TABLE 1. *A magic square from Jābir b. Ḥaiyān (d. 776), 'Book of Ways' (after W. Ahrens, 1917: 186)*

4	9	2
3	5	7
8	1	6

TABLE 2. *The 'jadwal', 'da'wat, 'al-shams'. This 49-cell table is given in Doutté (1909: 154) and variants are found in various Arabic sources (e.g. Al-Būnī): its sources are Chaldean, Christian and Jewish*

Line	Contents
1	7 magic signs
2	7 letters not found in the first 7 verses of the Qur'ān
3	7 of the 99 names of God
4	7 angels
5	7 demon kings (*jinn*)
6	7 days of the week
7	7 planets

The influence of literate magic depended on a recognition of the fact that writing represented a discovery of prime importance, which could be used to communicate with and control *jinn* and other agencies, just as in the case of human beings. The efficacy of the Book of Magic and the Book of God both depended upon the concrete achievements of the written word.

Nevertheless, features of the kind I have described restrict the development of widespread literacy. The skill of writing is a scarce resource, even though the technology is at a point where it is potentially available to all. The situation of socially restricted literacy is often similar to the technological restrictions imposed by non-phonetic systems of writing, where the sheer difficulties of learning the skill mean that it can be available only to a limited number of people.

There is a further restriction upon literacy which we referred to (see below, p. 41) but did not elaborate, namely the materials used to preserve communication. Impressing a stylus on wet clay tablets is clearly a more cumbrous way of writing than putting pen to paper and one which tended to limit the fluency of composition. Nor are the clay tablets themselves so easy to handle as missives, being heavier and easily broken. Clearly one of the great advantages that China possessed as against the early empires of the Fertile Crescent was the simple means of writing with brush, ink and paper, not to speak of the later use of print.

Few of the 'traditional' societies discussed in this book can be described as non-literate; they possessed not only writing but alphabetic writing. Nevertheless they were not literate societies in the Greek sense. Of course, literacy is everywhere a variable quantity and one which can be measured by various indices: a central concern of Schofield's chapter is the extent of literacy in post-reformation England, a problem which has general implications for those interested in the relationship of literacy to the economic take-off, the *démarrage*.

But I am here concerned with rather cruder distinctions, partly because the figures are lacking and the data too limited to set up a more sensitive scale. Given the rough measures at our disposal, we have to recognize an important class of society in which the implications of literacy are only partly developed, one where the oral tradition continues to play a dominant part in spheres that are potentially literary. We need to remind ourselves, though not with the retrogressive desires that characterize much thinking of the Wordsworthian, Back-to-the-Village, Culture-and-Environment schools, that this carried gains as well as losses. It was a society of this kind which Parry found in Yugoslavia when he went to study the features of 'oral poetry' with a view to throwing light on the Homeric compositions. It is the illiteracy of the epic singers 'which determines the particular form their composition takes, and which thus distinguishes them from the literary poet. In societies where writing is unknown, or where it is limited to a professional scribe whose duty is that of writing letters and keeping accounts, or where it is the possession of a small minority, such as clerics or a wealthy ruling class (though often this latter group prefers to have its writing done by a servant), the art of narration flourishes, provided that the culture is in other respects of a sort to foster the singing of tales... On the other hand, when writing is introduced and begins to be used for the same purposes as the oral narrative song, when it is employed for telling stories and is widespread enough to find an audience capable of reading, this audience seeks its entertainment and instruction in books rather than in the living songs of men, and the older art gradually disappears' (Lord 1960: 20).

WRITING AND THE ALPHABET

The main problems arising out of a discussion of our earlier paper have to do with a central theme of this collection, the social restrictions on alphabetic literacy—in other words, the reasons why the breakthrough did not elsewhere have the same concomitants as in the eastern Mediterranean. These restrictions I have discussed in the previous section and again in my essay on northern Ghana.

But there is another general point that needs making. The variable we earlier considered was changes in the media, in the technology of communication, and specifically 'widespread literacy' resulting from a simplified system of writing, such as the alphabet which was first developed in ancient Greece. But in Greece it was not only the alphabet that was being introduced but writing of any kind (at least, for the first time for some 500 years). Some of the features of Greek culture we associated with 'widespread literacy' should possibly be linked with writing itself. In other words, we gave less explicit credit to the potentialities of non-phonetic writing than is deserved. In China considerable technical advances were made under these conditions; works of speculative thought, historical writing of a kind, even a form of novel (Bishop 1955–56), all these appeared from the pens of the literate few. It was writing rather than alphabetic writing that permitted these developments. Likewise, in administration it was logographic writing that helped to maintain and extend the system of political control, as the Chinese themselves were aware. The Great Commentary on the *Book of Changes* says: 'In primitive times people knotted cords in order to govern. The holy men of a later age introduced written documents instead, as a means of governing the various officials and supervising the people' (Wilhelm and Baynes 1951: I, 360)[1]. The philosophers of the

[1] For this and other references on China I am indebted to Mark Elvin. It is clear that in our original article we overestimated the difficulties of learning Chinese script and underestimated the potentialities of non-alphabetic writing.

Chou dynasty (1027?–249 B.C.), the bureaucrats of the Ch'in (246–207 B.C.), the achievements of the Han (200 B.C.–A.D. 220) in history, medicine, mathematics, astronomy, botany and chemistry, the poetry of the T'ang (A.D. 618–906), the drama and novels of the Mongul dynasty, all utilized a non-phonetic script.

It was for scientific rather than artistic achievement that creative writing was most effectively used in the Bronze Age societies of the Fertile Crescent. Certain fields such as mathematics depend upon a graphic medium but phonetic transcription is irrelevant; the mathematical methods of Mesopotamia stand up well to the accomplishments of all other civilizations up to the middle of the second millennium A.D., i.e. for more than three thousand years (Oppenheim 1964: 306). Astronomy and much of medicine also require records of information about the universe, but the nature of the script is of little import. Nevertheless the advent of a simpler writing system and a larger reading public were clearly factors of great social and intellectual importance in the Mediterranean world and it is not accidental that at the present day so much stress is laid on literacy in programmes of social development.

TABLE 3. *The Uses of Writing in Mesopotamia*
(*after Oppenheim 1964: 230 et seqq.*)

1	Recording data for future use	(a) administrative purposes (b) codification of law (c) formulation of a sacred tradition (d) for annals (e) and ('eventually') for scholarly purposes
2	Communication of data on a synchronic level	(a) letters (b) royal edicts (c) public announcements (d) texts for training scribes
3	Communication with gods	secret texts, amulets, etc.

Even today questions arise in the determination of literacy and the degree of ability in reading or writing that is 'functional' in a particular society. Clearly the problem is much greater when we are dealing with historic societies or little-known areas. In her comments on our earlier paper Dr Gough suggests that in parts of India (which of course had an alphabetic script) up to half the men and one-sixth of the women (i.e. 33 per cent of the population) were literate and that 'a similar level of literacy may have characterized the periods of high culture in China' (p. 71, below). Exact figures are of course not available. But certainly for China the percentage seems to have been significantly less. In his book on *Nationalism and Language Reform in China*, the main authority in English, de Francis, writes: 'Rough statistics tell us merely that only ten or fifteen per cent of the population now and only one or two per cent throughout most of Chinese history have been bound together by literacy in the ideographic script' (1950: 222).

Estimates of the extent of literacy in China can differ widely. Writing of the number of *literati* (here, persons who had passed the county and prefectural examinations, 'scholar-commoners'), Freedman quotes estimates of 0·2 per cent for the province of Fukien in the nineteenth century and 0·1 for the New Territories of Hong Kong. But schooling was of course much more widespread and 'a great many villages in the area had schools of some sort; there the rudiments of reading and writing were taught' (Freedman 1966: 71). It was the more advanced schools or 'studies' that provided the training for the literati, and such schools seem to have been restricted to sons of the well-to-do.

At the ordinary schools, generally found in ancestral halls, boys were taught to read and write the characters. But they did not spend much time in study and those who afterwards went into trade or handicrafts only remained there from two to four years, 'during which time they acquire sufficient knowledge of the characters to carry on business, write letters and make out accounts'.[1]

The great range of literate accomplishments in China makes any assessment of literacy very difficult; behind the limited number of scholar-commoners stood an indefinite number of readers of agricultural almanacs and minor specialists keeping their own accounts. Estimates of this larger category of limited literates fluctuate considerably, but it would seem that de Francis' figure understates the actual numbers.

The sharp pyramid of learning is found in societies marked by religious literacy and possessing an alphabetic script. In China the difficulties appear to be more fundamental. Traditionally, children were taught the simpler characters first and then extended their range by the memorization of new ones, linking form and sound. 'When the pupils reached the age of 7 or 8...the teacher usually began to explain the meanings of characters. As soon as a pupil had learned about a thousand characters, he began to read from textbooks for children' (Gray 1956: 33). Most of the guidance was given individually, the teacher reading a passage and getting the pupil to repeat it. This was done several times; afterwards the pupil returned to his desk where he read aloud to himself until he had memorized the passage

[1] R. Krone, 1859, 'A Notice of the Sanon District', Article v, *Trans. China Branch, R. Asiatic Soc.* vi, p. 94, quoted Freedman 1966: 73.

and then went to the teacher's desk to show what he had learned. 'If the recitation was fluent and uninterrupted, a new passage was assigned.'

These procedures were necessitated largely by the nature of the script and the tonal quality of the language. And while the non-phonetic character of the system did ensure that *literati* speaking different dialects could communicate in writing throughout the Empire and in this sense provided the technological basis for the bureaucratic administration developed under the Ch'in rulers (246–207 B.C.), it came under increasing criticism. At the beginning of the present century phonetic symbols were widely introduced as aids in learning the characters, a process that was helped by the movement towards a standard national pronunciation. Quick methods of reading enabled a student to learn to read the newspaper in 300 hours. But despite these improvements, there were nevertheless strong pressures towards the total abandonment of logographs on social grounds.

Many scholars of China have seen a connection between a low literacy rate and the use of a non-alphabetic script. At the end of the nineteenth century, the Protestant missionary, J. C. Gibson, considered that the 'ideographic script had limited literacy to an upper-class minority' and the Reverend W. N. Brewster claimed that a serious indictment against the classical script was that 'it develops a *privileged class*... So China has a government of the literati, for the literati, and by the literati' (de Francis 1950: 27).

Nor were these remarks confined to foreign missionaries. Many Chinese radicals thought that the high rate of illiteracy was connected with the script and pressed for an alphabetic system. One of the most active workers in favour of latinization (already described by Lenin as 'the great revolution of the East') was Ch'ü Ch'iu-pai, Moscow representative of the Chinese Communist Party in 1928, who wrote: 'The "Chinese script" of China is certainly too difficult for the masses and only the gentry class can have time enough to learn it, so that politically and culturally it is an enormous impediment' (de Francis 1950: 93). And the revolutionary poet, Hsiao San, wrote, 'In reality the Chinese hieroglyphic script is nothing but an archaic survival of feudal ages, a symbol of centuries-old slavery, a tool for the enslavement of the working masses by the governing class' (de Francis 1950: 95). Lu Hsün, perhaps the greatest Chinese writer of modern times, asked, 'Shall we sacrifice ourselves for the ideographs?' (de Francis 1950: 113). And Ch'ien Hsüan-t'ung, a well-known philologist and later a founder of the Chinese Communist Party, wrote that 'if you want to abolish Confucianism you must first abolish the Chinese script' (de Francis 1950: 68).

The movement for writing reform was strongly resisted by many Kuomintang officials in the 1930s, but was taken up by student groups.

The manifesto of the Shanghai Society to Study the Latinization of Chinese Writing claimed: 'It is necessary to expend several years' time and several tens or hundreds of dollars before it is possible to acquire even a superficial knowledge of [the ideographs]. The masses...lack the time and the money to divert themselves with this pastime' (de Francis 1950: 118). This movement for reform was taken up by the Chinese in Russia and by the Communists themselves. In 1951 Mao Tse-tung himself declared: 'The written language must be reformed; it should follow the common direction of phoneticization which has been taken by the world's languages' (Mills 1955–56: 517).

Why had such a script not been adopted earlier? The Chinese were well aware of the alphabetic systems on their doorstep and recognized their simplicity; but even the spread of Buddhism failed to induce them to abandon their own script. The answer is implicit in the verdict of Cheng Ch'iao, a well-known encyclopaedist of the Sung dynasty (A.D. 960–1280): 'The world is of the opinion that people who know ideographs are wise and worthy, whereas those who do not know ideographs are simple and stupid' (de Francis 1950: 10). In other words, the Chinese script enabled knowledge to be confined to a small percentage of people—though in terms of the reading public the numbers were large because of the size of the population. But a nationwide literacy rate does not give a very realistic picture of the distribution of the reading public, for, as Gough points out for India, this may be concentrated in towns (or in monastic institutions) which act as centres for the transmission and development of the written culture.

Despite the considerable achievements of Chinese and Indian society, we can have little doubt of the restricted character of their literate cultures. In India, the potentialities of the alphabet were limited by the religious tradition. In China, the restrictions of the non-alphabetic script were severe. Though the twenty years we earlier gave as the time required for the acquisition of full literacy in Chinese (see below, p. 36) was an overestimation, reformers have no doubt at all that the earlier script takes considerably longer to learn than an alphabetic one. Lattimore speaks of 'the Egyptian obscurity of writing', and the concomitants were significant; de Francis writes: 'Extremely low literacy, a characteristic of pre-industrial society everywhere, abetted the tendency towards preciosity, antiquarianism, and other forms of literary exclusiveness which characterize inbred scholarship in general' (1950: 8).

INTRODUCTION

PRESENT AIMS

This series of essays derives from an interest in communications, in media (it is difficult to avoid the merely fashionable implications) and their effect upon human intercourse. And primarily this concern with the technology of the intellect centres upon the effect of literacy on human culture, especially in 'traditional' or pre-industrial societies.[1]

In most of the essays the effects of literacy are considered from the local level, from the standpoint of the fieldworker interested in the ways in which written learning is transmitted, in the position of literates in a predominantly oral community, in the general uses of literacy under conditions of this kind.[2] One aim is to provide a series of case studies illustrating the uses of literacy in 'traditional' societies, not simply in those societies where partial literacy has been long established, but also the impact of writing, both 'traditional' and 'modern', upon non-literate societies;[3] I have myself examined the impact of writing on northern Ghana, while Meggitt analyses the role of European writing in the New Guinea movements known as Cargo cults. But each author has approached the problem in a slightly different way. Tambiah has discussed literacy in a Thai village; Gough has examined a region of India, while Wilks has discussed a group that specialize in literacy and trading, the nearest African equivalent to the learned castes of the Asian continent.

The significance of writing varies widely among the societies discussed. But even among pastoral peoples like the Somali, even in societies long cut off from the mainstream of literate cultures, like the Merina of Madagascar, even in religiously very mixed areas, like the western Sudan, the book is an important feature of social life, because it provides a reference point for individual and social behaviour, especially that kind of verbal behaviour we think of specifically as 'symbolic', magico-religious,

[1] I do not wish to imply for one moment any opposition between the use of field methods and the study of documentary materials—a glance at papers by Wilks and Schofield will show the irrelevancy of such a suggestion. Although their practitioners often view them as alternative and incompatible ways of arriving at satisfactory explanations of human behaviour, sociology, history and anthropology (to mention only three possibilities) represent little more than partial techniques for attacking a problem. Serious scholarship will do well to avoid the irrelevant question of into whose domain a solution falls.

[2] We are fully aware of the unsatisfactory nature of the term 'traditional' in this context but could discover no alternative that would suit our book. The adjective should simply be taken as an indicator of a general direction.

[3] We have not attempted to deal with the consequences of literacy arising from the introduction or development of the secular school—the most dramatic instrument of social change at man's disposal—simply because our field of study is already wide enough. Besides which, the advantage of studying non-European forms of literacy is that one has a better chance of isolating the effects of the technique as distinct from the content of writing, though clearly such an aim can never be fully realized.

mythopoeic or cosmological—though our given categories do us a great disservice here. So that when Hébert offers us a 'structural analysis' of divinatory systems in Madagascar and in Africa (it is even less easy to perceive the force of 'structural' here than in most usages of this term), he is pointing to certain features of a system of divination, crystallized in writing, that is carried out from Kano to Calcutta, from Tananarive to Samarkand, a 'symbolic' system that has little or no intrinsic connection with the myths, beliefs and categories of the peoples among whom they are found. Even supposing that all the societies in question were equally committed to 'orthodox' Islam and acknowledged the Islamic elements in the system of divination (such as the use of the names of caliphs and archangels and the sacred names of God), many elements in the system (e.g. the 9-cell squares) have quite a different derivation, a much wider distribution, which makes them as much (and as little) an intrinsic part of specifically Gonja or Hausa symbolic structures as the mathematical theory of groups is of specifically Japanese or Belgian thought. For the 9-cell square not only derives from pre-Islamic sources connected with the growth of Babylonian mathematics, it is also equally at home in China and India. The significance of the number 9 may vary from society to society but it always has a fixed point of reference in these arithmetical calculations. Likewise, the precise significance of 7 (from the number of planets in Chaldean astronomy) varies throughout Eurasia and the Islamic world; but it has certain constant features which may be linked only in a relatively loose way with the other customary beliefs and actions of a specific society. Unfortunately the twin concepts of function and structure (as usually interpreted) tend to leave too little room for an assessment of the degree of entailment of a particular aspect of behaviour with the remaining features of social life.[1]

[1] I am grateful to the members of the seminar on literacy at the African Studies Centre Cambridge in 1967 for their lively interest and comments and especially to Edward Shils, Audrey Richards and Esther Goody. Mark Elvin, Mathew Hodgart, Ian Watt and Wunderley Stauder have made helpful comments and suggestions.

THE CONSEQUENCES OF LITERACY

by JACK GOODY *and* IAN WATT

The accepted tripartite divisions of the formal study of mankind's past and of his present are to a considerable extent based on man's development first of language and later of writing. Looked at in the perspective of time, man's biological evolution shades into prehistory when he becomes a language-using animal; add writing, and history proper begins. Looked at in a temporal perspective, man as animal is studied primarily by the zoologist, man as talking animal primarily by the anthropologist, and man as talking and writing animal primarily by the sociologist.

That the differentiation between these categories should be founded on different modes of communication is clearly appropriate; it was language that enabled man to achieve a form of social organization whose range and complexity were different in kind from that of animals; whereas the social organization of animals was mainly instinctive and genetically transmitted, that of man was largely learned and transmitted verbally through the cultural heritage. The basis for the last two distinctions, those based on the development of writing, is equally clear: to the extent that a significant quantity of written records are available, the prehistorian yields to the historian; and to the extent that alphabetical writing and popular literacy imply new modes of social organization and transmission, the anthropologist tends to yield to the sociologist.

But why? And how? There is no agreement about this question, nor even about what the actual boundary lines between non-literate and literate cultures are. At what point in the formalization of pictographs or other graphic signs can we talk of 'letters', of literacy? And what proportion of the society has to write and read before the culture as a whole can be described as literate?

These are some of the many reasons why the extent to which there is any distinction between the areas and methods peculiar to anthropology and sociology must be regarded as problematic; and the difficulty affects not only the boundaries of the two disciplines but also the nature of the intrinsic differences in their subject matter.[1] The recent trend has been for

[1] Some writers distinguish the field of social anthropology from that of sociology on the basis of its subject matter (i.e. the study of non-literate or non-European peoples), others on the basis of its techniques (e.g. that of participant observation). For a discussion of these points, see Siegfried F. Nadel, *The Foundations of Social Anthropology* (London, 1951), p. 2.

anthropologists to spread their net more widely and engage in the study of industrial societies side by side with their sociological colleagues. We can no longer accept the view that anthropologists have as their objective the study of primitive man, who is characterized by a 'primitive mind', while sociologists, on the other hand, concern themselves with civilized man, whose activities are guided by 'rational thought' and tested by 'logico-empirical procedures'. The reaction against such ethnocentric views, however, has now gone to the point of denying that the distinction between non-literate and literate societies has any significant validity. This position seems contrary to our personal observation; and so it has seemed worthwhile to enquire whether there may not be, even from the most empirical and relativist standpoint, genuine illumination to be derived from a further consideration of some of the historical and analytic problems connected with the traditional dichotomy between non-literate and literate societies.

THE CULTURAL TRADITION IN NON-LITERATE SOCIETIES

For reasons which will become clear it seems best to begin with a generalized description of the ways in which the cultural heritage is transmitted in non-literate societies, and then to see how these ways are changed by the widespread adoption of any easy and effective means of written communication.

When one generation hands on its cultural heritage to the next, three fairly separate items are involved. First, the society passes on its material plant, including the natural resources available to its members. Secondly, it transmits standardized ways of acting. These customary ways of behaving are only partly communicated by verbal means; ways of cooking food, of growing crops, of handling children may be transmitted by direct imitation. But the most significant elements of any human culture are undoubtedly channelled through words, and reside in the particular range of meanings and attitudes which members of any society attach to their verbal symbols. These elements include not only what we habitually think of as customary behaviour but also such items as ideas of space and time, generalized goals and aspirations, in short the *Weltanschauung* of every social group. In Durkheim's words, these categories of the understanding are 'priceless instruments of thought which the human groups have laboriously forged through the centuries and where they have accumulated the best of their intellectual capital' (Durkheim 1915: 19). The relative continuity of these categories of understanding from one generation to another is primarily ensured by language, which is the most direct and comprehensive expression of the social experience of the group.

The transmission of the verbal elements of culture by oral means can be visualized as a long chain of interlocking conversations between members of the group. Thus all beliefs and values, all forms of knowledge, are communicated between individuals in face-to-face contact; and, as distinct from the material content of the cultural tradition, whether it be cave-paintings or hand-axes, they are stored only in human memory.

The intrinsic nature of oral communication has a considerable effect upon both the content and the transmission of the cultural repertoire. In the first place, it makes for a directness of relationship between symbol and referent. There can be no reference to 'dictionary definitions', nor can words accumulate the successive layers of historically validated meanings which they acquire in a literate culture. Instead, the meaning of each word is ratified in a succession of concrete situations, accompanied by vocal inflections and physical gestures, all of which combine to particularize both its specific denotation and its accepted connotative usages. This process of direct semantic ratification, of course, operates cumulatively; and as a result the totality of symbol–referent relationships is more immediately experienced by the individual in an exclusively oral culture, and is thus more deeply socialized.

One way of illustrating this is to consider how the range of vocabulary in a non-literate society reflects this mode of semantic ratification. It has often been observed how the elaboration of the vocabulary of such a society reflects the particular interests of the people concerned. The inhabitants of the Pacific island of Lesu have not one, but a dozen or so, words for pigs (Powdermaker 1933: 292; Henle 1958: 5–18), according to sex, colour, and where they come from—a prolixity which mirrors the importance of pigs in a domestic economy that otherwise includes few sources of protein. The corollary of this prolixity is that where common emphases and interests, whether material or otherwise, are not specifically involved, there is little verbal development. Malinowski reported that in the Trobriands the outer world was only named in so far as it yielded useful things, useful, that is, in the very broadest sense;[1] and there is much other testimony to support the view that there is an intimate functional adaptation of language in non-literate societies, which obtains not only for the relatively simple and concrete symbol-referents involved above, but also for the more generalized 'categories of understanding' and for the cultural tradition as a whole.

In an essay he wrote in collaboration with Mauss, 'De quelques formes

[1] Bronislaw Malinowski, 'The Problem of Meaning in Primitive Languages', in C. K. Ogden and I. A. Richards, *The Meaning of Meaning* (London, 1936), pp. 296–336, esp. p. 331. But see also the critical comments by Claude Lévi-Strauss, *La Pensée sauvage* (Paris, 1962), pp. 6, 15–16.

primitives de classification',[1] Durkheim traces the interconnections between the ideas of space and the territorial distribution of the Australian aborigines, the Zuni of the Pueblo area and the Sioux of the Great Plains. This intermeshing of what he called the collective representations with the social morphology of a particular society is clearly another aspect of the same directness of relationship between symbol and referent. Just as the more concrete part of a vocabulary reflects the dominant interests of the society, so the more abstract categories are often closely linked to the accepted terminology for pragmatic pursuits. Among the LoDagaa of northern Ghana, days are reckoned according to the incidence of neighbouring markets; the very word for day and market is the same, and the 'weekly' cycle is a six-day revolution of the most important markets in the vicinity, a cycle which also defines the spatial range of everyday activities.[2]

The way in which these various institutions in an oral culture are kept in relatively close accommodation one to another surely bears directly on the question of the central difference between literate and non-literate societies. As we have remarked, the whole content of the social tradition, apart from the material inheritances, is held in memory. The social aspects of remembering have been emphasized by sociologists and psychologists, particularly by Maurice Halbwachs.[3] What the individual remembers tends to be what is of critical importance in his experience of the main social relationships. In each generation, therefore, the individual memory will mediate the cultural heritage in such a way that its new constituents will adjust to the old by the process of interpretation that Bartlett calls 'rationalizing' or the 'effort after meaning'; and whatever parts of it have ceased to be of contemporary relevance are likely to be eliminated by the process of forgetting.

The social function of memory—and of forgetting—can thus be seen as the final stage of what may be called the homeostatic organization of the cultural tradition in non-literate society. The language is developed in intimate association with the experience of the community, and it is learned

[1] *L'Année sociologique*, VII (1902–3), pp. 1–72. See also S. Czarnowski, 'Le morcellement de l'étendue et sa limitation dans la religion et la magie', *Actes du congrès international d'histoire des religions* (Paris, 1925), I, pp. 339–59.

[2] Jack Goody, unpublished field notes, 1950–2. See also E. E. Evans-Pritchard, *The Nuer* (Oxford, 1940), chap. 3, 'Time and Space', and David Tait, *The Konkomba of Northern Ghana* (London, 1961), pp. 17 ff. For a general treatment of the subject, see A. Irving Hallowell, 'Temporal Orientations in Western Civilisation and in a Preliterate Society', *American Anthropologist*, XXXIX (1937), pp. 647–70.

[3] *Les Cadres sociaux de la mémoire* (Paris, 1925); 'Mémoire et société', *L'Année sociologique*, 3e série, I (1940–8), pp. 11–177; *La Mémoire collective* (Paris, 1950). See also Frederic C. Bartlett on the tendency of oral discourse to become an expression of ideas and attitudes of the group rather than the individual speaker, in *Remembering* (Cambridge, 1932), pp. 265–7, and *Psychology and Primitive Culture* (Cambridge, 1923), pp. 42–3, 62–3, 256.

by the individual in face-to-face contact with the other members. What continues to be of social relevance is stored in the memory while the rest is usually forgotten: and language—primarily vocabulary—is the effective medium of this crucial process of social digestion and elimination which may be regarded as analogous to the homeostatic organization of the human body by means of which it attempts to maintain its present condition of life.

In drawing attention to the importance of these assimilating mechanisms in non-literate societies, we are denying neither the occurrence of social change nor yet the 'survivals' which it leaves in its wake. Nor do we overlook the existence of mnemonic devices in oral cultures which offer some resistance to the interpretative process. Formalized patterns of speech, recital under ritual conditions, the use of drums and other musical instruments, the employment of professional remembrancers—all such factors may shield at least part of the content of memory from the transmuting influence of the immediate pressures of the present. The Homeric epics, for instance, seem to have been written down during the first century of Greek literature between 750 and 650 B.C., but 'they look to a departed era, and their substance is unmistakably old' (Finley 1954: 26).

With these qualifications, however, it seems correct to characterize the transmission of the cultural tradition in oral societies as homeostatic in view of the way in which its emphasis differs from that in literate societies. The description offered has, of course, been extremely abstract; but a few illustrative examples in one important area—that of how the tribal past is digested into the communal orientation of the present—may serve to make it clearer.

Like the Bedouin Arabs and the Hebrews of the Old Testament, the Tiv people of Nigeria give long genealogies of their forebears, which in this case stretch some twelve generations in depth back to an eponymous founding ancestor.[1] Neither these genealogies, nor the Biblical lists of the descendants of Adam, were remembered purely as feats of memory. They served as mnemonics for systems of social relations. When on his deathbed Jacob delivered prophecies about the future of his twelve sons, he spoke of them as the twelve tribes or nations of Israel. It would seem from the account in Genesis that the genealogical tables here refer to contemporary groups rather than to dead individuals;[2] the tables presumably serve to

[1] Laura Bohannan, 'A Genealogical Charter', *Africa*, XXII (1952), pp. 301–15; Emrys Peters, 'The Proliferation of Segments in the Lineage of the Bedouin of Cyrenaica', *Journal of the Royal Anthropological Institute*, XC (1960), pp. 29–53. See also Godfrey and Monica Wilson, *The Analysis of Social Change* (Cambridge, 1945), p. 27.

[2] Ch. 49; further evidence supporting this assumption is found in the etymology of the Hebrew term *Toledot*, which originally denoted 'genealogies', and assumed also the meaning of 'stories and accounts' about the origin of a nation. 'In this sense the term was also applied to the account of the creation of heaven and earth' (Solomon Gandz,

regulate social relations among the twelve tribes of Israel in a manner similar to that which has been well analysed in Evans-Pritchard's work (1940) on the Nuer of the southern Sudan and Fortes' account (1945) of the Tallensi of northern Ghana.

Early British administrators among the Tiv of Nigeria were aware of the great importance attached to these genealogies, which were continually discussed in court cases where the rights and duties of one man towards another were in dispute. Consequently they took the trouble to write down the long lists of names and preserve them for posterity, so that future adminstrators might refer to them in giving judgement. Forty years later, when the Bohannans carried out anthropological field work in the area, their successors were still using the same genealogies.[1] However, these written pedigrees now gave rise to many disagreements; the Tiv maintained that they were incorrect, while the officials regarded them as statements of fact, as records of what had actually happened, and could not agree that the unlettered indigenes could be better informed about the past than their own literate predecessors. What neither party realized was that in any society of this kind changes take place which require a constant readjustment in the genealogies if they are to continue to carry out their function as mnemonics of social relationships.

These changes are of several kinds: those arising from the turnover in personnel, from the process of 'birth and copulation and death'; those connected with the rearrangement of the constituent units of the society, with the migration of one group and fission of another; and lastly those resulting from the effects of changes in the social system itself, whether generated from within or initiated from without. Each of these three processes (which we may refer to for convenience as the processes of generational, organizational and structural change) could lead to alterations of the kind to which the administration objected.

It is obvious that the process of generation leads in itself to a constant lengthening of the genealogy; on the other hand, the population to which it is linked may in fact be growing at quite a different rate, perhaps simply replacing itself. So despite its increasing length the genealogy may have to refer to just as many people at the present time as it did fifty, a hundred, or perhaps two hundred years ago. Consequently the added depth of lineages caused by new births needs to be accompanied by a process of genealogical shrinkage; the occurrence of this telescoping process, a common example of the general social phenomenon which J. A. Barnes

'Oral Tradition in the Bible' in *Jewish Studies in Memory of George A. Kohut*, ed. Salo W. Baron and Alexander Marx, New York, 1935, p. 269).

[1] 'A Genealogical Charter', p. 314.

has felicitously termed 'structural amnesia', has been attested in many societies, including all those mentioned above (Barnes 1947: 48–56; Fortes 1944: 370).

Organizational changes lead to similar adjustments. The state of Gonja in northern Ghana is divided into a number of divisional chiefdoms, certain of which are recognized as providing in turn the ruler of the whole nation. When asked to explain their system the Gonja recount how the founder of the state, Ndewura Jakpa, came down from the Niger Bend in search of gold, conquered the indigenous inhabitants of the area and enthroned himself as chief of the state and his sons as rulers of its territorial divisions. At his death the divisional chiefs succeeded to the paramountcy in turn. When the details of this story were first recorded at the turn of the present century, at the time the British were extending their control over the area, Jakpa was said to have begotten seven sons, this corresponding to the number of divisions whose heads were eligible for the supreme office by virtue of their descent from the founder of the particular chiefdom. But at the same time as the British had arrived, two of the seven divisions disappeared, one being deliberately incorporated in a neighbouring division because its rulers had supported a Mandingo invader, Samori, and another because of some boundary changes introduced by the British administration. Sixty years later, when the myths of state were again recorded, Jakpa was credited with only five sons and no mention was made of the founders of the two divisions which had since disappeared from the political map.[1]

These two instances from the Tiv and the Gonja emphasize that genealogies often serve the same function that Malinowski claimed for myth; they act as 'charters' of present social institutions rather than as faithful historical records of times past (1926: 23, 43). They can do this more consistently because they operate within an oral rather than a written tradition and thus tend to be automatically adjusted to existing social relations as they are passed by word of mouth from one member of the society to another. The social element in remembering results in the genealogies being transmuted in the course of being transmitted; and a similar process takes place with regard to other cultural elements as well, to myths, for example, and to sacred lore in general. Deities and other supernatural agencies which have served their purpose can be quietly dropped from the contemporary pantheon; and as the society changes, myths too are forgotten, attributed to other personages, or transformed in their meaning.

One of the most important results of this homeostatic tendency is that

[1] Jack Goody, unpublished field notes, 1956–7; the heads of the divisions who could not succeed to the paramountcy also claimed descent from sons of the founding ancestor, Jakpa, but this was not an intrinsic part of the myth as usually told, and in any case their number remained constant during the period in question.

the individual has little perception of the past except in terms of the present; whereas the annals of a literate society cannot but enforce a more objective recognition of the distinction between what was and what is. Franz Boas wrote that for the Eskimo the world has always been as it is now.[1] It seems probable, at least, that the form in which non-literate societies conceive the world of the past is itself influenced by the process of transmission described. The Tiv have their genealogies, others their sacred tales about the origin of the world and the way in which man acquired his culture. But all their conceptualizations of the past cannot help being governed by the concerns of the present, merely because there is no body of chronologically ordered statements to which reference can be made. The Tiv do not recognize any contradiction between what they say now and what they said fifty years ago, since no enduring records exist for them to set beside their present views. Myth and history merge into one: the elements in the cultural heritage which cease to have a contemporary relevance tend to be soon forgotten or transformed; and as the individuals of each generation acquire their vocabulary, their genealogies, and their myths, they are unaware that various words, proper names and stories have dropped out, or that others have changed their meanings or been replaced.

KINDS OF WRITING AND THEIR SOCIAL EFFECTS

The pastness of the past, then, depends upon a historical sensibility which can hardly begin to operate without permanent written records; and writing introduces similar changes in the transmission of other items of the cultural repertoire. But the extent of these changes varies with the nature and social distribution of the writing system; varies, that is, according to the system's intrinsic efficacy as a means of communication, and according to the social constraints placed upon it, that is, the degree to which use of the system is diffused through the society.

Early in prehistory, man began to express himself in graphic form; and his cave paintings, rock engravings and wood carvings are morphologically, and presumably sequentially, the forerunners of writing. By some process of simplification and stylization they appear to have led to the various kinds of pictographs found in simple societies (Gelb 1952: 24). While pictographs themselves are almost universal, their development into a self-sufficient system capable of extended discourse occurs only among the Plains Indians (Voegelin 1961: 84, 91).

Pictographs have obvious disadvantages as means of communication.

[1] Franz Boas, 'The Folklore of the Eskimo', *Journal of American Folklore*, LXIV (1904), p. 2. Lévi-Strauss treats the absence of historical knowledge as one of the distinctive features of *la pensée sauvage* in contrast to *la pensée domestiquée* (*La Pensée sauvage*, p. 349).

For one thing a vast number of signs are needed to represent all the important objects in the culture. For another, since the signs are concrete, the simplest sentence requires an extremely elaborate series of signs: many stylized representations of wigwams, footprints, totemic animals and so on are required just to convey the information that a particular man left there a few days ago. Finally, however elaborately the system is developed, only a limited number of things can be said.

The end of the fourth millennium saw the early stages of the development of more complex forms of writing, which seem to be an essential factor in the rise of the urban cultures of the Orient. The majority of signs in these systems were simply pictures of the outside world, standardized representations of the objects signified by particular words; to these were added other devices for creating word signs or logograms, which permitted the expression of wider ranges of meaning. Thus, in Egyptian hieroglyphics the picture of a beetle was a code sign not only for that insect but also for a discontinuous and more abstract referent 'became' (Voegelin 1961: 75–6).

The basic invention used to supplement the logograms was the phonetic principle, which for the first time permitted the written expression of all the words of a language. For example, by the device of phonetic transfer the Sumerians could use the sign for *ti*, an arrow, to stand for *ti*, life, a concept not easy to express in pictographic form. In particular, the need to record personal names and foreign words encouraged the development of phonetic elements in writing.

But while these true writing systems all used phonetic devices for the construction of logograms (and have consequently been spoken of as word-syllabic systems of writing), they failed to carry through the application of the phonetic principle exclusively and systematically.[1] The achievement of a system completely based upon the representation of phonemes (the basic units of meaningful sound) was left to the Near Eastern syllabaries, which developed between 1500–1000 B.C., and finally to the introduction of the alphabet proper in Greece. Meanwhile these incompletely phonetic systems were too clumsy and complicated to foster widespread literacy, if only because the number of signs was very large; at least six hundred would have to be learned even for the simplified cuneiform developed in Assyria, and about the same for Egyptian hieroglyphs (Gelb 1952: 115; Diringer

[1] C. F. and F. M. Voegelin classify all these systems (Chinese, Egyptian, Hittite, Mayan and Sumerian-Akkadian) as 'alphabet included logographic systems'; because these make use of phonetic devices, they include, under the heading 'self-sufficient alphabets', systems which have signs for consonant-vowel sequences (i.e. syllabaries), for independent consonants (IC), e.g. Phoenician, or for independent consonants plus independent vowels (IC+IV), e.g. Greek. In this paper we employ 'alphabet' in the narrower, more usual, sense of a phonemic system with independent signs for consonants and vowels (IC+IV).

1948: 48, 196). All these ancient civilizations, the Sumerian, Egyptian, Hittite and Chinese, were literate in one sense and their great advances in administration and technology were undoubtedly connected with the invention of a writing system; but when we think of the limitations of their systems of communication as compared with ours, the term 'protoliterate', or even 'oligoliterate', might be more descriptive in suggesting the restriction of literacy to a relatively small proportion of the total population.[1]

Any system of writing which makes the sign stand directly for the object must be extremely complex. It can extend its vocabulary by generalization or association of ideas, that is, by making the sign stand either for a more general class of objects or for other referents connected with the original picture by an association of meanings which may be related to one another either in a continuous or in a discontinuous manner. Either process of semantic extension is to some extent arbitrary or esoteric; and as a result the interpretation of these signs is neither easy nor explicit. One might perhaps guess that the Chinese sign for a man carries the general meaning of maleness; it would be more difficult to see that a conventionalized picture of a man and a broom is the sign for a woman; it's a pleasing fancy, no doubt, but not one which communicates very readily until it has been learned as a new character, as a separate sign for a separate word, as a logogram. In Chinese writing a minimum of 3000 such characters have to be learned before one can be reasonably literate (Moorhouse 1953: 90, 163) and with a repertoire of some 50,000 characters to be mastered, it normally takes about twenty years to reach full literate proficiency. China, therefore, stands as an extreme example of how, when a virtually non-phonetic system of writing becomes sufficiently developed to express a large number of meanings explicitly, only a small and specially trained professional group in the total society can master it, and partake of the literate culture.

Although systems of word signs are certainly easier to learn, many difficulties remain, even when these signs are supplemented by phonemic devices of a syllabic sort. Other features of the social system are no doubt responsible for the way that the writing systems developed as they did;

[1] 'Protoliterate' is often employed in a rather different sense, as when S. N. Kramer ('New Light on the Early History of the Ancient Near East', *American Journal of Archaeology*, LII, 1948, p. 161) uses the term to designate the Sumerian phase in Lower Mesopotamia when writing was first invented. There seems to be no generally accepted usage for societies where there is a fully developed but socially restricted phonetic writing system. Sterling Dow ('Minoan Writing', *American Journal of Archaeology*, LVIII, 1954, pp. 77–129) characterizes two stages of Minoan society: one of 'stunted literacy', where little use was made of writing at all (Linear A); and one of 'special literacy', where writing was used regularly but only for limited purposes (Linear B). Stuart Piggott refers to both these under the name of 'conditional literacy' (*Approach to Archaeology*, London, 1959, p. 104).

but it is a striking fact that—for whatever ultimate causes—in Egypt and Mesopotamia, as in China, a literate élite of religious, administrative and commercial experts emerged and maintained itself as a centralized governing bureaucracy on rather similar lines. Their various social and intellectual achievements were, of course, enormous; but as regards the participation of the society as a whole in the written culture, a wide gap existed between the esoteric literate culture and the exoteric oral one, a gap which the literate were interested in maintaining. Among the Sumerians and Akkadians writing was the pursuit of scribes and preserved as a 'mystery', a 'secret treasure'. Royalty were themselves illiterate; Ashurbanipal (668–626 B.C.) records that he was the first Babylonian king to master the 'clerkly skill' (Driver 1954: 62, 72). 'Put writing in your heart that you may protect yourself from hard labour of any kind', writes an Egyptian of the New Kingdom: 'The scribe is released from manual tasks; it is he who commands' (Childe 1941: 187–8; 1942: 105, 118). Significantly, the classical age of Babylonian culture, beginning under Hammurabi in the late eighteenth century B.C., appears to have coincided with a period when the reading and writing of Akkadian cuneiform was not confined to a small group, or to one nation; it was then that nearly all the extant literature was written down, and that the active state of commerce and administration produced a vast quantity of public and private correspondence, of which much has survived.

These imperfectly phonetic methods of writing continued with little change for many centuries;[1] so too did the cultures of which they were part.[2] The existence of an élite group, which followed from the difficulty of the writing system, and whose continued influence depended on the maintenance of the present social order, must have been a powerfully conservative force, especially when it consisted of ritual specialists;[3] and so, it may be surmised, was the nature of the writing system itself. For pictographic and logographic systems are alike in their tendency to reify the objects of the natural and social order; by so doing they register, record, make permanent the existing social and ideological picture. Such, for

[1] 'Egyptian hieroglyphic writing remained fundamentally unchanged for a period of three thousand years', according to David Diringer (*Writing*, London, 1962, p. 48). He attributes the fact that it never lost its cumbrousness and elaboration to 'its unique sacredness' (p. 50).

[2] Many authorities have commented upon the lack of development in Egypt after the initial achievements of the Old Kingdom: for a discussion (and a contrary view), see John A. Wilson in *Before Philosophy*, ed. H. Frankfort and others (London, 1949), pp. 115–16 (pub. in U.S.A. as *The Intellectual Adventure of Ancient Man*, Chicago, 1946).

[3] 'The world view of the Egyptians and Babylonians was conditioned by the teaching of sacred books; it thus constituted an orthodoxy, the maintenance of which was in the charge of colleges of priests' (Benjamin Farrington, *Science in Antiquity*, London, 1936, p. 37. See also Gordon Childe, *What Happened in History*, p. 121.

example, was the tendency of the most highly developed and longest-lived ancient writing system, that of Egypt, whose society has been described with picturesque exaggeration as 'a nation of fellahin ruled with a rod of iron by a Society of Antiquaries'.

This conservative or antiquarian bias can perhaps be best appreciated by contrasting it with fully phonetic writing; for phonetic writing, by imitating human discourse, is in fact symbolizing, not the objects of the social and natural order, but the very process of human interaction in speech: the verb is as easy to express as the noun; and the written vocabulary can be easily and unambiguously expanded. Phonetic systems are therefore adapted to expressing every nuance of individual thought, to recording personal reactions as well as items of major social importance. Non-phonetic writing, on the other hand, tends rather to record and reify only those items in the cultural repertoire which the literate specialists have selected for written expression; and it tends to express the collective attitude towards them.

The notion of representing a sound by a graphic symbol is itself so stupefying a leap of the imagination that what is remarkable is not so much that it happened relatively late in human history, but rather that it ever happened at all. For a long time, however, these phonetic inventions had a limited effect because they were only partially exploited: not only were logograms and pictograms retained, but a variety of phonograms were used to express the same sound. The full explicitness and economy of a phonetic writing system 'as easy as A B C' were therefore likely to arise only in less advanced societies on the fringes of Egypt or Mesopotamia, societies which were starting their writing system more or less from scratch, and which took over the idea of phonetic signs from adjoining countries, and used them exclusively to fit their own language.[1] These phonetic signs could, of course, be used to stand for any unit of speech, and thus be developed either into syllabaries or into alphabets. In a few cases, such as Japanese, the particular nature of the language made it possible to construct a relatively simple and efficient syllabary; but as regards the great majority of languages the alphabet, with its signs for individual consonants and vowels, proved a much more economical and convenient instrument for representing sounds. For the syllabaries, while making writing easier, were still far from simple;[2] they were often combined with logograms and

[1] Gelb, *Study of Writing*, p. 196, maintains that all the main types of syllabary developed in just this way. Driver rejects the possibility that the Phoenician alphabet was invented on Egyptian soil, as it would have been 'stifled at birth' by the 'deadweight of Egyptian tradition, already of hoary antiquity and in the hands of a powerful priesthood' (*Semitic Writing*, p. 187).

[2] 'Immensely complicated', Driver calls the pre-alphabetic forms of writing Semitic (*Semitic Writing*, p. 67).

pictographs.[1] And whether by necessity or tradition or both, pre-alphabetic writing was still mainly restricted to élite groups. The Mycenaean script disappeared completely after the twelfth century B.C., a fact which was possible because of the very restricted uses of literacy and the close connection between writing and palace administration (Chadwick 1958: 130; 1959: 7–18). It is doubtful whether any such loss could have occurred in Greece after the introduction of a complete alphabetic script, probably in the eighth century B.C.

The alphabet is almost certainly the supreme example of cultural diffusion (Diringer 1948): all existing or recorded alphabets derive from Semitic syllabaries developed during the second millennium. Eventually there arose the enormous simplification of the Semitic writing system, with its mere twenty-two letters; and then only one further step remained: the Greek script, which is, of course, much closer than the Semitic to the Roman alphabet, took certain of the Semitic signs for consonants which the Greek language didn't need, and used them for vowels, which the Semitic syllabary did not represent.[2] The directness of our inheritance from these two sources is suggested by the fact that our word 'alphabet' is the latinized form of the first two letters of the Greek alphabet, 'alpha', derived from the Semitic 'aleph', and 'beta', from the Semitic 'beth'.

The reason for the success of the alphabet, which David Diringer calls a 'democratic' script as opposed to the 'theocratic' scripts of Egypt, is related to the fact that, uniquely among writing systems, its graphic signs are representations of the most extreme and most universal example of cultural selection—the basic phonemic system. The number of sounds which the human breath stream can produce is vast; but nearly all languages are based on the formal recognition by the society of only forty or so of these sounds. The success of the alphabet (as well as some of its incidental difficulties) comes from the fact that its system of graphic representation takes advantage of this socially conventionalized pattern of sound in all language systems; by symbolizing in letters these selected phonemic units the alphabet makes it possible to write easily and read unambiguously about anything which the society can talk about.

The historical picture of the cultural impact of the new alphabetic writing is not altogether clear. As regards the Semitic system, which was widely adopted elsewhere, the evidence suggests that the social diffusion of writing was slow. This was caused partly by the intrinsic difficulties of the system but mainly by the established cultural features of the societies which

[1] For Hittite, see O. R. Gurney, *The Hittites* (London, 1952), pp. 120–1. For Mycenaean, see John Chadwick, *The Decipherment of Linear B* (Cambridge, 1958).

[2] *The Alphabet*, pp. 214–18. On the 'accidental' nature of this change see C. F. and F. M. Voegelin, 'Typological Classification', pp. 63–4.

adopted it. There was, for one thing, a strong tendency for writing to be used as a help to memory rather than as an autonomous and independent mode of communication; and under such conditions its influence tended towards the consolidation of the existing cultural tradition. This certainly appears to be true of India and Palestine.[1] Gandz notes, for example, that Hebrew culture continued to be transmitted orally long after the Old Testament had begun to be written down. As he puts it, the introduction of writing

> did not at once change the habits of the people and displace the old method of oral tradition. We must always distinguish between the *first introduction* of writing and its *general diffusion*. It often takes several centuries, and sometimes even a millennium or more, until this invention becomes the common property of the people at large. In the beginning, the written book is not intended for practical use at all. It is a divine instrument, placed in the temple 'by the side of the ark of the covenant that it may be there for a witness' (Deuteronomy xxxi. 26), and remains there as a holy relic. For the people at large, oral instruction still remained the only way of learning, and the memory—the only means of preservation. Writing was practised, if at all, only as an additional support for the memory...

It was not, in fact, until some six centuries after the original Hebrew adoption of the Semitic writing system that, at the time of Ezra (*c.* 444 B.C.), an official 'generally recognized text' of the Torah was published, and the body of the religious tradition ceased to be 'practically...a sealed book' and became accessible to anyone who chose to study it (Gandz 1935: 253–4).

Even so, of course, as the frequent diatribes against the scribes in the Gospels remind us,[2] there remained a considerable gap between the literati and the laymen; the professionals who plied their trade in the market-place belonged to 'families of scribes', perhaps organized as guilds, within which the mystery was handed down from father to son.[3]

Anything like popular literacy, or the use of writing as an autonomous mode of communication by the majority of the members of society, is not found in the earliest societies which used the Semitic writing system; it was, rather, in the sixth and fifth centuries B.C. in the city states of Greece and Ionia that there first arose a society which as a whole could justly be characterized as literate. Many of the reasons why literacy became widespread in Greece, but not in other societies which had Semitic or, indeed, any other simple and explicit writing systems, necessarily lie outside the scope of this essay; yet considerable importance must surely be attributed to the intrinsic advantages of the Greek adaptation of the Semitic alphabet,

[1] According to Ralph E. Turner, *The Great Cultural Traditions* (New York, 1941), I, pp. 346, 391, the Hebrews took over the Semitic system in the eleventh century B.C., and the Indians a good deal later, probably in the eighth century B.C.

[2] E.g. Luke xx; Matthew, xxiii; in the seventh century B.C., even kings and prophets employed scribes, Jer. xxxvi, 4, 18.

[3] Driver, *Semitic Writing*, pp. 87–90, where he instances the case of one scribe who, having no son, 'taught his wisdom to his sister's son'.

an adaptation which made it the first comprehensively and exclusively phonetic system for transcribing human speech.[1] The system was easy, explicit and unambiguous—more so than the Semitic, where the lack of vowels is responsible for many of the cruces in the Bible: for instance, since the consonant in the Hebrew words is the same, Elijah may have been fed by 'ravens' or 'Arabs'.[2] Its great advantage over the syllabaries lay in the reduction of the number of signs and in the ability to specify consonant and vowel clusters. The system was easy to learn: Plato sets aside three years for the process in the *Laws*,[3] about the time taken in our schools today; and the much greater speed with which alphabetic writing can be learned is shown, not only by such reports as those of the International Institute of Intellectual Cooperation in 1934,[4] but also by the increasing adoption of the Roman script, and even more widely of alphabetic systems of writing, throughout the world.

The extensive diffusion of the alphabet in Greece was also materially assisted by various social, economic and technological factors. In the first place, the eighth century saw a great burst of economic activity following the revival of the eastern trade which had declined after the Mycenaean collapse in the twelfth century (Starr 1961: 189–190, 349). Secondly, while the Greek society of the period had, of course, its various social strata, the political system was not strongly centralized; especially in the Ionic settlements there appears to have been a good deal of flexibility and in them we discern the beginnings of the Greek city state. Thirdly, the increased contact with the East brought material prosperity and technological advance. The wider use of iron, the advent of the true Iron Age, was perhaps one of the results (Starr 1961: 87–8, 357). More closely connected with literacy was the fact that trade with Egypt led to the importation of papyrus; and this made writing itself easier and less expensive, both for the individual writer and for the reader who wanted to buy books; papyrus was obviously much cheaper than parchment made from skins, more permanent than wax tablets, easier to handle than the stone or clay of Mesopotamia and Mycenae.

The chronology and extent of the diffusion of literacy in Greece remain a matter of debate. With the Mycenaean collapse in the twelfth century,

[1] 'If the alphabet is defined as a system of signs expressing single sounds of speech, then the first alphabet which can justifiably be so called is the Greek alphabet' (Gelb, *Study of Writing*, p. 166).

[2] 1 Kings xvii. 4–6; see *A Dictionary of the Bible*...ed. James Hastings (New York, 1898–1904), *s.v.* 'Elijah'.

[3] 810a. From the age of ten to thirteen.

[4] *L'Adoption universelle des caractères latins* (Paris, 1934); for more recent developments and documentation, see William S. Gray, *The Teaching of Reading and Writing: An International Survey*, *Unesco Monographs on Fundamental Education*, x (Paris, 1956), esp. pp. 31–60.

writing disappeared; the earliest Greek inscriptions in the modified Semitic alphabet occur in the last two decades of the eighth century (Starr 1961: 169). Recent authorities suggest the new script was adopted and transformed about the middle of the eighth century in northern Syria.[1] The extensive use of writing probably came only slowly in the seventh century, but when it finally came it seems to have been applied in a very wide range of activities, intellectual as well as economic, and by a wide range of people.[2]

It must be remembered, of course, that Greek writing throughout the classical period was still relatively difficult to decipher, as words were not regularly separated (Kenyon 1951: 67); that the copying of manuscripts was a long and laborious process; and that silent reading as we know it was very rare until the advent of printing—in the ancient world books were used mainly for reading aloud, often by a slave. Nevertheless, from the sixth century onwards literacy seems to be increasingly presumed in the public life of Greece and Ionia. In Athens, for example, the first laws for the general public to read were set up by Solon in 594–3 B.C.; the institution of ostracism early in the fifth century assumes a literate citizen body—6,000 citizens had to write the name of the person on their potsherds before he could be banished (Carcopino 1935: 72–110); there is abundant evidence in the fifth century of a system of schools teaching reading and writing (*Protagoras*, 325d) and of a book-reading public—satirized already by Aristophanes in *The Frogs*;[3] while the final form of the Greek alphabet, which was established fairly late in the fifth century, was finally adopted for use in the official records of Athens by decree of the Archon Eucleides in 403 B.C.

ALPHABETIC CULTURE AND GREEK THOUGHT

The rise of Greek civilization, then, is the prime historical example of the transition to a really literate society. In all subsequent cases where the widespread introduction of an alphabetic script occurred, as in Rome for example, other cultural features were inevitably imported from the loan country along with the writing system; Greece thus offers not only the first instance of this change, but also the essential one for any attempt to isolate the cultural consequences of alphabetic literacy.

[1] L. H. Jeffery, *The Local Scripts of Archaic Greece* (Oxford, 1961), p. 21; R. M. Cook and A. G. Woodhead, 'The Diffusion of the Greek Alphabet', *American Journal of Archaeology*, LXIII (1959), pp. 175–8. For north Syria, see Sir Leonard Woolley, *A Forgotten Kingdom* (London, 1953).

[2] Chester Starr speaks of its use by 'a relatively large aristocratic class' (p. 171) and Miss Jeffery notes that 'writing was never regarded as an esoteric craft in early Greece. Ordinary people could and did learn to write, for many of the earliest inscriptions which we possess are casual graffiti' (p. 63).

[3] l. 1114; in 414 B.C. See also Plato, *Apology*, 26d, and the general survey of Kenyon, *Books and Readers in Ancient Greece and Rome*.

The fragmentary and ambiguous nature of our direct evidence about this historical transformation in Greek civilization means that any generalizations must be extremely tentative and hypothetical; but the fact that the essential basis both of the writing systems and of many characteristic cultural institutions of the Western tradition as a whole are derived from Greece, and that they both arose there simultaneously, would seem to justify the present attempt to outline the possible relationships between the writing system and those cultural innovations of early Greece which are common to all alphabetically literate societies.

The early development of the distinctive features of Western thought is usually traced back to the radical innovations of the pre-Socratic philosophers of the sixth century B.C. The essence of their intellectual revolution is seen as a change from mythical to logico-empirical modes of thought. Such, broadly speaking, is Werner Jaeger's view; and Ernst Cassirer writes that 'the history of philosophy as a scientific discipline may be regarded as a single continuous struggle to effect a separation and liberation from myth'.[1]

To this general picture there are two kinds of theoretical objection. First, that the crucial intellectual innovations—in Cassirer as in Werner Jaeger—are in the last analysis attributed to the special mental endowments of the Greek people; and in so far as such terms as 'the Greek mind' and 'genius' are not simply descriptive, they are logically dependent upon extremely questionable theories of man's nature and culture. Secondly, such a version of the transformation from 'unphilosophical' to 'philosophical' thought assumes an absolute—and untenable—dichotomy between the 'mythical' thought of primitives and the 'logico-empirical' thought of civilized man.

The dichotomy, of course, is itself very similar to Lévy-Bruhl's earlier theory of the 'prelogical' mentality of primitive peoples, which has been widely criticized. Malinowski and many others have demonstrated the empirical elements in non-literate cultures,[2] and Evans-Pritchard (1937) has carefully analysed the 'logical' nature of the belief systems of the Azande of the Sudan;[3] while on the other hand the illogical and mythical

[1] *The Philosophy of Symbolic Forms* (New Haven, 1955), II, p. xiii; and *An Essay on Man* (New York, 1953), esp. pp. 106–30, 281–3. For Werner Jaeger, see esp. *The Theology of the Early Greek Philosophers* (Oxford, 1947).

[2] 'Magic, Science and Religion' in *Science, Religion and Reality*, ed. Joseph Needham (New York, 1925), reprinted *Magic, Science and Religion* (New York, 1954), p. 27. For an appreciation of Lévy-Bruhl's positive achievement, see Evans-Pritchard, 'Lévy-Bruhl's Theory of Primitive Mentality', *Bulletin of the Faculty of Arts, University of Egypt*, II (1934), pp. 1–36. In his later work, Lévy-Bruhl modified the rigidity of his earlier dichotomy.

[3] See also Max Gluckman's essay, 'Social Beliefs and Individual Thinking in Primitive Society', *Memoirs and Proceedings of the Manchester Literary and Philosophical Society*, XCI (1949–50), pp. 73–98. From a rather different standpoint, Lévi-Strauss has analysed 'the logic of totemic classifications' (*La Pensée sauvage*, pp. 48 ff.) and speaks of two distinct modes of scientific thought; the first (or 'primitive') variety consists in 'the

nature of much Western thought and behaviour is evident to anyone contemplating either our past or our present.

Nevertheless, although we must reject any dichotomy based upon the assumption of radical differences between the mental attributes of literate and non-literate peoples, and accept the view that previous formulations of the distinction were based on faulty premises and inadequate evidence, there may still exist general differences between literate and non-literate societies somewhat along the lines suggested by Lévy-Bruhl. One reason for their existence, for instance, may be what has been described above: the fact that writing establishes a different kind of relationship between the word and its referent, a relationship that is more general and more abstract, and less closely connected with the particularities of person, place and time, than obtains in oral communication. There is certainly a good deal to substantiate this distinction in what we know of early Greek thought. To take, for instance, the categories of Cassirer and Werner Jaeger, it is surely significant that it was only in the days of the first widespread alphabetic culture that the idea of 'logic'—of an immutable and impersonal mode of discourse—appears to have arisen; and it was also only then that the sense of the human past as an objective reality was formally developed, a process in which the distinction between 'myth' and 'history' took on decisive importance.

Myth and history

Non-literate peoples, of course, often make a distinction between the lighter folk-tale, the graver myth, and the quasi-historical legend (e.g. the Trobriands; Malinowski 1926: 33). But not so insistently, and for an obvious reason. As long as the legendary and doctrinal aspects of the cultural tradition are mediated orally, they are kept in relative harmony with each other and with the present needs of society in two ways: through the unconscious operations of memory, and through the adjustment of the reciter's terms and attitudes to those of the audience before him. There is evidence, for example, that such adaptations and omissions occurred in the oral transmission of the Greek cultural tradition. But once the poems of Homer and Hesiod, which contained much of the earlier history, religion and cosmology of the Greeks, had been written down, succeeding generations were faced with old distinctions in sharply aggravated form: how far was the information about their gods and heroes literally true? How could its patent inconsistencies be explained? And how could the beliefs and attitudes implied be brought into line with those of the present?

The disappearance of so many early Greek writings, and the difficulties

science of the concrete', the practical knowledge of the handy man (*bricoleur*), which is the technical counterpart of mythical thought (p. 26).

of dating and composition in many that survive, make anything like a clear reconstruction impossible. Greek had of course been written, in a very limited way, during Mycenaean times. At about 1200 B.C. writing disappeared, and the alphabet was not developed until some four hundred years later. Most scholars agree that in the middle or late eighth century the Greeks adapted the purely consonantal system of Phoenicia, possibly at the trading port of al Mina (Poseidon?). Much of the early writing consisted of 'explanatory inscriptions on existing objects—dedications on offerings, personal names on property, epitaphs on tombs, names of figures in drawings' (Jeffery 1961: 46). The Homeric poems were written down between 750 and 650 B.C., and the seventh century saw first the recording of lyric verse and then (at the end) the emergence of the great Ionian school of scientist philosophers.[1] Thus within a century or two of the writing down of the Homeric poems, many groups of writers and teachers appeared, first in Ionia and later in Greece, who took as their point of departure the belief that much of what Homer had apparently said was inconsistent and unsatisfactory in many respects. The logographers, who set themselves to record the genealogies, chronologies and cosmologies which had been handed down orally from the past, soon found that the task led them to use their critical and rational powers to create a new individual synthesis. In non-literate society, of course, there are usually some individuals whose interests lead them to collect, analyse and interpret the cultural tradition in a personal way; and the written records suggest that this process went considerably further among the literate élites of Egypt, Babylon and China, for example. But, perhaps because in Greece reading and writing were less restricted to any particular priestly or administrative groups, there seems to have been a more thoroughgoing individual challenge to the orthodox cultural tradition in sixth-century Greece than occurred elsewhere. Hecataeus, for example, proclaimed at about the turn of the century, 'What I write is the account I believe to be true. For the stories the Greeks tell are many and in my opinion ridiculous' (Jacoby 1931), and offered his own rationalizations of the data on family traditions and lineages which he had collected. Already the mythological mode of using the past, the mode which, in Sorel's words, makes it 'a means of acting on the present' (Hulme 1941: 136; Redfield 1953: 125), has begun to disappear.

That this trend of thought had much larger implications can be seen from the fact that the beginnings of religious and natural philosophy are

[1] 'It was in Ionia that the first completely rationalistic attempts to describe the nature of the world took place' (G. S. Kirk and J. E. Raven, *The Presocratic Philosophers*, Cambridge, 1957, p. 73). The work of the Milesian philosophers, Thales, Anaximander and Anaximenes, is described by the authors as 'clearly a development of the genetic or genealogical approach to nature exemplified by the Hesiodic *Theogony*' (p. 73).

connected with similar critical departures from the inherited traditions of the past; as W. B. Yeats wrote, with another tradition in mind: 'Science is the critique of myths, there would be no Darwin had there been no *Book* of Genesis' (Hone 1942: 405, our italics). Among the early pre-Socratics there is much evidence of the close connection between new ideas and the criticism of the old. Thus Xenophanes of Colophon (*fl. c.* 540 B.C.) rejected the 'fables of men of old', and replaced the anthropomorphic gods of Homer and Hesiod who did 'everything that is disgraceful and blameworthy among men' with a supreme god, 'not at all like mortals in body and mind',[1] while Heraclitus of Ephesus (*fl. c.* 500 B.C.), the first great philosopher of the problems of knowledge, whose system is based on the unity of opposites expressed in the *Logos* or structural plan of things, also ridiculed the anthropomorphism and idolatry of the Olympian religion.[2]

The critical and sceptical process continued, and, according to Cornford, 'a great part of the supreme god's biography had to be frankly rejected as false, or reinterpreted as allegory, or contemplated with reserve as mysterious myth too dark for human understanding' (Cornford 1923: xv–xvi; Burnet 1908: 1). On the one hand the poets continued to use the traditional legends for their poems and plays; on the other the prose writers attempted to wrestle with the problems with which the changes in the cultural tradition had faced them. Even the poets, however, had a different attitude to their material. Pindar, for example, used *mythoi* in the sense of traditional stories, with the implication that they were not literally true; but claimed that his own poems had nothing in common with the fables of the past (1st Olympian Ode). As for the prose writers, and indeed some of the poets, they had set out to replace myth with something else more consistent, with their sense of the *logos*, of the common and all-encompassing truth which reconciles apparent contradictions.

From the point of view of the transmission of the cultural tradition, the categories of understanding connected with the dimensions of time and space have a particular importance. As regards an objective description of space, Anaximander (b. 610 B.C.) and Hecataeus (*fl. c.* 510–490), making use of Babylonian and Egyptian techniques, drew the first maps of the world (Warmington 1934: xiv, xxxviii). Then their crude beginnings were

[1] Hermann Diels, *Die Fragmente der Vorsokratiker* (Berlin, 1951), fr. 11, 23; see also John Burnet, *Early Greek Philosophy* (2nd ed. London, 1908), pp. 131, 140–1, and Werner Jaeger, *The Theology of the Early Greek Philosophers* (Oxford, 1947), pp. 42–7; Kirk and Raven, *The Presocratic Philosophers*, pp. 163 ff.

[2] Diels, *Fragmente der Vorsokratiker*, fr. 40, 42, 56, 57, 106; see also Francis M. Cornford, *Principium Sapientiae: The Origins of Greek Philosophical Thought* (Cambridge, 1952), pp. 112 ff.; Kirk and Raven, *The Presocratic Philosophers*, pp. 182 ff.

subjected to a long process of criticism and correction—by Herodotus (*History*: IV, 36–40) and others; and from this emerged the more scientific cartography of Aristotle, Eratosthenes and their successors (Warmington 1934: xvii, xli).

The development of history appears to have followed a rather similar course, although the actual details of the process are subject to much controversy. The traditional view gave priority to local histories, which were followed by the more universal accounts of Herodotus and Thucydides. Dionysius of Halicarnasus writes of the predecessors of these historians who, 'instead of co-ordinating their accounts with each other,...treated of individual peoples and cities separately...They all had the one same object, to bring to the general knowledge of the public the written records that they found preserved in temples or in secular buildings in the form in which they found them, neither adding nor taking away anything; among these records were to be found legends hallowed by the passage of time...' (Pearson 1939: 3).

Jacoby, however, has insisted 'the whole idea is wrong that Greek historiography began with local history' (1949: 354). As far as Athens is concerned, history begins with the foreigner Herodotus, who, not long after the middle of the fifth century, incorporated parts of the story of the town in his work because he wanted to explain the role it played in the great conflict between East and West, between Europe and Asia. The aim of Herodotus' *History* was to discover what the Greeks and Persians 'fought each other for' (*History*: I, 1; Finley 1959: 4); and his method was *historia*, personal inquiry or research into the most probable versions of events as they were to be found in various sources. His work rested on oral tradition and consequently his writings retained many mythological elements. So too did the work of the logographer, Hellanicus of Lesbos, who at the end of the fifth century wrote the first history of Attica from 683 to the end of the Peloponnesian war in 404. Hellanicus also tried to reconstruct the genealogies of the Homeric heroes, both backwards to the gods and forwards to the Greece of his own time; and this inevitably involved chronology, the objective measurement of time. All he could do, however, was to rationalize and systematize largely legendary materials (Pearson 1939: 193, 232). The development of history as a documented and analytic account of the past and present of the society in permanent written form took an important step forward with Thucydides, who made a decisive distinction between myth and history, a distinction to which little attention is paid in non-literate society (Malinowski 1922: 290–333). Thucydides wanted to give a wholly reliable account of the wars between Athens and Sparta; and this meant that unverified assumptions about the past had to be excluded. So Thucydides rejected, for example, the chronology that Hellanicus had worked out for the prehistory of Athens, and confined himself very largely to his own notes of the events and speeches he related, or to the information he sought out from eyewitnesses and other reliable sources (Thucydides: I, 20–2, 97).[1]

And so, not long after the widespread diffusion of writing throughout the Greek world, and the recording of the previously oral cultural tradition, there arose an attitude to the past very different from that common in non-literate societies. Instead of the unobtrusive adaptation of past tradition to present needs, a great many individuals found in the written records, where much of their traditional cultural repertoire had been given permanent form, so many inconsistencies in the beliefs and categories of understanding handed down to them that they were impelled to a much more conscious, comparative and critical attitude to the accepted world picture, and notably to the notions of God, the universe and the past. Many individual solutions to these problems were themselves written down, and these versions formed the basis for further investigations.[2]

In non-literate society, it was suggested, the cultural tradition functions as a series of interlocking face-to-face conversations in which the very conditions of transmission operate to favour consistency between past and present, and to make criticism—the articulation of inconsistency—less likely to occur; and if it does, the inconsistency makes a less permanent impact, and is more easily adjusted or forgotten. While scepticism may be present in such societies, it takes a personal, non-cumulative form; it does not lead to a deliberate rejection and reinterpretation of social dogma so much as to a semi-automatic readjustment of belief.[3]

In literate society, these interlocking conversations go on; but they are

[1] For a picture of note-taking (*hypomnemata*) among Athenians, see *Theaetetus*, 142c–143c.

[2] Felix Jacoby notes that 'fixation in writing, once achieved, primarily had a preserving effect upon the oral tradition, because it put an end to the involuntary shiftings of the *mnemai* (remembrances), and drew limits to the arbitrary creation of new *logoi* (stories)' (*Atthis*, 1949, p. 217). He points out that this created difficulties for the early literate recorders of the past which the previous oral *mnemones* or professional 'remembrancers' did not have to face; whatever his own personal view of the matter, 'no true Atthidographer could remove Kekrops from his position as the first Attic king...Nobody could take away from Solon the legislation which founded *in nuce* the first Attic constitution of historical times.' Such things could no longer be silently forgotten, as in an oral tradition.

The general conclusion of Jacoby's polemic against Wilamowitz' hypothesis of a 'pre-literary chronicle' is that 'historical consciousness...is not older than historical literature' (p. 201).

[3] As writers on the indigenous political systems of Africa have insisted, changes generally take the form of rebellion rather than revolution; subjects reject the king, but not the kingship. See Evans-Pritchard, *The Divine Kingship of the Shilluk of the Nilotic Sudan* (The Frazer Lecture, Cambridge, 1948), pp. 35 ff.; Max Gluckman, *Rituals of Rebellion in South-East Africa* (The Frazer Lecture, 1952), Manchester, 1954.

no longer man's only dialogue; and in so far as writing provides an alternative source for the transmission of cultural orientations it favours awareness of inconsistency. One aspect of this is a sense of change and of cultural lag; another is the notion that the cultural inheritance as a whole is composed of two very different kinds of material; fiction, error and superstition on the one hand; and, on the other, elements of truth which can provide the basis for some more reliable and coherent explanation of the gods, the human past and the physical world.

Plato and the effects of literacy

One area of this process can be described as the replacement of myth by history; but of course *historia* in the Greek sense, meaning 'inquiry', can be envisaged much more broadly as an attempt to determine reality in every area of human concern; and in many of these areas it was the Greeks who provided us with the fundamental premises of our present categories of understanding.

The actual role of writing in the development of this conceptual framework is more largely a matter of inference than in the particular case of history proper; but when we turn from the processes of collective development and transmission in their chronological perspective to the particular process of transmission from one individual to another, we can find something a little more definite than inference to go on; for in the writings of the Greek who shows most consciousness of the difference between oral and literate thoughtways, Plato, the greater completeness and intensity of oral transmission are discussed and emphasized.

Plato was born about 427 B.C., long after the widespread diffusion of the alphabet in the Greek world. Many of the characteristic institutions of literate culture had already appeared: there were schools for children from the age of six and upwards (Marrou 1948: 76–152); and professional scholars and philosophers, such as the Sophists, had replaced the traditional expounders of the lore of the past, such as the *Eupatridai*, noble families in whom had earlier been vested the right to interpret the laws. Both the schools and the Sophists are discussed in an early Platonic dialogue, the *Protagoras*, where Socrates is shown to be suspicious of the new professional teachers and authors who have turned wisdom into a market-place commodity, a commodity which is dangerous unless the buyer already has 'understanding of what is good and evil' (*Protagoras*, 313e). But it is in the *Phaedrus* and the *Seventh Letter* that we find the most explicit criticism of writing as a means of conveying thoughts and values.

In the *Phaedrus*, Socrates takes up the 'nature of good and bad speaking and writing' and tells how the Egyptian king Thamus rebuked the God Theuth for claiming that his invention of writing would provide 'a recipe for memory and wisdom': '...If men learn this,' Thamus concludes, 'it will implant forgetfulness in their souls; they will cease to exercise memory because they rely on that which is written, calling things to remembrance no longer from within themselves, but by means of external marks; what you have discovered is a recipe not for memory, but for reminder. And it is no true wisdom that you offer your disciples, but only its semblance; for by telling them of many things without teaching them you will make them seem to know much, while for the most part they know nothing; and as men filled, not with wisdom, but the conceit of wisdom, they will be a burden to their fellows.'[1]

The emphasis on memory, the repository of the cultural tradition in oral society, is significant; and it is appropriate that Socrates should deliver his attack on writing in the form of a fable or myth, in a distinctively oral and non-logical mode of discourse (Notopoulos 1938: 465–93). The ensuing discussion, and several other discussions, of which the most important occurs in the *Seventh Letter*, make clear that the objections to writing are twofold: it is inherently shallow in its effects; and the essential principles of truth can only be arrived at dialectically.

Writing is shallow in its effects because reading books may give a specious sense of knowledge, which in reality can only be attained by oral question and answer; and such knowledge in any case only goes deep when it 'is written in the soul of the learner' (*Phaedrus*, 276a). The reasons which Plato, or his spokesman Socrates, gives for holding dialectic to be the true method of pursuing essential knowledge are very close to the picture given above of the transmission of the cultural tradition in oral society. For the dialectic method is, after all, an essential social process, in which the initiates pass on their knowledge directly to the young; a process, indeed, in which only a long personal relationship can transcend the inherent incapacity of mere words to convey ultimate truths—the forms or ideas which alone can give unity and coherence to human knowledge. As Plato puts it in the *Seventh Letter*, such knowledge can be passed on only when, 'after personal assistance in these studies from a guide, after living for some time with that guide, suddenly a flash of understanding, as it were, is kindled by a spark that leaps across, and once it has come into being within the soul it proceeds to nourish itself'.[2]

What is at issue here is not only the intimate understanding which comes

[1] 259e; 274–5. From Reginald Hackforth's translation in his *Plato's Phaedrus* (Cambridge, 1952).

[2] 341c–d (trans. R. S. Bluck, *Plato's Life and Thought*, London, 1949).

from long personal contact, but also the inherent advantages which living speech is given over the written word by virtue of its more immediate connection with the act of communication itself. The first advantage is that possible confusions or misunderstandings can always be cleared up by question and answer; whereas 'written words', as Socrates tells Phaedrus, 'seem to talk to you as though they were intelligent, but if you ask them anything about what they say, from a desire to be instructed, they go on telling you just the same thing for ever'. The second intrinsic advantage is that the speaker can vary his 'type of speech' so that it is 'appropriate to each nature...addressing a variegated soul in a variegated style...and a simple soul in a simple style'. And so, in the *Phaedrus*, Socrates concludes that 'anyone who leaves behind him a written manual, and likewise anyone who takes it over from him, on the supposition that such writing will provide something reliable and permanent, must be exceedingly simple-minded' (*Phaedrus*, 275d; 275c; 277c).

To some extent Plato's arguments against writing are specific reflections of the incapacity of words alone to convey the Ideas, and of the initiate's usual reluctance to share his esoteric lore except on his own terms (David-Neel and Yongden: 1959); while in the perspective of the later history of epistemology, Plato's position must be seen as an indication of his prescient awareness of the danger of using abstract words about whose referents no common agreement or identity of understanding has been established. Plato's reservations about writing must also be seen in relation to the preference which Greek culture shares with Roman for the more living quality of the spoken as opposed to the written word (Green 1951: 23–59): the general argument at this particular point in the *Phaedrus* is concerned with the advantages of extempore as compared with written speeches.

Nevertheless, the *Phaedrus* and the *Seventh Letter* seem to provide good evidence that Plato considered the transmission of the cultural tradition was more effective and permanent under oral conditions, at least as regards the individual's initiation into the world of essential values. The endless ferment of new ideas at the end of the fifth century in Athens, and the growing scepticism about religion and ethics, bore eloquent witness to how writing down the accumulated lore of the past had fostered a critical attitude; but whatever the dismay of Plato at some features of the process, he himself could not escape it. Plato, of course, was largely critical in his thought. The majority of his dialogues are arguments against the views of other philosophers; and even his most practical and constructive writings, such as the *Republic* and the *Laws*, are in large part continuations of the debates which had begun with the pre-Socratic criticisms and rationalizations of the anthropomorphism of the body of traditional myths; myths which were sanctified by the pre-eminent authority of Homer, from whom, as Plato wrote in the *Republic*, 'all men have learned from the beginning' (Jaeger 1947: 42, 211; Cornford 1952: 154–5).

It would be wrong, therefore, to represent Plato as a whole-hearted protagonist of the oral tradition. Neither he nor Socrates was an intransigent enemy of literate culture; Socrates did not write books himself, but Xenophon tells us that he would 'turn over and peruse in company with his friends...the treasures of the wise men of old, which they have left written in books';[1] while the scale, the complexity of organization, and the high literary finish of the *Republic* led Wilamowitz-Moellendorff to hail Plato as the first true author (1919: 1, 389). One must assume, therefore, a much more complex attitude to the new problems of the literate culture: the increase both in the number of books and readers and, consequently, in the public awareness of historical change which books fostered had made the problems inescapable by the end of the fifth century in Athens; and Plato was torn between his interest and understanding of the prosaic, analytic and critical procedures of the new literate thoughtways on the one hand, and his occasional nostalgia for the 'unwritten customs and laws of our ancestors',[2] along with the poetic myths in which they were enshrined.

Logic and the categories of understanding

The importance of Plato in the later history of philosophy, of course, lies primarily in that aspect of his work which looks forward, and which did much to define the methods of Western thought; the present argument therefore requires a brief consideration of how far these are intrinsically connected with writing. Obviously the great majority of Greek ideas have their roots in the specific historical and social circumstances, for many of which one can find earlier sources and analogues in the great civilizations of the Near East and elsewhere. Yet it does not seem to be merely a matter of ethnocentric prejudice to say that in two areas at least the Greeks developed intellectual techniques that were historically unique, and that possessed intrinsic empirical advantages which led to their widespread adoption by most subsequent literate cultures: the first area is epistemological, where the Greeks developed a new kind of logical method; and the second area is that of taxonomy, where the Greeks established our accepted categories in the fields of knowledge—theology, physics, biology and so forth.

[1] *Memorabilia*, i, 6, 16. See also *Phaedo*, 98–9; *Phaedrus*, 230d–e.

[2] See esp. Plato's *Laws* 793a–c. Plato is shown to represent both the old veneration and the new distrust of Homer in H. V. Apfel's 'Homeric Criticism in the Fourth Century B.C.', *Transactions of the American Philological Association*, LXIX (1938), p. 247.

In the former, Plato is essentially an heir of the long Greek enterprise of trying to sort out truth, *episteme*, from current opinion, *doxa*. This epistemological awareness seems to coincide with the widespread adoption of writing, probably because the written word suggests an ideal of definable truths which have an inherent autonomy and permanence quite different from the phenomena of the temporal flux and of contradictory verbal usages. In oral cultures, words—and especially words like 'God', 'Justice', 'Soul', 'Good'—may hardly be conceived of as separate entities, divorced from both the rest of the sentence and its social context. But once given the physical reality of writing, they take on a life of their own; and much Greek thought was concerned with attempting to explain their meanings satisfactorily, and to relate these meanings to some ultimate principle of rational order in the universe, to the *logos*.

It was, of course, Plato and Aristotle who conceived that there might be a special intellectual procedure for this process; who imagined the possibility of a system of rules for thinking itself, rules which were quite distinct from the particular problem being thought about and which offered a more reliable access to truth than current opinion. In the *Phaedrus*, for example, Socrates is made to speak of the proper method for arriving at the truth in general; and this method consists in disregarding the body of popular assumptions and, instead, analysing each idea by an initial definition of terms, followed by the development of a unified argument with 'a middle and extremities so composed as to suit each other and the whole work'. This is to be achieved by 'divisions and collections', by analysis of a problem into its constituent elements, and by subsequent rational synthesis (*Phaedrus*: 264c; 265d–266b; 277b–c).

This logical procedure seems essentially literate. On general grounds, because, as Oswald Spengler put it, 'writing...implies a complete change in the relations of man's waking consciousness, in that it *liberates it from the tyranny of the present*;...the activity of writing and reading is infinitely more abstract than that of speaking and hearing' (1934: II, 149). On more practical grounds too, because it is difficult to believe that such a large and complex series of arguments as are presented in the *Republic*, for instance, or in Aristotle's *Analytics*, could possibly be created, or delivered, much less completely understood, in oral form.

There is also some fairly convincing evidence to suggest a more directly causal connection between writing and logic. The Greek word for an 'element' was the same word as for a 'letter of the alphabet'; and in the *Statesman* Plato compares the basic principles of his philosophy with the child's first contact with the alphabet,[1] on the grounds that each principle

[1] *Statesman*, 278. See also *Cratylus*, 424b–428c.

or letter is the key to an infinitely greater number of words or ideas than the particular ones through which it is learned. Plato develops this idea in the *Theaetetus* when Socrates compares the process of reasoning to the combination of irreducible elements or letters of the alphabet into syllables which, unlike their constituent letters, have meaning: 'the elements or letters are only objects of perception, and cannot be defined or known; but the syllables or combinations of them are known and...apprehended'.[1] From this it is not far to the way the letters of the alphabet are used to symbolize the manipulation of general terms in Aristotelian logic; the set sequence of the premises, arguments and conclusions of a syllogism has been represented by letters of the alphabet ever since Aristotle so used them in the *Analytics*. It is further significant that Aristotle felt that he had made his greatest philosophical contribution in the field of logic; for, as he says in *De Sophisticis Elenchis*, 'on the subject of reasoning we had nothing else of an earlier date to speak of at all'.[2]

The same process of dissection into abstract categories, when applied not to a particular argument but to the ordering of all the elements of experience into separate areas of intellectual activity, leads to the Greek division of knowledge into autonomous cognitive disciplines which has since become universal in Western culture and which is of cardinal importance in differentiating literate and non-literate cultures. Plato made one important step in this direction, for he developed both the word and the notion of theology to designate a separate field of knowledge (Jaeger 1947: 4–5). This kind of strict separation of divine attributes from the natural world, and from human life, is virtually unknown among non-literate peoples (Goody 1961: 142–64). Neglect of this fact has led to much misunderstanding of the non-empirical and magico-religious aspects of their culture; but the neglect is itself a tribute to the depth of the literate tradition's acceptance of the categories of understanding which it has inherited from Greece.

Plato, however, was too much the disciple of Socrates to take the compartmentalization of knowledge very far. This was left to his pupil, Aristotle, and to his school (Taylor 1943: 24–39); by the time of the death of Aristotle in 322 B.C. most of the categories in the field of philosophy, natural science, language and literature had been delineated, and the systematic collection and classification of data in all of them had begun.

With Aristotle the key methods and distinctions in the world of knowledge were fully, and for the most part permanently, established; and so, of

1 *Theaetetus*, 201–202. The analogy is continued to the end of the dialogue.

2 184b. There were, of course, many precursors, not only Plato and his laws of the dialectic but the Sophists and grammarians with their semantic interests (see John Edwin Sandys, *A History of Classical Scholarship*, Cambridge, 1921, I, pp. 27, 88 ff.).

course, were its institutions. It was Aristotle, according to Strabo,[1] who was the first man to collect books, and who taught the kings of Egypt to set up libraries; and although there had actually been earlier private collectors of books, Aristotle's library is the first of which much is known; it is from his collections that our word 'museum' derives; and if 'academy' commemorates the school of Plato, *lycée* carries us back to Aristotle's *Lyceum.*

LITERATE CULTURE: SOME GENERAL CONSIDERATIONS

It is hardly possible, in this brief survey, to determine what importance must be attributed to the alphabet as the cause or as the necessary condition of the seminal intellectual innovations that occurred in the Greek world during the centuries that followed the diffusion of writing; nor, indeed, does the nature of the evidence give much ground for believing that the problem can ever be fully resolved. The present argument must, therefore, confine itself to suggesting that some crucial features of Western culture came into being in Greece soon after the existence, for the first time, of a rich urban society in which a substantial portion of the population was able to read and write; and that, consequently, the overwhelming debt of the whole of contemporary civilization to classical Greece must be regarded as in some measure the result, not so much of the Greek genius, as of the intrinsic differences between non-literate (or protoliterate) and literate societies—the latter being mainly represented by those societies using the Greek alphabet and its derivatives. If this is so, it may help us to take our contrast between the transmission of the cultural heritage in non-literate and alphabetically literate societies a little further.

To begin with, the ease of alphabetic reading and writing was probably an important consideration in the development of political democracy in Greece; in the fifth century a majority of the free citizens could apparently read the laws, and take an active part in elections and legislation. Democracy as we know it, then, is from the beginning associated with widespread literacy; and so to a large extent is the notion of the world of knowledge as transcending political units; in the Hellenic world diverse people and countries were given a common administrative system and a unifying cultural heritage through the written word. Greece is therefore considerably closer to being a model for the world-wide intellectual tradition of the contemporary literate world than those earlier civilizations of the Orient which each had its own localized traditions of knowledge: as Oswald Spengler put it, '*Writing is the grand symbol of the Far*' (1934: II, 150).

[1] *Geography*, 608–9, *cit.* Sandys, *History of Classical Scholarship*, I, p. 86. See also *ibid.* pp. 76–114, and James Westfall Thompson, *Ancient Libraries* (Berkeley, 1940), pp. 18–21.

Yet although the idea of intellectual, and to some extent political, universalism is historically and substantively linked with literate culture, we too easily forget that this brings with it other features which have quite different implications, and which go some way to explain why the long-cherished and theoretically feasible dream of an 'educated democracy' and a truly egalitarian society has never been realized in practice. One of the basic premises of liberal reform over the last century and a half has been that of James Mill, as it is described in the *Autobiography* of his son, John Stuart Mill:

> So complete was my father's reliance on the influence of reason over the minds of mankind, whenever it is allowed to reach them, that he felt as if all would be gained if the whole population were taught to read, if all sorts of opinions were allowed to be addressed to them by word and in writing, and if, by means of the suffrage, they could nominate a legislature to give effect to the opinions they adopted [p. 74].

All these things have been accomplished since the days of the Mills, but nevertheless 'all' has not been 'gained'; and some causes of this shortfall may be found in the intrinsic effects of literacy on the transmission of the cultural heritage, effects which can be seen most clearly by contrasting them with their analogues in non-literate society.

The writing down of some of the main elements in the cultural tradition in Greece, we say, brought about an awareness of two things: of the past as different from the present; and of the inherent inconsistencies in the picture of life as it was inherited by the individual from the cultural tradition in its recorded form. These two effects of widespread alphabetic writing, it may be surmised, have continued and multiplied themselves ever since, and at an increasing pace since the development of printing. 'The printers', Jefferson remarked, 'can never leave us in a state of perfect rest and union of opinion,'[1] and as book follows book and newspaper newspaper, the notion of rational agreement and democratic coherence

[1] *Cit.* Harold A. Innis, 'Minerva's Owl', *The Bias of Communication* (Toronto, 1951), p. 24. Harold Innis was much occupied with the larger effects of modes of communication, as appears also in his *Empire and Communications* (Oxford, 1950). This direction of investigation has been taken up by the University of Toronto review *Explorations*; and the present authors are also indebted to the then unpublished work of Professor E. A. Havelock on the alphabetic revolution in Greece. Among the many previous writers who have been concerned with the Greek aspect of the problem, Nietzsche (*Beyond Good and Evil*, Edinburgh, 1909, p. 247), and José Ortega y Gasset ('The Difficulty of Reading', *Diogenes*, XXVIII (1959), pp. 1–17) may be mentioned. Among those who have treated the differences between oral and literate modes of communication in general, David Reisman ('The Oral and Written Traditions', *Explorations*, VI, 1956, pp. 22–8, and *The Oral Tradition, the Written Word and the Screen Image* (Yellow Springs, Ohio, 1956)) and Robert Park ('Reflections on Communication and Culture', *American J. of Sociology*, XLIV, 1938, pp. 187–205) are especially relevant here.

among men has receded further and further away, while Plato's attacks on the venal purveyors of knowledge in the market-place have gained increased relevance.

But the inconsistency of the totality of written expression is perhaps less striking than its enormous bulk and its vast historical depth. Both of these have always seemed insuperable obstacles to those seeking to reconstruct society on a more unified and disciplined model: we find the objection in the book-burners of all periods; and it appears in many more respectable thinkers. In Jonathan Swift, for example, whose perfectly rational Houyhnhnms 'have no letters', and whose knowledge 'consequently...is all traditional'.[1] These oral traditions were of a scale, Swift tells us, that enabled 'the historical part' to be 'easily preserved without burthening their memories'. Not so with the literate tradition, for, lacking the resources of unconscious adaptation and omission which exist in the oral transmission, the cultural repertoire can only grow; there are more words than anybody knows the meaning of—some 142,000 vocabulary entries in a college dictionary like the *Webster's New World*. This unlimited proliferation also characterizes the written tradition in general: the mere size of the literate repertoire means that the proportion of the whole which any one individual knows must be infinitesimal in comparison with what obtains in oral culture. Literate society, merely by having no system of elimination, no 'structural amnesia', prevents the individual from participating fully in the total cultural tradition to anything like the extent possible in non-literate society.

One way of looking at this lack of any literate equivalent to the homeostatic organization of the cultural tradition in non-literate society is to see literate society as inevitably committed to an ever-increasing series of culture lags. The content of the cultural tradition grows continually, and in so far as it affects any particular individual he becomes a palimpsest composed of layers of beliefs and attitudes belonging to different stages in historical time. So too, eventually, does society at large, since there is a tendency for each social group to be particularly influenced by systems of ideas belonging to different periods in the nation's development; both to the individual, and to the groups constituting society, the past may mean very different things.

From the standpoint of the individual intellectual, of the literate specialist, the vista of endless choices and discoveries offered by so extensive a past can be a source of great stimulation and interest; but when we consider the social effects of such an orientation, it becomes apparent that the situation fosters the alienation that has characterized so many

[1] *Gulliver's Travels*, part IV, chap. 9, ed. Arthur E. Case (New York, 1938), p. 296.

writers and philosophers of the West since the last century. It was surely, for example, this lack of social amnesia in alphabetic cultures which led Nietzsche to describe 'we moderns' as 'wandering encyclopaedias', unable to live and act in the present and obsessed by a '"historical sense" that injures and finally destroys the living thing, be it a man or a people or a system of culture' (1909: 9, 33). Even if we dismiss Nietzsche's views as extreme, it is still evident that the literate individual has in practice so large a field of personal selection from the total cultural repertoire that the odds are strongly against his experiencing the cultural tradition as any sort of patterned whole.

From the point of view of society at large, the enormous complexity and variety of the cultural repertoire obviously creates problems of an unprecedented order of magnitude. It means, for example, that since Western literate societies are characterized by these always increasing layers of cultural tradition, they are incessantly exposed to a more complex version of the kind of culture conflict that has been held to produce *anomie* in oral societies when they come into contact with European civilization, changes which, for example, have been illustrated with a wealth of absorbing detail by Robert Redfield in his studies of Central America.[1]

Another important consequence of alphabetic culture relates to social stratification. In the protoliterate cultures, with their relatively difficult non-alphabetic systems of writing, there existed a strong barrier between the writers and the non-writers; but although the 'democratic' scripts made it possible to break down this particular barrier, they led eventually to a vast proliferation of more or less tangible distinctions based on what people had read. Achievement in handling the tools of reading and writing is obviously one of the most important axes of social differentiation in modern societies; and this differentiation extends on to more minute differences between professional specializations so that even members of the same socio-economic groups of literate specialists may hold little intellectual ground in common.

Nor, of course, are these variations in the degree of participation in the literate tradition, together with their effects on social structure, the only causes of tension. For, even within a literate culture, the oral tradition—the transmission of values and attitudes in face-to-face contact—nevertheless remains the primary mode of cultural orientation, and, to varying

[1] *Chan Kom, a Maya Village* (Washington, D.C., 1934); *The Folk Culture of Yucatan* (Chicago, 1941); *A Village that Chose Progress: Chan Kom Revisited* (Chicago, 1950); and for a more general treatment, *The Primitive World and its Transformations* (Ithaca, New York, 1953), pp. 73, 108. See also Peter Worsley, *The Trumpet Shall Sound* (London, 1957). For the concept of *anomie*, see Emile Durkheim, *Le Suicide* (Paris, 1897), book II, chap. 5.

degrees, it is out of step with the various literate traditions. In some respects, perhaps, this is fortunate. The tendency of the modern mass-communications industries, for example, to promote ideals of conspicuous consumption which cannot be realized by more than a limited proportion of society might well have much more radical consequences but for the fact that each individual exposed to such pressures is also a member of one or more primary groups whose oral converse is probably much more realistic and conservative in its ideological tendency; the mass media are not the only, and they are probably not even the main, social influences on the contemporary cultural tradition as a whole.

Primary group values are probably even further removed from those of the 'high' literate culture, except in the case of the literate specialists. This introduces another kind of culture conflict, and one which is of cardinal significance for Western civilization. If, for example, we return to the reasons for the relative failure of universal compulsory education to bring about the intellectual, social and political results that James Mill expected, we may well lay a major part of the blame on the gap between the public literate tradition of the school and the very different and indeed often directly contradictory private oral traditions of the pupil's family and peer group. The high degree of differentiation in exposure to the literate tradition sets up a basic division which cannot exist in non-literate society: the division between the various shades of literacy and illiteracy. This conflict, of course, is most dramatically focused in the school, the key institution of society. As Margaret Mead (1943: 637) has pointed out: 'Primitive education was a process by which continuity was maintained between parents and children...Modern education includes a heavy emphasis upon the function of education to create discontinuities—to turn the child...of the illiterate into the literate.' A similar and probably even more acute stress develops in many cases between the school and the peer group; and, quite apart from the difficulties arising from the substantive differences between the two orientations, there seem to be factors in the very nature of literate methods which make them ill suited to bridge the gap between the street-corner society and the blackboard jungle.

First, because although the alphabet, printing, and universal free education have combined to make the literate culture freely available to all on a scale never previously approached, the literate mode of communication is such that it does not impose itself as forcefully or as uniformly as is the case with the oral transmission of the cultural tradition. In non-literate society every social situation cannot but bring the individual into contact with the group's patterns of thought, feeling and action: the choice is between the cultural tradition—or solitude. In a literate society, however, and quite apart from the difficulties arising from the scale and complexity of the 'high' literate tradition, the mere fact that reading and writing are normally solitary activities means that in so far as the dominant cultural tradition is a literate one, it is very easy to avoid; as Bertha Phillpotts (1931: 162–3) wrote in her study of Icelandic literature:

> Printing so obviously makes knowledge accessible to all that we are inclined to forget that it also makes knowledge very easy to avoid...A shepherd in an Icelandic homestead, on the other hand, could not avoid spending his evenings in listening to the kind of literature which interested the farmer. The result was a degree of really national culture such as no nation of today has been able to achieve.

The literate culture, then, is much more easily avoided than the oral one; and even when it is not avoided its actual effects may be relatively shallow. Not only because, as Plato argued, the effects of reading are intrinsically less deep and permanent than those of oral converse; but also because the abstractness of the syllogism and of the Aristotelian categorizations of knowledge do not correspond very directly with common experience. The abstractness of the syllogism, for example, of its very nature disregards the individual's social experience and immediate personal context; and the compartmentalization of knowledge similarly restricts the kind of connections which the individual can establish and ratify with the natural and social world. The essential way of thinking of the specialist in literate culture is fundamentally at odds with that of daily life and common experience; and the conflict is embodied in the long tradition of jokes about absent-minded professors.

It is, of course, true that contemporary education does not present problems exactly in the forms of Aristotelian logic and taxonomy; but all our literate modes of thought have been profoundly influenced by them. In this, perhaps, we can see a major difference, not only from the transmission of the cultural heritage of oral societies, but from those of protoliterate ones. Thus Marcel Granet relates the nature of the Chinese writing system to the 'concreteness' of Chinese thought, and his picture of its primary concentration on social action and traditional norms suggests that the cultural effect of the writing system was in the direction of intensifying the sort of homeostatic conservation found in non-literate cultures; it was indeed conceptualized in the Confucian *tao-'tung*, or 'orthodox transmission of the way'. In this connection it may be noted that the Chinese attitude to formal logic, and to the categorization of knowledge in general, is an articulate expression of what happens in an oral culture (Granet 1934: vii–xi, 8–55; Hu Shih 1922). Mencius, for example, speaks for the non-literate approach in general when he comments: 'Why I dislike holding to one point is that it injures the *tao*. It takes up one point and disregards a hundred others' (Richards 1932: 35).

The social tension between the oral and literate orientations in Western society is, of course, complemented by an intellectual one. In recent times the Enlightenment's attack on myth as irrational superstition has often been replaced by a regressive yearning for some modern equivalent of the unifying function of myth: 'Have not', W. B. Yeats asked, 'all races had their first unity from a mythology that marries them to rock and hill?' (1955: 194).

In this nostalgia for the world of myths Plato has had a long line of successors. The Rousseauist cult of the Noble Savage, for instance, paid unwitting tribute to the strength of the homogeneity of oral culture, to the yearning admiration of the educated for the peasant's simple but cohesive view of life, the timelessness of his living in the present, the unanalytic spontaneity that comes with an attitude to the world that is one of absorbed and uncritical participation, a participation in which the contradictions between history and legend, for example, or between experience and imagination, are not felt as problems. Such, for example, is the literary tradition of the European peasant from Cervantes' Sancho Panza to Tolstoy's Platon Karataev. Both are illiterate; both are rich in proverbial lore; both are untroubled by intellectual consistency; and both represent many of the values which, it was suggested above, are characteristic of oral culture. In these two works, *Don Quixote* and *War and Peace*, which might well be considered two of the supreme achievements of modern Western literature, an explicit contrast is made between the oral and literate elements of the cultural tradition. Don Quixote himself goes mad by reading books; while, opposed to the peasant Karataev, stands the figure of Pierre, an urban cosmopolitan, and a great reader. Tolstoy writes of Karataev that—in this like Mencius or like Malinowski's Trobrianders—he

> did not, and could not, understand the meaning of words apart from their context. Every word and every action of his was the manifestation of an activity unknown to him, which was his life. But his life, as he regarded it, had no meaning as a separate thing. It had a meaning only as part of a whole of which he was always conscious [*War and Peace*].

Tolstoy, of course, idealizes; but, conversely, even in his idealization he suggests one major emphasis of literate culture and one which we immediately associate with the Greeks—the stress upon the individual; Karataev does not regard 'his life...as a separate thing'. There are, of course, marked differences in the life histories of individual members of non-literate societies: the story of Crashing Thunder differs from that of other Winnebago (Radin 1926, 1927); that of Baba of Karo from other Hausa women (Smith 1954); and these differences are often given public recognition by ascribing to individuals a personal tutelary or guardian spirit. But on the whole there is less individualization of personal experience in oral cultures, which tend, in Durkheim's phrase, to be characterized by 'mechanical solidarity'[1]—by the ties between like persons, rather than by a more complicated set of complementary relationships between individuals in a variety of roles. Like Durkheim, many sociologists would relate this greater individualization of personal experience in literate societies to the effects of a more extensive division of labour. There is no single explanation; but the techniques of reading and writing are undoubtedly of very great importance. There is, first of all, the formal distinction which alphabetic culture has emphasized between the divine, the natural, and the human orders; secondly, there is the social differentiation to which the institutions of literate culture give rise; third, there is the effect of professional intellectual specialization on an unprecedented scale; lastly, there is the immense variety of choice offered by the whole corpus of recorded literature; and from these four factors there ensues, in any individual case, the highly complex totality deriving from the selection of these literate orientations and from the series of primary groups in which the individual has also been involved.

As for personal awareness of this individualization, other factors doubtless contributed, but writing itself (especially in its simpler, more cursive forms) was of great importance. For writing, by objectifying words, and by making them and their meaning available for much more prolonged and intensive scrutiny than is possible orally, encourages private thought; the diary or the confession enables the individual to objectify his own experience, and gives him some check upon the transmutations of memory under the influences of subsequent events. And then, if the diary is later published, a wider audience can have concrete experience of the differences that exist in the histories of their fellow men from a record of a life which has been partially insulated from the assimilative process of oral transmission.

The diary is, of course, an extreme case; but Plato's dialogues themselves are evidence of the general tendency of writing to increase the awareness of individual differences in behaviour, and in the personality which lies behind them;[2] while the novel, which participates in the autobiographical and confessional direction of such writers as St Augustine, Pepys and Rousseau, and purports to portray the inner as well as the outer life of

[1] Emile Durkheim, *The Division of Labor in Society*, trans. G. Simpson (New York, 1933), p. 130.

[2] In the *Theaetetus*, for example, emphasis is placed on the inner dialogue of the soul in which it perceives ethical ideas 'by comparing within herself things past and present with the future' (186b).

individuals in the real world, has replaced the collective representations of myth and epic.

From the point of view of the general contrast between oral and alphabetically literate culture, then, there is a certain identity between the spirit of the Platonic dialogues and of the novel:[1] both kinds of writing express what is a characteristic intellectual effort of literate culture, and present the process whereby the individual makes his own more or less conscious, more or less personal selection, rejection and accommodation among the conflicting ideas and attitudes in his culture. This general kinship between Plato and the characteristic art form of literate culture, the novel, suggests a further contrast between oral and literate societies: in contrast to the homeostatic transmission of the cultural tradition among non-literate peoples, literate society leaves more to its members; less homogeneous in its cultural tradition, it gives more free play to the individual, and particularly to the intellectual, the literate specialist himself; it does so by sacrificing a single, ready-made orientation to life. And, in so far as an individual participates in the literate, as distinct from the oral, culture, such coherence as a person achieves is very largely the result of his personal selection, adjustment and elimination of items from a highly differentiated cultural repertoire; he is, of course, influenced by all the various social pressures, but they are so numerous that the pattern finally comes out as an individual one.

Much could be added by way of development and qualification on this point, as on much else that has been said above. The contrast could be extended, for example, by bringing it up to date and considering later developments in communication, from the invention of printing and of the power press to that of radio, cinema and television. All these latter, it may be surmised, derive much of their effectiveness as agencies of social orientation from the fact that their media do not have the abstract and solitary quality of reading and writing, but on the contrary share something of the nature and impact of the direct personal interaction which obtains in oral cultures. It may even be that these new modes of communicating sight and sound without any limit of time or place will lead to a new kind of culture: less inward and individualistic than literate culture, probably, and sharing some of the relative homogeneity, though not the mutuality, of oral society.

To speculate further on such lines would be to go far beyond the purposes of this essay; and it only remains to consider briefly the consequences of

[1] Jaeger, *Paiedeia* (Oxford, 1939), II, p. 18, speaks of the dialogues and the memoirs by many members of the circle of Socrates as 'new literary forms invented by the Socratic circle...to re-create the incomparable personality of the master'.

the general course of the argument for the problem as it was posed at the outset in terms of the distinction between the disciplines primarily (though not exclusively) concerned in the analysis of non-literate and literate societies, that is, anthropology and sociology.

One aspect of the contrast drawn between non-literate and alphabetic culture would seem to help explain one of the main modern trends in the development of anthropology: for part of the progress which anthropology has made beyond the ethnocentrism of the nineteenth century surely derives from a growing awareness of the implications of one of the matters discussed above: an awareness, that is, of the extent to which, in the culture of oral societies, non-Aristotelian models[1] are implicit in the language, the reasoning, and the kinds of connection established between the various spheres of knowledge. The problem has been approached in many ways; particularly illuminating, perhaps, is Dorothy D. Lee's contrast between the 'lineal' codifications of reality in Western culture and the 'non-lineal' codifications of the Trobriand Islanders; and there, incidentally, although Aristotle is not mentioned, his characteristically analytic, teleological and relational thinking is recognizable in the governing attitudes that Dorothy Lee presents as the typical literate mode of thought in contrast to that of the Trobrianders.[2] Benjamin Lee Whorf makes a similar point in his contrast of Hopi with SAE (standard average European). He sees the 'mechanistic way of thinking' of Europeans as closely related to the syntax of the languages they speak, 'rigidified and intensified by Aristotle and the latter's medieval and modern followers' (Whorf 1956: 238). The segmentation of nature is functionally related to grammar; Newtonian space, time and matter, for example, are directly derived from SAE culture and language (1956: 153). He goes on to argue that 'our objectified view of time is... favourable to historicity and to everything connected with the keeping of records, while the Hopi view is unfavourable thereto'. And to this fact he links the presence of:

1. Records, diaries, bookkeeping, accounting, mathematics stimulated by accounting.
2. Interest in exact sequences, dating, calendars, chronology, clocks, time wages, time graphs, time as used in physics.
3. Annals, histories, the historical attitude, interest in the past, archaeology, attitudes of introjection towards past periods, e.g. classicism, romanticism.[3]

[1] Just as it has been argued that a proper understanding of Homer depends upon a 'non-Aristotelian literary criticism' which is appropriate to oral literature: James A. Notopoulos, 'Parataxis in Homer: a New Approach to Homeric Literary Criticism', *Transactions of the American Philological Association*, LXXX (1949), pp. 1, 6.

[2] 'Codifications of Reality: Lineal and Nonlineal', in *Freedom and Culture* (Englewood Cliffs, New Jersey, 1959), pp. 105–20; see also her 'Conceptual Implications of an Indian Language', *Philosophy of Science*, v (1938), pp. 89–102.

[3] *Op. cit.* p. 153.

Many of these features are precisely those which we have mentioned as characteristic of societies with easy and widespread systems of writing. But while Whorf and other anthropological linguists have noted these differences between European institutions and categories on the one hand and those of societies like the Trobriands and the Hopi on the other, they have tended to relate these variations to the languages themselves, giving little weight to the influence of the mode of communication as such, to the intrinsic social consequences of literacy.[1]

On the other hand, what has been said about literacy and the consequent developments of Greek thought leading to the logical methods, and the categories, of Aristotle may seem to attribute to one individual, and to the civilization to which he belonged, a kind of absolute claim to intellectual validity to which neither the philosopher, the anthropologist, nor the historian of ancient civilization is likely to assent. The currency of such diffuse assumptions in general long ago moved John Locke to an unwonted burst of wintry humour: 'God has not been so sparing to men to make them barely two-legged creatures, and left it to Aristotle to make them rational' (*Essay Concerning Human Understanding*, bk. IV, chap. 17, 84). Nevertheless, Locke's own treatment of the 'forms of argumentation' and of 'the division of the sciences' is itself recognizably within the tradition that derives from Aristotle and his time; and so, in some important ways, is the literate culture, not only of the West, but of the civilized world today. There is obviously some more or less absolute efficacy in the organization of human knowledge which appears in the thoughtways of the first substantially literate culture, although its definition (which could hardly be more difficult) is well beyond the scope of this paper. Max Weber saw as the essential differentiating factor of Western civilization the 'formal rationality' of its institutions; and this, in turn, he regarded as a more fully developed and more exclusively practised version of the ordinary human tendency to act reasonably—to behave with 'substantive rationality'. For Weber 'formal rationality' was merely an institutionalized form of this general tendency working through 'rationally established norms, by enactment, decrees, and

[1] For example, in his paper 'A linguistic consideration of thinking in primitive communities' (*Language, Thought and Reality*, pp. 65–86), Whorf discusses Lévy-Bruhl's account of the thinking of primitive man as characterized by *participation mystique*, and suggests that the differences are related to the structure of language. No mention is made of the role of writing and he seems to see language itself as the independent variable, although in his later paper on 'Habitual thought' he does make a passing reference to writing, as well as to the *interdependence* of language and culture (p. 153). Lévi-Strauss, who is much concerned with the linguistic aspects of the problem, makes no mention of the role of literacy in his analysis of the differences between *la pensée sauvage* and *la pensée domestiquée*, but again the actual process of domestication is peripheral to his study (1962).

regulations'[1] rather than through personal, religious, traditional or charismatic allegiances. Weber's differentiation in some respects parallels the differentiation made above between oral and alphabetic culture, and in various places he anticipates part of the argument advanced in this paper.[2]

The present study, then, is an attempt to approach a very general problem from one particular point of view. In that perspective it suggests one reason for what has been widely remarked upon in the comparison between anthropology and sociology: the relative incompleteness of sociological analyses as compared with those of anthropology, and the tendency for anthropologists studying European societies to limit their observations to village communities or family groups. For, quite apart from differences of scale and complexity of social structure, there are two other dimensions of analysis which can in practice be largely disregarded by the anthropologist but not by the student of literate societies.

First, the reifying of the past in written record means that sociology must inevitably be the more deeply concerned with history. The kinds of practical and theoretical issues involved here are numerous, for the great importance of the historical dimension, with its very different kind of impact on various social groups, obviously poses acute methodological problems. At the most general level, the analytic model of the sociologist must take into account the fact that from one point of view his data include materials accumulated from earlier cultures and periods, and that the existence of these records greatly increases the possible alternative ways of thinking and behaving for the members of the society he is studying, as well as influencing their action in other ways. This added complexity means that certain aspects of the past continue to be relevant (or at least potentially so) for the contemporary scene; and it also means that when functional theoretical models are used, the interconnections can hardly be as direct or immediate as those the anthropologist might expect in non-literate societies.

Secondly, the sociologist must in any case recognize that, since in alphabetic society much of the homeostatic function of the oral tradition works at the inward and individual rather than at the overt and public level, sociological descriptions, which inevitably deal primarily with collective

[1] *From Max Weber: Essays in Sociology*, trans. H. H. Gerth and C. Wright Mills (New York, 1946), pp. 298–9. See also *The Theory of Social and Economic Organisation*, trans. A. M. Henderson and Talcott Parsons (New York, 1947), pp. 184–6.

[2] Especially in the 'Author's Introduction' to *The Protestant Ethic*, trans. Talcott Parsons (London, 1930), pp. 13–31, where Weber gives a rapid but comprehensive survey of the problem of 'what combination of circumstances' made some aspects of Western civilization 'lie in a line of development having *universal* significance and value'. See also his lecture 'Science as a Vocation' (*From Max Weber*, esp. pp. 138–43).

life, are considerably less complete than those of anthropology, and consequently provide a less certain guide to understanding the behaviour of the particular individuals of whom the society is composed.

SUMMARY

Recent anthropology has rightly rejected the categorical distinctions between the thinking of 'primitive' and 'civilized' peoples, between 'mythopoeic' and 'logico-empirical' modes of thought. But the reaction has been pushed too far: diffuse relativism and sentimental egalitarianism combine to turn a blind eye on some of the most basic problems of human history. Where the intellectual differences in the cultural traditions of complex and simple societies are given adequate recognition, the explanations offered are unsatisfactory. In the case of Western civilization, for example, the origins are sought in the nature of the Greek genius, in the grammatical structure of the Indo-European languages, or, somewhat more plausibly, in the technological advances of the Bronze Age and the associated developments in the division of labour.

In our view, however, insufficient attention has been paid to the fact that the urban revolution of the Ancient Near East produced one invention, the invention of writing, which changed the whole structure of the cultural tradition. Potentially, human intercourse was now no longer restricted to the impermanency of oral converse. But since the first methods of writing employed were difficult to master, their effects were relatively limited, and it was only when the simplicity and flexibility of later alphabetic writing made widespread literacy possible that for the first time there began to take concrete shape in the Greek world of the seventh century B.C. a society that was essentially literate and that soon established many of the institutions that became characteristic of all later literate societies.

The development of an easy system of writing (easy both in terms of the materials employed and the signs used) was more than a mere precondition of the Greek achievement: it influenced its whole nature and development in fundamental ways. In oral societies the cultural tradition is transmitted almost entirely by face-to-face communication; and changes in its content are accompanied by the homeostatic process of forgetting or transforming those parts of the tradition that cease to be either necessary or relevant. Literate societies, on the other hand, cannot discard, absorb, or transmute the past in the same way. Instead, their members are faced with permanently recorded versions of the past and its beliefs; and because the past is thus set apart from the present, historical enquiry becomes possible. This in turn encourages scepticism; and scepticism, not only about the legendary past, but about received ideas about the universe as a whole. From here the next step is to see how to build up and to test alternative explanations; and out of this there arose the kind of logical, specialized, and cumulative intellectual tradition of sixth-century Ionia. The kinds of analysis involved in the syllogism, and in the other forms of logical procedure, are clearly dependent upon writing, indeed upon a form of writing sufficiently simple and cursive to make possible widespread and habitual recourse both to the recording of verbal statements and then to the dissecting of them. It is probable that it is only the analytic process that writing itself entails, the written formalization of sounds and syntax, which make possible the habitual separating out into formally distinct units of the various cultural elements whose indivisible wholeness is the essential basis of the 'mystical participation' which Lévy-Bruhl regards as characteristic of the thinking of non-literate peoples.

One of the problems which neither Lévy-Bruhl nor any other advocate of a radical dichotomy between 'primitive' and 'civilized' thought has been able to resolve is the persistence of 'non-logical thinking' in modern literate societies. But, of course, we must reckon with the fact that in our civilization writing is clearly an addition, not an alternative, to oral transmission. Even in our *buch und lesen* culture, child rearing and a multitude of other forms of activity both within and outside the family depend upon speech; and in Western cultures the relation between the written and the oral traditions must be regarded as a major problem.

A consideration of the consequences of literacy in these terms, then, throws some light not only upon the nature of the Greek achievement but also upon the intellectual differences between simple and complex societies. There are, of course, many other consequences we have not discussed—for instance, the role of writing in the running of centralized states and other bureaucratic organizations; our aim has only been to discuss in very general terms some of the more significant historical and functional consequences of literacy.[1]

[1] The authors are much indebted to John Beattie, Glyn Daniel, Lloyd Fallers, Moses Finley, Joseph Fontenrose, Harry Hoijer, the late Alfred Kroeber, Simon Pembroke and Nur Yalman for reading and commenting upon earlier versions of this paper. They are also grateful to the Center for Advanced Studies in the Behavioral Sciences, California, for the opportunity of working together on the manuscript in the spring of 1960.

IMPLICATIONS OF LITERACY IN TRADITIONAL CHINA AND INDIA

In the following paper, Dr Gough discusses the suggestions put forward in 'The Consequences of Literacy' with reference to India and China. She points out that we are dealing with necessary rather than sufficient causes; with this we are in entire agreement, doubting whether there are any 'sufficient causes' which can account for the complex aspects of human behaviour.

She also suggests certain modifications in our original hypothesis and these I have discussed in the introduction. We tended to overestimate the difficulties of Chinese writing and underestimate the achievements of its literary culture. And as far as alphabetic cultures are concerned, a central theme of this volume is that more consideration needs to be given to factors restricting the use of writing, both in terms of the extent of the audience and the nature and circulation of the literary products.

Dr Gough makes a number of comments upon our earlier paper that help to clarify the problems raised there. She suggests that a thoroughgoing dichotomy between natural and supernatural did not emerge until the beginnings of experimental science in modern times; clearly this has been a progressive differentiation. She also points out that elimination from the written corpus does of course occur. Little is known about large sections of the history of the literate Middle East because documents have not survived. Equally, oral materials can be kept in circulation, unchanged, over the centuries. Nevertheless the different scale of storage capability that writing provides justifies us in assigning it an important role in the great progress man has made since the Bronze Age; nor is it simply a matter of capacity, for the material so stored is relatively indestructible.

Her remarks on democracy are apposite, though we were thinking here simply in terms of large-scale and informed participation in the processes of government; here literacy seems an essential prerequisite. In discussing the tendency of writing to produce 'a vast proliferation of more or less tangible distinctions based upon what people had read' and in discussing the problem of alienation (where we saw literacy as only one factor), we were not thinking primarily of classes or defined social strata of any kind. The individualization, alienation, distinctiveness we were thinking of had to do with the capacity to extend one's experience through time and space by what one reads, thus providing an intellectual history that is different, often radically so, for each individual in the society. Clearly, literacy is, as always, a precondition; we do not look for monolithic explanations of human behaviour and we would be reluctant to oppose literacy to capitalism or bureaucracy as alternative causes. But the change in the nature of the media does seem to us to have important implications for individual experience.

IMPLICATIONS OF LITERACY IN TRADITIONAL CHINA AND INDIA

by KATHLEEN GOUGH

In order to test and expand the hypotheses put forward by Goody and Watt it is necessary to have accounts of the uses of literacy in a wide range of societies. In what follows I shall first discuss their suggestions at a very general level in the light of comparisons with India and China. In a later chapter I describe the uses of literacy in the kingdoms of Kērala in south-west India from the early sixteenth to the mid-eighteenth century, and end with a brief account of some changes in the uses and implications of literacy in modern Kērala.

'WIDESPREAD' LITERACY

An initial difficulty arises over the meaning of 'widespread literacy'. Was literacy more widespread in sixth-century Ionia or fifth-century Attica than, for example, in the heartlands of the Maurya or Gupta empires or in Han or Sung China? Granted that the majority of Greek citizens of the fifth century B.C. constituted a book-reading public, it is uncertain how widespread literacy was among non-citizens. McNeill, quoting Beloch and Gomme, concludes that 'adult male citizens in Athens probably numbered between 35,000 and 50,000 on the eve of the Peloponnesian War, and the total population of Attica was probably between 250,000 and 350,000, of which somewhat less than half were slaves and disfranchised foreigners'.[1] With a majority of women in classical Greece illiterate, it is possible that Gupta India of the fourth and fifth centuries A.D., or even the central region of the Maurya empire (fourth and third centuries B.C.), had almost as high a percentage of literate people, at least in the areas round their capitals.

In these empires, as in later, medieval India, literacy appears to have been universal among men of the two upper classes of society, the Brahmans (priests, lawgivers and scholars) and the Kshattriyas (rulers and military). Literacy was probably widespread, also, among the middle-ranking Vaishyas (traders, craftsmen and some of the peasantry), for early inscriptions re-

[1] William H. McNeill, *The Rise of the West* (University of Chicago Press, 1962), p. 256 n. 2. Parsons estimates that 'the Athens of the Periclean Age had only about 30,000 citizens, including women and children, in a total population of about 150,000' (Talcott Parsons, *Societies: Evolutionary and Comparative Perspectives*, Foundations of Modern Sociology Series, Prentice-Hall, 1966, p. 105).

cord donations by wealthy merchants and craftsmen to religious causes. It was, moreover, the trading classes who favoured Buddhism and Jainism, with their rejection of Vēdic literature and rites and their promulgation of vernacular sacred writings. These three upper classes, the 'twice-born', certainly had legal access to most of the writings of Hinduism, Jainism and Buddhism if they cared to make use of them.

The fourth class, of Sūdras or manual labourers, ranked much lower. They formed an 'unclean', largely servile category, forbidden by law to amass wealth or to hear or recite the Sanskrit Vēdas. It seems probable that the Sūdras, together with the still lower-ranking Untouchables or exterior castes, were largely illiterate in ancient as in medieval north India. Even so, some Sūdras in ancient north India did acquire wealth and, although they were forbidden to study the Vēdas, there was no prohibition on their studying the later epics and *purānas* or reading the devotional vernacular literature of post-Mauryan times. In south India, again, the early Tamil kingdoms of the first to fourth centuries honoured poets from the Sūdra and even the Untouchable castes, as did the later Tamil kingdom of Chōla in the tenth to twelfth centuries (Basham 1954: 142–4; Sāstri 1955: 132).

While quantitative estimates are hazardous, it is possible that up to half of the men, and perhaps one-fifth or one-sixth of the women, were literate in the periods of greatest prosperity and brilliance of both the north and south Indian irrigation-based empires. As I shall suggest later, the percentages may have been even higher in the small kingdoms of Kērala, based on rainfall agriculture and overseas commerce, in the sixteenth to eighteenth centuries.

As in Greece, writing in India was rapid and materials easily available, the most common being processed leaves of the talipot and palmyra palms. Birch-bark, sized cotton, silk, and thin slips of bamboo or wood were also used locally. Ink was applied with a reed pen in northern and central India. In the south, the letters were scratched with a stylus and the leaf then rubbed with powdered lamp-black (Basham 1955: 194, 198–9; Sāstri 1955: 132).

A similar level of literacy may have characterized the periods of high culture in China after the introduction of brush-writing and the standardization and simplification of letters in the Ch'in empire of the third century B.C. Needham notes that Han China of about 145 B.C. provided for the education of at least some peasants in local schools, to a level below that required of scholars intended for the bureaucracy. Hundreds of books written on wood, bamboo tablets, silk and paper were stored in libraries, and by 145 B.C. university chairs were established for each of the major divisions of learning. The peak of pre-modern Chinese learning was apparently reached in the Sung period of the tenth to thirteenth centuries A.D. Printing was widespread by A.D. 980, and a rapid form of cursive writing, comparable in speed to shorthand, was known by the tenth century and practised by Chinese scholars as far afield as Baghdad (Needham 1954: I, 101–2, 111, 219).

While the evidence of literacy rates is extremely unsatisfactory, we must, I think, place both the Indian and Chinese high civilizations, along with the Greek, in Parsons' category of 'advanced intermediate' societies. As such, they contrast with Parsons' 'archaic' societies, possessing an esoteric craft literacy confined to small, highly specialized groups, usually of religiosi or magical practitioners (Parsons 1966: 51).

Parsons defines advanced intermediate cultures as those having full literacy for adult males of an upper class. Such societies usually organize their cultures around a set of sacred writings, knowledge of which is expected of all educated men. He argues that only modern industrial societies institutionalize literacy for a majority of both men and women. It could perhaps be argued that fifth- and fourth-century Greece had a higher proportion of literacy than any other pre-modern society. Lacking adequate evidence, however, I am obliged to class the high cultures of India and China along with that of Greece on grounds of qualitative criteria such as the existence of universities, libraries, public inscriptions and village schools. More precise research may, however, reveal quantitative differences in literacy which are in fact crucial for some of the cultural differences to be discussed.

THE ALPHABET

Assuming that Greek, Indian and Chinese societies were all 'advanced intermediate' with *relatively* widespread literacy, we come next to the question of the alphabet. The most salient fact is, of course, that although alphabetic writing has been known to the Chinese since the second century A.D., they have refused to accept it right up to the present time. The Chinese presumably rejected the alphabet because, by the time it was presented to them, their own more cumbersome script—a combination of ideographic and rebus symbols—had, over centuries, become the medium for a large body of literature, as well as being intertwined with religious institutions and accepted as the hallmark of the educated gentry.[1]

[1] Kroeber argues that it was the greater power and prestige of Chinese institutions, and thus of the Chinese script, that prevented the triumph of alphabetic writing in Korea as well, even though the Koreans twice developed a phonetic symbol-system—in the seventh century, in the form of a phonetic syllabary based on Chinese characters, and in 1446, of an alphabet derived, perhaps, from Pali (Alfred L. Kroeber, 'The Story of the Alphabet', in *Anthropology*, Harcourt, Brace, 1948, p. 495).

Chinese retention of predominantly ideographic writing seems to undercut some of the claims made for the alphabet by Goody and Watt. First, as I have argued, it is possible that literacy may have been almost as widespread in some periods of traditional China as was alphabetic writing in classical Greece. Second, this is certainly the case today. Universal literacy is an immediate goal in China, yet the Communist government, although it has devised a simplified script, has not instituted the alphabet. Widespread literacy does not, therefore, require the alphabet, although there can be little doubt that an alphabet, coupled with easily used writing instruments, greatly facilitates literacy. The fact that alphabetic writing, invented and permanently accepted only once in history, eventually spread from Phoenicia throughout the literate world with the exception of the extreme Far East, suggests that alphabetic writing has usually prevailed over ideographic because of its greater simplicity and analytic utility. The Chinese exception indicates, however, that ideographic writing *can* yield widespread literacy, and has done so where it was already deeply engrained before the advent of the alphabet.

It should perhaps be mentioned that the various Indian scripts are also not alphabetic in the strictest sense of the term, but semi-syllabic, a trait attributable to their direct Semitic origin (Kroeber 1948: 532). Only initial vowels have special characters, and the characters for consonants carry the vowel *a* unless a special diacritical sign is used to remove it. Where two consonants precede a vowel, they are condensed into a single character. Vowel sounds other than *a* are represented by a variety of diacritical marks attached to the character for the preceding consonant. Most Hindu scripts are distinguishable from Semitic in having twice as many letters, new symbols having been devised not only for compound consonants but for sounds which occur in Indian and not in Semitic languages. Thus Sanskrit has forty-eight letters; Malayālam, the Dravidian language of Kērala, fifty-three.

The letters of Indian scripts are arranged in a phonetic and logical order, in which groups of sounds formed against the back and front palates, gums, teeth and lips, follow each other in sequences. Kroeber regards this arrangement as evidence that phonetics and grammar had developed into sciences in India before writing was introduced (Kroeber 1948: 533). Apart from the early, undeciphered Indus script, it is true that no known Indian inscriptions date from before the mid-third century B.C. Basham, however, thinks it possible that writing was introduced from Mesopotamia by merchants in the Aryan period before 600 B.C. (Basham 1954: 43). Kosambi believes writing was introduced by 700 B.C. in view of the evidence of urban routines, trade, and accurately weighed silver coinage by that date

(Kosambi 1966: 88). I am unable to judge whether or how the semi-syllabic character of Indian writing, or its probable introduction by merchants and early rejection by the priesthood, may have influenced Indian modes of thought. Certainly, the Brahmans, like Plato, have always regarded written transmission of knowledge as inferior to oral. The orthodox maintain this attitude to the present day. It is for this reason that, in spite of the vast bulk of Hindu religious literature, the Vēdas themselves are still transmitted and memorized orally in villages—often, it must be noted, with very little understanding of their meaning. Indeed, they are not known to have been regularly written down or systematically edited before the second half of the fourteenth century (Kosambi 1966: 78).

I turn now briefly to the implications of literacy for modes of thought, as discussed by Goody and Watt. The remarks that follow are tentative, both because of the imprecision of some of the concepts and, even more, my limited knowledge of Indian and Chinese literatures. A beginning may, however, be attempted.

The distinction between myth and history

India is noted for its dearth of historical records. It can probably be said that myth and history scarcely diverged before the Muslim period. The reason most commonly given is the theocratic character of Hindu society in most periods and the supremacy of the Brahmans. In Buddhism and Jainism too, although Brahman supremacy and the belief in gods were rejected, the material world continued to be denigrated or even seen as unreal. The search for truth continued to mean primarily spiritual truth to be found through meditation and right living. In such a society, where the highest aim of the dominant literary class was to lift its eyes from both the natural and social worlds towards other-worldly realities, it is perhaps not surprising that historiography failed to develop.

In China, by contrast, a this-worldly approach emphasizing profound interest in correct social relations was fostered by secular monarchs and bureaucracies of literati. Perhaps because of this, reliable historical research and exact chronological records appeared by the time of the first major empire (Han). According to McNeill, 'the very bulk of surviving materials complicates the task of ascertaining the main lines of Chinese development, while giving (Chinese) political history an unrivalled precision' (1962: 304–5). Needham concludes that 'the Chinese have one of the greatest historiographical traditions in the world' (1954: I, 74).

Lineal conceptions of time

Like all literate peoples, the Indians and Chinese had several conceptions of time, utilized in different intellectual contexts and by different social strata or occupational groups. In many contexts in both societies, especially among the common people, significant events were thought of as occurring cyclically, without precise measurement or chronology. This view of time applies of course to the succession of night and day, the light and dark halves of the moon, the annual seasons, the female menstrual cycle, and both the lunar and solar years. The Indians elaborated it to describe the four ages of human life and also the cycles of rebirth through which souls, both animal and human, were believed to pass.

Both Indians and Chinese thought of the universe, too, as existing in cyclical time, in contrast, for example, to the Hebrew view of time as a linear passage from the creation to the end of the world. The Hindus saw the universe as passing through cycles (*kalpas*), each divided into fourteen secondary cycles (*manvantaras*) of 306,720,000 years. Each secondary cycle comprised seventy *mahāyugas* (aeons) and each *mahāyuga*, four *yugas*. Chaos supervened at the end of each *mahāyuga*, with the earth destroyed by flood or fire. The whole universe was thought to be eclipsed and recontained within the body of Brahma, the creator, at intervals within each *kalpa*. The Buddhists took a similar scheme of *kalpas* to China, together with a characteristically Indian view of the infinity of space and time, the plurality of worlds, and vast distances, comparable to light years, existing between the worlds. The Neo-Confucians of the Sung period also believed in time cycles, each terminated by chaos and each composed of a dozen ages.

As Leach points out (1958: I, 116), cyclical conceptions of time are in general characteristically primitive, since they do not require records or the notion of chronology. In the cycles of ages, however, the Indian and Chinese literati elaborated these primitive concepts through calculations of vast numbers. Since these numbers did not refer to empirical events they constituted a pseudo-scientific, 'magical numerology'. But they did set forth a view of the universe similar to the modern one in its stress on the magnitude of distances between planets and the infinity of time and space. Such conceptions of what Leach calls 'magical time' are evidently widespread in early literate societies, the Babylonian and Mayan systems being comparable examples.

As might be expected from their greater concern with history, the Chinese had a stronger sense of chronology and thus of 'linear time' than did the Indians. They were interested both in recording the correct chronological sequences of events, especially political events (what Leach calls 'historical time') and also in accurately measuring the sequences in ten-year and sixty-year periods. Thus, although the Chinese, like the Indians, referred to events in terms of dynasties, their chronology of major events is judged accurate by modern historians back to 900 B.C., and is carried back with less certainty to 2,000 B.C., whereas Indian dynasties and major events can be dated only tentatively before the Muslim period. Both Indians and Chinese developed a number of calendars dating back to the beginning of particular dynasties, some of them of short duration. Both, of course, developed methods of measuring short divisions of the day through sundials, hour-glasses, etc., but the Chinese elaboration of water-clocks and clockwork seems to show a greater concern with exact measurement of small units of time than was found in India.

In both countries, astronomy early became established as a science. Western classical astronomy influenced both countries, especially India, but both made advances on Greek astronomy as a result of their improvements in mathematics. The invention of the zero in India by the fifth or sixth century A.D., and its rapid transmission to China, was of course crucial in this respect and ideally requires a separate treatment in any discussion of the effects of systems of writing. It seems probable to me, indeed, that the presence or absence of the zero may be of greater significance for the development of several kinds of knowledge (astronomy, algebra, arithmetic and, ultimately, of course, the whole of modern experimental science) than is the distinction between ideographic and alphabetic writing. The subject is, however, too complex to be undertaken here.

As in ancient Greece, and in Europe generally until the seventeenth century, astronomy in both China and India remained bound up with astrology, as part of a belief in what Leach calls 'magical time' (1958: I, 116). The movement of the heavenly bodies being believed to be co-ordinated with the fortunes of men, specialists made calculations from the planets to predict and guide actions both in the state and in the lives of individuals. Auspicious times had to be fixed for marriages, journeys, and other important undertakings, and portions of the day were regarded as favourable or unfavourable for particular activities.

Summing up, both India and China fit Goody and Watt's theories that societies with widespread literacy have some interest in exact time sequences and time-keeping devices, and some development of a linear concept of time. But cyclical and magical conceptions of time were also prominent in both countries, and in India, as contrasted with China, interest in the chronology of societal events was extraordinarily weakly developed.

Objective descriptions of space

Maps were prevalent in China from the third century B.C. Scientific cartography began with Phei Hsiu (A.D. 224–71), whose work has been compared with that of Ptolemy. The science developed in the Sung period, especially with the eleventh-century invention of the magnetic compass. By the fourteenth century Chinese maps were superior to European and comparable in accuracy to those of the Arabs (Needham 1954: III, 556). Chinese sailing charts were also highly developed, especially from the fifteenth century, with the scientific exploration of the South Seas and the Indian Ocean.

By contrast, Indian geography and cartography are poorly developed in the extant literature, although pilgrims, military conquerors, seamen and merchants must have had a sound practical knowledge of India and the neighbouring regions. Religious cosmography and geography dominated the scene, although a small élite of Indian scientists recognized that the earth was spherical, and Brahmagupta (seventh century A.D.) gave its circumference with fair accuracy (Basham 1955: 488). In China, religious cosmography seems to have been confined to Buddhism and Taoism and to have been overshadowed by scientific cosmography and geography from early times (Needham 1954: III, 566). Both civilizations developed exact land records, and Indian astronomers, like Chinese, had a fairly accurate knowledge of the longitudes of important places in their own country. The scientific exploration and recording of space, like that of time, was evidently more advanced in pre-modern China than in India.

The sceptical questioning of traditions and the conscious search for objective truth

Forms of scepticism and of reverence for tradition vary, so that it is difficult to assess this criterion. I would judge India to have been more tradition-bound and less sceptical than China, but both civilizations incorporated both attitudes. Orthodox Brahmanical Hinduism placed the greatest possible emphasis on the sacredness of oral traditions, on otherworldly preoccupations and on the observance of traditional ritual and custom. Hence, probably, the weak development of geography, experimental physics and chemistry, as well as the comparative lack of interest in chronologies of social events. On the other hand, Indian medicine and surgery surpassed those of the Greeks in some respects, developing through the Hindu interest in yogic exercises and the Buddhist concern with charity hospitals. The science of bureaucratic politics also had at least one famous expression in the *Arthasāstra* of Kautilya, supposedly a Brahman adviser of Chandragupta, India's earliest great emperor, of the fourth century B.C. Indians also went far in mathematics, phonetics, grammar, astronomy and other knowledge concerned with non-textual experience. Some schools of philosophical sceptics, in both Hinduism and Buddhism, questioned the existence not only of God but of the material universe itself. Those who chose mysticism as the path to salvation have also usually denied the validity of ritual and myth. Indian science was not, however, systematically experimental until modern times.

With its emphasis on secular and social learning, Chinese scepticism entered more pervasively into scientific history and geography, attacks on myth and on traditional knowledge, and the recording and comparison of physical and social events. Wang Chhung, philosopher-scientist of the first century, systematically questioned much of the received knowledge of his time, including beliefs in ghosts and immortality, the anthropocentrism of nature, and the connection between ethical and cosmic irregularities. After Wang Chhung the sceptical rationalist tradition became incorporated into much of Confucian thought, and persistently combated both old superstitions and the new ones that appeared with the rise of Buddhism. Needham argues that traditional Chinese scepticism found its fullest development in humanistic studies, textual criticism and archaeology (1954: II, 390). China also outstripped other cultures at various periods in some branches of natural science, especially magnetic science, botany, zoology and pharmaceutics. Medieval Chinese science, in fact, contributed much that was essential to the groundwork of modern European science. Natural science in the Ming period was impeded from flowering to the extent that it did in Europe because of the Chinese failure to mathematize scientific hypotheses and to test them by experiment. Needham holds that the Chinese social structure, with its weaker development of overseas commercialism and its stricter separation of functions between mental and practical workers, was responsible for the failure to develop modern natural science. The same would be even truer of India, but there the scholarly élite was unconcerned not only with practical applications of most knowledge but also with the actual exploration of many facets of the material and social worlds.

Branches of knowledge

The development of scientific logic came early in both India and China, supporting Goody and Watt's theory that writing (although not necessarily alphabetic writing) encourages sequential thought and the development of syllogisms. Both cultures divided knowledge into autonomous cognitive disciplines similar to those established by the Greeks, although, as we have seen, they emphasized and excelled in different fields. There was clear recognition of a world of knowledge transcending political units—especially in India, where empires were smaller and of shorter duration than in China. The question of the separation of natural and divine worlds, and of theology and science, is difficult in that early Buddhism, Confucianism and Taoism, as well as some schools of Hinduism, were in theory atheistic. If we shift the question to one of the extent of separation of the supernatural and the natural worlds, and of their study, this separation seems to have occurred, but to have been less complete in India and China than in modern Europe. Both in India and in China there were philosophers and scientists who disregarded or ridiculed the 'knowledge' of religious specialists when it contradicted their own researches. On the other hand, such pseudo-sciences as alchemy, astrology and other forms of divination had an honourable place in the world of learning and appear to have been regarded by most scholars as inseparable from their cognate sciences such as chemistry and astronomy. I would question, in fact, whether the separation between supernatural and natural science has been as thoroughgoing anywhere in the past as it became in modern Europe with the application of mathematics to experimental science.

Social and psychological effects of widespread literacy

Substantially widespread literacy has not produced or been accompanied by 'democracy as we know it' in either China or India, with the possible exception of India since 1947. The concept seems too vague to test in its present form, although it may eventually be possible to relate specific uses of literacy to specific forms of the state. It does seem improbable that centralized states containing more than about a million people can exist, or can hold together easily, without some use of writing for political administration. Beyond this it is hard to generalize directly from literacy to political structure. Pre-modern states with substantial literacy have included aristocratic, oligopolistic and democratic city-states, feudal regimes, and bureaucratic despotisms of the 'Oriental' type. Modern mass society includes both fascism and parliamentary democracy, as well as military regimes with varying popularity, in the capitalist bloc, and both highly bureaucratic centralism and more decentralized forms of popular participation in the communist world. There is little doubt that both the Maurya and the Han empires offered less popular participation in government than did sixth- and early fifth-century Athens. It seems doubtful, however, whether this difference can be ascribed to differences in literacy rates, for Athens' overseas expansion from about the mid-fifth century was accompanied by the growth of marked wealth differences and a more authoritarian political system. As Kosambi points out, moreover, a simple contrast between the ideals of the *Arthasāstra* and Plato's *Republic* or Aristotle's *Politics* is 'pretentious irrelevance', for 'Aristotle's royal pupil Alexander did not put the learned Stagirite master's political ideas into action. Athenian democracy failed after a singularly brief span, for all the supposed practical wisdom of its constitution, precisely because of Plato's closest friends' (Kosambi 1966: 141). I am inclined to emphasize ecology and external political and economic relations as causal factors in the development of political systems rather than the spread of literacy. On the other hand, the distribution of literacy between social and occupational classes may well be, in large measure, a *result* of the political and economic systems. The society's values and idea system, which are themselves heavily conditioned (although not, I think, entirely determined) by its current technology and social structure, may also act back to some extent to shape political forms and the uses of literacy.

Thus, it can be argued that ancient Athens developed political democracy mainly because of its small size coupled with the industrial and commercial character of its economy—indeed, its incipient capitalism (Polanyi 1957: 64–96); whereas China and India developed their centralized bureaucratic empires on the basis of their agrarian irrigation economies. There was, however, in all these societies a particular kind of 'set' to the idea system, which may itself have been determined in large measure both by past history and by the character of the political economy and of men's reactions to its strictures. Thus in India, from at least the sixth century B.C., a strong strain of other-worldly asceticism made for the formation of small communities of scholarly ascetics, who went to live separately in the forests under relatively democratic forms of self-government. Such men pursued their own research into the nature of the good life independently of the main political structure, and in a sense lived above it. Later, monasteries were built for such communities of both Hindu and Buddhist ascetics, and, in course of time, in both India and China, monastic communities often acquired wealth and developed their own hierarchical administrations. But in both Hinduism and Buddhism the ideal persisted of the small community of scholars living in voluntary poverty apart from the public domain. In ancient Greece, as in early China, by contrast, scholars who were out of power or alienated from the political scene, as were Socrates, Plato and Confucius, nevertheless studied politics and society rather than other-worldly salvation, for it was unthinkable in their societies that wise men would be unconcerned with public administration (McNeill 1962: 232–66).

A measure of democratic self-government also existed *within* some other occupational classes of traditional India and China, for example some merchant and peasant communities. But such institutions are probably not attributable to widespread literacy. Among south Indian Hindus, for example, the most egalitarian and democratic caste assemblies tend to be found among the lowest castes of Harijans, almost all of whom were until recently illiterate. We cannot therefore simply attribute democracy to widespread literacy, although it is perhaps difficult for large-scale representative democracies—like large-scale dictatorships or bureaucracies—to function in the absence of substantial literacy.

Similarly, it does seem probable that widespread literacy tends to be accompanied by an interest in record-keeping. This interest was strongly developed in the political sphere in both India and China. Here again, however, I would argue that literacy in itself is a necessary but not a sufficient condition. Literacy, along with high economic productivity, makes possible complex political economies, which in turn require a more or less great emphasis on record-keeping.

Again, I would not precisely agree with Goody and Watt that widespread literacy of itself necessarily produced 'a vast proliferation of more or less tangible distinctions based on what people had read' (see p. 58). Nor would I agree that the development of widespread literacy necessarily produces the psychological alienation of the modern specialist. I would argue that classes, whether modern or ancient, are based primarily on division of labour and relationships to the means of production, and that differences in levels of literacy and reading habits tend to spring from these arrangements rather than giving rise to them. Further, it does not seem to be true that literate society has no system of elimination and thus no structural amnesia, as Goody and Watt argue. Many books do, after all, go out of print, and it is possible for literate societies, like primitive ones, to ignore phases of their own histories or to reinterpret their histories in the light of current concerns. Similarly, the alienation of overspecialization may be, I suspect, a feature of highly bureaucratized modern industrial states (whether socialist or capitalist) rather than pre-eminently of an over-accumulation of literature. In future, with the development of cybernation and thus of prolonged leisure periods, it may be possible to overcome much modern alienation by broadening the interests of the highly literate, breaking down the separation between mental and manual work, and creating wider areas of self-government.

At all events, psychological alienation can certainly result from other causes than literate specialization. Confucius, Buddha and Plato apparently all experienced acute alienation, but in each case this seems to have stemmed mainly from political impotence and disapproval of the goals of their own societies, rather than from the overspecialization of the scholar. In short, alienation seems to stem from particular forms of complex political and economic structures rather than intrinsically from the spread of literacy.

The individualization of experience and the liking for privacy, again, do not seem to me necessarily to characterize literate society in general, although literacy may well be a necessary precondition for a high evaluation of privacy and individualism. In both China and India, the main body of literati evidently conformed rather strictly to the mores of their class and were discouraged from unwonted expressions of individual experience. Thus Granet writes of Chinese literate society in Han times:

> Civic morality, having gravitated towards an ideal of strained politeness, seems to tend solely to organizing among men a regulated system of relations, in which the actions befitting each age are fixed by edict, as are also those for each sex, each social condition and each actual situation. Finally, in political life, where the stage is reached of advocating the principle of government by history, it appears that it is claimed as sufficient for everything to follow solely the virtues of a traditionalist conformity. [Granet 1959: 427].

Compare Basham on the Sanskrit literati of classical Hindu society:

> The poets lived in a comparatively static society, and their lives were controlled in detail by a body of social custom which was already ancient and which had the sanction of religion behind it. They were never in revolt against the social system, and Indian Shelleys and Swinburnes were lacking. Most of this literature was written by men well integrated into their society and with few of the complex psychological difficulties of the modern literary man; hence the spiritual anguish of a Cowper, the heart-searchings of a Donne, and the social pessimism of a T. S. Eliot, are almost entirely absent. [1954: 415–16].

The main exceptions to these pictures of the conforming literati were, of course, the wandering mystics. Their devotional literature, tends, however, to deal with the relationship between devotee and supreme spirit rather than with unique or intimate interpersonal relations. Neither traditional Indian nor Chinese literature contains personal diaries, although Chinese has novels and numerous biographies, and some of the Indian dramas and narrative tales depict character with realism. The dialogue was also a preferred medium in the early philosophical literature of Hinduism, Buddhism, Taoism and Confucianism, as in ancient Greece. In all these cases the dialogue seems to me, however, the medium of a society where much learning is still transmitted orally, rather than necessarily an expression of the individualized experience of a highly complex literate society.[1]

[1] Goody and Watt argue for a particular affinity between the Platonic dialogues and the novel as a literary form, since both stress the need for personal selection, among conflicting ideas and attitudes, of an individual approach to one's culture. This may be

In general I would suggest that the intense individualism of modern western society is chiefly (albeit indirectly) a product of capitalism rather than intrinsically of widespread literacy. To the extent that the Greeks anticipated it, this, too, may have resulted indirectly from the commercialism and incipient capitalism of their economy and the consequently high degree of individual action and experience enjoyed by the literate community.

CONCLUSIONS

Contemporary China indicates that, although advantageous, the alphabet is not essential for widespread literacy. We cannot say whether *alphabetic* writing has particular effects: China lacks the alphabet, and India has semi-syllabic scripts. The literacy rates for traditional China and India are unknown, but both, like Greece, had substantial if not widespread literacy and are classifiable as 'advanced intermediate' literate civilizations.

Widespread writing does not necessitate a clear distinction between myth and history, as India shows. It may require some degree of 'linear' codification of time and of reality generally, but this is variable: cyclical conceptions of time can co-exist with linear, or even remain dominant, in quite highly literate societies. The scientific exploration of space is also widely variable as between comparably literate civilizations. So, too, is the sceptical questioning of authority. Both China and India reveal a conscious striving for objective truth which seems to spring from literacy and from the consequent emergence of scientific logic; but in India the search took primarily 'inner' and mystical forms, while in China it produced an extreme interest in societal verities and in history. In neither did it turn toward the application of mathematics to experimental science. China and India both suggest that widespread literacy may automatically produce distinctions between the main branches of knowledge similar to those found in the West. They also indicate, however, that these may be developed with widely varying emphases.

Apart from some concern with record-keeping and some tendency to develop large and complex political units, societies with substantial literacy do not appear necessarily to produce particular forms of political structure. Widespread literacy may be necessary for large scale representative democracy to function easily, but it certainly does not necessarily produce democracy. As literacy develops and the number of written works

true, but it is also true, as the authors point out (above pp. 49–52) that Plato expressed disapproval of written as opposed to oral communication and that the Platonic dialogue, like the Upanishads and the Confucian and Taoist dialogues, issues from a society in which, in general, much learning was still transmitted orally.

increases, social classes and occupational groups are necessarily divided from each other partly on the basis of reading habits. I would not, however, regard this as a primary *source* of division between social classes, and it can apparently occur with quite variable amounts of social mobility. Widespread literacy does not necessarily, so far as I can see, produce extreme individualization, a marked need for privacy, or alienation. It is suggested that, in their modern forms, these spring more from capitalism or (in the case of alienation) from the bureaucratization and personal impotence experienced in modern industrial society, rather than intrinsically from literacy.

Writing, like other communications media, is problematic because it forms part of both the technological and the ideological heritage of complex societies, as well as being intricately involved with their social structures. Difficulties arise because it is hard to disentangle the implications of literacy from those of other techniques (for example, plough agriculture, settled cultivation, rapid transport or power industries), or of other institutions (for example, specialized priesthoods or powerful governments) commonly found in advanced societies. Literacy appears to be, above all, an *enabling* factor, permitting large-scale organization, the critical accumulation, storage and retrieval of knowledge, the systematic use of logic, the pursuit of science and the elaboration of the arts. Whether, or with what emphases, these developments will occur seems to depend less on the intrinsic knowledge of writing than on the overall development of the society's technology and social structure, and perhaps, also, on the character of its relations with other societies. *If* they occur, however, there seems little doubt of Goody and Watt's contention that the use of writing as a dominant communications medium will impose certain broad forms on their emergence, of which syllogistic reasoning and linear codifications of reality may be examples. The partial supersession of writing by new communications media will no doubt throw into relief more and more of the specific implications of literacy.

LITERACY IN A BUDDHIST VILLAGE IN NORTH-EAST THAILAND

The studies of writing in its social context begin with Dr Tambiah's account of a Buddhist village in northern Thailand. Here he considers what information is stored in written form, the uses that are made of it, and the personnel involved in literate activities. He describes the functions of the village temple and of its permanent and temporary monks, and discusses the roles within the village's social field that demand some attainment of literacy, either in the local secular script used for the vernacular or in the special scripts used for the ritual language of Pali. He also discusses the way in which the village is articulated to the other towns and villages by means of the written word, in terms both of literary input into the local community and of the contribution of that community to the wider literary culture. He points to the high prestige of literate ritual practitioners in a partially literate society; as other contributors note, writing presents the ritual specialist with a superior means of communication with the supernatural powers (below, p. 237) and with access to secrets not known to others as a whole. Moreover, in this Buddhist community the uses of writing are highly ritualized.

Tambiah also stresses the need to distinguish between the acquisition of the skills of reading and writing, which are often taught serially rather than concomitantly as is done in contemporary Western schools. Schofield later points out that until recently it was the case in England that the decoding of other people's thoughts was taught before the encoding of one's own; one was instructed how to receive before one could give. In addition, before the introduction of mechanical means of reproduction, the distribution of books and their storage in libraries could be accomplished only by the laborious task of copying the original by hand. Again the stress was on repetition or commentary rather than on creation. But in Thailand there was some creative use of writing in the composition of folk plays and operas. And one of the main sources of this 'popular' literature was the stories contained in the more formal literary tradition of monk and temple.

LITERACY IN A BUDDHIST VILLAGE IN NORTH-EAST THAILAND

by S. J. TAMBIAH

INTRODUCTION

The subject I deal with is the literacy that existed in a village prior to the implementation by the Government of Thailand in the 1930s of a national scheme of primary education and also prior to the incorporation of villages in the 1940s in a system of administration that required the keeping of certain kinds of demographic and administrative records by village headmen. This literacy exists today as a continuing tradition because some of the literates of the previous era are still alive and play indispensable roles and, more so, because the major agency of literacy in the past—the Buddhist temple (*wat*[1])—functions intact and undiminished.

The phrase 'continuing tradition' used in respect of the village in question is not meant to convey the idea of historical depth running into centuries. It merely encompasses the time period normally taken into account in the usual anthropological studies and expressed by the phrase 'the anthropological present', i.e. time as remembered and experienced by the oldest living members of the society studied. The paradox of a literate civilization, such as the one represented by this village, is that it is largely ahistorical—in the sense that it was not necessary for the knowledge written down and transmitted to be chronologically dated. Most of the literature existing in the village, especially that of a religious nature, is undated and is believed to have been handed down from the distant past. Texts have been continually copied and recopied, but are considered to be reproductions of ancient models. Yet such a village was not entirely anonymous, for it was affected by grand political, religious and literary events that can be dated from other sources. Nor was it necessarily intellectually static for in the course of generations its local literati might have creatively added to derived knowledge.

The village is called Ban Phran Muan (the village of Muan the hunter). It is situated in north-east Thailand, west of the Mekong river, between the provincial capital of Udorn and the border market town of Nongkhai.

[1] The *wat* will hereafter be translated as 'temple'. It should be noted that it comprises a complex of buildings including the *bod* (chapel), *sala* (preaching hall), *khuti* (monks' quarters), etc. The temple cluster is set apart from the village settlement; at the same time it is the social and religious centre of the village.

Although Udorn was only seventeen kilometres away, in the past the villagers had little contact with it; traditionally, they had commercial dealings with the trading centre of Nongkhai and social relations extending east of the Mekong river into Laos, which is today politically a separate country but culturally similar to north-east Thailand.

The villages of north-east Thailand are depressed by Thai standards. They used to subsist primarily on one annual rice crop, which was dependent on uncertain monsoon rains. In recent years, for politico-economic reasons, a few main roads have been built, new towns have sprung up and certain cash crops like jute have spread. But hardly ten years ago, most villages in the region were isolated, remote and fed by poor communications. Many remain in this position today from the point of view of administrative control and accessibility to motor vehicles.

The villages are normally quite large, clustered and separated from one another by a distance of a few kilometres. In 1961, the village of Ban Phran Muan had 149 households comprising 182 families, with a total population of 932 persons. The villages in a particular locality, up to, say, a radius of a dozen kilometres, had social contact with one another as judged by marriages made and the spread of kin. But extra-village marriages were a minority. The widest spread of contact was religious, in that nearby villages participated and attended one another's Buddhist festivities and fairs held in the village temples. The fact that Buddhism is the focus of the widest network of social interaction and regional cultural identity is critical for our understanding of traditional literacy. For each village of any size and standing had its temple; this was both a religious and a social imperative.

Two features of the social structure of the village are particularly relevant to the recruitment of literates. The structure of kinship is bilateral and for most people the number of kinsmen within the village is large. The village scheme of social categorization places emphasis on the asymmetrical relationships between the superordinate senior and the subordinate junior generations (into which the total community is divided) rather than on defined dyadic relationships within demarcated kin groups. Secondly, there is no marked economic differentiation within the village. There are no steep differences in land-ownership, landlord–tenant categories are unimportant, and standards of living are markedly egalitarian. This is a poor, economically non-hierarchical society; socially, the hierarchy of generations is the important one.

A poor, until recently remote, and little-stratified village of this kind is often the object of fallacious judgements, especially in this era when development and progress are conscious aims of both natives and foreigners. Thus, today, when it is a part of the creed of national governments and international agencies that universal primary and secondary education be carried to the people, villages such as Phran Muan are apt to be labelled illiterate. Alternatively, when the creed is that scientific information should be disseminated to masses steeped in religious superstition, it is thought that any learning has been confined to a closed sacerdotal group with closed minds. We shall see that the situation in the village of Phran Muan was more complex than this.

The first complexity is related to the linguistic and political background; a second to the different kinds of script in which certain kinds of its traditional knowledge and thought were written; the third to the variety of literate specialists, their recruitment, their training, the content and the uses of their literacy, and, finally, the transmission of the knowledge.

THE LINGUISTIC BACKGROUND

The Thai family of languages is widely spoken between the Yangtse and Shan Burma, and between Siam and the Gulf of Tongking. It is often contrasted with the Mon-Khmer languages of Burma and Cambodia. Although at one level the Thai family can be said to be a homogeneous group which provides no total barrier to mutual understanding, yet it is internally differentiated into dialects with different degrees of mutual intelligibility.

Thus the dominant people of Thailand and Laos, the Thai/Lao, are often described as being divided into some four regional groups on the basis of language, geographical location and cultural variation: the Central Thai, people of the Chao Phraya valley around and north of Bangkok, who comprise the majority; Thai (or Lao) Yuan of the north around Chiengmai; Thai Korat in the Korat province; and the Lao (Thai) of the north-east of Thailand and of the kingdom of Laos (who comprise the second largest category).

The village of Phran Muan is situated in the last of the four regions mentioned above, a region which today stretches over two separate political units, Thailand and Laos.[1]

North-east Thailand, by virtue on the one hand of cultural and linguistic affinity with Laos, and on the other of political incorporation in Thailand (which in turn gave rise to many kinds of contact with the Central Thai),

[1] By the end of the fourteenth century there were three Thai kingdoms established in the area, the Thai kingdom of Ayutthaya, the Yuan kingdom of Lanna or Chiengmai, and the Laotian kingdom of Lan Xang, which included most of the middle Mekong valley and the Khorat plateau. The first, second and part of the third were united in the nineteenth century to form modern Thailand, while the kingdom of Laos, east of the Mekong river, remained separate.

presents some curious problems as regards the language spoken and the scripts in use. Conflicting and confusing views have been advanced on these matters by writers (e.g. Blanchard 1958, and Finot 1959), but the situation seems to be as follows.

Language

The Lao language of the north-east and the Thai language of the Central Plain (or Bangkok Thai) can be said to be different dialects. Thai is not completely intelligible to a Lao-speaker and vice versa.[1] It needs to be noted, however, that considerable blurring has occurred in recent times, primarily because of the educational policy of the Thai government which has decreed that central Thai should be the national medium of instruction. This is a conscious policy of assimilating all minority groups to a common national culture. Thus in the north-east today most male adults and school-children are bilingual. But in the village a simple opposition is still by-and-large valid. The language of dialogue amongst villagers is north-eastern Lao; the language of traditional ritual and regional literature is the same. The language officially taught in the schools is Thai, which is also the language of communication between the villagers and the administrative officers of the central government. More men are bilingual than women. The fact that central Thai is fast spreading into the area today has, as we shall see, implications for traditional literacy.

Scripts

Complications set in when we examine the scripts traditional to the north-east and to Laos. We have to see this problem of scripts in a wider setting and in terms of historical events which have left a permanent imprint on the civilizations of south-east Asia and moulded the pattern of their traditional literacy. Two formative and interrelated events were the migrations from India and the impact of Hinduism and Buddhism. For writing as such, the significant process was the eastward movement from India of the Brahmi script, largely as a result of the spread of Buddhism. It

[1] On the other hand, it would be wrong to think that the Laotian language is uniform. Like Thai, Laotian has no settled inflections, which are sometimes completely reversed in two localities. As Finot has said '...the Laotian that is spoken on the right bank of the Mekong is not the same as what one hears in the hinterland of the left bank' (1959). However, the distinction between central Thai and north-eastern Lao is of greater degree and complexity. When discussing the language spoken in the Udorn region, research colleagues, versed in Bangkok Thai, not only found differences in words produced by transpositions and tonal differences, but also a number of unfamiliar words and usages. About a month was needed before they were sure of reasonable understanding, but problems were always encountered, especially with villagers who knew little central Thai, and more particularly among the old women.

seems that the Brahmi scripts in question were the south Indian varieties (Grantha scripts), which were the basis of all the scripts in the region. Mercantile, cultural and religious colonization by India was well established by the first half of the first millennium A.D. (Diringer 1962). Pali Buddhism made its entry into south-east Asia *via* Ceylon much later, in the eleventh century, and has contributed numerous Pali words to the vocabulary of the languages. Any examination of the traditional literacy and literature of the civilizations of south-east Asia must take as its point of reference the spread and influence of Buddhism and to a lesser extent of Hinduism.

The history and the exact nature of the scripts of Thailand and Laos (and the neighbouring countries of Burma and Cambodia) is a complex matter not yet fully unravelled by scholars. However, as far as the traditional literature of north-east Thailand is concerned, the following three points are relevant for our purposes:

(1) The sacred or ritual literature was written in the Tham or Lao Tham script.

(2) At the same time there was a secular Lao script connected primarily with the state and administrative matters; it was also the alphabet of poetic and romantic literature.

(3) Since the political incorporation of the north-east by Siam in the nineteenth century, the Thai script has also been introduced.

The basic differentiation is between the Tham on the one hand and the secular Lao and Thai scripts on the other. It would appear that secular Lao writing is in fact an extension of the Thai script. This writing is said to have been 'invented' by King Rama Kamhen Sukhodaya in A.D. 1283 and represents a cursive form of the epigraphic writing of Cambodia (Khmer). This Sukhodaya writing was transmitted with few alterations to Laos and to the Siamese kingdom of the central plain.

But the sacred Tham writing of the north-east and Laos is a branch of Shan writing rather than Sukhodaya writing. According to Finot, there are at the present time three local varieties of Shan writing—Tham used throughout Laos, Lur confined to the northern extremity of Laos, and Yuon of Chiengmai (north Thailand). The word Tham derives from the Pali word *Dhamma* which means Buddhist doctrine and the corpus of sacred texts. As its name indicates, the Tham script is used solely for religious writing, and is the script that figures importantly in this essay. As a type of writing it is a mixed form influenced by Mon writing rather than by the Khmer form.[1] In the north-east today all religious writings

[1] Corresponding to the Tham script of the north-east and Laos is the Korm script (Khmer) of central Thailand, which was traditionally the script in which Siamese Buddhist

are referred to as *nansy Tham* (i.e. *Dhamma* books), but this label is interpreted widely.

The literature found and used in the village temple is *nansy Tham*. It includes not only chants and Buddhist texts but also *nitarn*, stories of a purely regional origin which are recited as sermons by monks and therefore included in the category of *nansy Tham*. A good portion of the texts of ceremonies performed by laymen (e.g. *khwan* rites) and texts relating to medicine are also written in Tham. However, judging from texts which I collected in Phran Muan village,[1] the literature can sometimes be written in a mixture of sacred Tham and secular Lao scripts. The key would be the type of person at the village level who did the actual copying: a Buddhist monk would in the past have tended to employ Tham; while a lay copyist would have been more flexible.

In the village there is also another type of literature, folk opera (*mau lum*) and 'wise sayings' (*phaya*), which is usually written in the secular script. Traditional literature in the village thus appears to have been written in a range of scripts; at the one end is Tham for sacred and ritual literature, which is by far the major category; in the middle are mixed forms; and at the other end is the secular Lao type. Traditionally, the village temple was the place where both scripts, but more especially the Tham script, were learned.

In the village of Phran Muan, the documents which I refer to are of two sorts: palm-leaf manuscripts (*bai lan*) and paper manuscripts. The palm-leaf texts are by far the more frequent. Writing was incised on palm leaves with a sharp instrument; ink or black powder was applied and then rubbed off, leaving the scratches filled and visible; the leaves were then strung together to form a book. In elaborate books the leaf edges were gilded or painted in vermilion and the leaves put between lacquered or painted wooden covers. Most ritual literature was written and preserved in this form. The second kind of manuscript is a long strip of cardboard; if left in its natural yellow-white colour, the writing was done with Chinese ink.

literature was written. Thus a monk in central Thailand has to learn the sacred Korm script in order to have access to scriptural writings. This situation is changing today with the increasing use of Thai script for printing sacred literature. It is also relevant to note that traditionally in Siamese court circles the Khmer language, civilization and kingship provided the model for Thai court culture. Words of Thai-Lao origin were considered less polite than words of Khmer origin, and the language of the aristocracy had its euphemisms and hierarchical nuances (Graham, 1912, p. 568). Such phenomena are of course common to many aristocracies and hierarchical societies.

The Khmer script and language, which belongs to the larger family of Cham-Khmer languages, achieved its maturity between the ninth and twelfth centuries, when the Khmer civilization rose to its peak.

[1] I am indebted to Mr Stuart Simmonds for identifying the script in which these texts are written.

This latter kind of paper was well suited for colour illustration and diagrams, and some of the astrological texts are written in this form. The paper could also be blackened, and written on with a soft yellow pencil.

VILLAGE LITERACY

The village specialists, their literacy and their social rank

A starting point for describing traditional literacy is to take a general view of the specialist statuses in the village and to inquire which of them require literacy and are normally associated with it. A pertinent question to consider also is: what kind of literacy?

In Appendix III I have divided the specialists into ritual and secular kinds for purposes of convenience. The basic distinction I want to bring out here is that some of them require and are associated with literacy and others not. The village monk, the *acharn wat* (the lay leader of the Buddhist congregation), the *mau khwan* or *prahm* (the officiant at *khwan* rites), the *mau ya* (the physician) and the *mau du* (the astrologer) can read texts in Tham, Lao and Thai alphabets with varying degrees of competence. In fact, apart from the monk's, the other roles are lay, and it is possible for the same man to practise all of them, or some of them, concurrently. All these specialist roles are interlocked in a manner which, in general terms, can be stated as follows. Except in the case of a few persons, monkhood is of temporary duration. Some of the ex-monks who have reached the required level of literacy can and do become lay ritual experts whose art is dependent on the reading and consultation of ritual texts. Buddhism and Buddhist rites are allied to those practised by the *mau khwan* (and the art of the physician) because they are rites of auspicious 'charging' and do not traffic with malevolent spirits (*phi*). The monk does not practise *khwan* rites; but he is not opposed to them and can himself be the client or patient.

In contrast, all the ritual specialists like *mau song* (diviner), *jum*, *tiam* (intermediary and medium of village guardian spirits) and *mau tham* (exorcizer), and *mau lum phi fa* (medium of the sky spirit) are distinguished as dealing with spirits (*phi*) with whom both doctrinally and in practice monks have no truck and to whom Buddhism is 'opposed'. Reading (and, much less, writing) ability in any script is not required of these practitioners; their art consists of either manipulating objects and memorizing divining codes, or spells, or forms of invocation and thanksgiving; mediumship especially, in so far as it stands for possession by a spirit, is furthest removed from the monk or ritual expert who is associated with learning and with texts.

In the light of this, it is understandable that in the village the ritual specialists who are literate have higher prestige than those who are not literate; partly because Buddhism and its allied rituals are ethically superior and opposed to the spirit cults; partly because the former's art is associated with specially valued learning and literacy *per se*. This distinction is not merely a matter of prestige; it directly impinges upon leadership. The most important village elders (*puthao* or *thaokae*—both words mean 'old persons' and 'mediators'/'witnesses') are those who are *acharn wat*, *mau khwan* and *mau ya*. Together with the abbot, they are members of the village temple committee which organizes Buddhist festivities and manages the finances of the temple. They are also the officiants at marriages and other rites of passage (except death, which is the province of the monk), the settlers of disputes, and the witnesses to marriage and divorce transactions.

No specialist in the cult of the spirits (*phi*) is a village elder or leader in this sense. He may be individually respected but he is not a leader in the community. This is as much an evaluation in the contemporary context of the lesser respect due to his cult as of his lower level of personal achievement in both a technical and a moral sense.

Now to comment briefly on the list of secular specialists. The headman is primarily an intermediary with the Government district office. He has also certain duties of maintaining order and of compiling village statistics. Hence a certain competence in reading and writing of Thai is required. The headman's office is not in this village an envied one, although he must be an elder to occupy it.

The *mau lum*, both male and female singers of folk opera, have to be able to read and copy texts in Lao and Thai scripts and sometimes in Tham. Many of their songs are written down and have to be memorized. We shall see later that the content of their songs—tales and local myths—is not so far removed from some of the sermons preached in the Buddhist temple. The village schoolteacher, especially in the capacity of a government officer, teaching in Thai and dispensing compulsory primary education, belongs to the new literacy, not the older ('traditional') one. As teacher, he has replaced the monk. But he is also a new kind of intermediary between the villagers and the outside world and usually lacks interest in the older forms of literacy.

At this stage an important point about the notion of literacy has to be made explicit. In considering traditional literacy we must distinguish the ability to read from the ability to write; and within writing itself, we have to distinguish between the ability to copy from the ability to compose creatively. The primary qualification required of the traditional literate specialist in the village is that he be able to read; writing usually went with reading, but its chief use, if acquired well, was in copying. The emphasis was on calligraphic skill, not on creative composition. Thus village monks are never known to have written new texts or commentaries. The texts therefore become 'fixed' and comprise a sacrosanct body of knowledge, transmitted 'unchanged' through time. This applies particularly to *nansy Tham*, the sacred literature in Tham script. But of course villagers who could write in Lao or Thai script had other uses for their writing—but even here copying took procedence over creative additions to old texts.

It has already been mentioned that the acquisition of literacy, which gives access to ritual texts, is *via* the village temple. The progression of traditional literacy was from *dekwat* (temple boy) to *nen* (novice) to *phra* (monk) to layman ex-monk who functioned as a ritual expert (e.g. *mau khwan*). Until the introduction of compulsory primary education by the government, children attended the temple school, run by a Buddhist monk, to acquire the rudiments of education which prepared those interested for novicehood and monkhood.

Thus in earlier times attendance at a temple school was an essential first step in the ladder, and the initial schooling it provided was integrated into a programme of learning that was primarily religious and ritual in purposes. This emphasis has changed in recent times—at least as regards primary education—with the establishment of government schools and the employment of professional teachers; but at the same time the traditional features of the temple as an institution inculcating religious education for its novices and monks continues today.

In examining the ladder of literacy in detail I begin with a history of the village primary school over the last fifty years, with special emphasis on its earlier structure.

History of village school (c. *1916–66*)

The history of the village school can be usefully related to the course of national events in the sphere of education. In 1887, during the reign of King Chulalonghorn, a Department of Education was established under the direction of Prince Damrong. The activities of this department had little or no impact on village life, especially in the region we are considering. In 1921 King Vajiravudh promulgated a decree concerning compulsory primary education, but this law began to be systematically enforced throughout the country only after 1935. It is in recent years, especially since UNESCO'S Karachi Plan, that a determined effort has been made to provide the facilities that would make universal primary education a reality.

At the turn of this century the village school was situated in the old temple (which was later abandoned). The temple had an abbot, called *acharn* (teacher) Wanthong, and two or three other monks. It was the abbot alone who taught children, sometimes helped by a layman (an ex-monk). The teaching was voluntary and the abbot received no pay from the government.

The school had a very limited number of students—about six or seven. Almost all of them were male and were boys who lived in the temple and ministered to the monks' needs as pages (*dekwat*), though occasionally a girl might be included. Education was not compulsory. There were no grades, no examinations, and no child studied for more than two years. What the children were taught was the rudiments of reading, writing and arithmetic. It is interesting to note that at this stage the children were taught to read and write the Thai script. The techniques were learning by rote and writing on paper. Judging from educational techniques in the village today, the method has not changed appreciably; children collectively repeat aloud in unison and memorize.

When the abbot teacher, Wanthong, reached the age of 30, he gave up his robes to resume lay life. This was about the time of King Vajiravudh's proclamation, when state help and interest were forthcoming.

Abbot Wanthong was succeeded as village teacher by a novice whom he had trained; this novice was later ordained and became abbot (*chao wat*). He was *acharn* Pumma. By this time (*c.* 1930) compulsory primary education had been proclaimed by the state and existing schools received some support. The support in this instance was a payment of four *baht* (about one shilling and sixpence in today's money) to the teacher. Children were expected to join the school at 9 years and leave at 14; there was no system of grades and no examinations.

About eighty children of both sexes attended school, though attendance must have been sporadic and instruction not very systematic since there was only one teacher. However, some living elders claim that they had five years of schooling, and such persons are literate in Thai even today. What is of particular interest in this course of events is that it was no longer necessary to become a temple boy to receive the rudiments of learning. Villagers say that from this time the institution of *dekwat* declined, and only a few who were their kin served the monks; it was the novices themselves who were now expected to serve their senior monks.

Acharn Pumma, at the age of 30 years, gave up his robes to get married; this spelled temporary disaster for the school, which was closed down for a year because of the lack of a teacher. The government remedied the situation by appointing the village's first secular teacher at a salary of eight *baht* per month. From this time the school was a government-sponsored institution.

The school that was re-established and expanded in 1933 continued to function in the *sala* (preaching hall) of the old temple. From this date until 1966 it had a total of three teachers. In 1951, the old temple was abandoned in favour of the present one (which itself was old and had been remodelled), and the school too was shifted to the new temple. In 1966 the school moved for the first time into a building of its own and a fourth teacher was appointed. The teachers are now salaried; the syllabus and curriculum are controlled on a national level; and the medium of instruction is Thai alone.

If we take traditional literacy to relate to the time before the 1930s, then it would appear that a small number of boys, usually temple boys, were taught to read and write Thai for a couple of years (or more) by the village abbot; this educational phase rarely went beyond 12–14 years of age. The next stage in literacy was being ordained as novice in the late teens, usually 17–18 years of age, which implied that there was a time gap between primary schooling and novicehood.

NOVICEHOOD AND MONKHOOD

In another essay I have elucidated in some detail the meaning and function of novicehood and monkhood in village life. I shall therefore make only a brief statement of these aspects and devote my attention to these institutions only as they bear on literacy and the transmission of knowledge.

Novicehood precedes monkhood; it is entered upon in adolescence between the ages of 12 and 18 years. In the past most novices were ordained in late adolescence. The normal time for becoming a monk is early adulthood (20–21 years of age) prior to marriage.

In terms of numbers, novicehood has not been a popular form of religious service, for (and this is critical for literacy) novices stayed in the temple for a couple of years primarily to learn, and a good number of them continued in service to become monks at the age of 20. In other words, novicehood is entered upon as a prelude to monkhood of some duration, if not lifelong vocation. The serious business of acquiring religious knowledge starts at the novice stage. There is, however, a temporary novicehood of a few weeks that is entered upon by grandsons or sons to make merit for a dead grandparent or parents; this form should be considered separately.

Monkhood *per se* has somewhat different implications, as is evident from the well-known Thai custom in the central plain and in the north-east whereby every year a group of young men become ordained as monks and the vast majority resume lay life after the duration of one 'Lent' (from 3 to 6 months). This institution, which is not related to lifelong vocation, is in a sense a rite of passage; the young men make merit for themselves, but more importantly for their parents, as a filial duty. Sociologically, then, the institution of temporary monkhood can be seen as a relation of reciprocity between the generation of parents and their sons; for the latter it is a valued period of temporary asceticism and denial of sexuality before entering upon marriage. The minority who continue as monks for some years tend to have novicehood behind them.

These assertions can be given some quantitative form in regard to the village of Ban Phran Muan itself. In 1961–2, a sample of 106 households out of a total of 182 families produced the following figures: a little over half the family heads had served as monks, about a third as novices and nearly a fifth as both. We can safely assume that from the point of view of literacy it is the fifth who served as both novice and monk who constituted the pool from which the literates emerged.

To present some further figures of intake of novices and monks in recent years:

(1) 1961. Novices: three adolescents (two aged 17 and the third 18) were initiated and continued into the following year.
Monks: three young men (21, 21, 23 years respectively) were ordained in June/July and resumed lay life in November at the end of Lent. In the same year, the abbot, who had served some years, and another monk, ordained in the previous year, represented the more permanent core.

(2) 1963. Novices: seven (ages ranging from 12 to 17 years) were ordained; their period of stay in the temple varied from 4 months (two cases), 8 months (two cases), 10 months (two cases) to 16 months (one case).
Monks: five were ordained (three aged 20, two aged 21): all of them had resumed lay life, after about 6 months, in January, in time for the harvesting.

(3) 1966. During the Lent of this year, there were six monks and five novices in the temple, of whom five monks and four novices were newly ordained.

Because secular schooling, especially secondary education, is available, it is clear that novicehood itself is becoming increasingly shorter, although it still represents apprenticeship to professional monkhood. The biographical facts relating to three elders of the village—its most illustrious citizens—illustrate the path of literacy in the past. I shall name the persons, because they will figure again later. *Pautu Phan* (Grandfather Phan), who is over 70 (1966), is the village's most renowned physician (*mau ya*) as well as *mau khwan* (lay ritual officiant at *khwan* ceremonies) and a leader of the lay congregation at Buddhist rites. From the age of 12, and for the next 4 years, he was a novice and became thoroughly literate in Tham and Lao dialects. At the age of 21 he became a monk and continued for 3 years of service and study. *Acharn Pun* is an ex-abbot of the temple and a leader of the congregation. He is 64 years old. He went to the temple school as *dekwat* from the age of 10 to 12 years; at the age of 18 he became a novice for 2 years and then a monk, which he remained for 7 years. He became the abbot after being a monk for 3 years. After some years he resumed lay life, and is now a householder. *Pau* (*father*) *Champi*, aged 59, is perhaps the most respected elder of the village and the successor of Pautu Phan, who is now too old to be active. Champi started to go to the village school at the time compulsory education was first proclaimed and studied there for 5 years (from the age of 9 to 14); at 17 he became a novice, and stayed on in the temple to become a monk 3 years later. He gave up his robes after one year as monk.

Abbot Tongloon, the present abbot, a young man only 27 years old, continues in the same tradition and is one of the few professional monks produced by the village. He had his normal village primary schooling from 9 to 14; immediately afterwards he became a novice, and remained so until he was 20. He was then ordained monk. He has passed three *nagtham* examinations (p. 104), and after his second was given permission by the clerical authorities to teach monks and novices in the village.

Content and mode of learning of novices and monks; transmission to congregation and audience participation

We are now in a position to examine the content and mode of learning among the novices and monks. This account deals with the situation fifty years ago, as described by elders, as well as with that prevailing today. Both time periods can be dealt with together, because teaching and learning techniques and the content of learning have remained largely the same. Whatever changes there are relate to script rather than content. Fifty years ago the village school was run on a voluntary basis by the abbot. As temple boys, the candidates for novicehood had their primary schooling and learned to read and write Thai. Today boys become theoretically novices only after completing grade 4 in the government primary school; in any case they have had 4–5 years of schooling and have learned the rudiments of reading and writing Thai.

In the past the education of the novices had three parts: first, learning to read *nansy Tham* and to write the Tham script; second, memorizing a collection of chants (*suad*); and third, practising the art of rendering sermons (*ted*).

Study of nansy Tham. Novices had to learn to both read and write the Tham script. Learning was done after breakfast. First of all, the abbot wrote the alphabet on paper and read out the letters. When the novices had learned the letters, they practised reading: each student in the class held the palm-leaf book in his hands and read aloud, while the teacher, standing behind him, checked his reading. After reading had been mastered, writing was practised on paper. This was secondary to reading.

Every month, or once in two months, the abbot tested his pupils; physical punishment with a stick was administered if mistakes were made.

Today (1966) certain changes have taken place in the learning of *nansy Tham*. The teaching of both monks and novices to read *nansy Tham* takes place primarily during Lent when the school is active, but learning to read it is not compulsory. Those who want to learn are taught by the abbot, and the technique of learning is precisely the same as it was fifty years ago. The voluntary learning of *nansy Tham* is a major change and most novices (and monks) can no longer read the Tham texts. However, those who propose to spend more than a year in the temple will in fact have to learn to read sermons, most of which are still in the Tham script, though increasingly it is being displaced by the Thai script. However, what is not acquired today is the ability to write *nansy Tham*, because, with the advent of the printing press, the copying of manuscripts is no longer necessary.

Memorizing chants. In many religions, especially the 'higher literate' religions, a feature of the priest or religious virtuoso, be he Buddhist monk or Brahmin priest or Islamic *mallam*, is his remarkable command of chants and texts which he has memorized. Since a large part of the training of village religious specialists consists primarily in memorizing texts (without a corresponding accent on the understanding of them), I shall discuss briefly the method of learning chants.

In the past (as well as today), it was on memorizing chants that a novice or a newly ordained monk was likely to spend most of his time. Every religious occasion in the temple, or a major rite of passage like death, or a rite of house-blessing, requires chanting by monks. Village monks and novices are expected to memorize a certain body of chants (*suad mon*) that are recited on these occasions. In addition, they must commit to memory chants which are used in the daily worship of the Buddha (*tham watr*), and other texts such as the Pattimokka ('confession' based on the rules of the Vinaya, which they recite fortnightly). The second category relates to the monastic regime and concerns monks alone.

In Appendix IV I give a list of the major chants which novices were, and are, expected to learn during their normal two-year period of study. They can be divided into two categories: *suad mon* and *tham watr*. If the reader notes the occasions at which the *suad mon* chants are rendered, he will get an idea of the ritual role of the monks in relation to the layman. Monks are concerned with the transfer of merit to laymen at collective temple festivals, at rites of passage, and at merit-making household rites such as house-warming and house-blessing. Together with blessing go protection and the removal of danger; these effects are achieved by the *paritta* chants. Contrary to the ideas of some observers, village Buddhism is not solely concerned with the other world as opposed to this world.

The technique of learning chants is as follows. The *tham watr* are not memorized from printed texts. Since they are chanted by monks in the early morning and at night, a newcomer repeats what he hears and memorizes them fairly quickly. But essentially the *suad mon* chants and the Pattimokka confessional are learnt by the pupils not only collectively in school but also privately, with the aid of printed texts.

The abbot gives each student the task of learning a set of chants. After about five days, at a common class, each student is asked to recite in turn. The task in question is not merely a matter of learning words but of chanting them according to certain tunes. Early morning before school, or after school in the afternoon, novices and monks practise chants individually in their cubicles (*khuti*).

The fact that Buddhism is aesthetically a musical religion, and that the memorizing of words is closely linked to musical rhythms, gives us a clue to the technique and the way in which novices and monks are in fact capable of memorizing an impressive amount of words in their correct order.

There are essentially three musical rhythms employed in chanting. The Magadha form breaks up the chant into phrases. The Samyoka style, on the other hand, is somewhat staccato; stops are made irrespective of meaning in those cases where words are joined by certain consonants like *k*, *c*, *t*, *p*, *d*. Both these styles are employed in the chanting of *mangala* (auspicious) chants. A third style is Sarabhanna, which employs a higher pitch of voice and also lengthens the speed of chanting, again breaking the chant into phrases; the Sanghaha is a similar mode of 'lengthened' chanting. Sarabhanna chanting is essentially employed on *avamangala* (inauspicious) occasions, such as immediately after death, when its slow and mournful grandeur suits the occasion.

The verbal structure of the verses (*gatha*, *sutra*) has discernible implications for facilitating memorization. The chants use the method of repetitions in stylized form. As Rhys Davids wrote:

> Two methods were adopted in India to aid this power of memory. One adopted chiefly by the grammarians, was to clothe the rules to be remembered in very short enigmatical phrases (called *sutras* or threads), which taxed the memory

but little, while they required elaborate commentaries to render them intelligible. The other, the method adopted in the Buddhist writings (both Sutta and Vinaya), was, firstly, the use of stock phrases, of which the commencement once given, the remainder followed as a matter of course and secondly, the habit of repeating whole sentences, or even paragraphs, which in our modern books would be understood or inferred, instead of being expressed [1881: xxiii].

It is clear, then, that the Buddhist *gathas* (like the Vedic prayers) initially belonged to the oral tradition and were designed in a particular form to facilitate transmission. Committing them to writing came later.

In village religion the Buddhist chants present a problem for interpretation. The language of the chants is Pali. Traditionally they were written in Tham script; today they are available in printed books in the Thai alphabet, which is one reason why the study of Tham is declining. Whether written in Tham or Thai alphabet, the Pali language itself is alien to most village novices and monks; some who stay in robes for a length of time may actually learn Pali, but this is infrequent. In effect, most village novices and monks do not understand the chants, or at best understand them imperfectly. The lay congregation, all the women and most of the men, are in greater ignorance about the actual content of chants. However, many of them can recognize particular chants (especially those recited frequently), and often know which chant is appropriate for which occasion; some men who were previously novices have a better idea of the content.

If this is the actual situation, there are two questions we may ask. To what extent does the knowledge of chants which are in Pali (and to a lesser extent, the ability to read *nansy Tham*) constitute an esoteric and exclusive body of knowledge confined to the clergy? Secondly, if Pali chants are essential at ritual performed by monks and novices and if at the same time they are largely unintelligible to the laity, what, then, is communicated in the rites?

The first question I shall attempt to answer later, because it is a general problem, related to the recruitment of clergy, their period of office, and their roles after giving up the robes.

The answer to the second is briefly as follows. The Buddhist monks in the village are agents for transferring merit to the laity. Monk and layman stand in a particular relation. By virtue of his asceticism and way of life the monk is partially aggregated to the world of death and final release of the kind Buddha stands for. The layman, an inferior being on the path to salvation, is emphatically in this world. Through proper ritual procedures the monk, as mediator, can transfer Buddha's conquest of the dangers inherent in human existence and transmute it into prosperity and mental states free of pain and charged with merit. The words of the chants, little understood by the laity, and insufficiently understood by most village monks themselves, are considered powerful in themselves; they are words of the Buddha, they embody his power, and the recitation of them brings effects. The blessing as such at the end of the chanting is the 'pay-off' for the laity; and it is effective because it is the monk by virtue of his ascetic style of life and his knowledge who has proper and sanctioned access to the sacred words. Simple access to the sacred words is not enough; the two intervening links are right conduct and discipline by the monk and right intention and merit-making on the part of the layman.

Sermons (*ted*). Sermons are also chanted and therefore require practice. The quality of recitation itself, apart from the words, is a matter of great aesthetic appreciation on the part of the congregation.

In the village, sermons are not free creations of the novice (or monk) who gives them. They are standardized and there is an appropriate one for each particular occasion or set of occasions, written down in palm-leaf manuscripts. In the past the writing was inscribed by human hand; today, one frequently sees palm-leaf documents on which the words are printed. The latter applies to documents in the Thai script, which are increasingly supplementing the older Tham texts.

Types and content of sermons. (1) The first kind are those which enumerate or 'tell' the advantages of making merit (*bog anisonk*), which in fact means giving gifts to the monks and the village temple. Typical occasions when merit-making is extolled are:

Bun prasard pueng: making merit for a dead person after the cremation rites are over by carrying a palanquin of gifts to the monks and also feasting them.

Bun kathin: giving of gifts by the village to the monks after they have completed Lent seclusion (during the rains), and emerge again into the world. It is after this ceremony that the temporary monks resume lay life.

(2) Another set of sermons are rather specialized and are reserved for the celebration of the opening of newly constructed (or repaired) *khuti* (monks' living quarters), *sala* (preaching hall), *wiharn* or *bod* (sacred place of worship). These are buildings constructed by the laymen.

(3) It is to the third category of sermons that I want to give special attention. They are called *ted nitarn* (sermons which relate stories), and these sermons have implications not only for the villagers' understanding of the morality and ethics of Buddhism but also represent the focus of genuine audience participation and a channel of cultural transmission beyond the narrowly religious.

Traditionally, the *ted nitarn* constitute a major component of *nansy Tham* (sacred palm-leaf books). *Ted nitarn* can be differentiated as follows: (*a*) *Pathom Sompote.* These are stories concerning the life of the Buddha, especially his birth, renouncing of his kingly life, achievement of *nirvana*, and also the episodes of his previous lives embodied as Chadok (Jataka) stories. These stories are a common substance of sermons, and are widely known throughout Thailand, but each region has its own version or adaptation. The sermons mentioned here are thus north-eastern creations. (*b*) *Lum Phrawesandaun.* This is a story of the same category as (*a*) above but deserves special mention because it is a work of many chapters, based on the great and moving story of Buddha's penultimate life, as related in the *Wessaundon Chadok* (Vessantara Jataka). It is the major sermon listened to (the reading takes a full day) on the occasion of Bun Phra Wes, which is the village's largest religious and secular festival staged after harvest. The north-eastern version of this story has its counterpart in the *Maha Chad* (Great Story) known in central Thailand. (*c*) Stories (*nitarn*) which are primarily local and regional (north-eastern) myths and folktales and which are not found elsewhere. These are particularly appreciated by the listeners, for whom their moral significance is secondary to their dramatic value as stories. The best known stories are, to give examples, Pha Daeng Nang Ai, Tao Sowat, Tao Phi Noi, Tao Chan Samut, Tao Ten Don, and Tao Nokrajog.

All these three kinds of sermons called *ted nitarn*, which consist of the reading of stories and their explanation, are given on the occasion of the major collective calendrical temple festivals or are read by monks to laymen during the Lent season. Lum Phrawesandaun is read on the last day of the three-day Bun Phrawes: categories (1) and (3) are preached at Org Phansa (the conclusion of Lent and the 'coming out' of the monks) and Bun Khaw Chi (making merit for the dead with puffed rice). Some of them also comprise minor sermons during Bun Phra Wes.

I have argued before that the Pali chants as such have little meaning content for the layman; the chanting of them on certain occasions is regarded as efficacious in a magical sense. In comparison, the various sermons read and explained in the north-eastern language are understood by the listeners. It is interesting to note that on merit-making occasions, it is the villagers who choose the sermon they would like to hear, and it was reported by the abbot that for the major festivals the villagers invariably choose a story of category (3).

Whereas stories of the life of the Buddha are universal in Thailand and are heard in variant forms by all Buddhist congregations, we see that the propagation and transmission of tales which have originated in, or at least are confined to, the north-east (and perhaps Laos) help to maintain regional cultural identity *vis-à-vis* other cultural regions of Thailand.[1] The temple, of course, is not the only channel of transmission—folk opera (*mau lum*) transmits the same stories through a different medium; furthermore, literate villagers may themselves possess copies of *nitarn* and read them at funeral wakes to entertain the mourners and guests.

In recent times, as may be expected, the sermons of categories (1) and (2), which are common to Thai Buddhism in general, have tended to become standardized by virtue of their being written or printed in the Thai alphabet. Increasingly the north-eastern stories (*nitarn*) themselves are also being printed in the Thai alphabet while linguistically retaining the local dialectal form.

The education of monks. From the point of view of learning and literacy, village monks are of two kinds: a minority, who have been novices and are then ordained as monks (intending to stay for some time in the temple), and the majority, who are ordained temporarily for one Lent season.

For the first type the period of monkhood is a continuation of their liturgical and philosophical learning. A novice in the course of his second year of service would normally prepare for the *nagtham* examinations (*nagtham* means one who is versed in the precepts and doctrines of the religion) held by the district ecclesiastical authorities. Preparation for becoming *nagtham* is intensified, and in many village temples engaged in only during Lent when the clerical school functions systematically.

The *nagtham* syllabus may be said to consist of four parts. Pupils are required (i) to show competence in writing essays in the Thai language, and to study (ii) the life of the Buddha (as embodied in stories of his life), (iii) the essentials of the Buddhist doctrine (*Dhamma*), and (iv) the 227 rules of the Vinaya, which are the rules of conduct that apply to monks; included in this is the study of the Navakowad, which is the admonition given to a new monk (*bhikku*) about the rules of the Vinaya.

The *nagtham* examinations range from grade 3 (lowest) to grade 1 (highest). In the lowest grade the study of the above syllabus is begun at an elementary level, and in the next two grades more advanced study is made. Most village monks from Ban Phran Muan do not get beyond grades 3 and 2; the abbots nowadays may pass grade 1 in the course of time, but this was not necessarily so for abbots in the past. In 1962, for instance, only the abbot and one novice had passed the second grade; four out of

[1] It is very probable that the Central Plain and the north have their own tales and myths which are culturally transmitted through the temple. Examples for the Central Plain are Ramakien (Ramayana) epic, Unarud, Nang U Thay, Mahasot, Worawongs, Wetyasunyin, etc. (Graham (1912), pp. 569–70).

five monks had passed the lowest grade 3, and the fifth none; two of the novices had failed the lowest grade. In subsequent years the abbot passed the highest grade 1 and is now officially entitled to run a school in the Lent season.

The three *nagtham* grades do not include the study of Pali as such, the language of the chants and Buddhist doctrinal texts. Pali studies are conducted separately and the relevant examinations are called *prayog*, which consist of seven grades (3–9). In theory a monk may embark on Pali studies concurrently with *nagtham* studies or after concluding them. In practice Pali studies are not easy to engage in because, even if the monk or novice is motivated to learn, he faces the difficulty of finding a competent monk to teach him. Few village monks are versed in Pali and therefore this specialized learning is infrequent. It is for these reasons that I have argued that the majority of village monks or novices are largely ignorant of Pali (or at least have a shaky knowledge) and therefore of the content of Pali chants and Pali doctrinal texts. While the latter are accessible in local script, the chants cannot be reduced into the words of the local language, for then they would lose their sacredness and their efficacy.

A monk whose service is a continuation of novicehood enlarges his repertoire of chants and takes up for special study the Navakowad (the 227 *vinai* precepts) and the Pattimokka (confession in Pali, which is based on the *vinai* rules).

What does a monk study who serves only for one Lent? He is expected to acquire the following competence: he is trained in *tham watr* (morning and evening worship of the Buddha), in giving the Five and Eight Precepts to the laity (*haj sin dai*); he tries to memorize the *suad mongkhon* chants and is also taught the *vinai* rules. It is not an exaggeration to say that temporary monks primarily take back to lay life a limited repertoire of Pali chants which they will never use again. But while in robes they will have participated in many temple and household rites where the chants will have been recited. The case of the novice who later becomes a monk and spends some years in the temple can be, as we have seen, quite different.

The temple library

The temple is the major repository of manuscripts and texts in the village. These collections have been accumulated over a long period of time: each generation of monks add to the existing collection by themselves copying texts which were freely borrowed from other temples. It is a merit-making act for lay donors on ceremonial occasions, especially at house-blessing rites, to give texts to the local temple. Many modern texts preserve the format of the old palm-leaf books; sermons especially are printed on palm leaves. But paper books in Thai script about Buddhist doctrine and chants and other subject matter of relevance to Buddhist Thailand are increasingly making their appearance in the village. I am not sure how laymen were able to get texts in the old days in order to make gifts: apart from texts inherited, there must have been ways of acquiring them from copyists, either monks or ex-monks.

In 1966 the village temple possessed about ninety separate texts, most of which were meant to be read as sermons (*ted*). The vast majority of them belonged to the category of tales (*nitarn*). I could not catalogue all of them, but a count of about thirty-five texts gave the following breakdown:[1]

(1) Tales that are local (north-eastern) in origin = 15.
(2) Stories about the life of the Buddha = 7.
(3) Texts about the teachings and doctrines of Buddha = 5.
(4) Texts concerning monks' discipline (*vinai*) = 3.
(5) Sermons (and chants) for special ceremonies (e.g. mortuary rites) = 3.
(6) Other (e.g. history of the coming of Buddhism to Thailand) = 2.

Monasteries in the towns, which have large numbers of resident monks and are centres for Buddhist studies, tend to have not only fairly large but also well-maintained libraries. But the village collections are usually inadequately stored and, because of the large turnover of monks, the texts in their possession are not known in full and are used only when ceremonial occasion demands. As I have indicated in the section on the education of novices and monks, in the past those who were in robes for some length of time actually read many of the *nansy Tham* texts, especially the *nitarn* for sermons, but today with the limited use of *nansy Tham* and the increasing dependence on a few printed books the old libraries have little relevance for the new monks, and the texts are in danger of being neglected and stored away in dark corners. It is possible that the same fate is striking the libraries of the traditional urban temples, the centres of monastic learning in Thailand, especially in regard to the old texts written in Tham, Yuon and Korm scripts.

[1] Examples are: (1) Nang Taeng On, Tao Lin Tong, Tao Sowat, Pha Daeng Nang Ai, Tao Khun Tueng and Nang Ag Kai, Tao Ten Don, Tao Nogkrajog and Nang Chan Ton, Tao Kum Phra Phi Noi, Tao Khu Lu Nang Ua. (2) Lum Phra Wesandaun, 'Buddha cuts his hair', 'Buddha visits the sinners', Tao Chun Samut and Nang Hom Hu. (3) No information available. (4) Sang Hom That (Books I–IV and V–XI); Vinai (both of which concern the discipline of monks). (5) Kai Nakon (concerning the four elements in the human body), Buddha's first sermon, Book of Sermons for Ceremonial Occasions, Chapana Kich (for funeral ceremony); Chaturong Sannibat Tessana (preached at Makha Bucha).

THE EX-MONK RITUAL LEADERS

In Appendix III and its accompanying comments I have already separated the lay ritual specialists who are literate from those for whom literacy is not essential.

The three kinds of literate specialist I shall take up for detailed consideration here are the *acharn wat* (lay leader of Buddhist congregation), *mau ya* (physician) and the *mau khwan* or *prahm* (officiant at *khwan* rites). The purist can legitimately criticize my inclusion of medicine under ritual specialisms. My reasons for doing so are that: the literacy in question was learned in the temple; a single man can combine all three specialisms; the folk science of medicine has ritual frills; often, in village Thailand, monks practise medicine and may later function as lay *mau ya* or while in robes teach medicine to lay students.

I shall discuss these three specialists in terms of the actual village personalities who enact these roles, Acharn Pun, Pau Tu Phan and Pau Champi, whose paths of literacy and educational backgrounds have been already stated (pp. 97–8).

Acharn wat

By virtue of their familiarity with monkish life, literacy and knowledge of chants, all three persons are eminently suited to being leaders of congregation at Buddhist worship. When all three are present together, then Acharn Pun is likely to be chosen as the leader by virtue of his previous abbotship.

The role of the *acharn* is to invite (*aratana*) the monks on behalf of the congregation to give precepts, or to chant, or to make a sermon, and to receive food and other gifts presented by laymen. Every merit-making occasion which monks attend requires the chanting of invitations in the Pali language.

The following chants of invitation are some of the most frequent that an *acharn* recites:

aratana sil: to invite monks to give the Five or Eight Precepts.
aratana tawai sankatarn: to invite monks to accept food.
aratana pahung: to invite monks to chant before alms are given to them, followed by breakfast.
aratana thed: invitation of monk or monks to give a sermon. In the festival of Bun Phrawes, there is a special invitation requesting monks to read Lum Phrawesandaun.
aratana Uppakrut: invitation of Phra Uppakrut (a mythical being who lives in the swamp) to accompany villagers to the temple before the Bun Phrawes proceedings start.

Mau ya and mau khwan (prahm)

The village's most prominent *mau ya* (expert in medicine) is Pau Tu Phan, who, more than fifty years ago, was novice for four years and monk for three years. Phan is also the village's most celebrated *mau khwan/prahm* (officiant at *sukhwan* rites).

Let us see how he became a medical expert, remembering that at the age of 23 he had left the temple to resume lay life and to marry.

It was at the age of 30 years that Phan started to learn medicine from his mother's younger brother, who held the position of doctor for the commune (*tambon*), a position recognized by government. According to Phan he studied medicine with his mother's brother for 'many years' and himself became a *mau ya* only after the death of his teacher, about forty years ago.

His teacher apparently took him into the forest and identified roots and herbs and explained their uses; he also gave Phan medical texts, which dealt with the curing of stomach-ache, the bleeding of the mother after childbirth, nausea, tuberculosis, food poisoning, venereal diseases, etc. He was also taught the technique of diagnosis—to feel the patient's pulse and question him about symptoms.

Pau Tu Phan has been a successful practitioner who has had many patients from nearby villages; two years ago he gave up visiting patients, who now come to him. Fees were charged but they varied with the ability of the patient to pay. Pau Tu Phan is one of the richest men in a poor village and his superior income was in part derived from his medical practice; but it must also be emphasized that curing is a highly philanthropic role and in most cases the fee is only a token sum, the maximum being six *baht* (about two shillings) plus the initial offering or *kaj* of five pairs of candles and flowers (*khan ha*). We may thus conclude that one of the rewards of literacy (the ability to read) is the possibility of becoming a highly valued medical expert. Apart from its money returns, this position is a prestigious one because of its philanthropic character.

Let us now examine how Pau Tu Phan became *mau khwan*. This is not the place to describe the rites as such, but it is highly relevant to note that the prime emphasis of the *khwan* and associated ceremonies is on words which are recited in the Lao dialect (the texts being written in Tham alphabet). The *khwan* is the spiritual essence of a human being which at certain crises (e.g. pregnancy, rites of passage like marriage and ordination, during certain kinds of affliction, or even on occasions like setting out on a journey, etc.) may leave the body, and thereby cause illness. The essence of the *khwan* rite is to call the *khwan* back and bind it to the body. This is symbolized by the tying of a thread on the wrist. The ceremony restores the morale of the celebrant and the ritual effect is achieved by reciting the words in the presence of elders who play a vital supporting role.

It was only when Phan was about 50 years old that he was invited by a relative of his grandparental generation (who was too old to officiate and wanted a successor) to go to his native village of Chiengpun and study the art of performing *khwan* and associated ceremonies for removing bad luck and for inducing prosperity. Phan went and resided in Chiengpun for a year and studied with his teacher.

About 12–13 years ago, Pau Tu Phan decided that his ritual duties were more than he could shoulder alone. Not only are the occasions on which these rites are held innumerable, but there is also very little monetary reward deriving from their performance—just one or two *baht* plus the ritual opening gift of flowers and candles. He therefore picked Pau Champi, a distant kinsman (*yad harng*), as his successor.

Now 59 years old, Pau Champi is the village's most respected leader. He is a former headman, monk and novice, and is the leader of the temple committee. It so happens that Pau Champi's father also performed *khwan* ceremonies but died before teaching his son; however, he left some texts which Champi inherited. Having given up his robes at the age of 21 and although fully literate, Pau Champi did not commence his ritual activity until he was 46 years old; but his interest had been roused by his father, and, being a great reader, he had previously read many texts. He assisted (*puchuay*) Pau Tu Phan at rites and, having gone through his apprenticeship, began to perform by himself these simple rites which have minimal acts of object manipulation and maximum emphasis on words as such. Pau Champi now performs all *khwan* and *sia kro* (dispelling bad luck) ceremonies in the village.

Certain points stand out in the facts presented. The practice of medicine and *khwan* and associated rites requires literacy of the type acquired in the temple; yet a person who has been a novice and monk does not automatically become a medical or ritual expert. Traditionally these arts have to be learned from an existing practitioner, who is likely to nominate and train a kinsman to succeed him; the apprentice usually waits until his teacher is ready to give up before he himself practises on his own. This appears to be the professional etiquette within the village in the cases described.

Thus this two-sided equation of teacher and chosen disciple means that recruitment for the learning of the arts of *mau khwan* and *mau ya* was not completely open nor a simple commercial transaction. The eligibility and suitability of the candidate were assessed by the teacher, and such qualities of character were intrinsic to the role of ritual elder.

It is instructive to compare the recruitment and training of the literate specialists with that of the non-literate specialists like *mau song*, *mau tham*, and *mau lum phi fa*.

The diviner (*mau song*) also learns his art from a teacher. The villagers' foremost diviner actually learned the art from his own father; he started to learn at the age of 25 and was an apprentice for 7 years. But his own father learned from a friend in Laos with whom he had cattle dealings. Though literacy is not required of him, the diviner is recruited and trained in a manner similar to literate specialists, but he may entirely lack the preliminary training as monk and novice, and he does not consult or read texts in the practice of divination.

The recruitment and training of a *mau tham* (exorcizer) is somewhat different. For the payment of a fee the magical art of exorcism can be learned from a specialist, provided the student can demonstrate his sensitivity to 'possession' or going into trance. The learning consists of the memorizing of a few potent charms and chants; their 'meaning' as such is irrelevant to the specialist. We may note the commercial nature of the acquisition of the knowledge. There is also no restriction on practice by the recruit while his teacher is living or professionally active. Finally, *jum*, *tiam*, *phi fa* are 'chosen' by possession, or through affliction and cure. They are essentially mediums and intermediaries of spirits. Here the personal, idiosyncratic element alone is the most important one in initial recruitment; but the art of performing the rituals has to be learned from other specialists and is accompanied by gifts and fees. No texts are used. Certain modes of address and propitiation are memorized; but there is no emphasis on verbal exactitude. The teacher is always invoked at the beginning of the ritual by the *mau tham* and *mau lum phi fa*, and the *jum* and *tiam* have their apprentice periods when they assist the acknowledged experts.

The texts of the mau khwan, prahm and mau ya

The *mau khwan/prahm* officiates at innumerable ceremonies, the most important of which are *khwan* rites performed on numerous occasions. Each occasion has a special type of ritual text attached. The language of the texts is always north-east Lao, the spoken tongue. In the village of Ban Phran Muan the *mau khwan* always reads from a palm-leaf text. There is no improvisation of words; and committing the texts to memory will be a herculean task to men who are ordinarily farmers and only part-time ritual specialists. The words of the texts are critical for two reasons: for the officiant they constitute a store of ritual information because the texts describe the ritual procedure as such; they are also critical for the listeners, for the ritual effects are created through the words, which are well understood. The *mau ya* also possesses texts relating to particular illnesses which he may consult at a particular diagnosis or read in his leisure time in order to master their contents.

This means that these specialists must have in their possession private collections of texts; they also should be in a position to borrow each other's texts if occasion demands. Borrowing is possible because the texts as such do not constitute secret knowledge; it is the ability to read that restricts access.

In Appendix 1 I give lists of texts found in the possession of some villagers. One list enumerates texts in the common possession of two ritual experts; another shows the texts inherited by a man whose father was a ritual specialist. The contents of the texts are indicated so that the reader can take note of the kinds of rituals at which the *mau khwan* presides. The texts can be divided into the following major subject groups: (1) medical texts, (2) texts of *khwan* rites, (3) texts for dispelling inauspicious omens and afflictions which are not attributed to the action of spirits (*phi*), (4) astrological texts. It is quite likely that private collections may also include regional myths and folktales and folk poetry.

The manner in which the texts were acquired leads us back to the point already stressed. In the past it was the temple that acted as library and its personnel as copyists. This emphasizes the point that these rituals come within the wider fold of Buddhism. Although the monk in robes could not be the officiant at the rites in question, yet he was interested in the texts as essential to have when he would give up his robes and play an important lay role. As far as healing was concerned, a monk could practise medicine and therefore the temple was sometimes the storehouse and transmitter of this knowledge.

I shall illustrate these points with some concrete examples. Acharn Pun, the ex-abbot, said that when he gave up his robes he had a collection of ritual texts relating to *khwan* ceremonial, astrology (how to find the auspicious day for building a house, performing a marriage, etc.) and ceremonies for removing bad luck caused by unnatural events, e.g. lightning striking a house, a vulture alighting on the roof. He said that when he was a novice and monk these texts were in the possession of his abbot and that he had copied them himself. Either one inherited texts or copied them as a novice or monk; none were for sale. However, in his time, certain printed books of Buddhist chants (seven Tamnan and twelve Tamnan) became available for purchase, but not the texts of rites which I am describing here.

Pau Larng, about 58 years old, inherited a large number of texts from his father-in-law, who had copied them himself when he was a monk.

Pau Larng never used the texts, and in 1966 when I visited him I found them rotting away in his hut. This was the state of affairs despite the fact that Pau Larng was fully able to read *nansy Tham*, having been a monk himself.

Traditional literacy: some quantitative aspects

I shall conclude this discussion of traditional literacy of novices, monks and lay ritual experts (who were ex-monks) by commenting on the number of people who travelled on the traditional path of literacy and emerged literate. In modern educational jargon, I am considering the problem of 'educational wastage' from the point of view of literacy, not in terms of other benefits.

In the figures given earlier on the number who became novices and monks, I have indicated that although more than half of the male family heads had seen some kind of religious service in the temple, only about a fifth of the total number had been both novices and monks, and therefore could be assumed to have had the time and training for mastering the art of reading *nansy Tham* and documents in the secular Lao/Thai scripts. But even this minority could not be assumed to have retained their ability to read when they resumed lay life. There are many elderly persons in the village today who, although they had studied *nansy Tham* in their youth, have virtually lost their literacy.

In 1966 a very rough count was made of the number of laymen who were versed in the traditional Tham and Lao scripts. Seven elders were mentioned by villagers as having this capacity. Of these only three were lay ritual leaders and medical practitioners of the type we have discussed: *acharn wat*, *mau khwan*, and *mau ya*. The other four, although able to read the odd literature that came to hand, were not using their literacy in a manner that had any visible impact on the village.

This leads us to other facts already cited. A former novice or monk does not automatically acquire lay ritual and medical skills; after a lapse of years he may learn from a practitioner who is willing to have him as his successor. Interest and effort on the part of the recruit (individual factors) as well as the right kinship connections (ascribed criteria) come into play.

In the village, then, monkhood and novicehood as such are not restricted; they are virtually open to any male, and it is not beyond the means of most villagers to have their sons ordained. In fact, in Ban Phran Muan ordination is a collective rite to which the entire village contributes financially. However, certain individual or idiosyncratic factors primarily determine which of the many young men will serve long enough in the temple to attain literacy and religious knowledge. Once lay life is resumed again, individual factors of interest and personal effort as well as restrictive criteria (e.g. finding a teacher who will pass on knowledge to a chosen or approved successor) play their part in determining the total number of men who in their middle age will become ritual experts, highly appreciated in the village.

What are the implications for traditional ritual and medicine of the fact that in recent years there have been hardly any young men in the village who can read the traditional manuscripts, both because of the government's educational policy of teaching children only in the Thai language and because the novices and monks of today need not, and in the main do not, master the Tham script?

Village elders consciously see this as a problem, for the number of *mau khwan* and *mau ya* in the region is dwindling, but not, as yet, the public demand for their services. For instance, *khwan* rites are widely practised at the moment. Most villagers are treated by their own village physicians rather than by government doctors. Nevertheless, the loss of traditional literacy will seriously affect the emergence of future specialists. Already, the death of elderly specialists is causing a visible shortage.

But in recent years there has been a countertrend the precise implications of which I am unable to judge. In the north-eastern towns like Udorn and Khon Kaen (and no doubt in others), particularly in shops that sell Buddhist ritual articles and literature, are displayed for sale very cheap printed booklets and books of north-eastern tales (*nitarn*), customs and ritual texts (e.g. *sukhwan* texts). They are printed in the Thai alphabet but the language is the local north-eastern dialect. In theory the modern literate who does not know Tham should be able to read and use this literature just as he has access to strictly Buddhist writings in the same form. I myself purchased copies of these printed texts and tales and showed them to villagers; some had heard of them or seen them; none possessed them (although some had a few of the new printed Buddhist texts); and the ritual experts of the village were of the view that the printed ritual texts were incorrect. The texts were printed in the town of Khon Kaen several miles away and the printers had used local manuscripts found there which differed in some details from those known in the Udorn region. The fact is that, if they are viewed as being incorrect, there is little chance of their being used in the village.

SECULAR LITERACY

Mau lum (folk opera)

Mau lum means both folk opera and drama as well as their performers. Folk opera is the most popular form of entertainment in north-eastern Thailand. A measure of the contemporary appreciation of it is that wherever the radio has spread into villages the programme most avidly listened to is *mau lum*. In the villages in the Udorn locality there are said to be two kinds of *mau lum*: *mau lum klaun*, which is singing in verse, and *mau lum ryang*, which is dramatic presentation of stories in prose. The former requires only one or two singers and a flutist, while the latter requires a troupe of actors. The village of Ban Phran Muan has a couple, man and wife, who perform *klaun*; he plays the bamboo flute instrument (*kan*) while she sings and dances.

The entertainment appeal of *mau lum* stems from the fact that much of its content is drawn from the pool of north-eastern tales and myths (*nitarn*) which we have discussed before. Although referred to as 'verse', the *klaun* would appear to be rather flexibly constructed rhyming songs, without the strict rules known in the 'higher' literary form also called *klaun*.[1] These songs are transmitted both orally and in written form. Furthermore, there is room for free creation because a good *mau lum* singer should be able to improvise and be adept at repartee.

The occasions when *mau lum* performers are usually heard by villagers are the annual collective Buddhist ceremonies which every village stages—Bun Kathin, Bun Phrawes, and the ordination of novices and monks, which is combined with Bun Bang Fai (rocket-firing ceremony). It is usual for such merit-making occasions to be accompanied at night by a fair in the temple grounds. The *mau lum* troupe, which performs from about 9 p.m until 5.30 a.m. the following morning, is paid out of the revenue collected by the temple committee from contributions of devotees and from renting stalls to shopkeepers. The performers travel quite widely in the north-east; for example, the village singers said that they had been invited to perform not only in the other villages of their district but also in other districts in their province and the neighbouring Loey province. The fees range from 200 to 600/700 *baht* depending on the distance travelled.

The village *mau lum* players named the following as their repertoire:

(1) Klaun Kheo: verses on courtship and love.

(2) Story of the town of Vieng Chan, capital of Laos.

(3) Klaun Nitarn: stories of Tao Sowatr, Pha Daeng Nang Ai, Tao Khu Lu and Nang Ua. All these three categories are regional north-eastern or Laotian tales.

(4) History and geography of the Thai people and its regions, which corresponds to traditions of Thai origins and migrations held widely in Thailand.

(5) (*a*) Klaun Khun Chang Khun Phan; (*b*) Klaun Phra Abhai. These two stories are part of Thai literature in general and are widely known, especially in central Thailand. Thus (4) and (5) belong to national traditions.

(6) Klaun Phra Wes (the story of the penultimate life of the Buddha).

[1] I am indebted to Mr Stuart Simmonds for this information.

(7) Klaun Pathom Sompote (stories of the life of Buddha). (6) and (7) are again Buddhist stories known throughout the country.

The above list allows us to make several inferences. A large proportion of the *mau lum* songs are based on *nitarn* (both Buddhist and local tales) which in another context and form are preached as sermons by monks. Unlike *nansy Tham* texts, however, the *mau lum* texts are usually written in the secular Lao script. Since *mau lum* performances are typically given at merit-making activities in the temple and to a lesser extent the household, it might seem inaccurate to view *mau lum* as 'secular' entertainment. But although *mau lum* is often performed on temple grounds, monks are forbidden to attend, which emphasizes the opposition of this entertainment to the monks' ascetic mode of life.

Actually the repertoire of *mau lum* is wider than that of sermons. It includes courtship and love poetry, burlesque and earthy, bawdy jokes: it echoes and stimulates the romantic sentiments of the young men and women (*phubao* and *phusao*).

The *mau lum* singers not only preserve and propagate regional traditions; they are also the channels through whom certain stories and epics, popularly known and appreciated in central and northern Thailand, are passed on to north-eastern villagers. They sing stories about the life of the Buddha which are nationally known and are heard in a different form in the temple. Today they appear to be agents for disseminating ideas and slogans of national importance.

The 'nationalizing' role of *mau lum* singers may be compared to the role of radio and television as communication media. The village *mau lum* singer informed us that in Udorn she had recently bought *mau lum* texts for about 100 *baht*, put out by the government in cooperation with certain American agencies. These new texts have as their themes rural development, animal husbandry, government slogans for various development drives, anti-communist propaganda, nuclear rockets (*jarnad nuclear*!), psychological warfare (*songram chittavitya*), and provincial reorganization of the north-east. These texts have been specially written as *mau lum klaun* and, to the extent to which the singers readily take to them, a truly grass-roots propaganda machine will have been harnessed by the government to promote its political and socio-economic policies.

The *mau lum* singer is relevant to the technical problem of literacy in this way. The audience need not be literate, but the singer must be able to read the secular Lao and, today, the Thai scripts, because he or she depends on texts a great deal for obtaining his or her songs. No doubt some songs are orally transmitted from singer to singer, teacher to pupil. Furthermore, in the course of their career singers will themselves improvise, adapt and add to the original texts. The oral and written traditions are not separate but supplement each other, and the latitude tradition gives to the singer should not make us underestimate the fact that a *mau lum* singer is in the first place trained to sing, and, in the second, has a wide repertoire of songs the memorizing of which is dependent on the possession of texts. The list of *klaun* I have already given is of actual texts in the possession of the woman *mau lum* of the village. When one singer trains and transmits his (or her) songs to his student, his own creative additions are committed to writing in the texts copied. Thus free creation of songs and their subsequent incorporation in written texts are continuous complementary processes which result in cumulative addition to old texts, the emergence of variant forms, and the corruption of classical forms.

The training undergone was described by the village singer as follows. She is 36 years old and she was born in the border town of Nongkhai. At the age of 12, when she had completed her primary schooling (grade 4) and had acquired elementary literacy, she was sent by her parents to the town of Khon Kaen to study *mau lum* with a male teacher (*khruba*). She lived in the teacher's house and studied with him for seven months.

In the daytime she copied verses and memorized them; in the evening and the night she practised singing and dancing with the teacher. When she had completed her studies, the teacher taught her certain magical verses which she must recite and the accompanying ritual which she must carry out before every performance she gave as a professional singer. The words in question are *au pong*, which are recited to ensure the songs can be easily memorized and not forgotten when singing, and *au lum*, which are recited to enamour listeners and make them appreciative of her singing and dancing and to be a preventive against loss of voice (*sai gun*). In fact the first ritual she performed, called *taeng kaj hian* (*rian*) *kaj au*, was her investiture, in which she both paid respect and gave a prescribed ritual gift (*kaj*) to her teacher, and then recited the spells which would promote and protect her professional skill. This same ritual is performed on every subsequent occasion on which she goes on stage, though of course the ritual articles are not given again to the teacher.

At the conclusions of studies the teacher was paid 800 *baht* (£13–14) for tuition and 400 *baht* for the texts of songs and stories (*klaun lum*). *Mau lum* training is a professional business, given for a fee; in turn the trained singer exacts fees whenever she performs, in the manner of professional entertainers. This transaction is in quite a different idiom from the philanthropic non-commercial services of a *mau khwan* and even a *mau ya*, who are given prescribed gifts of small monetary value.

The songs and stories of the *mau lum* shade off into the folksongs, love poetry and popular tales known by the villagers at large, sometimes found in written texts, often transmitted orally. Written texts of myths and tales are sometimes possessed by individuals who, if they know the Lao or Tham script, read them at funeral wakes and other occasions when people gather together. Much of the folk poetry revolves around love. In the past, evening courtships of maidens (*aew sao*) by groups of young men were occasions for formalized competitive love songs; some songs are the laments of separated lovers or deal with the inconstancy of affections.

THE PATH OF LITERACY OF THE SCHOLAR-MONK: FROM VILLAGE BUDDHISM TO HIGHER BUDDHISM

In this last section I shall look beyond the narrow universe of village Buddhism and briefly discuss two features of extra-village literacy in order, on the one hand, to remind the reader of the confines of my discussion of village literacy and, on the other, to indicate the complex educational network that spreads out from an isolated village.

Clearly in Thailand a network of monastic educational institutions exists on a regional level with urban and historic rural centres being focal points. In turn these networks converge upon Bangkok, the national capital. Apart from famous monastic schools, Bangkok has two universities for monks which teach subjects ordinarily taught in secular universities.

Village youths, especially novices who are promising and keen, may leave their village temples and go to district monastic centres. From there again they may be sent to historic provincial centres of learning and even finally find their way to Bangkok. This path of literacy is made possible by certain features peculiar to monkhood. First, a young novice or monk always has assigned to him an older monk as preceptor (called by the younger man *luang phi*, i.e. 'respected elder brother') who teaches, sponsors and supports him. This relationship between *upacha* (preceptor) and pupil monk can be an important one for mobility within the order. Secondly, the abbot of a village temple has contacts with other abbots and with his district head, so that he can find a place for a keen student in a monastic centre which gives superior education. Further, the status of novice or monk is a 'detached' one and in theory any such religious person can be mobile, going from temple to temple, provided he can find a place through the active collaboration of his preceptor and sponsor. Placement in other communities through kinship in the secular world is more circumscribed than the mobility that is possible for a monk. Here is a transformation of the concept of 'homeless wanderer' of pristine Buddhism.

That such networks are used and that village youths of promise have climbed the ladder of literacy is attested by writers (e.g. Klausner 1964). In Appendix II I give the educational career of an extraordinary monk who was born in a north-eastern village, not in Ban Phran Muan but in the province of Mahasarakam, and who has reached the apex of monastic learning in Thailand and is currently engaged in Sanskrit studies in the University of Cambridge. This appendix describes in detail many of the points I can merely mention here: the network and levels of monastic centres of learning, the institution of preceptor–pupil relationship, the number of novice/monk pupils in these centres, and finally the kind of instruction in Pali studies given at the centres.

Now it is clear that, compared with the story in that account, the village of Ban Phran Muan is undistinguished and has not systematically nurtured gifted young men who have then entered the network of higher learning. But I must hasten to add that Ban Phran Muan in fact falls into the lowest and largest category of villages in the hierarchy of traditional learning in north-east Thailand; its situation is shared by many others.

In estimating in a crude way the efficacy of monastic educational networks and the proportion of novices and monks who go beyond the elementary *nagtham* studies to Pali studies it is relevant to note the following facts. There is no systematic recruitment of novices or monks from villages into higher centres of learning. The point is rather that a gifted student, adequately sponsored, can find his way into the upper reaches. The system does not work in the manner of contemporary national educational systems which channel students from primary schools to secondary schools to universities.

Another way of saying the same thing is that the vast majority of village novices and monks do not aspire to become learned in Pali studies. This is due not only to the nature of temporary religious service. Even those who stay in robes for some length of time do not in the main aspire to become Pali scholar-monks.

There are many reasons for this. The role of the monk in a village is primarily a ritual one: we have already seen that in order to perform his parish and monastic role he needs to acquire only a certain amount of literacy in the sacred Tham and secular languages and to memorize a body of oft-used chants. Pali studies are not essential for this purpose.

Furthermore, a monk who becomes engaged in Pali doctrinal studies is in all probability also one who becomes increasingly committed to following that kind of doctrinal Buddhism which, if taken seriously, results in progressive detachment from the world and involves practising meditation and self-control and entering into mystical realms which promise Nirvana. In other words, he tends to become a world-renouncer, and only a few are capable of engaging in this higher pursuit.

From the point of view of literacy, a most relevant consideration is that which stands in contrast to the situation of the Islamic *mallam*. In Islam Arabic studies are a necessary vehicle for mastery of legal, judicial and other codes which have a direct secular significance. The learned man is an interpreter of law and a judge and counsellor of men in everyday affairs. The Pali doctrinal texts of Buddhism have no implication for the laws and customs of everyday life of the laity. For a village monk, we have seen, his pay-off is primarily ritual eldership in the village, for which he requires a kind of literacy (other than mastery of Pali) which he acquired in the past at the village level.

It is for these reasons that few monks take their *nagtham* studies seriously or enter upon the more complex Pali studies. Some do learn Pali, for it confers prestige and entitles them to conduct village religious schools. Thus centres of learning feed back into the villages their pupils. But such monks rarely go beyond the first few grades of Pali studies. It is not a matter of importance to the village congregation that they should have in their midst a Pali scholar—it is enough that someone is available in the neighbourhood.

However, a professional monk may wish to climb the religious hierarchy; he may aspire to become abbot of his village temple and then become a district head (*chaokana amphur*). Such a monk must have a certain amount of intellectual training and service in other temples. While the village of Phran Muan has never produced a scholar-monk, it has produced one monk in recent times who has climbed the clerical hierarchy. He is Phra Khru Anurak Punnaket, 48 years of age, and at present the ecclesiastical head of Pen District. He is the son of Pau (father) Puay, an ordinary and undistinguished farmer in Phran Muan village. Phra Anurak spent about fifteen years in a temple at the provincial capital of Udorn and several years in Bangkok, then returned as abbot to his native village from where he received his promotion. He has some knowledge of Pali but would not consider himself a scholar. His local influence is great because of his position, his varied experience and his wide network of contacts, both ecclesiastical and secular.

CONCLUSION

I have focused on the nature of traditional literacy and the kinds of traditional literati in a remote north-eastern village in Thailand which, when viewed in relation to towns, historic monastic centres and the prosperous villages of the rice-bowl plains of central and northern Thailand, would normally be considered remote, isolated, poverty-stricken, uncouth and illiterate. But even this village in a backwater region was in the path of the grand civilizational streams associated with the coming and flourishing of Buddhism and within the orbit of the sophisticated political kingdoms that rose and fell in this part of south-east Asia. The village is hardly an island by itself, even less a fossilized deposit of an ancient civilization. It is a vital going concern, that partakes of a regional religious, artistic and intellectual culture; from within, it produces personnel who are the carriers and transmitters of wider traditions.

The village of Phran Muan eloquently explodes two popular myths about communities of its type—that they are traditionally illiterate and therefore learning has to be taken to them for the first time; or that, if they had learning, it was exclusively religious and confined to religious personnel, the monks. These assertions need to be refined.

One point about traditional literacy in the village is that there was of course no mass literacy, but a literacy of specialists who were in touch with the higher learning of Buddhism, with gods, with codified curative knowledge, and in more recent times with the government.

In this literacy of specialists, the main agency of transmission (though not necessarily the only one) has been the village temple. The largest portion of village literature was ritualistic and it was written in the sacred Tham script. However, there was some literature in the secular Lao or even in mixed Tham/Lao forms. We should note that all literature was not narrowly 'religious': the range included medical texts, local myths and tales, and folk poetry and songs. Conspicuous by their absence are codifications of laws; practical crafts there always were, but they, like customs, were transmitted orally and by example. Whatever the form of writing, literacy was gained largely through service in the temple, which transmitted a large portion of the traditional literature, especially through sermons at festivals; it also provided the occasion and the stage for the enjoyment of folk opera.

The rungs on the ladder of literacy were, first, temple boy (or student) in the temple primary school, then novicehood, concluding with monkhood. When a man resumed lay life, literacy was essential for expertise in conducting the important *khwan* rites, which in fact were concerned with the initiation into and replacement and maintenance of the statuses of village society; literacy was also essential for the practice of medicine and for conducting the arts of entertainment. Literacy required of the last was usually but not necessarily linked to the educational machinery of the temple.

The leadership and prestige hierarchy of the village placed great emphasis on literacy. Here I refer not so much to monks, who were indeed respected but who belonged to a domain set apart from lay life, but to the respected elders (*puthao*) of the village, who were primarily ritual and medical specialists. Their literacy was indissolubly linked with their ethical and religious training in their youth. Their lay ceremonial roles come under the umbrella of Buddhism. For these reasons they are distinguished from and are superior to the non-literate ritual specialists.

The literacy required of the specialists and imparted to them by the temple was in some ways a restricted one. This is partly attributable to the content of traditional literacy and its uses. Novices and monks were primarily trained to read the scripts and only secondarily to write. Writing was not so much creative composition as copying. The literature read and copied was composed of religious texts or traditional tales which could not in theory be changed, only transmitted. This realm of traditional knowledge was very much a combination of both fixed literary form and oral transmission. Thus the emphasis in the training of novices and monks and lay specialists, whose art depended on the use of words, was on memorizing and on effective recitation, delivery and elocution. But we should not ignore the creative latitude possible in certain segments of the literary–oral traditions. The folk tales in fact have several variants which must surely be the result of changes resulting from oral and written transmission; folk poetry obviously portrays creative additions; *mau lum* songs have always included the improvisations and elaborations of its gifted artists. Because writing exists, these creative additions and modifications are at some point written down. These literary forms thus stand at the opposite end of the Buddhist Pali chants and doctrinal texts, which are in fact fixed; the intellectual freedom of the monk is exercised in the exposition and elucidation of texts which themselves cannot be changed.

Language, as such, is of critical importance in village ritual. Ritual uses words together with manipulation of objects to transmit messages and achieve effects in the devotee, celebrant or patient. Especially in the rituals conducted by the literate specialists (Buddhist monks and the *mau khwan*) words as such are pre-eminent, and the recitation of texts forms the core of ceremonies. But we have observed that words do not play a similar role in the rites. The Buddhist monk recites sacred Pali chants which are largely not understood by the congregation, nor indeed by many of the temporary monks themselves; however, their recitation in itself is supposed to confer blessings and protection. The words are sacred and effective because they are the words of the Buddha and are recited by ascetic disciplined monks who lead a religiously valued life. In the case of sermons rendered by monks, the words are understood and have necessarily to be understood because they are meant to educate morally and to entertain. The *mau khwan* recites texts which again have to be understood by the celebrant because the words achieve their effects in him through an uplift of morale and a conveying of confidence and support by the assembled dignified and mature village elders. At the other extreme, the *mau dharm* or exorcizer recites charms and spells unintelligible to himself and the patient, but here the words are an element in a therapy which uses shock effects and are the secret possession of a specialist who exercises dangerous but potent power over the spirits. The *mau dharm* and the monk are in one sense similar in that they use in their chants or spells unintelligible words, but are completely opposed in their ethical endowment, their way of life, and their relation to the supernatural. Finally in the sphere of entertainment, the folk-opera performers communicate with their audience in a manner that is required of all successful theatrical performances.

The institution of temporary monkhood, the annual ordination of a band of village sons, and the maintenance of the temple and its religious personnel in common by the village necessarily mean that recruitment to novicehood and monkhood is open. Monks at the village level do not comprise a closed monopolistic group. But we have seen that, although entry to literacy is open, in fact selectivity functions in a different form. It is only a youth willing and able to submit himself to the discipline of some years of novicehood and monkhood who secures an adequate level of literacy to become a lay specialist in later life. But the assumption of ritual leadership in lay life is not automatic. Individual interest and aptitude play their part; and certain particularistic features, such as kinship connections, are operative in the choice of candidates who will be trained as their successors by existing practitioners. But the particularistic features are by no means inordinately restrictive in a society in which bilateral kinship reckoning is interpreted in a wide sense and the ideology of mutual aid and merit-making is widespread.

The old literacy of the village had no implication for the art of government and politics and the transmission of manual skills. Village headmen, we are told, are traditional to Thailand. But it was only in 1947 that village government was firmly integrated with district government and the agencies of central government. The recording of disputes, collection of village statistics, transmission of government orders to villagers are tasks that require literacy, but this is a feature of the new literacy and hence excluded in this essay. For the same reason are excluded the prime representatives of new literacy, the village schoolteachers, who since the 1930s have become increasingly significant in rural Thailand as agents of government, as carriers of new knowledge and new orientations.

Finally, if one looks from the village outwards, one discovers links between village temple and district monastic centres of learning, and between these and national centres. They provide the channels for the exceptionally gifted monk or novice of village origin who becomes the scholar-monk or an eminent monk in the religious hierarchy. A certain number of these return to their village temples. It is only by taking into account this network that one can assess the nature of traditional literacy in Thailand as a whole. It would be an error to extrapolate from the village of Phran Muan to the entire country. However, my arguments as to why I think few village monks aspired to enter this network, especially to master the Pali language, tell us a great deal about the nature of traditional village literacy and its firm mooring in village interests.

APPENDIX I: PRIVATE COLLECTIONS OF PALM-LEAF TEXTS IN PHRAN MUAN VILLAGE

Case 1: The joint collection of Pau Tu Phan and Pau Champi

Phan is the most celebrated physician and *mau khwan* officiant at the various ceremonies for recalling the 'spirit essence'. Champi is Phan's successor to the position of *mau khwan*. Phan inherited medical texts from his teacher, who was his mother's brother—the texts relate to the curing of stomach-ache, prevention of bleeding of women after childbirth, curing nausea, tuberculosis, food poisoning and venereal diseases.

Phan inherited the *khwan* and related ritual texts from his other teacher, also a kinsmen. Since Champi, a distant kinsman, was chosen by Phan as his apprentice and successor, Phan's ritual texts are used by Champi, who himself inherited a few texts from his own father. Champi will probably inherit Phan's texts after Phan dies. The following is the list of ritual texts in the common possession of Phan and Champi. I indicate with the symbol (C) the texts inherited by Champi; the rest belong to Phan. The texts, which are all-important in the actual rites, bear the names of the ceremonies.

(1*a*) *Taengkae mae marn:* to dispel bad luck in a pregnant woman and to call her *khwan*. The ceremony is usually performed in the seventh or eighth month, and is compulsory for the birth of the first child. (*b*) *Sukhwan mae marm:* the calling of the *khwan* of a pregnant women. This ceremony is less elaborate than (*a*) above, and is performed before every childbirth. (2) *Sukhwan thamada:* 'ordinary' *khwan* ceremony, performed when a man goes on or returns from a trip, when a man recovers from slight illness, etc. (3) *Sukhwan nag: khwan* ceremony for a person going to be ordained as novice or monk. (4) *Sukhwan phua mia mai: khwan* ceremony performed at marriage for bridegroom and bride. (5) *Sukhwan luang:* a major *khwan* ceremony for good health and prosperity (*ju dee mee haeng*). (6) *Sukhwan phra: khwan* ceremony performed for monks by lay elders before they go into retreat in Lent season. (7) *Taeng kae promchati* (C): a long-life ceremony in which Thaen—the heavenly creators of human beings—are propitiated for cure of illness and prolongation of life. (8) *Kae kamlerd* (C): to dispel sickness in children caused by 'former mothers' (*mae gao mae larng*). (9) *Baeng khaw baeng kai* (cutting into halves of rice balls and boiled eggs): this ceremony is performed when a child under ten years suffers prolonged illness owing to the fleeing of its *khwan*. (10) *Sia kroh luang:* ceremony to dispel misfortune or bad luck caused by very inauspicious 'unusual' events such as lightning striking a tree in the house compound, or the house itself; a vulture alighting on the roof; a toad entering the house; or the domestic buffalo lying down in the mud under the wash place (*hong nam*). (11) *Taeng bucha choke* (C): requesting good fortune. (12) *Bucha tua sawoei:* ceremony for the animal of the year in which one is born. In the village the life chart is made up of 8-year cycles represented by the following animals: tiger, *garuda* (*krut*), rat, elephant, ox, *naga* (serpent), cat and lion. There is an alternative system based on the 12-year cycles using different planetary and other symbols. (13) *Sutra khwan luang* (C): a *khwan* ceremony for continuation of life performed for an adult who is suffering from a serious and prolonged illness. It is performed while the patient is asleep. (14) A short astrological text for finding good days for initiating house-building.

All the texts (1–14) listed are in the Lao language but written in Tham, or Tham-Lao mixed scripts. The combined collection has the following range: (*a*) *khwan* rites, (*b*) rites for dispelling bad luck/illness, (*c*) astrological texts, (*d*) medical texts.

Case 2: Private collection of texts in the possession of Pau Larng

Pau Larng inherited these texts from his father-in-law, who was versed in rituals but does not conduct rituals himself.

(1) *Sia kroh gae ubad:* to drive away inauspicious and unusual happenings. (2) *Rerg thang thang:* auspicious days and times. (3) *Sado kroh thang thang:* to dispel many kinds of misfortune. (4) *Phaya:* proverbs and wise sayings. (5) *Taengkae thugyang:* to drive away all kinds of misfortune; similar to (3). (6) *Bucha kroh:* ceremony to avert misfortune; similar to (3) and (5). (7) *Gae ubad:* similar to (1). (8) *Gae Rahu:* to dispel misfortune caused by Rahu, one of the planetary forces. (9) *Gae mae gao mae larng:* to drive away misfortune caused by 'former mothers' of children. (10) *Jubyarng thang thang:* to find the auspicious time by astrology. (11) *Rerg thang thang:* to find auspicious times for initiating projects; similar to (10). (12) *Bucha tua sawoei:* ceremony for the animal of the year of birth. (13) *Tham raya kae buad sisa:* medical text for curing headache. (14) *Tham raya lai yarng:* medical texts for curing many kinds of illnesses. (15) Text for making love magic.

It was impossible to identify two more texts because they were in a state of decay. This collection has a wide range: apart from the four kinds listed in case 1, it also includes proverbs. Pau Larng also used to have a text of the story of Nang Prakosob (the spirit of the rice goddess).

APPENDIX II: THE BIOGRAPHY OF A SCHOLAR MONK

Phra Maha Sathienpong was born in the village of Ban Huay Kaen in Mahasarakam province (north-east Thailand) in 1940. His father was a farmer and Sathien was the second of six children, the third and fourth also being boys.

The village in question is an exceptional one because the village temple (Wat

Ambawan: the Temple of the Mango Grove) was one of the three big centres of monastic learning in the province. A second big centre was also located in a village, in Naung Waeng Nang. A third centre, not of the same calibre, was in the capital of the province itself. This was Wat Maha Chai, the seat of the provincial ecclesiastical head (Chaokana Changwat). The provincial capital also had other monastic educational institutions of minor importance.

Thus Sathien's village, which was no bigger than the average, had an historic temple which was to play a crucial role in his life. At the time Sathien himself became a novice about a hundred novices and monks, the former predominating, resided in this temple. Most of them had come from other villages in the province in order to engage in religious studies. There were about seven teacher-monks, three who prepared students for the *nagtham* examinations, and four who taught the Pali language and Pali texts. Of these four Pali teachers, two had the title of Phra Maha which is conferred on monks who have passed at least one of the Pali examinations (Prayog), which are divided into seven grades (3–9).

For most of us, especially in our youth, the conscious reasons for choice of future career have no simple connections with the complex circumstances that shape our lives. Like other boys of his village, Sathien attended the primary school and by the age of 12 successfully completed his four grades (Prathom 4). His father contemplated sending him on to study in the district secondary school, and consulted the boy. Sathien, however, chose to be ordained as a novice.

It is interesting to note that Sathien reports that his urge to be ordained as novice had nothing to do with academic aspirations. As a boy who had various household and farming chores, he envied the young novices in the temple who had a leisurely life and received gifts of food and fruits from the villagers ('As an act of merit villagers always give fruits to monks and novices before they themselves eat'). He wished to become a novice to enjoy what seemed to a little boy an attractive life. Sathien's father and mother were pleased with his decision; they therefore sponsored his ordination, aided by relatives and fellow villagers. As is the village custom, Sathien was ordained as novice in a group ceremony in which four candidates took part.

Sathien passed his first *nagtham* examination in the course of the year, and also began his preliminary studies in Pali grammar. He was a novice in the temple for two years when he went to another similar monastic centre in the town of Nakorn Phanom.

This move was dictated by the obligations and ties arising out of a special relationship. Each novice is attached to a monk (*bhikku*) who acts as his mentor and whose practical needs the novice looks after. The mentor is usually referred to by the novice as *luang phi* ('respected elder brother'). Sathien's *luang phi*, who had himself passed the first Pali examination, decided to change his monastic institution and chose to go to Nakorn Phanom, where Sathien followed him.

The monastic institution at Nakorn Phanom was not as large as the one in Sathien's village, but it was a famous centre of learning and practised a somewhat restrictive policy in recruiting students. It had about sixty student novices and monks (the former category being the larger), and three Pali teachers who were all Phra Maha, plus others who taught the *nagtham* syllabus.

Sathien resided in Nakorn Phanom for only one year—he was requested by his father to return to his native village because his parents wanted him to be near them. When, therefore, he left Nakorn Phanom he had already passed his second *nagtham* examination and his first Pali examination (Prayog 3). He now assumed the title of Samanera Paurian conferred on novices who had passed any one of the Pali examinations; Paurian is derived from the word *parinna*, which means wisdom.

Back in his village, Sathien continued his religious studies. He reports that by now he had become seriously dedicated to intellectual and religious pursuits. He demonstrated his brilliance by passing the third and highest Nagtham examination (Nagtham Eg) and the second Pali examination (Prayog Si). At the age of 15 his achievement was remarkable, and his teacher and abbot at the temple of Ambawan, Phra Maha Buddhi, felt that he could no longer teach him and decided to send him to a monastic centre in Bangkok, the national capital.[1] Sathien's own keenness, plus the backing of the abbot, was enough to secure the consent of Sathien's parents.

Sathien came to Bangkok at the age of 15 to stay temporarily in the temple of Pichaiyat (near Sapan Put) until Abbot Phra Buddhi could find him a place of residence. It is always difficult for a novice or monk to find a place in a Bangkok temple, especially one which is a centre of monastic learning. This difficulty is greater in the case of novices or monks who want to come to Bangkok from the provinces. After a few months, in the succeeding Lent season (when the monastic schools function in earnest), Sathien went to study at the famous centre of learning, the temple of Thong Nopakun in Thonburi. The teacher here, Chao Khun Kittisara Sobhana, impressed with the brilliance of the young novice, invited him to take up residence in the *wat*. This was a great privilege and a stroke of good fortune. Having secured permission from his *luang phi* in the temple of Pichaya, Sathien went to reside in the temple of Thong, which has up to this day been his temple.

At Bangkok Sathien's academic career was remarkable. With clock-work regularity he passed a *prayog* examination each year, and by the age of 21 years he passed the highest Pali examination (Prayog Gao). In his final year, he was the only novice in the entire country to pass the examination; the other eight successful candidates were older ordained monks. In fact, in the history of the present Ratanakosin Dynasty (since the late eighteenth century) only two other novices had climbed to the same academic peak. The Sangaraja (Patriarch), Kittisobhana, of the temple of Benchama Bopit (Marble) was one.

The Sangaraja who is in charge of Pali studies in the country, impressed with Sathien's qualities, recommended that the King himself sponsor Sathien's ordination. This royal favour was bestowed on Sathien, and the Sangaraja acted as *upachaya* (preceptor) at the ceremony with the King acting in his lay capacity.

After ordination (and indeed even before) Sathien taught at the temple of Thong together with his own teacher, Kittisara. This monastic school, the most famous in Bangkok, usually has about 100 resident monks and novices, and in addition teaches several who daily come from other temples. In the Prayog 5

[1] It is interesting to note that Sathien's teacher, Phra Maha Buddhi, gave up robes at the age of 33/34 and is now a government officer in Nakorn Phanom.

and 6 classes there are about 200–300 candidates, but the numbers drop drastically beyond this grade.

In 1965 Sathien was sent to England to engage in further studies, primarily in Sanskrit. Having spent a year in London learning English, he is now enrolled in Cambridge University as an undergraduate. At the age of 27 the career of this remarkable scholar-monk has just begun and he will no doubt reach greater heights.

According to Phra Maha Sathien, Pali studies are first and foremost a study of Pali as a sacred language. Literary appreciation and the mastery and evaluation of doctrine as such are secondary, in that the mastery of the language is a vehicle for the latter. Furthermore, doctrinal study is possible through reading edited Thai texts.

In this scheme of studies, the pupil first masters the grammar of the Pali language and the etymology of words and concurrently practises translation from Pali into Thai (Grades 3–4). In the second stage the pupil concentrates on composition which translates from Thai into Pali (Grades 5–7). In the final stage the scholar would be able to write creative compositions (poems and essays) in the Pali language (Grades 8–9). As a by-product of such language training, Pali Buddhist concepts, doctrinal texts and commentaries will have been read and mastered.

The following is a brief account of Prayog syllabi for grades 3–9 (3 being the first grade).

Prayog Sam (3)

Study of Pali grammar and the etymology (*sampandha*) of Pali words. The texts used are the eight volumes of *Dhammapada Atthakatha* (commentary on the *Dhammapada* written by Budhagosa). The examination consists of four papers: (1) literal and free translation from Pali to Thai; (2) Pali grammar; (3) etymology of Pali words; (4) composition in the Thai language.

Prayog Si (4)

A close textual study of volume 1 of the *Dhammapada*, and a study of *Mangalattha Dipani* (a commentary written by a Thai scholar-monk). The examination consists of two papers: (1) arranging Pali words in their grammatical sequence; (2) translating *Mangalattha Dipani* from Pali to Thai.

Prayog Ha (5)

At this stage starts the more difficult mastery of writing in the Pali language itself. There are two papers for this grade: (1) translation of *Samantapasadika* (commentary of the *vinaya*) by Buddaghosa (5 vols.): Pali into Thai; (2) an essay translation from Thai into Pali based on the *Dhammapada* (vols. 1–5).

Prayog Hog (6)

Two papers are taken: (1) translation from Pali to Thai of texts in *Mangalattha Dipani* (2 vols.); (2) an essay from Thai into Pali based on passages in *Dhammapada* (vols. 6–8).

Prayog Jet (7)

Two papers again. The texts are varied but the examination is in the same vein as for grades 5 and 6: (1) translation from Pali into Thai of passages from *Samantapasadika* (part 2); (2) a composition from Thai into Pali based on the *Mangalattha Dipani* texts.

Prayog Pad (8)

At this level a far greater mastery of the Pali language is required. The examination consists of two papers: (1) the composition in Pali of poems (*chanda*), about three in number, in different metres on a set theme concerning the life of the Buddha and his teaching; (2) translation (Pali into Thai) from *Visuddhimagga*, a commentary written by Buddaghosa.

Prayog Gao (9)

This is the highest grade and the two papers are: (1) an essay written in Pali based on an extract from a modern Thai literary piece; (2) translation (Pali into Thai) from *Abidhammattha Vibhavini*, a sub-commentary on the *Abidhamma* written by a Ceylonese monk, Sumangala Thera.

APPENDIX III: SPECIALISTS IN PHRAN MUAN VILLAGE

(*A*) *Ritual specialists for whom literacy is essential*

(1) *Phra* (*monk*):

Number in village temple during Lent 1966 = abbot+5 monks+4 novices. Traditionally novices and monks who had been in robes for some years could read fluently Tham, secular Lao and Thai scripts. Competence in writing, however, was variable, again depending on length of service. The learned monks, especially the abbots (*chao wat*), tend to be proficient writers, today in Lao and Thai scripts, in the past in Tham as well.

(2) *Acharn wat* (ex-abbot or ex-monk and lay leader of Buddhist congregation):

Number in 1965 = 3. Always an ex-monk whose literacy was good as far as reading of Tham, Lao and Thai scripts went. Usually could write in Lao and Thai scripts, but ability was variable and not essential. Strictly speaking, the title is conferred only on ex-abbots.

(3) *Mau khwan/prahm* (lay officiant at *khwan* (spiritual essence) rites):

Number in 1966 = 2+1 occasional practitioner. *Khwan* rites are typically threshold rites and rites of passage, especially at birth, marriage, ordination and pregnancy. They also extend into rice cultivation, and rites of affliction. The officiant was invariably an ex-monk. Reading ability of Tham and Lao scripts essential; usually could write Lao and Thai scripts, but not necessarily Tham.

(4) *Mau ya* (physician):

Number in 1966 = 1. Attainments similar to *maukhwan* (3). Ability to read medical and ritual texts in Tham and Lao scripts essential. Indigenous medicine includes ritual frills and techniques of ritual healing as supplement to herbal and other medicines to cure organic illnesses.

(5) *Mau Du* (astrologer):
Number in 1966 = 3, possibly more. Usually has same qualifications as (3) and (4) above. Should be able to read charts and make simple calculations.

(*B*) *Secular specialists for whom literacy is required*

(1) *Puyaiban* (headman):
Number in 1966 = 1. Traditionally literacy not required; today, in theory required. Primary role is mediating between village and district administration. Today, usually versed in Lao and Thai scripts, though, since records kept are minimal, writing competence is not advanced. Has usually been a monk, and can be a village elder with the prestige and qualifications of *mau khwan.*
(2) *Mau lum* (folk-opera entertainers):
Number in 1966 = 2. Entertainers are both male and female. Reading and copying ability in Lao and, today, Thai scripts required, but not Tham script; special emphasis on memorization of words. Elementary schooling is essential but not service as monk/novice.
(3) *Khru* (schoolteacher):
Number in 1966 = 4. As a professional specialist he is quite recent (since the 1930s) and has replaced the teaching monk. He has to teach Thai in the Thai script in village school. Perfectly fluent—both in reading and writing—in Lao and Thai scripts, but not in Tham sacred script which gives access to traditional regional Buddhist and other ritual texts. Teachers are not interested in the forms of literacy of the *maukhwan* type. Since Buddhist texts are today being increasingly printed in Thai script, they are versed in Buddhism.

(*C*) *Ritual specialists for whom literacy is not required*

(1) *Mau song* (diviner):
Number in 1966 = 3 or 4. The diviner's art consists of manipulating ritual objects (e.g. looking through an egg or into a mirror) and interpreting signs. His techniques do not require writing and calculating on paper. He need not have been a monk and reading ability is not required; is usually quasi-literate as far as reading is concerned.
(2) *Jum* and *Tiam* (intermediary and medium, respectively, of village and temple guardian spirits = Tapuban and Chao Pau Tongkyang).
Number in 1966 = 1+1; a village can have only 1 of each kind. Only memorization of a few words of address to the guardian spirits is required. Reading ability in any script not essential; same as *mau song* (1) above. Usually these personnel have never been novices or monks in the Buddhist temple.
(3) *Mau tham* (exorcizer of malevolent spirits):
Number in 1966 = 2. Memorizes charms and spells; some of them are portions of Buddhist *pali* chants, others are magical formulae without explicit meaning. Literacy not required; invariably has never been a novice or monk, and usually has very poor reading and writing competence in any script. However, exceptions can be found—there are none in Phran Muan village—of persons who possess, read and use magical texts; these persons significantly have learned to read

esoteric texts and to practise their arts from certain 'extraordinary' monks or lay teachers (*guru*).

(4) *Mau lum phi fa* (medium of sky spirit):

Number in 1966 = 1. Usually female. Memorizes words and chants, but accuracy not important. Reading ability not required. Excluded from monkhood by virtue of sex. Village medium is illiterate.

APPENDIX IV

CHANTS FREQUENTLY MEMORIZED AND RECITED BY NOVICES ('NEN') AND MONKS ('PHRA')

The language of the chants is Pali, written in the past in Tham script and increasingly in Thai today. The following are the collections of chants that a monk or novice is required to memorize, and which comprise the repertoire adequate for everyday purposes.

(1) *Tham watr:* This is a collection of chants recited by monks in the temple in their morning and evening worship of Lord Buddha. This worship is part of the monk's religious discipline and regime, quite apart from his parish role *vis-à-vis* the laity.

(2) The second category of chants are recited by monks at collective merit-making rites at the temple (*gnan bun*) in which the laity participate or at the houses of laymen or other locations outside the temple (e.g. cemetery) where ceremonial is held. The chants are divided into two groups: *avamangala* and *mangala*. *Avamangala* refers to inauspicious occasions or occasions which have to be 'desacralized' and *mangala* to occasions which are auspicious or at which 'sacralization' or 'charging' with blessing takes place.

(*a*) *Suad kusala:* This is an *avamangala* chant, which is recited in a funeral house *immediately* after a person dies.

(*b*) *Suad monghkon* are an important and frequently recited collection of *paritta* (verses or portions of *sutra*, discourses of the Buddha) which give protection from misfortune as well as positive blessing.

The *suad mongkhon* are also referred to as *suad mon yen* and *suad mon chaw* (evening and morning chants). At any merit-making festival at the temple, e.g. *Bunkathin* (collective village offerings to monks at the end of Lent) or at home, or after the completion of cremation, monks will first recite at night and then on the following morning chant the blessing, during which laymen fill their bowls with food and give them gifts. The sequence is 'protection' followed by 'blessing' and 'gift-giving'. In the case of post-cremation sacralization, monks chant for three consecutive nights in the funeral house and are feasted on the fourth morning.

The following are an example of the collection of *paritta* that comprise *suad mon yen* (evening chants):

(1) Either *namo pad* or *sum putte.*

(2) *Mangla sutra* (*asevana*), usually in abbreviated form.

(3) *Ratana sutra*, usually in abbreviated form.

(4) *Karaniya metra sutra* (*suad karanee*), either in full or in abbreviated form.
(5) *Vipassis.*

The concluding *suad mon chaw* (morning chant), which transfers blessings to the laity, is usually referred to as *suad pahung*; the best known is the victory blessing *chayamangala katha*. The morning chant (*suad pahung*) is also chanted by monks at the *wat* on *wan sil* (Buddhist sabbath) during the presentation of food to the monks (*sai bart/tak bart*).

The research upon which this essay is based was sponsored by the Bangkok Institute for Child Study. I thank UNESCO and the Government of Thailand for giving me the opportunity to work in Thailand for three years, my colleagues in the Institute whose assistance in the field was invaluable, and two successive Directors of the Institute, Dr Hugh Philp and Dr Lamaismas Saradatta, who supported the research in every way. I also thank the University of Cambridge for giving me a Hayter grant to visit Thailand in 1966.

LITERACY IN KĒRALA

In her paper on Kērala, Dr Gough takes a much wider canvas, spatially and temporally, than the village; she discusses the history of the South Indian state of Kērala including the busy cosmopolitan sea-ports of Calicut and Cochin, which provided a haven for merchants from the Middle East. Long before the arrival of the Portuguese, groups of Jews, Christians and Muslims, all with religions of the 'Book', had settled on the coast and today form 40 per cent of the population. Much of their written material was magico-religious.

Among the Hindus, this religious bias was yet more apparent since traditional learning was in the hands of the Brahman aristocracy, consisting of some 2 per cent of the population (this is the figure De Francis estimates as the literate percentage in China). And the function of this scholarship was essentially conservative and traditionalist.

But writing was not confined to the sacred language, Sanskrit; it had made the important breakthrough to the vernacular—a breakthrough that in West Africa does not seem to have occurred until the nineteenth century. A high degree of competence in literacy extended down the hierarchy of caste to the matrilineal Nāyars, forming a further 19 per cent of the population, most of whom, Gough reckons, were literate in the local language, Malayālam, and some in Sanskrit as well. From the sixteenth century this group made an increasing contribution to literature. The immediate function of Nāyar literacy, in contrast to that of the Brahmans, 'pertained chiefly to government, politically administered trade and the feual administration of fiefs and villages'.

In addition to Brahmans and Nāyars, a number of lower castes required a knowledge of writing in order to act, for example, as astrologers or doctors, making use of a simplified Brahman lore. Many low-caste peasants and artisans also acquired a rudimentary literacy. All in all, Kērala had 'an unusually high proportion' of literates in comparison with the rest of India.

Nevertheless Kērala did not display the array of features that Watt and I saw as potential consequences of widespread literacy, which did nothing either to break down caste barriers or to foster a strong interest in history or science.

Despite the failure to develop in these ways, literacy was of great significance. It assisted in maintaining kingdoms of a large size both by increasing the communication links between centre and periphery and by facilitating the collection and recording of taxes. It also allowed the emergence of various specialisms, and Gough suggests that even the fundamental dichotomy between priests and rulers 'may depend upon literacy'. At least it made possible 'a vast complexity of sumptuary laws' and other ways of differentiating social status.

While writing did not lead to history in the usual sense, it was used for recording genealogies, local chronicles of aristocratic lineages, towns and villages, and semi-mythological 'histories' of Kērala, and hence provided some of the raw material of history. But perhaps the most important factor that distinguishes 'traditional' from 'modern' literacy is its sacral character; it is this that seems to have provided the main brake on the realization of the potentialities of a demotic script.

LITERACY IN KĒRALA

by KATHLEEN GOUGH

ORIGINS OF LANGUAGE AND SCRIPTS

Kērala or Chēra, on the south-west coast of India, emerges in history as an independent kingdom in the third century B.C. Its people spoke ancient Tamil, a Dravidian language ancestral to modern Tamil and Malayālam. Together with the Tamil kingdoms of Chōla and Pāndya in south-east India, Kērala traded with the Middle East and with Rome, developed a prosperous small 'empire', and gave birth to a brilliant early Tamil literature in the first to fourth centuries A.D. From about the ninth century the south-west empire collapsed and Kērala broke up into four small coastal kingdoms—Kolaṭṭunād, Kōzhikode, Cochin and Travancore—each centred on a major port. Inland, in the foothills of the Western Ghāts, lay a large number of more or less independent petty principalities. The political structure had strong resemblances to the feudalism of late eleventh-century western Europe. The kings obtained their revenues mainly from overseas-administered trade, first with China and the Arabs until the sixteenth century, then with Portugal, and later, in the seventeenth and eighteenth centuries, with the Dutch, French and English East India Companies (Panikkar 1960; Nilakanta Sāstri 1955: 110–41).

With modifications, the feudal structure persisted until the second third of the eighteenth century, when Travancore and Cochin abolished their fiefs and introduced standing armies and elementary bureaucracies. In the 1760s, Kolaṭṭunād and Kōzhikode were overrun by Muslim armies from Mysore and partially bureaucratized. The whole region passed under British rule in the 1790s. 'Traditional Kērala' refers to the feudal kingdoms from the mid-fifteenth to the mid-eighteenth century.

After the collapse of the Chēra empire Tamil literature declined in Kērala. In the Middle Ages, with the rise of the feudal kingdoms, Sanskrit became the chief medium of literature, and the highest caste of Nambūdiri Brahmans its chief exponents. Tamil remained, however, both the official and the everyday language of the courts and common people. During the Middle Ages the Tamil of Kērala, under the heavy influence of Sanskrit, diverged more and more from Tamil east of the Ghāts. By the sixteenth century, the two modes of speech had attained virtually their present form, with the West Coast language coming to be known as Malayālam.

The first extant Malayālam work, a narrative poem called the *Uṇṇunīli*

Sandēsam, belongs to the fourteenth century. It is written in a somewhat artificial literary language, *maniprāvalam*, with a large admixture of Sanskrit words. In the fifteenth and sixteenth centuries Malayālam became an increasingly popular literary medium with a widening public, and a unique Malayālam poetic form, the *kilippāṭṭu*, developed. Tunjath Ezhuttacchan, the most famous Malayālī writer, together with a group of illustrious contemporaries, rendered the most famous Sanskrit works into Malayālam and gave their characteristic form to original Malayālam poetry and philosophical literature. Ezhuttacchan's dates are disputed but he probably wrote some time in the late sixteenth or early seventeenth century (Sāstri 1955: 402; Ayyar 1938: 306). It is significant that Ezhuttacchan was a Nāyar of a rather low sub-caste of schoolteachers, and not a Brahman. His work is evidence that by the late sixteenth century the Sanskrit literature of the Brahmans (except for the Vēdas) was being transmitted to the Nāyars, the highest non-Brahman caste of nobles and landed military retainers. Some Nāyars, in turn, were by this time composing original Sanskrit works of their own but, even more important, they were helping to create a synthesis between Sanskrit and Tamil literary forms which ushered in a quite distinctive popular 'national' Malayālam literature (Sāstri 1955: 399–402; Ayyar 1938: 296–310). Comparable developments were taking place in music, drama and painting, notably in the development of *kathakali*, the famous dance-drama of Malabar. In this process of synthesis and creativity the royal courts of the kingdoms, and the palaces of some of the lesser princes, played of course a paramount role. So too, in all probability, did the fact that at some time during the Middle Ages it became common for the younger sons of Nambūdiri Brahman patrilineal households to take consorts in various echelons of the matrilineal Nāyar caste. The children of such unions were Nāyars of the mother's lineage, and the Nambūdiri father observed strict rules of ritual pollution and social distance in relation to his children and to the family of the Nāyar consort at whose home he was a nocturnal visitor. Nevertheless, much of the Sanskrit culture of the Brahmans did no doubt pass to the Nāyars through these channels, and above all to the matrilineal royal and princely lineages, almost all of whose womenfolk had liaisons with Nambūdiris. In addition to the Nambūdiris themselves, many of the most prominent Sanskrit writers of the age were princes, and a few were princesses, of various royal houses.

Ancient Tamil had been written with the *vaṭṭezhuttu* script.[1] It derived

[1] For the evolution of scripts in Kērala and south India generally see A. L. Basham, *The Wonder that was India* (Macmillan, 1954), pp. 396–9; A. Sreedhara Menon, *Kērala District Gazetteers, Trivandrum* (Trivandrum, 1962), pp. 261–2.

almost certainly from the north Indian Brahmi script, which had acquired distinctive south Indian forms by the third century B.C. Modifications of *vaṭṭezhuttu* were used for records of the palaces of Kērala throughout the medieval period, and in Travancore until 1860. The Īzhavas and other low-caste Hindus used the *vaṭṭezhuttu* script until the end of the eighteenth century. Māppilla (Muslim) merchants continued to use it until the early twentieth century. A distinctive form of *vaṭṭezhuttu*, called *kōlezhuttu*, evolved in the royal courts during the traditional period.

From about the ninth century, Brahmans in south India used a script called *grandha*, derived from the north Indian *dēvanāgari*, to write Sanskrit. The Nambūdiri Brahmans in Kērala used it extensively in their Sanskrit literary compositions. As more and more Sanskrit words were incorporated into the vernacular of Kērala, high-caste non-Brahmans added *grandha* characters to their *vaṭṭezhuttu* script to represent sounds, especially aspirates, found in Sanskrit but not in Tamil. Tunjath Ezhuttacchan and his contemporaries produced the present Malayālam script, derived largely from *grandha* but with a number of *vaṭṭezhuttu* characters. It became the medium of literary Malayālam for high-caste Hindus, and gradually spread to the lower castes and the non-Hindus during the British period, especially with the popularization of printing after the mid-nineteenth century. The spread of government-sponsored village schools during the British period also helped to gain universal acceptance for the Malayālam script.

Malayālam has fifty-three characters, compared with Tamil's twenty-eight. The difference stems mainly from the use of characters to handle the aspirates found in Sanskrit words that have been incorporated into the language. The script is round and cursive and, a number of words being joined to one another, it is written rapidly. Writing is from left to right. The traditional writing materials were an iron stylus and leaves of the palmyra palm, cut into long narrow strips of about two by eighteen inches. The leaves were soaked and dried before use to season and harden them. Books were formed by passing two small pegs of wood or iron, or a thread, through holes at one end of a bundle of such strips. Thin boards of the same size as the leaves formed the binders, and a long string fastened to one of the leaves served to hold them together. To examine a book, the reader unfastened the string, removed the pegs, and released the leaves from one another. Old Malayālam and Sanskrit books exist in quantity in government record offices, private homes, and the libraries of former royalty, Brahmans and nobles. The leaf and stylus remained in use in some villages for government records until the 1930s.

When a person wrote a letter, he folded the inscribed leaf and placed it in an outer covering on which he wrote the address. The two ends of the outer leaf were cut and fastened together by a small knot which served as a seal. Letters varied in length and breadth according to the caste rank or political dignity of the sender—an example of Kērala's almost innumerable sumptuary laws.

Solemn and important documents, for example grants of land or dignities from kings to nobles, Brahmans or merchant communities, were inscribed on copper plates. The oldest extant copper plates belong to Jewish and Syrian Christian communities, who received land grants with rights of self-government, trade and the use of sumptuary goods from kings of Kērala, probably in the late eighth and early ninth centuries (Logan 1951: I, 265–70, II, cxix–cxxvi; Pothan 1963: 32–6). Metal plates were also—and in remote areas may still be—used to inscribe magical formulae or cabalistic designs which may be buried near a house or a person in order to protect them or to bring them harm. Astrologers supplied villagers with small cylindrical amulets of gold, silver or brass containing pieces of leaf inscribed with charms. These were—and are—worn on a thread at the waist or round the upper arm to ward off illness.

In addition to Sanskrit, Kērala had four other sacred languages in the traditional period, namely Syriac, Arabic, Hebrew and Latin; for Hindus formed only about 70 per cent of the population. The Syrian Christian community of Cochin and Travancore dates back to the fourth, or possibly to the first, century. Traders, landlords, cultivators and soldiers, Syrians held high social rank and were divided into orthodox Syrians (Jacobites) and Catholics converted by the Portuguese. Both groups used a Syriac script derived from Aramaic, and the Syriac language, for their devotions, sacred books and amulets.[1] The Portuguese destroyed most of the ancient Syrian books in the sixteenth century, but new texts were made.

In addition to the older Syrian Christians, the Portuguese converted low-caste Hindu coastal communities, especially of fishermen, placed them under separate bishops, and gave them the Latin rite. Even after the departure of Portuguese traders in the seventeenth century, moreover, European Catholic bishops, priests and monks remained in some coastal towns together with communities of Catholic artisans and servants of Indian or Eurasian descent. In their monasteries, schools and colleges these ecclesiastics trained their followers in Latin and various modern European tongues. As their trading companies settled on the coast, groups of French, Dutch and English factors, soldiers and missionaries also formed their own

[1] See K. P. Padmanabha Menon, *History of Kērala* (Cochin Government Press, Ernakulam, 1929), II, pp. 443–503, for a discussion of the history, literature and customs of the Syrian Christians.

small communities, with schools in which they gave rudimentary education to native or Eurasian converts. Malayālam remained, however, the main language and written medium of all these native communities.

At Cochin in the centre of the coast, a small group of one to two thousand Jews retained Hebrew bibles and other ancient texts in their synagogues. Like the Syrians, the Jews had their religious centres sacked and their books burned by the Portuguese in the early sixteenth century. They possess, however, at least one late sixteenth-century copy of the Pentateuch, inscribed on vellum, in their synagogue at Mattāncheri in Cochin today. Small numbers of Jewish newcomers from Portugal, Spain, Amsterdam and Egypt in the sixteenth to eighteenth centuries may have replenished the Jews' sacred literature.[1]

In the northern half of Kērala larger numbers of Muslims (Māppillas) occupied their own coastal and inland riverine communities.[2] They descended from Arab merchants and native low-caste converts of the ninth to sixteenth centuries, when Middle Eastern merchants dominated the coastal trade of Kolaṭṭunād and Kōzhikode. After the Portuguese drove most Arabs from the coast the Māppillas turned to cultivation, fishing and inland trading. A few held fiefs under the Rājas, governed coastal communities or retained ships for overseas trade. The Māppillas may have formed 10 per cent of Kērala's population until the mid-eighteenth century. It is probable that most of them were literate in Malayālam, while many had a smattering of Arabic, and a few religious leaders were Arabic scholars. The Mysorean invaders of the 1760s to 1780s forcibly converted many to Islam. In the nineteenth century both the Māppilla and the Latin Catholic communities were further augmented by converts from the lower Hindu castes, many of whom were illiterate. Today, the Muslim and Christian groups altogether form some 40 per cent of Kērala's population. Most of the men and most younger women are now literate, but Muslims as an ethnic group lag behind both Christians and Hindus in general education.

THE DISTRIBUTION AND USES OF LITERACY IN TRADITIONAL KĒRALA

Muslims, Christians and Jews

I have mentioned that a large majority of Christians, Jews and Muslims were probably literate in the traditional period. This statement applies to men. In every literate ethnic group a smaller proportion of women than of

[1] See Menon, pp. 504–31, for a discussion of the Cochin Jews' culture and literature.

[2] See Menon, pp. 532–63, for a discussion of Māppilla history and culture; also Logan, *Malabar*, I, pp. 191–9; C. A. Innes, *Malabar and Anjengo*, Madras District Gazetteers (The Government Press, Madras, 1908), pp. 189–99.

men received formal education. Nevertheless, all of the literate groups contained some female scholars and there was no prohibition on a woman learning to read. Māppilla girls received less regular instruction in schools than did Christians or Jews. What they did receive was terminated before puberty, when they entered a modified form of purdah. But almost all the men of these trading groups, and a high proportion of Jewish and Christian women, appear to have been educated in simple Malayālam, arithmetic and the rudiments of religious knowledge. Māppillas used the old Tamil script, at least for their trading records, and retained a larger proportion of Tamil words in their everyday speech, for example their kinship terms.

As among Hindus, children attended village schools on the verandahs of homes or in thatched sheds, run by teachers of their own religious group. In the Māppilla schools, called *pāyals* or *ooṭṭu-pallis*, the local *mulla* or leader of the mosque taught children to recognize the Arabic letters, carved on wooden planks. He gave instruction in Malayālam grammar and syntax, logic, the traditions of the prophet, and the chanting of the Qur'ān. The Qur'ān and other sacred books were translated into Malayālam, but it seems probable that a majority of Māppilla children, then as now, learned to recite Arabic verses without literally understanding their meaning. The wealthier trading and landowning families employed tutors to educate their children. Some of these learned to speak and write Arabic fluently.

As a community the Māppillas did not, however, produce any significant literature in either Arabic or Malayālam. Their literacy was apparently geared to storing and retrieving religious, legal, magical and folk knowledge and to keeping records and accounts of revenues, taxes and trade.

Māppillas had certain officials with specialized functions requiring literacy. I have mentioned the *mulla* who, well versed in Arabic, led the Friday services and schooled the children. He was appointed from the mosque's congregation by the *kāzi*, a hereditary headman of the Māppilla village community. This official, also literate in both Arabic and Malayālam, preached or read the Friday sermon, registered marriages, and arbitrated religious and small civil disputes in accordance with his own and other elders' interpretations of Qur'ānic law. In multi-caste villages the *kāzi* was responsible to the Nāyar village headman or local noble for such matters as trade taxes and the reporting of more serious disputes and crimes. In Calicut and perhaps other large ports a hereditary official called a *kutval* collected trade and house taxes and administered Muslim law among the Māppillas, under the higher jurisdiction of a Nāyar town governor or *talacchannavar*. In some ports Muslim merchants owned ships which gave feudal services to the king in time of war. In Cannanore, a Muslim noble family, the Āli Rājas, held large estates and served as ministers and treasurers of the king of Kolaṭṭunād. All of such offices required literacy for purposes of accounting, legal administration, official letter-writing, or the writing and registration of legal documents.

The Jews and Christians, like the Māppillas, were predominantly traders, and literacy seems to have had similar uses among them. Carmelite Friars maintained schools for both Latin and Syrian Catholics near Cranganore, where they taught, besides these languages, theology, mathematics, and geography (Panikkar 1960: 320). Non-Catholic Syrians, or Jacobites, had their centre of learning at Kottayam, and village schools where the priest, who was often hereditary, played a major role. The Syrians possessed, in addition to their sacred texts, three famous Malayālam books: the *Parisman*, the *Wāpustakam* or Book of Utterances, and the *Palapustakam* ('Time Book') (Pothan 1963: 95–6, 107–10). The *Parisman* contained astrological information and lists of unlucky days, for Christians, like their Hindu forebears, cast horoscopes and believed in omens. The latter two books contained lists of short maxims and predictions from which the reader picked at random to obtain divine counsel in conducting his affairs. Although details are not known to me, it seems probable that the Māppillas had similar works, for they, too, believed in omens and astrology. Both Muslims and Christians had the horoscopes of newborn children cast by the local Hindu astrologer. Both groups, like the Hindus, also had collections of proverbs which were either written down and copied, or else learned by rote, in the village schools.

In addition to this folk wisdom, priests or other trained religiosi in both communities studied the sacred literatures in colleges and libraries and maintained contact through pilgrimages and missionaries with religious centres in the Middle East. The literary lore of Christians and Muslims in Kērala seems, however, to have been almost entirely that of trading and peasant peoples. They were attached through their literacy to foreign 'great traditions', but regarded these as completed and somewhat mysterious repositories of knowledge from which they had only to draw sayings, divinations, and legal and ethical instructions for the conduct of their daily lives.

The Brahmans

The Hindu castes fell into four broad categories. The first of these were the indigenous Nambūdiri Brahmans and the lower-ranking, immigrant, Tamil and Kaṇṇada Brahmans, comprising altogether some 2 per cent or more of the population.[1] The Nambūdiris, spiritually supreme in Kērala,

[1] Brahmans were fewer than 2 per cent of the population of Malabar, Cochin and Travancore in 1931, the last date on which separate figures were compiled for the different Hindu

owned landed estates and managed temples and colleges. They performed public ceremonies on behalf of the kingdom, advised and fathered the matrilineal royalty and nobility, and transmitted and augmented the heritage of Malayālam and Sanskrit literature. Kaṇṇada Brahmans were almost all village temple priests of low social rank. Although literate in Sanskrit, Malayālam, and Kaṇṇada, they do not appear to have contributed to the literature of Kērala in traditional times. Tamil Brahmans filled a variety of literate occupations, as inland traders with the regions east of the Ghāts, and as tutors, accountants, messengers, bailiffs and scholars in the houses of the wealthier families of Nambūdiris, royalty and Nāyars. A few Tamil Brahmans were notable poets and dramatists of Kērala, among them Uddānda of the fifteenth century and Chidambara Kāvi of the seventeenth.

Nambūdiri Brahmans comprised ranked sub-castes distinguished by their power, wealth, occupations and religious privileges.[1] Those of the highest rank, Ādhyans, included two rival families of spiritual heads over other sections of Nambūdiris, the Azhuvanchēri and Kalpanchēri Tamburakkals;[2] and below them, a number of great landlords. Some of these were religious dignitaries, learned in the Vēdas; others, secular aristocrats possessing fiefs and armies like the Nāyar nobility.

Below the Ādhyan aristocracy the main body of the caste, called Āsyans, included, first, Agnihōtris or groups of Brahmans learned in the Vēdas and *sāstras*, who specialized in performing Vēdic sacrifices on behalf of the kingdom. The Bhaṭṭatiris, similar in rank to the Agnihōtris, included Vādhyans or teachers of logic, philosophy, theology, grammar and ritual in Sanskrit colleges. Other Bhaṭṭatiris, called Vaidīgans and Smārttas, administered the laws of caste within the kingdoms, fixed penances, and judged cases of outcasting for serious offences.

All of these Brahmans owned large estates and occupied honoured positions. Some served as ministers or as ambassadors between kingdoms. All were closely affiliated with and patronized by the royal lineages and the lesser rulers of principalities. Although neighbouring kings were at war with one another throughout most of the traditional period, Brahmans had

castes. Nambūdiri Brahmans were less than 1 per cent of the population. It is possible, however, that they were more numerous in early centuries. The custom whereby only the eldest son of a Nambūdiri family is allowed to marry a Brahman girl and beget children for his own family has probably caused the Nambūdiri population to decline somewhat over the centuries.

[1] Accounts of Nambūdiri Brahman sub-castes, and their distinguishing features, are given in K. P. Padmanabha Menon, *History of Kērala*, III, pp. 35–46; L. K. Ananthakrishna Iyer, *Cochin Tribes and Castes*, II (Higginbotham, Madras, 1912), pp. 172–6.

[2] The Azhuvanchēri Tamburakkal lived in Ponnāni in the Kōzhikode kingdom, and the Kalpanchēri Tamburakkal in the kingdom of Cochin. The Kalpanchēri family died out in the nineteenth century, leaving the Azhuvanchēri Tamburakkal as the supreme spiritual head among the Nambūdiris.

the right of pilgrimage and peaceful transit from kingdom to kingdom. Brahmans were, moreover, subject to their own legal institutions and not to those of the kingdoms, although they also served as legal advisers of the kings. Many of them lived on separate estates called *sankēdams*, surrounding their greater temples, where committees of Brahmans managed the temple, governed their own caste fellows, and administered their servants of the lower Hindu castes. Brahman scholars throughout Kērala were permitted to attend the Vēdic colleges at Trichur in the kingdom of Cochin. Famous Brahman scholars and poets, while usually attached to the court of a particular king, attended cultural gatherings and religious debates in other kingdoms and might move from one royal patron to another.

Below the ranks already mentioned, a majority of the Āsyan Nambūdiris owned smaller estates, usually single villages, and were occupied not in Vēdic study but in other special pursuits. Some performed daily ceremonies in temples or directed festivals for temple deities. Others specialized in professional magic and exorcism, in astronomy and astrology, or in the public recitation of Sanskrit *purānas* or narrative poems.

Of still lower rank than the general run of Nambūdiris were a number of specialists whose work degraded them below the ritual rank of ordinary Brahmans, namely, physicians and surgeons, household priests who performed ancestral ceremonies on behalf of the Nāyars, and minor priests who carried the idol in temple processions, prepared rice for temple offerings, and cleaned the inner sanctum of the deity.

This occupational list of Kērala's traditional scholars shows that literacy was not designed primarily to investigate the natural world through scientific methods, nor to record historical events, nor yet to experiment with social innovations. Its chief functions were to conserve custom, to organize and sanction the feudal kingdom, and to provide artistic entertainment and religious and philosophical enlightenment to the ruling castes. Brahman lore also served to maintain elaborate ranks within the society, instilled in men's minds a reverence for other-worldly experiences, and produced an atmosphere of mystery, esoteric knowledge and special powers around those who guided the society's destiny and buttressed the authority of its princes.

It is interesting that Brahman families practising medicine ranked so low as to qualify only as borderline Brahmans. Yet medicine, apart from astronomy, seems to have been the only scholarly pursuit bearing any relationship to natural science. A similarly low status was given leeches and folk doctors in the villages. They ranked below the cultivators and combined their science either with laundry work or with astrology and exorcism. Notwithstanding these limitations, medicine did make progress in traditional Kērala. By the eighteenth century it was probably as advanced as anywhere in traditional India.

We must not assume from this picture that Kērala's society was stationary. The traditional period saw the expansion of overseas commerce, the introduction of new cash crops such as tapioca (cassava) and cashew-nuts, the scientific mass-production of coconuts, pepper, cinnamon and other indigenous cash crops for export, the adoption of new weapons and of gunpowder by the kings, and the growth of new classes of artisans in the ports. Nevertheless, the authorities of Kērala remained on the whole traditionalist and backward-looking until the 1730s. The Nambūdiris, especially, monopolized much of the land and virtually controlled the law courts, centres of learning and organs of public propaganda. With their obsession with details of ritual prohibition and performance, and their contempt for trade, experimental science or any form of social innovation, they epitomized the type of conservative religious influence that India's Brahmans have exercised during most of the main periods of Hindu rule.

After the 1730s, the impact of the new warfare, of the growing commercial classes, and of the competition for markets and pressures for political centralization exerted by the European companies brought new classes to power in Kērala and wrecked the feudal polity and the Nambūdiris' supremacy. In the south, the Mahārājas of Travancore and Cochin centralized their kingdoms, dispossessed most of the nobles, and raised Nāyar commoners and Tamil immigrants to the level of a new bureaucratic class. The kings also struggled to gain monopolies over foreign trade and to hold their own against the European companies. As in the old kingdoms, Nambūdiris received wealth and honour, but they were no longer in control of the direction of policy. In Kolaṭṭunād and Kōzhikode, the Muslim-manned armies of the Mysore kingdom burst through the mountains to the coast. They devastated the coastal polities, raised to leadership the indigenous Māppillas, captured monopolies of the overseas trade, and executed, forcibly converted or expelled the Brahmans, royalty, and much of the Nāyar nobility. None of these powers could, however, withstand British pressures to conquer the whole of India, its markets and its raw materials. All were submerged under colonial rule by the 1790s, although Cochin and Travancore kept their Mahārājas and remained as Native States under British hegemony.

The British restored the Brahmans and many of the secular nobles to their lands, pomp and religious authority. Later, they used them as props against revolutionary change on the part of the growing Malayālī bourgeoisie, the impoverished peasantry, and the landless wage-workers of the colonial society. The Nambūdiris and their religious esoterica thus gained a new lease on life for 150 years. As pensioners competing for authority with colonial administrators, Christian missionaries, capitalist entrepreneurs and English schools and colleges, however, the Nambūdiris entered a backwater and never regained the legal and moral dominance that had been theirs in feudal times.

Most of Kērala's literature was written by Nambūdiri Brahmans before the sixteenth century, and much of it thereafter.[1] It included Sanskrit prose works on ritual, grammar, law, astrology, philosophy and logic; and both Sanskrit and Malayālam narrative poems, poetic renderings of the ancient Sanskrit epics and mythological stories, and devotional poems to favourite deities. Another large class of Malayālam works was monologues, stories and dramas designed for recitation or singing at festivals inside high-caste temples by special non-Brahman classes of temple servants. These were based on mythological episodes but incorporated witty satires on current events in high society. Such performances in Brahmanical temples were open only to Brahmans, royalty, temple servants and high-class Nāyars. A more popular dance drama was the miming play *kathakali*, performed by troops of Nāyar and temple-servant actors and musicians at the courts of royals and nobles or at the houses of wealthy Brahmans. These dramas, too, comprised incidents from the Sanskrit *purānas* or mythological stories, and the accompanying recitations were chiefly written by Nambūdiris.

Until the seventeenth century, history in Kērala was confined to local and family chronicles. They were written by scholars attached to the royal courts or the greater temples, or by the heads of Nāyar matrilineages of noble rank. In the seventeenth century, however, appeared two generalized 'histories' of Kērala, the *Kērala Mahātmyam* in Sanskrit and the *Kēralolpatti* in Malayālam (Logan 1951: I, 221–45). They are a blend of mythology, historical fact and conjecture, with little or no attention to chronology. Both were probably written by Nambūdiris, since they greatly glorify that caste. Although unscientific and semi-mythological, they appear to reflect the birth of a 'national' or regional Malayālī culture and consciousness. As Namboodiripād has argued, this development of a regional consciousness probably resulted from the unifying impact of European commerce and the growth of a regional market (Namboodiripād 1967: 66–7). The historians themselves may also have been indirectly influenced by Portuguese and Dutch histories. Many of Kērala's princes and nobles learned the languages of the European companies with whom they made treaties. Some read widely in European literature. Royal patrons may have influenced the work of their Brahman scholars even though the latter

[1] See K. M. Panikkar, *A History of Kērala* (1960), pp. 426–34, for an account of the main types of literature in Kērala and the social origins of their authors.

considered themselves prohibited by their religious laws from learning non-Indian tongues.

Certain sub-castes of Nambūdiris kept to themselves the advanced study of the Vēdas. These are, of course, the first four books of Sanskrit literature containing hymns and spells which date, most probably, from between 1500 and 1000 B.C. Throughout India, only Brahmans studied the Vēdas, although Kshattriyas and Vaisyas were permitted to hear them and to have them recited by Brahman priests in their household ceremonies. In Kērala some of the royal and princely lineages were early accorded the rank of Kshattriyas. Boys of these lineages underwent initiation rites (*upanāyanam*) modelled on those of the Brahmans, wore the sacred thread, and were permitted to hear the Vēdas. Princes of lower ranks, and Nāyar commoners, were recognized only as Sūdras and so prohibited from hearing the Vēdas, although the body of later Sanskrit epic, dramatic, ritual and philosophical literature was freely available to them. Kērala had no indigenous Vaisyas, all the castes below Nāyars being regarded in Brahman theory as, strictly speaking, *avarnas*, outside the orthodox Hindu fold.

Nambūdiris specializing in Vēdic study attended one or another of the Vēdic colleges at Trichūr or Tirunāvāya, *sankēdams* respectively located in the kingdoms of Cochin and Kōzhikode. As elsewhere in India, the Vēdas were passed on orally and memorized *in toto*, little use being made of writing and much attention paid to correct pronunciation.

In general the oral transmission of learning by a *guru* to one or a small group of disciples played a more prominent role among Brahmans than in the castes below them. Brahman boys, like those of other castes, were initiated into letters by their father or a teacher at the age of five. The ceremony, called *vidhyārambam*, involved the teacher's writing the alphabet on the boy's tongue with a gold ring or other gold object. After this the child was made to trace the letters with his finger in rice on the ground.[1] As in all castes, he first traced the letters of an invocation to the gods Vishnu, Lakshmi and Ganapati, whose blessings were required for intellectual achievements. After this ceremony a Brahman boy learned writing and other subjects for two years with his father or a teacher in his home. At seven, however, he underwent a second and more important initiation, the *upanāyanam* or donning of the sacred thread. This ceremony bound him to a *guru* or religious preceptor, in theory, and often in practice, for

[1] Children of non-Brahman castes traced the letters in sand sprinkled on the floor of the verandah or shed in which the ceremony was held. In the non-Brahman village schools children customarily wrote with the finger in sand until they had mastered the art sufficiently to use palm leaves. Pietro della Valle described a group of boys learning arithmetic by this method further north along the coast near Honavar in 1623 (*The Travels of Pietro della Valle in India*, ed. Edward Grey (Burt Franklin, New York, 1942), II, pp. 227–8).

the space of nine years. During this period, called *brahmachāryam*, the youth lived simply and ascetically, often in his *guru's* home. He received daily instruction in reciting the particular Vēda of his sub-caste. The period of Vēdic study ended with a ceremony called *samāvarthanam*, after which the youth was qualified to perform the daily and household ceremonies of a Brahman. After the *samāvarthanam* a youth was free to marry or—in the case of younger sons—to have liaisons with women of the matrilineal castes.

Brahmans specially trained for longer periods in the Vēdic colleges became experts in Vēdic recitation and engaged in public competitions at festivals of the greater temples. Other Brahmans versed in Vēdantic philosophy, poetry or monologues debated or recited for prizes at festivals in the royal courts. Thus, although Brahmans contributed more than other castes to the permanent literature of Kērala, they retained a still higher evaluation of the spoken word and of dialogues as modes of learning. Among the Nāyars, greater emphasis seems to have been placed on skill in writing. It is possible in fact that the literary compositions of Kērala were mainly recorded by Nāyars, who provided the professional clerks in the palaces.

Brahman women occupied a low social and legal status in this patriarchal caste, and were strictly segregated within their homes. Their education was confined to learning *slōkas* and proverbs, and few if any of them appear to have been literate.

The Nāyar group

Kērala's second category of castes comprised the royalty, the secular nobility and their retainers. All followed matrilineal descent. The royal matrilineages ranked immediately below the Brahmans. They were mostly fathered by Nambūdiris of high rank, who married the princesses. The temple servants formed a group of small castes—musicians, dramatists, flower-gatherers, and stewards attached to the great temples of the Sanskrit deities Siva, Vishnu and their consorts, which were owned by Brahmans or royalty. The Nāyars constituted the lesser nobility, village headmen, military retainers and clerks attached in service relationships to the Brahmans, nobles and kings. Below the Nāyars proper came several still lower-ranking matrilineal castes. Their members provided craft goods for the temples and palaces and various personal or menial services for the Nāyars and their superiors.

The Brahman and Nāyar groups were the 'high', 'good' or 'clean' castes of the kingdoms. A wide gap separated them from the two lower categories, with whom they were forbidden to eat, cohabit or consort freely in any way. The high castes—who observed meticulous ranks among themselves—lived outside the towns and occupied separate areas of the villages.

They were socially segregated from the merchant groups of alien religion as well as from the lower castes.

Kērala's Nāyar group today forms about 19 per cent of the population, and may have done so traditionally. It is probable that virtually all the men and most women were literate in Malayālam. Many, especially in the royal and noble lineages, also learned Sanskrit. Some princesses, as well as princes, became famous grammarians, philosophers and poets.[1]

From the sixteenth century, the Nāyars contributed increasingly to literature, especially to Malayālam drama and to narrative and lyric poems. At some time in the sixteenth century the Nāyar poets of Nīranam in central Travancore, and, somewhat later, Tunjath Ezhuttacchan of the Kōzhikode kingdom, composed Malayālam renderings of the *Ramāyana*, *Mahābhārata*, the *Bhārata Purana*, and other famous Sanskrit works, copies of which spread widely and today can be found in most Nāyar homes. From that time Nāyars, even of comparatively low rank, produced a rich and popular poetic and dramatic literature in Malayālam.

Although royalty were tutored in the palaces, the Nāyar group as a whole received education in village schools. Both sexes were ceremonially initiated into letters at five. Hereditary teachers called *ezhuttacchans* or *āsāns* drilled the pupils in thatched sheds or on the verandahs of the larger joint family homes. They taught the Malayālam and Sanskrit characters, grammar, arithmetic, and reading of epic and devotional poems. As in the other castes, much emphasis was placed on memorizing proverbs relating to ethics and the shrewd conduct of one's daily life. Girls ceased to attend school after the ritual marriage ceremony (*tālikeṭṭukalyānam*), usually at the age of nine to twelve. Boys divided their time between lessons and military training in village gymnasia from the age of seven. Students who wished to specialize in astrology, philosophy or medicine attended special teachers in their homes.[2]

All Nāyars received military training and could be required to fight in the private army of their king or of a lesser feudal lord to whom they were attached as retainers. Many Nāyar commoners, however, served as scribes in the royal palaces or the households of lesser princes. Duarte Barbosa, a Portuguese envoy, describing their work at the beginning of the sixteenth century, wrote:

[1] One of the best known was Manorama Tamburatti of the Kōzhikode royal lineage, 1760–1828. She fled to Travancore during the Mysorean invasions, and kept up a correspondence in Sanskrit with the Travancore Mahārāja Kārtika Tirunāl. She was a grammarian and poetess and wrote commentaries on the *purānas* (Ayyar, *The Zamorins of Calicut* (1938), p. 310).

[2] See M. S. A. Rao, *Social Change in Malabar* (Popular Book Depot, Bombay, 1957), pp. 161–75, for a summary of most of the known information on traditional Kērala schools.

The King of Calicut continually keeps a multitude of writers in his palace, who sit in a corner far from him; they write upon a raised platform, everything connected with the King's Exchequer and with the justice and governance of the realm. They write on long and stiff palm leaves, with an iron style without ink... And there are seven or eight more, the King's private writers, men held in great esteem, who stand always before the King, with their styles in their hands and a bundle of leaves under their arms. Each one of them has a number of these leaves in blank, sealed by the king at the top. And when the king desires to give or to do anything as to which he has to provide he tells his wishes to each of these men and they write it down from the royal seal to the bottom, and thus the order is given to whomsoever it concerns.[1]

Of the Calicut Record Office, Pyrard de Laval wrote as follows:

Hard by [the palace] is a block of buildings allotted to the secretary and clerk to the King, for keeping all the registers. The order and system is most admirable herein; and I have oftentimes wondered to see the great number of men with no other duty or work all day but writing and registering. These posts are of much honour; the clerks all reside in the palace, but in different apartments, and they have different duties. Some make entry of all goods arriving for the King; others the dues and taxes paid day by day; others the expenditure of the King's household; others the most notable incidents of each day, both what happens at court and in the rest of the kingdom; in short, all news, for he has everything registered; and each clerk has his separate room. They keep also a register of all strangers who come there, taking their names and nationalities, the time of their arrival and the business that has brought them, and so they did with us. It is a wondrous thing to observe their number and the perfect order that exists among them, and how fast they write on their palm leaves.[2]

Clearly, the literacy of Nāyar commoners, as distinct from that of Brahmans, pertained chiefly to royal government, politically administered trade, and the feudal administration of fiefs and villages. The kings' greater vassals or *nāduvazhis*, like the smaller independent princes, had their own staffs of Nāyar writers, as did the *sankēdams*. In each village the hereditary village headman, with one or more bailiffs or younger men of his lineage to aid him, maintained records of tribute received from villagers or paid to his immediate lord, and of rents, mortgages, legal disputes and their settlement, and the accounts of the village temples.[3] Each village headman and each higher feudal noble was also obliged to keep records of the number of able-bodied Nāyars he could muster from his village for war. The kings

[1] *The Book of Duarte Barbosa*, Hakluyt Society, II (1510), pp. 18–19, quoted in Ayyar, *The Zamorins of Calicut*, p. 277.

[2] *The Voyage of Pyrard de Laval*, Hakluyt Society, I, pp. 412–13, quoted in Ayyar, *The Zamorins of Calicut*, pp. 277–8. In the Kōzhikode kingdom, most scribes were of the sub-caste of Agattu Charna Nāyars, and took the title 'Menon' after their personal names.

[3] For the duties of village headmen or *dēsavazhis*, see C. A. Innes, *Malabar and Anjengo*, pp. 351–3.

and lesser princes held customary rights to twenty-eight kinds of special fees and perquisites from their vassals (Ayyar 1938: 275–76), all of which had to be duly collected, recorded and submitted to the royal treasury or to the palace itself. Among these claims were, for example, the tails and skins of deer and tigers, cows with three or five udders, and a great variety of tolls, trade-taxes, fines, duelling fees, escheats, and fees for the military protection of traders and other travellers. On the kings' larger private estates, Nāyar bailiffs maintained complete accounts of all income, expenses and remittances to the treasury. A constant flow of letters and royal writs passed by messenger from the central and subordinate palaces to the houses of vassal nobles under the king's immediate authority, and from these latter to their village headmen. At the ports, a separate array of Nāyar officials are said by Laval to have recorded incoming and outgoing merchandise in the custom-houses and supervised its storage. In the capital towns of each kingdom still other staffs of writers were attached to the mint and the treasury.[1]

The Lower Castes

Two categories of castes ranked below the Nāyars in villages. Although each caste had its own community headman and body of elders for internal administration, the lower castes were excluded from government of the kingdom. Each household in these castes was hereditarily attached to a Nāyar or Brahman household of the village in a servile relationship, or else to the governing body of the village's Nāyar elders as a whole. The lower castes carried out most of the agricultural and menial work in their villages.

The lower of these two categories comprised a number of castes of agricultural slaves. Nāyar and Brahman households owned them as hereditary attachments to their estates, and, especially toward the end of the traditional period, they could be leased or sold for cash. These castes, together with certain other very low castes of itinerant beggars, basket-makers, snake-charmers and exorcists,[2] seem to have been entirely illiterate. Today they are Kērala's Harijans or Scheduled Castes, forming some 9 per cent of the population. In the early sixteenth century they may have been a larger proportion, for after that date some became Muslims or Latin Catholics. Conversion became still more common in the second half of the nineteenth century after the slaves had been freed. The slave population seems to have been the only large category of Malayālīs to whom literacy was forbidden.

[1] *The Voyage of Pyrard de Laval*, I, p. 361, quoted in Ayyar, *The Zamorins of Calicut*, p. 295.

[2] Pānans, Pulluvans, Nāyadis, Parayans and Malayans were among the more prominent of these castes.

Between the Nāyars and their slaves there existed, however, a category of semi-servile peasants, artisans and specialist castes with substantial literacy. By far the largest of these castes was the Īzhavas or Tiyyars. They did garden work, leased rice lands, tended coconut trees, and had hereditary attachments to Nāyar households. Culturally cognate with the Īzhavas were a number of small castes of village servants under the authority of the Nāyar village assembly at large. Blacksmiths, carpenters, goldsmiths, bell-metal workers, stonemasons, astrologers, fencing masters, bow makers, laundry workers and barbers were among the more prevalent.

Boys and girls of all of these lower castes attended schools in their own section of each village, run on lines similar to the Nāyar schools. The hereditary teachers in low-caste schools came from the caste of Kaḍupaṭṭans in Kōzhikode and from the Kaḷari Panikkars or gymnasium masters in Cochin. Both castes provided astrologers, physicians and exorcists as well as teachers, and Kaḷari Panikkars were fencing masters for the Īzhavas as well (Iyer 1912: 103–4; Aiyappān 1945: 127–35). Although culturally similar to the Īzhavas and ranking below them, both castes claimed descent from degraded sections of Tamil Brahmans. They ascribed to their Brahmanical origin their rudimentary knowledge of Sanskrit, astrology and medicine.

In many ways, indeed, these castes of astrologers and teachers played the roles of pseudo-Brahmans in relation to the lower castes. Like Brahmans in relation to royalty and nobles, they cast and read horoscopes, treated the sick, and chanted Sanskrit *mantras* to alleviate suffering or bring merit to households. They exorcized evil spirits and poltergeists, provided love charms, potions and protective amulets, and presided over a pantheon of village godlings capable of bringing all manner of benefits or troubles upon the villagers. Their lore was, of course, a much simplified version of Brahman lore. Through them, however, some of the elements of Sanskrit religious belief and practice were filtered to lower-caste people who could not attend high-caste temples or receive Brahmanical services. Such elements included offerings and prayers to deities, belief in rebirth and *karma*, faith in astrology and other forms of divination, and knowledge of the stories and ethical precepts of the Hindu epics. The castes of astrologers and teachers thus served as media for the Sanskritization of the lower castes (Srinivas 1966: 1–46), a process that appears to have been going on gradually, with increasing literacy, throughout the traditional period.

With the Sanskrit knowledge were mingled, of course, beliefs and practices connected with local, non-Sanskritic supernatural beings. The same castes propitiated some of these spirits on behalf of the Nāyars and their congeners as well as the lower castes. Correspondingly, the learning of low-caste teachers partook even more strongly of magical esoterica than did that of the Brahmans and involved much less in the way of logic, mathematics, philosophy, aesthetics or scientific enquiry. Among the low-caste teachers, for example, the recitation of whole Vēdas or the writing of books gave place to such activities as repetition of short, secret *mantras* possessed of magical powers, or the inscribing of *mantras* or *yantras* (cabalistic designs)[1] on metal plates or amulets designed to ward off dangers.

It is interesting to notice that still further down the caste scale, among the Untouchables, very low castes of exorcists and magicians reproduced on a still grosser scale some of the lore of the low-caste teachers. Among these castes the Pānans of central Kērala and the Malayans of Kolaṭṭunād were, for example, well known. At this level, however, magic dominated learning and the idea of literacy survived only in cabalistic figures, single characters or other secret supernatural designs. These castes 'controlled' still lower-ranking non-Sanskritic spirits of more evil character than those of the astrologers, and specialized in black magic, lycanthropy and exorcism. They were thus in some demand among both high and low castes to bring secret harm to enemies or to counter particular misfortunes and illnesses. As I have explained elsewhere, these powers of the lowest castes placed certain restrictions on the high castes' exercise of political and economic power (Gough 1959: 265).

Literacy among the lower castes of Īzhavas and village servants tended to serve special technical or social purposes rather than to open up to them the heritage of Sanskrit and Malayālam literature. Although most men of our third category could probably read and write simple sentences, few in these castes owned books or composed original literature. Most children combined manual work with school from the age of nine or ten. School subjects were confined to arithmetic, mythological stories, proverbs, and agricultural and ethical precepts related to daily life. Among adults, literacy seems to have been chiefly used to handle documents of land transfers, tenures or mortgages, or to keep accounts, or to read and transmit 'craft books' concerned with such special knowledge as house-building, skilled metal work, astrology, or ceremonies. There were also some written renderings of folk songs, ballads of local heroes and songs for harvest or women's festivals.[2] There were in addition long narrative songs about non-Sanskritic deities, some of them, such as the *teyyams* of Kōzhikode, of local

[1] For examples and a discussion of the uses of *mantras* and *yantras* to control spiritual beings for magical purposes, see Aiyappan, *Iravas and Culture Change*, pp. 136–51, and pl. x.

[2] Especially popular were (and are) women's songs for Onam, the harvest festival in September, and Tiruvādhira, a women's festival for Kāma Dēvan, the god of passion, in December. Among the folk ballads, that of Thacchōli Odēnan, a Nāyar warrior of Badagara in the Kadaṭṭunād principality north of Kōzhikode, is the most popular in the northern half of Kērala.

vintage, and others such as Bhagavati and Ayyappan, known throughout most of Kērala. These songs accompanied low-caste dramas and dances and formed a kind of folk version of *kathakali*, the dance drama of the higher castes. All of these compositions, transmitted partly orally and partly in writing, formed a rich legacy of Malayālam folk art which was shared by the low castes and by commoner Nāyars in villages, and much of which is perpetuated at the present time.

Although literacy was probably a marginal accomplishment for most people of the third category of Hindu castes, some persons of this group became scholars as a result of European influence. In the coast towns, many Īzhavas and artisans entered the service of Dutch, French and English merchants and settlers, who accorded them higher rank than did the high-caste Hindus. In Kolaṭṭunād a sizeable Eurasian population grew up as a result of marriages between Englishmen and women of the Tiyyar matrilineal caste. The offspring retained Hinduism and their matrilineal kinship system, but they learned English and some of them became prosperous military leaders, merchants, cash-crop farmers and professionals even before British rule. Other Īzhavas acquired modern learning through Dutch or French contacts. Itty Achutan, for example, an Īzhava of Cochin, helped the Dutch scholar Henrick Van Rheede to compile *Hortus Malabaricus*, the first scientific botanical work in Kērala (Panikkar 1960: 319).

IMPLICATIONS OF LITERACY IN TRADITIONAL KĒRALA

Compared with most of India, Kērala had an unusually high proportion of literate people in the traditional period. There may have been several reasons for this. Kērala's high agricultural productivity, connected with its heavy rainfall, permitted at least a quarter of the population to be set apart as literate specialists. The growth of overseas commerce, and thus of land sales, cash rents and mortgages, and cash wages for soldiers and urban artisans, fostered the use of simple literacy for accounting and legal documents. The Nāyars and other matrilineal castes gave their women a higher status in many respects than was customary in patrilineal India, and most of them learned to read. European settlers educated other, low-caste, people who might otherwise have remained illiterate. Although figures are not available, descriptions suggest that more than half the men and at least a quarter of the women may have been proficient in Malayālam in the early eighteenth century. While we may perhaps not call this 'widespread' literacy in the sense intended by Goody and Watt above, p. 40), Kērala certainly qualifies as an 'advanced intermediate' society in the Parsonian sense (Parsons 1966: 51).

Kērala had, however, only a few of the characteristics mentioned by Goody and Watt as perhaps resulting from widespread literacy. There was interest in the development of logic as a science, as well as some separation of cognitive disciplines. Grammar and syntax, logic, history, geography, arithmetic, medicine, physiology and astronomy were recognized as separate disciplines, but so also, of course, were ritual, magic, exorcism and astrology. Generalized history, as distinct from special chronicles, began to develop in the seventeenth century, but there was little or no attempt to separate history from myth, or theology from science. There was apparently little interest in the sceptical questioning of tradition or the conscious search for scientific, as distinct from mystical, truth. Democracy did not develop in any Western sense, although the assemblies of local elders within each caste had a strong democratic element.

Through the Nambūdiris, Kērala possessed a world of knowledge transcending its small feudal kingdoms and extending, indeed, to the whole of Hindu India. Christian, Islamic and Jewish literati also maintained links with their cultures of the Middle East and of Europe. There was rigid social stratification, and this was in part based on the extent of literacy and learning in the various castes. Wide gaps separated the Sanskrit literati of Brahman and royal vintage from the more plebeian of the Nāyars and temple servants, who knew only Malayālam. A similarly wide chasm separated the Nāyars, well versed in Malayālam, from the Īzhava group, most of whom knew only folk literature. The illiteracy and almost total lack of Sanskrit knowledge of the Untouchables were, in turn, both symptom and cause of the scorn in which they were held. On the other hand, relatively widespread literacy did not break down the strict rules of social distance obtaining between the various literate birth-status categories, nor, indeed, between the minute subdivisions within each category.

Kērala society did have a great interest in records: in accounting, book-keeping, and chronicles relating to particular institutions such as the court, the temple, the noble lineage and the village: for literacy was fully used in the running of the feudal kingdom and the ecclesiastical estate. In certain cultural areas there was also an interest in exact time sequences and in 'lineal' codifications of reality, although not in others. Thus, linear time-keeping and chronology appeared in the use of solar and lunar calendars and the recording of events in terms of the Malayālam era, commencing in A.D. 825. On the other hand, concepts of cyclical time appeared in villagers' calculations of the seasons or beliefs about the rotation of aeons and eras and the rebirth of souls and of worlds.

Finally, the traditional uses of literacy do not seem to have fostered individualism or alienation. There were no novels, and few heart-searching literary discussions of individual character, and even ascetics in Kērala lived mainly in corporate communities.

My discussion of literacy in traditional Kērala thus tends to bear out conclusions reached from a general consideration of China and India (see above, pp. 83–4). Literacy is for the most part an enabling rather than a causal factor, making possible the development of complex political structures, syllogistic reasoning, scientific enquiry, linear conceptions of reality, scholarly specialization, artistic elaboration, and perhaps certain kinds of individualism and of alienation. Whether, and to what extent, these will in fact develop depends apparently on concomitant factors of ecology, inter-societal relations, and internal ideological and social structural responses to these. In traditional Kērala considerable quantitative development of literacy occurred, but it was put to work mainly in the service of trade, political relations, the arts of the court, and the elaboration of priestly esoterica.

It is interesting to consider which facets of Kērala society could *not* have developed without literacy. The following are suggested. First, although decentralized and feudal in structure, Kērala's kingdoms were bigger than those usually found, for example, in preliterate Africa. The Zamorins' kingdom may have contained a million people in the sixteenth century, and the others between one-quarter of a million and a million. It is questionable, too, whether such a quantity of overseas trade could have been handled without writing, which facilitated international treaties, price-fixing and the payment of customs dues. Literacy certainly assisted book-keeping, collection of tribute and taxes, the development of a complex legal system, and other features of a centralized political system.

Literacy, coupled with high productivity and a leisure class, made possible the emergence of an array of educated 'specialisms' relating to ritual, philosophy, art, science and government, reflected in the elaborate proliferation of castes and sub-castes at the top of the social hierarchy. It may even be questioned whether the fundamental dichotomy between priests and rulers is likely to occur in the absence of literacy and of the elaborations of ritual and government that it permits. The confinement of specialized literate skills to the aristocracy also fostered a sharp division between mental and manual labour, and hence the wide social distance between 'good' and 'polluting' castes. Given, moreover, a traditionally oriented society based on birth-status groups, literacy provided an additional rigidity to differences of social status and privilege. Thus, writing made possible a vast complexity of sumptuary laws, laws relating to property and ceremonial privileges, and legal documents in general.

Writing also enabled royal and aristocratic lineages to record their genealogies and political histories. As a result, some of these lineage histories can today be reconstructed with apparently great accuracy to the fourteenth and fifteenth centuries. It is interesting to notice, however, that the recording of genealogical and other information does not seem to have caused aristocrats to question the relationships between genealogical segments and political or land rights except in cases of dispute. Recording genealogies did not, for example, prevent segments of lineages from conquering each other's territories or occupying each other's political offices, and did not preclude *selective* references to genealogies, and the development of myths and reinterpretations of history, to justify ongoing events. The development of critical, 'objective' history seems, therefore, to depend on circumstances other than literacy alone, especially the appearance of professional historians from other societies who have no axe to grind. Even then, it may of course be questioned whether the history of any place or period can ever be presented without bias.

A final point may be made regarding writing in traditional Kērala which distinguishes it from modern literacy. Perhaps because the Hindu kingdoms were themselves basically theocratic and the whole of social life in some sense sacred, writing appears to have been itself a sacred activity, carrying with it supernatural powers and fraught with mystical dangers. Initiation into letters began, as we saw, with the written invocation of Vishnu, Lakshmi and Ganapati. Among Hindus, it was forbidden to write any document or private communication without inscribing this invocation at the top of the page; other religious communities had similar observances. There were also grades of sacredness in learning and in things written, as well as things spoken, which corresponded with grades of religious purity in the caste system. Only Brahmans could read the Vēdas, and only the twice-born could hear them. Literacy in Sanskrit was confined to upper castes and to chosen specialists, chiefly astrologers, of the lower castes. Writing itself was forbidden to the Untouchables. Secret written prayers, words, or cabalistic designs, derived from individuals or castes of higher ritual status than one's own were at every level of society believed to be especially powerful and dangerous.

Writing was, finally, forbidden during periods of religious pollution following the death or birth of a close relative. My informants were unable to explain why this was so, but comparison with other such prohibitions suggests an answer. In general, the prohibitions surrounding death or birth pollution tend to fall into two categories. The first comprises observances, such as fasting or abstention from sex relations, which enhance the relative ritual purity, and thus safety from supernatural dangers, of the observer. The second category of prohibitions keeps the observer from polluting or offending other beings, objects or places through his own unwonted impurity, and thus from bringing human or supernatural punishments on himself. Examples are the prohibitions on entering temples or bathing pools of the caste or on touching one's caste fellows during ritual pollution. The prohibition on writing seems to fall in the latter category. It was abstention from a sacred activity, comparable to worship in temples, which, if performed while in a state of impurity, might bring divine punishment on the person infringing the rule.

LITERACY IN MODERN KĒRALA

It is not possible to explore fully here the implications of literacy in modern Kērala, but I shall try to indicate some important directions of modern change.

A. S. Menon argues that there was an 'alarming increase of illiteracy' early in the British period (Menon 1962: 651). This is almost certainly true. Schools and colleges were disrupted in the wars of the late eighteenth century, and the British, by introducing English as the medium of modern education, discouraged Sanskrit learning and vernacular village schools. Both in British Malabar and in the Native States of Cochin and Travancore, regular public instruction seems to have been firmly re-established only toward the end of the nineteenth century. In the 1860s, state-aided vernacular primary schools were opened for both sexes in most village clusters, and private high schools, using the English medium, began to receive grants-in-aid from the government.

As late as 1911, however, Cochin State led the rest of Kērala with an official literacy rate of only 20 per cent for males and 4 per cent for females. The figures are, however, too low; for 'literates' were defined as those who had passed the fourth standard in a government-recognized elementary school. Since most older people had never attended modern schools, and since most village girls and many boys left after the third standard, actual ability to read and write was much greater than the official literacy rate. In the age group 15–20, moreover, the official rate in Cochin in 1911 was 31·8 per cent for males and 9·7 per cent for females. After 1931, the census collectors were instructed to record actual rather than 'fourth standard' literacy. In 1941, partly as a result of this change, the recorded male literacy rate in Cochin rose to 79·3 per cent in the age-group 15–20, and the female rate to 58·6 per cent.

By 1951, four years after Independence, over 43 per cent of Cochin's total population was recorded as literate. Progress since Independence brought the overall literacy rate to 50·5 per cent in southern Cochin in

1961: 57·7 per cent for males and 43·3 per cent for females. In Kērala as a whole in 1961 the literacy rate was 46·9 per cent, while in India as a whole it was still only 24 per cent. 'Effective' literacy among people over the age of 4 was 59·5 per cent in southern Cochin in 1961; somewhat less, for Kērala as a whole (Menon 1962: 111–13). As formerly, literacy is least advanced among Untouchables and Muslims; most advanced among Syrian Christians and high-caste Hindus. Whereas very few Untouchables could read in 1949, however, I found many literate Untouchable children of 8 to 10 years of age on my return to Kērala in 1964. Most children of all ethnic groups under the age of 12 are now in at least part-time attendance at village schools.

It is difficult to discuss the implications of literacy in modern Kērala without also discussing its cultural and social concomitants. These include, especially, the use of English as the medium of instruction prevailing in high schools until the 1930s, and in colleges up to the present time. With this circumstance went, of course, the introduction of English art forms, of modern science and of Western learning in general. There was also the fact that in Kērala, although a state system of education developed in the nineteenth century, most high schools and colleges are still managed, and partly financed, by Christian churches, by caste or other ethnic associations, or by private individuals. These subjects have been explored to some extent elsewhere.[1] Without treating them in their own right, I shall focus on those features of modern Kērala society for which modern literacy has been a necessary, although not usually a sufficient, condition.

The fundamental technological change of modern times connected with literacy was, of course, the development of bulk printing. Its significance became felt in the 1880s with the popularization of daily newspapers and weekly journals. By 1947, at independence, almost every village had its reading-room, newspapers, novelettes, and printed copies of sacred books and famous Malayālam literature. At that date, high-caste Hindus and Christians tended to monopolize the patronage and use of reading-rooms and to own larger quantities of books than other castes, although Īzhavas and Muslims were consciously developing education through their modern ethnic associations. On my return to Kērala in 1964, it seemed that the whole state was flooded with newsprint, novels, political pamphlets, advertisements, wall-slogans, shop-signs, bill-boards, posters, letters, printed

[1] See, for example, Aiyappan, *Iravas and Culture Change*, pp. 151–7, 188–194; A. K. Gopalan, *Kērala, Past and Present* (Lawrence and Wishart, 1959), pp. 26–78; E. M. S. Namboodiripad, *Kērala Yesterday, Today and Tomorrow* (National Book Agency Private, Ltd., Calcutta 16, 1967), pp. 128–212; Kathleen Gough, 'Indian Nationalism and Ethnic Freedom', in *Concepts of Freedom in Anthropology*, ed. by David Bidney (Mouton and Co., 1963), pp. 170–207, and 'Kērala Politics and the 1965 Elections', in *The International Journal of Comparative Sociology* (1967), VIII, 55–88.

invitations and announcements. The growing interest since Independence of the lowest castes and the propertyless in all these materials was one of the more impressive changes. Even among Untouchables, for example, few today, however remote they are from the coast towns, do not read or hear sections of one of the many newspapers delivered by bus to the teashops, and discuss these animatedly with friends. More than through the growth of the numbers of the literate, Kērala society is today influenced by the sheer bulk of written and printed material and the flood of information that this brings, directly or indirectly, from the world at large to the whole of the citizenry. Since independence, the information flow has been further augmented by government-sponsored documentary films, public village radios, and mass political meetings of the major parties.

Bulk printing has made possible a number of social structural changes that would otherwise have been difficult or impossible. Early in the present century, newspapers and weeklies made possible the growth of the Indian nationalist movement among the new bourgeoisie of the higher Hindu castes. The same media facilitated the organization of all-Kērala caste associations and other ethnically based groups by the new middle classes. These associations aimed to build religious or caste solidarity between the former kingdoms and sub-castes, promote education and 'uplift', and compete for jobs, schools and positions in government service. The Muslim League in Malabar and the Īzhava S.N.D.P. Yōgam,[1] Nāyar Service Society and Nambūdiri Yōga Kshēmam were among the most prominent of these state-wide associations, while the Catholic church played a similar role among Christians. Other caste-unifying institutions developed among the new middle classes. Along with the growth of such powerful associations it became common, for example, for 'modern' families to advertise in newspapers for spouses for their children from all over Kērala, rather than to maintain traditional preferential marriage customs or to engage local go-betweens.

The growth of unified ethnic associations, coupled with bulk printing and expanding literacy, in turn hastened the downward spread of the 'great traditions' as well as the dissemination of various modern, and often Western, values. Thus, the Hindu ethnic associations all encouraged Sanskritic as opposed to local or low-caste rituals, while both Christian and Muslim associations propagated modern and cosmopolitan versions of their religions. All of the ethnic associations, moreover, published tracts which inculcated such modern capitalist virtues as thrift, saving, diligence and private enterprise. The fact that all of the ethnic associations, like the modern political parties, set up their own printing presses and

[1] The Srī Nārāyana Dharma Parapālana Yōgam, called after Srī Nārāyana Guru, a revered teacher among the Īzhavas, who died in 1922.

newspapers shows how clearly their leaders perceived the significance of literacy for modern forms of organization and culture change.

In the 1920s and 1930s the spread of literacy and especially of English learning to all castes, coupled with the uneven distribution of learning within each caste, facilitated the emergence of a number of class-based political parties in addition to the Indian National Congress and the Muslim League. Chief of these were, of course, the Communist Party and the various independent socialist groups. Each party was led by a group of literate mass organizers and espoused a body of social theory incorporated in books and newspapers which the party made it its business to propagate. Thus, with the modern development of printing as a mass medium came also mass propaganda and the whole concept of mass society. In Kērala, with its heavy development of export crop farming and processing, its rapid population increase, its widening gap between rich and poor, and its high proportion of wage labour, it was perhaps inevitable that mass society should also entail severe class struggle with, eventually, the spread of Marxist ideals of a classless society. It seems clear also that modern bulk printing and the spread of literacy to lower classes made possible, although they did not themselves necessitate, the introduction of the whole concept of political 'subversion' as well as that of representative democracy.

The uneven distribution of literacy among the lower castes and classes meant that literacy acquired special significance for Kērala's revolutionary parties, notably the Communist Party and such smaller groups as the Revolutionary Socialist Party. Thus, whereas literacy is not a necessary qualification for membership of the Indian National Congress Party, it is mandatory in Kērala for membership of the Communist Party. This difference seems to be related to the fact that in the Congress Party, a party committed to gradual change and to already legitimized authority, leadership automatically accrues to the existing upper classes of property owners. It is therefore unnecessary to stipulate literacy as a criterion for mere membership of the party, as distinct from leadership. Among the Communists, by contrast, the bulk of adherents are without property and were until recently illiterate. The ultimate goal is liquidation of private property and thus of the bourgeoisie as a class. The programme is, at least in theory, revolutionary, and some activities have therefore necessarily been secret.[1] It was thus appropriate that the party should constitute a small vanguard of literate persons capable of studying theories of revolution and of communicating in secret, who would form the leadership of a large body of propertyless and mostly illiterate labourers, and organize them into mass

[1] For an outline of Communist policies and fortunes in Kērala as seen from within, see E. M. S. Namboodiripad, *Kērala Yesterday, Today and Tomorrow*, pp. 168–252.

groupings such as trade unions and peasants' associations. In the past decade, however, there are signs that with the increasing spread of literacy in the low castes and propertyless classes, the élite relationship of the vanguard to its following is disintegrating. Non-party followers are, for example, competing for and often obtaining elected offices in both village and state governments with the sponsorship of the Communist Party. The split into Right and Left Communist Parties which took place in 1964 also tends to bring to the forefront newly literate, often low-caste, Communist supporters who are not party members; for each of the two new parties wishes to form a grass-roots following and to raise to local leadership intelligent village 'amateurs' who will spread its ideas among the people. If the present level of political consciousness persists, increasing literacy in Kērala may, therefore, bring a decline of vanguard parties and the growth of more loosely structured and participatory forms of mass movement. Whether these will take a revolutionary turn will depend, no doubt, not on literacy but on the extent of dissatisfaction and the outcome of class struggles within the society.

We must note, finally, that the period of bulk printing and modern literacy in Kērala *has* seen most of the features attributed by Goody and Watt to societies with widespread literacy. They include, in addition to those found traditionally, and those already mentioned, the modern distinction between myth and history; the separation of the divine and the natural worlds, and the growth of a secular society as a political ideal. Knowledge is now fully divided into the cognitive disciplines familiar in the West. There has been an expansion of linear codifications of reality to new areas, for example, increased interest in exact time-keeping and in scientific causality, as also in the cataloguing of historical events and the setting of targets and goals. Modern education has brought a greater emphasis on scepticism and systematic scientific enquiry. There has, finally, been a great growth of individualism and a need for increased privacy among the highly literate, as seen in the intense interest in and production of modern novels, movies and dramas of character, and in the development of individual property, intimate dyadic friendships, romantic love, and individually arranged marriages.

Directly or indirectly, it seems probable that bulk printing, and possibly some modern increase in the literacy rate, have played a role in fostering all of these developments. It is difficult to isolate this role, however, partly because we still lack adequate information on the traditional literacy rate, and partly because these familiar modern developments have come in the wake not only of bulk printing but of British conquest, modern power-based transport and industries, capitalist economic relations, and modern world-communications. More precise studies of the uses of literacy in other pre-industrial societies may shed light on the implications of these various causal factors. So also may studies of literacy in modern Communist societies, where the element of private enterprise is muted. Finally, we shall probably appreciate the full implications of literacy only as we pass into societies where other kinds of mass media overshadow the written and the printed word—a future which, for better or for worse, is already almost upon us (McLuhan 1964).

THE TRANSMISSION OF ISLAMIC LEARNING IN THE WESTERN SUDAN

The next four chapters deal with peoples who have been influenced by Islam and the written works that accompany its spread. Professor Wilks writes about the western Sudan, but he is concerned not so much with a specific 'culture' or 'society' in the usual sense as with the specialized trading groups of the Dyula, which also constituted a major channel of Muslim learning throughout a large part of the western Sudan. Settling in the midst of many different peoples, the Dyula maintained a network of communications that covered the pagan tribes and centralized states of the savannah hinterland. Wilks examines the way in which learning is handed down over the generations, the relationship between trade and learning (often, in the same family, one person is for scholarship, one for trade) and refers to the role of a universalistic written code in helping to establish the conditions for a flourishing long-distance trade crossing ethnic and linguistic frontiers.

THE TRANSMISSION OF ISLAMIC LEARNING IN THE WESTERN SUDAN

by IVOR WILKS

INTRODUCTION: THE DYULA TOWNS

In this paper[1] I am concerned with parts of the Western Sudan now within the republics of Mali, Guinea, Upper Volta, Ivory Coast and Ghana. The account I shall give of learning in this region is not to be regarded as equally applicable to other parts of Muslim West Africa. In particular, the situation in the Central Sudan—in Hausaland and Bornu—differs in many respects from that which I shall describe here. West African Muslims are themselves keenly aware of the difference between the Western and Central Sudanese traditions, which meet and to a limited extent interact roughly along a line between Timbuktu and Accra. Specifically, I shall here describe the spread of a knowledge of the Islamic sciences into a group of towns which includes Kong, Buna and Bonduku in the Ivory Coast, Bobo-Dioulasso and Safane in Upper Volta, and Wa and Banda in Ghana. Such towns will be referred to as Dyula, since all contain an important, and sometimes a dominant, Dyula element in their composition. *Dyula* is a Malinke word for 'trader', and those who describe themselves by it appear to be ultimately of Malian, i.e. Malinke and Soninke, origin. Dyula immigration into these towns has been taking place intermittently over half a millennium or more. While following many routes, it has occurred along two principal axes: the one easterly from the Upper Niger in the Kangaba area, and the other southerly from the Middle Niger around Jenne. Originally intimately concerned with the trade in gold between the great Western Sudanese entrepôts—termini of the Saharan caravan trails—and the distant and scattered centres of the extractive industry along the Black Volta and in the forests to its south (Wilks, in press: section 2), the Dyula subsequently broadened the basis of their enterprise until today,

[1] This paper is based upon field-work carried out between 1959 and 1966, largely sponsored by the Institute of African Studies, University of Ghana. Copies of field-notes are deposited in the Institute's library. I have been grateful throughout for the guidance of al-Ḥājj 'Uthmān b. Isḥāq Boyo, Senior Research Assistant at the Institute. My colleagues J. J. Holden and D. Gjertsen, both of the University of Ghana, joined me in many field trips. Mr Thomas Hodgkin, as Director of the Institute, gave unfailing support in this inquiry. I was afforded the opportunity to work on this material by the award of a Simon Senior Research Fellowship in the Department of Social Anthropology, Manchester University, 1966–7, and wish to thank Professor Max Gluckman and his colleagues there for their considerable encouragement.

in huge modern towns such as Accra and Abijan, Kumasi and Bouake, they are to be found dealing in anything from ball-point pens to ten-ton lorries. The Dyula often refer to themselves, and are referred to by others, as Wangara, a name of great antiquity.[1] 'Wangara', wrote the author of the sixteenth-century *Ta'rīkh al-fattāsh*, 'serves to describe the merchants who trade from country to country' (Maḥmūd Kāti 1913: 65). While many Dyula communities have now become involved in agriculture, they usually remain active in commerce, at the very least, as a dry-season occupation. Most Dyula still speak a dialect of Malinke. All Dyula persist in the use of Malinke and Soninke salutation-names: Tarawiri (Fr. Traoré), Sissay (Cissé), Kunatay (Konaté), Kamaghatay, Jabaghatay, and the rest. By and large the Dyula remain Muslim, as they have been from the beginnings of their dispersion. There are, however, communities of Dyula origin whose members have ceased all commercial activity, have apostasized, and no longer speak Malinke: they cannot be regarded as still in any real sense Dyula.

The region of Dyula settlement is characterized by a marked opposition between town and countryside. A Dyula town will have a number of associated Dyula villages, urban outposts spaced out along the trade paths connecting one major centre with another. In general, however, the countryside is dominated by groups—tribes—having little cultural community with the Dyula. Thus, for example, in the Buna subdivision in the Ivory Coast some 5,000 Muslims, mainly Dyula, live among some 40,000 non-Muslims, mainly Kulango and Birifor polytheists (CHEAM 1957). In the Wa local authority area in Ghana, of a total population of over 130,000, only about 20,000 are Muslim, and no more than half of these Dyula: that is, some conversion of the non-Dyula rural population has occurred (particularly of Chakalle and Wala), though not on a scale sufficient to destroy the basic correlation between urban and Muslim, rural and non-Muslim.[2] In a few areas, however, largely as a result of militant Muslim movements in the nineteenth century, much more extensive conversion of the rural population was achieved, and the opposition between town and countryside became correspondingly diminished. The subdivision of Ferkéssédougou in the Ivory Coast, of which Kong is part, has for example a Muslim/non-Muslim ratio of two to three.[3] In general, however, the Dyula are still to be found living in small urban and semi-urban communities separated

[1] See, for example, the mid-twelfth-century *Book of Roger* by al-Idrīsī.

[2] The Ghana population census of 1960. The only figures for religious affiliations are unreliable, being based upon the later 5 per cent post-enumeration sample census. The above estimates for the Muslim and Dyula population of the Wa area are, in consequence, my own.

[3] CHEAM 1957. In the case of Kong, the institution of the Sonangui (see Bernus (1960), pp. 290–3) was *inter alia* an agency of Islamization in the rural areas.

from each other by numerically preponderant non-Dyula and usually non-Muslim people, and certainly this was universally the case until the nineteenth century.

The trading towns of the Dyula attracted, over the centuries, the interest of some groups having a military rather than a mercantile tradition—of bands whose capital lay in their possession of horses and in their knowledge of the techniques of cavalry warfare. Such groups sometimes succeeded in establishing themselves in positions of political authority within state-systems which they created, each based upon one or more of the Dyula towns and as much of the surrounding countryside as could be pacified. Thus horsemen from the Mossi lands—from Dagomba, Mamprussi and perhaps Wagadugu—came to establish a number of settlements on the Middle Black Volta in the course of the seventeenth century, and in the early eighteenth century, with the support of the local Dyula, in two cases succeeded in converting their petty chiefdoms into small but viable states: Wa, to the east of the river, and Buna, to the west. At much the same time, likewise with the co-operation of the Dyula of such towns as Kong and Bobo-Dioulasso, other groups of Middle Niger (Malinke and Bambara) background were laying the foundations of the Watara kingdoms in the region of the headwaters of the Komoé and Black Volta rivers. In the pluralistic systems that arose in places like Wa and Buna or Kong and Bobo-Dioulasso, authority is found broadly distributed among the three major components of society: first, the cavalry people who assumed responsibility for both internal and external security; second, the Dyula, who retained control of commercial affairs; and, third, the 'autochthonous' groups which remained in ritual custody of the land.[1] Further to the south other Dyula communities, particularly those such as Bonduku and Banda which were offshoots of the ancient and important southerly centre of Bighu (Begho), came within the ambit of the rising Akan kingdoms (Wilks 1961; Goody 1965), but continued to enjoy a measure of local autonomy sufficient for the preservation of their Dyula identity. The Dyula towns are linked by common commercial interests and by joint commercial enterprise, by a network of alliances based upon kinship and marriage,[2] and by Islam. The high degree of social and economic interdependence has made conflict between Dyula communities almost unknown. It follows from what has been said, however, that no political superstructure binds together the

[1] There are few detailed studies of Dyula communities. But for Kong, see Bernus 1960; for the Dyula of Gonja, Goody 1967; for Bonduku, Tauxier 1921. A study of Wa by the writer is in preparation.

[2] Strong alliances are also formed between classmates, i.e. those attending the same school at the same time, and between ḥāj-mates, i.e. those making the pilgrimage to Mecca in the same year.

various towns, although a bid to unite them on the basis of Islam came within sight of success in the late nineteenth century, when the Almamy Samori Turay extended his power over the whole region. Had not the French systematically destroyed his empire, Samori might have become to the Dyula communities of the Western Sudan what 'Uthmān dan Fodio earlier in the century had been to the Hausa of the Central Sudan.

Each Dyula community has acquired in the course of time marked local characteristics as a result of limited cultural borrowing both from the surrounding rural people (from whom the Dyula often found it necessary to obtain wives), and from the locally prestigious chiefly groups such as the Watara of Kong, the Dagomba of Wa, and the Abron of Bonduku. Dyula particularism of this sort is sometimes acknowledged in the use of such terms as Dagari-Dyula and Bobo-Dyula to describe those living among the Dagari and Bobo (Fing) respectively. There is perhaps some basic relationship between the antiquity of a Dyula community in its locality and the extent of its adaptation to the local cultural milieu. A limiting case, of virtually complete assimilation, is exemplified by the Tagara (i.e. Tarawiri) of Jirapa in north-western Ghana, who, although apparently descended from early (perhaps sixteenth-century) Dyula settlers there, retain no Dyula characteristics other than the continuing use of the salutation-name and an awareness of distant kinship with the Tarawiri of Wa to the south (Goody 1954: 32; Rattray 1932: II, 472). This tendency towards assimilation, however, is usually counteracted by a constant and conscious concern for the renewal and reinvigoration of the Muslim content of Dyula culture —a process described by the Arabic term *tajdīd*. It is this process that is the central issue of the present paper, since the necessary preconditions of *tajdīd* are, first, the presence throughout society of a basic level of literacy and, second, the existence within society of an educated élite—the '*ulamā*'— able to maintain links with the wider Muslim community and, through the study and interpretation of basic expositions of the Islamic sciences, to preserve conformity between local practice and the general precepts of Islam. The existence of communities such as the Tagara of Jirapa shows that this programme was not always successful,—usually through shortages either of written works or of teachers competent in their exposition.

2. EDUCATION IN THE DYULA TOWNS

The Dyula send many of their sons and some of their daughters to school: granted, that is, that schools are available and that the family is able to maintain its economic viability without the full-time labour of its children. Between the ages of approximately 6 and 14 years the pupils acquire an elementary knowledge of Arabic based upon the recitation and copying of the Qur'ān. While non-Muslim writers have tended to deplore such instruction as of little pedagogical value (Tauxier 1921: 256–6; Marty 1922: 272), my own observations suggest that such judgements are probably partisan and certainly too severe. A talented and well-taught pupil will rapidly acquire a command of Arabic, and in his early teens may be studying grammar and syntax, and reading, for example, basic works of Mālikī law such as the *Risāla* of Ibn Abī Zayd al-Qayrawānī. Only a minority of students will achieve such progress, of course, but many will leave school able to read and write Arabic even if imperfectly. Adequate statistical material on literacy among the Dyula is unfortunately lacking. Such data as there are, however, show clearly that schooling is an important feature of society. Thus, around 1920 the Muslim population of Bonduku town, 2,078 persons, was served by eight elementary Qur'ānic schools with about 200 (mainly male) pupils (Tauxier 1921: 555; Marty 1922: 219). Although the age structure of Bonduku at the time is not known, the implication of these figures is that most boys were attending school. The same would appear true of Kong (Marty 1922: 189). Rough estimates made by the writer in Bonduku in 1959 suggested that the situation had remained unaltered: about 450 children (90 per cent boys) attended Qur'ānic schools, the total Muslim population of the town then being around 5,000.[1] The Ghana Census of 1960 shows that, of all male Wala children receiving elementary education of any sort in that year, 735, or 52 per cent, were attending 'Arabic' schools, while of the 1,160 Wala aged 25 or more in that year who had received full-time education, 1,020 or 88 per cent had been at 'Arabic' schools.[2] It is unfortunately impossible on the basis of the census to distinguish between the Wa Dyula and all others describing themselves as Wala, whether Muslim or otherwise. However, a study of two of the Dyula sections of Wa—Limamyiri with about 2,500 people and Tagarayiri with about 750—makes it clear that virtually all male children from the former attend Qur'ānic schools, and perhaps about 70 per cent from the latter.[3]

It should be noted that not only Dyula children go to the Dyula schools. Children from non-Dyula Muslim families are admitted as a matter of course, and it is not unknown for a non-Muslim family to request a teacher

[1] These estimates were based mainly on information from the Imām 'Alī b. Ibrāhīm Timitay, and his deputy, Muḥammad b. Ibrāhīm Timitay (the present imām).

[2] Ghana Census of 1960, Special Report E. The report unfortunately fails to define what is meant by 'Arabic' school.

[3] Estimates for female attendance have not been offered since their schooling tends to be intermittent. The Tagarayiri Dyula of Wa have been in the locality for perhaps four centuries or more, and the Limamyiri for about two and a half.

to take one of its children (Marty 1922: 268). In the past the Dyula also considered it an obligation of Islam to educate the children of their slaves. The French and British colonial administrations gave little official support to the Dyula schools. The post-colonial governments, on the other hand, often with an increasing political involvement with the Arab world, have shown some signs of encouraging the teaching of Arabic, which, in towns like Bobo-Dioulasso in Upper Volta and Wa in Ghana, is now offered not only in the traditional Qur'ānic schools but also in some grant-aided ones.

That Dyula culture was—in a way that will be more closely examined later—a literate one, was a matter that impressed the early travellers in the area. Thus of Salaga in Gonja, a town with an admixture of Dyula and Central Sudanese elements, David Asante noted in 1877:

> In this strongly Muhammadan town there are many houses of prayer, and private and public schools...As a result almost every Salaga man can read and write Arabic [Asante 1880–1].[1]

Of Kong, on the occasion of his visit in 1888, Binger observed:

> Education is highly developed at Kong. There are few illiterate persons. The Arabic which they write is not that which is the most pure; one is however astonished to see them so well educated... [Binger 1892: I, 236];

and in the same year Austin Freeman reported of Bonduku:

> Most of the elder better-class men have a rudimentary knowledge of Arabic, and may be seen at the close of the day sitting in the shadow of their houses, or in the market-booths, reading their prayers from small manuscripts, or copying them on to pieces of a thick drab paper... [Freeman 1892: 140].

In this paper I am particularly concerned with those who, having completed their elementary Qur'ānic education, subsequently go on to further studies and may themselves in time become teachers or functionaries of some sort—*imāms*, *qāḍīs*, or *muftīs*. These form a well-defined professional class within Dyula society, and are usually described by the Arabic term *'ulamā'*, the men of learning (singular, *'ālim*). A member of the *'ulamā'* class is addressed in Malinke as *karamoko*, literally 'one who can read', from Malinke *kara*, Arabic *qara'a*, 'to read, recite'. Not all literate persons, however, are described as *karamokos*, but only those who have carried their studies on to a stipulated advanced level. In practice there is considerable local variation in the requirements regarded as minimal for recognition as a *karamoko*. In areas where men of learning are few, for example, such as the economically impoverished parts of Gonja and of the Grunshi country where there is little to attract *'ulamā'* from more prosperous places, a person of very modest educational attainments may be accepted as a

[1] For writings in the Arabic script (and both Arabic and Hausa languages) from Gonja and particularly Salaga, see Goody and Wilks, below, pp. 241–58.

karamoko and encouraged to teach—one who in a town like Kong would be unlikely to obtain a single pupil. Nevertheless, a degree of uniformity is present in the system in principle, and is followed in practice in all the larger Dyula centres. There it is accepted that the title of *karamoko* is accorded only to those who have completed the study of three specific works, namely:

(1) the *Tafsīr al-Jalālayn* of al-Maḥallī (d. 1459) and al-Suyūṭī (d. 1505);[1]

(2) *al-Shifā' fī ta'rīf ḥuqūq al-Muṣṭafā* by 'Iyāḍ b. Mūsā b. 'Iyāḍ al-Sabtī (d. 1149); and

(3) the *Muwaṭṭā'* of Imām Mālik b. Anas (d. 795).

The first of these works is an advanced commentary on the Qur'ān; the second, broadly, an ethical work concerned with the rules of rightful conduct based upon the study of the life of the Prophet; and the third a comprehensive corpus of Muslim law—marriage, contract, inheritance, penal law, etc. I shall comment later on the significance of these works for the Dyula *'ulamā'* concerned with the regulation of the affairs of society.

These three works are frequently read together with one teacher. The student seldom starts work upon them until 30 years of age or more. Younger candidates are positively discouraged, the *'ulamā'* preferring to recruit only from those who have already shown evidence both of piety and of social responsibility.[2] It is not uncommon to meet students who are over 50 years, and even in their sixties. It is difficult to generalize about the length of time taken in study of the three works. Students may remain attached to their teacher for many years (thirty in one case that I met with), participating in the advanced classes but at the same time acting as teaching assistants for the elementary Qur'ānic groups. In cases in which a student spends only a few months with a teacher it is usually found that he has previously studied the works under another *karamoko* and is undertaking a second and briefer course with a more learned or pious tutor. In circumstances which may be considered broadly normal, however, a student will spend from three to five years on the *Tafsīr*, *al-Shifā'* and *Muwaṭṭa'*, though the formal instruction given by the teacher may be as little as three or four hours a day for five days of the week, the student dividing the rest of his time between his business or farming interests, on the one hand, and prayer and private study on the other.[3]

[1] In certain circumstances other commentaries may be substituted for the *Tafsīr al-Jalālayn*, but my material on this matter is incomplete.

[2] The general observations in this section are based upon data from various towns, 1959–66. For earlier accounts of Dyula education, see Delafosse (1910), pp. 177–206; Tauxier (1921), pp. 225–6; Marty (1922), ch. III.

[3] A 'normal' day for a devoted student will pass much as follows: 0200–0400 hours, private prayer and study; 0400–0600 hours, sleep; 0600–0700 hours, bathing, breakfast, etc.; 0700–0900 hours, formal instruction; 0900–1400 hours, farming, business, etc.;

I can offer no estimates of drop-out and failure rates; since no time limit is imposed on the student, most appear sooner or later to complete their readings to the satisfaction of the teacher. Those who do so are entitled to call themselves *karamokos* and to be addressed as such by others. Each is awarded a written certificate or *isnād*, and is also authorized to wear the turban—a band of white cloth bound tightly around the cap (Delafosse 1910: 178, 183–4; Marty 1922: 262–3). The institution of the turban as a mark of distinction for those completing the study of the three works is attributed, in West Africa, to al-Ḥājj Sālim Sūwarī (see, for example, *Dukhūl al-Islām*), a Malian jurisconsult probably of the fifteenth century to whom reference will be made later.

A *karamoko*, having obtained his turban and *isnād*, will commonly enter the teaching field, obtaining a position as assistant to an already established teacher or sometimes starting his own school. In the latter case he will either respond to an appeal from some small and probably remote village requiring an instructor, or will open classes for children from his own family—the extended group known in Dyula as the *so* or the less extended *lu* (Tauxier 1921: 216; Bernus 1960: 294). A few *karamokos*, however, will choose to continue with their studies, and at this stage will often be obliged to travel far from their home towns in search of instruction. The emphasis will now be upon *Fiqh*, law, and *Ḥadīth*, Traditions of the Prophet. The student will extend and deepen his knowledge of works of Mālikī law with which he will already have acquaintance—for example, the *Tuḥfat al-ḥukkām* of Ibn 'Āsim, the *Risāla* of Ibn Abī Zayd, the *Mukhtaṣar* of Khalīl, the *Mudawwana* of Saḥnūn, and the *Irshād al-Sālik* of Ibn Askār. He will also study commentaries on such works, including ones of local authorship,[1] and through these will move from the study of the principles of law to that of case law. He will also work systematically on the Traditions, and especially on the great collections of Bukhārī and Muslim (the two *Ṣaḥīḥs*), many of which he will be required to commit to memory. At the completion of such further studies the *karamoko* becomes entitled to carry a staff and to wear the *burnūs*, a highly decorative hooded gown. He may still choose to teach, but is likely to acquire a position as *imām*, *qāḍī* or *muftī*. (In many

1400–1600 hours, sleep; 1600–1800 hours, formal instruction; 1800–1900 hours, bathing, eating, etc.; 1900–2100 hours, private prayer and study; 2100–0200 hours, sleep. In the formal classes the students will read aloud, with the teacher, a passage of the work in question. The teacher will next explain points of grammar and syntax, and comment on the general significance of the passage. The students will then raise questions, and will be questioned by the teacher.

[1] Attention may be drawn to the lengthy commentary on the *Irshād al-Sālik* of Ibn Askār written by Ḥamid Bābā b. al-Fāmī b. 'Umar of Jenne. I found a manuscript of this work, in 1100 folios, in Bobo-Dioulasso, where it is highly valued. A few pages in photocopy are accessioned as IASAR/64 in the Arabic Collection, Institute of African Studies, University of Ghana.

communities in which hereditary imāmates exist, the staff is handed on as a badge of office regardless of the educational attainments of the successor, and thus loses its true significance. Similarly Muslim chiefs, although lacking advanced education, sometimes regard their function in Muslim terms as that of *qāḍī* or judge, and so adopt the *burnūs* as a ceremonial dress. In some areas their example has been followed by pagan rulers.[1])

Being a *karamoko*, then, is an achievement role. 'A man is a *karamoko*', the Dyula say, 'because of his chain (*isnād*) for learning, not his chain for birth.' Although the '*ulamā*' class, in the region here under consideration, is a component part of Dyula society as such, it is nevertheless the case that the individual *karamoko* may be non-Dyula. Indeed, there are instances of locally famous scholars who have been sons of non-Dyula and even non-Muslim parents.[2] On the other hand, the *karamoko* of non-Dyula origins is almost inevitably drawn into Dyula society: in the course of his studies he will acquire the language of his hosts, will adopt a Malinke salutation-name (usually that of his teacher), and will probably arrange marriages which will link him affinally with his teachers or Dyula fellow students by giving or promising them one or more of his daughters. Although recruitment to the '*ulamā*' class is in this sense open, nevertheless there is a tendency for a tradition of learning to develop particularly strongly within certain families, which thus, generation after generation, provide *imāms*, teachers and jurisconsults.[3] In such families a father will always attempt to free at least one of his sons for advanced education: which, and when, will depend upon the general economic state of the *lu*. Dyula enterprise, whether commercial, agricultural or other, is organized on the basis of a work unit consisting essentially of a set of brothers, married or unmarried; their father while in life; their sons; and sometimes one or two other males who have become attached, perhaps affines, perhaps non-kin (e.g. in the past, slaves). This is the male component of the Dyula *lu*. An economically strong *lu* may spare the senior member of the set of

[1] Kyerematen (1964), pp. 2 and 4, shows the non-Muslim chief of Navrongo and the Muslim chief of Wa, both in northern Ghana, wearing the *burnūs*. In some communities which have apostasized, the staff and the *burnūs* of an ancestor have been enshrined and so worshipped as sacred objects. I recorded one such case for a Sanu (Bobo-Dyula) group in Bobo-Dioulasso, see field-notes, 9 May 1966.

[2] Field-notes, Bobo-Dioulasso, 9 May 1966: Mule of Doguna was converted, as 'Uthmān Tarawiri, and educated by the Dyula in Bobo-Dioulasso (late eighteenth to early nineteenth century). His son Muḥammad Tarawiri became a highly respected *karamoko*, and his grandson was the very well-known teacher, writer, and Tijani *muqaddam* al-Ḥājj Ṣāliḥ of Jenene in Ghana (d. 1931). Field-notes, Kintampo, 14 April 1966: an Isala educated by the Dyula of Bonduku, where he took the name al-Ḥamadu Kamaghatay on conversion, later becoming one of the most active teachers in Kintampo in the early part of this century.

[3] A well-known example of this is the (Wangara) Baghayughu family of Timbuktu, treated at length in Maḥmūd Kāti's *Ta'rīkh al-fattāsh*.

brothers for advanced studies—or, in other words, a father sends his eldest son to a *karmoko* for schooling. Exceptionally (see section 5 below) a *lu* will allow most of its members, at staggered intervals in time, to study to become *karamokos*: such is a 'clerical' *lu*, a major part of its revenues deriving from the professional activities of its members. More commonly, however, older brothers are required by their father to trade and farm in order to maintain the economic viability of the *lu*, and it is only a younger brother who can be released for studies. (The tendency for the *'ulamā'*—like the Church of England—to recruit from younger sons produces, especially in a polygamous society such as that of the Dyula, odd quantitative features in dynasties of, for example, *imāms*: in one case I met with, in 1966, the father, had he lived, would have been 120 years of age, the son in office was 65 years, and the 'chosen' grandson was 8.)

At no level in the whole educational system is the student's indebtedness to his teacher expressed in any fixed scale of fees: such would be regarded as contrary to the precept that teaching is engaged in not for financial gain but for the glory of the Faith.[1] It is, however, customary for the student's family to make gifts—described as *ṣadaqāt*—to the teacher at intervals fixed not in time but with reference to the progress made. I was shown in Wa one schedule which lists thirteen points in the study of *Tafsīr* at which gifts should be made.[2] The amount of such donations, however, is never laid down, but is regarded as depending upon the prosperity of the student's family. I have noted cases in which, on completion of the reading of the Qur'ān, the family was able to give only a few kola nuts or two or three fowls; another case (in or about 1926) where, on the same occasion, *ṣadaqāt* amounted to one cow, one sheep, a *burnūs*, trousers, cap and sandals, and about £40 in cash.[3] Pupils in the elementary Qur'ānic classes frequently assist their teacher on his farms or with domestic work—carrying water, chopping firewood, and the like. Sometimes an ambitious student from an impoverished background, in order to continue with his studies, may place himself in bondage to his teacher, becoming virtually part of the *lu* and undertaking a full work-load within it, and only emerging many years later as a fully fledged *karamoko*.

[1] This observation has to be qualified in the light of some recent changes. In the Fongo Qur'ānic school in Wa, for example, pupils now pay 1*s*. per month, which is used to remunerate the ten teachers.

[2] This schedule was written into the *isnād* for the study of *Tafsīr* of al-Ḥājj 'Abd al-Mu'min b. Sa'īd Tarawiri of Wa. IASAR/48 is a similar schedule for the reading of the Qur'ān.

[3] Field-notes, Kintampo, 14 April 1966.

3. THE 'ISNĀDS' AND THE SAGHANUGHU

As noted above, on completion of his studies the *karamoko* is awarded an *isnād*. The following sections are based upon a study of forty-six *isnāds* collected randomly in the Ivory Coast, Ghana and Upper Volta. Photographic copies of many of these are deposited in the Arabic Collection, Institute of African Studies, University of Ghana.[1] Others it was necessary to examine in the field. All are in both Arabic script and language. None is awarded for the study of any work other than *Tafsīr*, *al-Shifā'* and *Muwaṭṭā'*. Some but not all are witnessed, and a few are adorned with a photograph of the student and sometimes of his teacher as a precaution against fraudulent use. All are greatly valued by their owners and are sometimes carried on the person, but more usually kept within the pages of the relevant book. In the nature of the case they are readily produced for inspection. The *isnāds* examined are listed at the end of this paper, and will be referred to by the serial letters ISN/.

An *isnād*, also often referred to as a *silsila* (with the same meaning in Arabic), is produced by adding the name of the student to the *isnād* of his teacher. It follows, then, that an *isnād* consists of a list of the names of successive teachers of a given work: with the exception of the most recent name in the chain, every person in it must have been taught by and must have taught at least one other person. An *isnād* may be stronger or weaker, that is, a chain is valued according to the esteem in which are held the various teachers whose names appear in it. It is not uncommon for a student who has obtained an *isnād* from one teacher subsequently to re-study the work under another and so obtain a second and stronger *isnād*; this may occur when the second teacher has himself a particularly high reputation or when the *isnād* which he issues is an especially estimable one. Althought the *isnād* itself seldom incorporates any useful assessment of a teacher's worth, descriptions such as *mu'allim*, *wālī*, *shaykh*, etc. being largely conventional, nevertheless an outstanding figure is usually independently commemorated through visits to his grave, poems in his praise, and prayers made in his name and written on scraps of paper which the devout carry about on their persons.[2]

The forty-six *isnāds* examined (see Appendix 1) all commence with living, or recently dead, persons. Six may be eliminated from further consideration, being second copies of others in the set.[3] Another six will be eliminated as

[1] Accessioned as IASAR/49; 50; 141; 162; 163; 175; 232; 295; 338; 339; 427; 438; 439; 444. Some of these contain more than one *isnād*.

[2] IASAR/164 has the names of twelve well-known early teachers. IASAR/446 has that of Muḥammad al-Muṣṭafā Saghanughu and his twelve sons. I have seen numerous copies of these and similar works.

[3] ISN/15 (ii); 16 (ii) and (iii); 17 (ii); 23 (ii); 37 (ii).

incomplete. One of these has only nine names, terminating in Muḥammad b. Aḥmad Taslīm (ISN/17(i)); three have only seven or eight names, terminating in Ṭāhir Saghanughu (ISN/34; 35; 36); and two have seven and nine names terminating in Abū Bakr Jabaghatay of Jenne (ISN/24; 37(i))—the latter a well-known figure probably of the late eighteenth century who appears among the teachers of al-Ḥājj Sālim Kasamba (*c.* 1745–1836/7) (Marty 1921: 107).[1] The remaining thirty-four *isnāds* are alike in all running back to Imām Mālik b. Anas (d. 795)—whose disciples founded the Māliki school of law—and through him to the Prophet. The unity of this group of *isnāds*, however, is more strongly evinced in their convergence on the later figure of Muḥammad al-Muṣṭafā b. al-ʻAbbās Saghanughu: that is, all include (allowing for copyists' errors) an identical list of nineteen teachers from Imām Mālik to Muḥammad al-Muṣṭafā inclusive, and only from that point onwards diverge into a number of different chains with between eleven and sixteen persons linking Muḥammad al-Muṣṭafā with living (or recently dead) *karamokos* (see Appendix II). The activities of Muḥammad al-Muṣṭafā, in other words, appear largely responsible for the form which the teaching of *Tafsīr*, *Muwaṭṭā'* and *al-Shifā'* has taken in the Dyula towns. Whatever other and perhaps earlier lines of transmission existed have been largely eliminated by a preference for *isnāds* through Muḥammad al-Muṣṭafā.

Fortunately Muḥammad al-Muṣṭafā Saghanughu is readily identifiable. He is to this day a figure highly revered by the Dyula, who frequently carry about with them prayers written in his name and in the names of each of his twelve sons. His grave at Boron in the north-central Ivory Coast is still a centre of local pilgrimage. Manuscript sources give the date of his death as 1190 A.H., 1776/7 A.D., and as 1168 A.H., 1754/5 A.D.[2] With reservations, I shall prefer the former date as the more compatible with what is known of the chronology of his sons. Muḥammad al-Muṣṭafā's father was al-ʻAbbās Saghanughu, whose grave is at Kani in the Ivory Coast, some forty-five miles west of Boron (*Dukhūl al-Islām*). One source reports the year of his death as 1178 A.H., 1764/5 (*Dukhūl al-Islām*). He is not regarded as having been a man of learning, and indeed the *isnāds* show that Muḥammad al-Muṣṭafā was taught not by his father but by his grandfather, Muḥammad al-Ḥāfiẓ Saghanughu (whose grave is at Koro, in the Ivory Coast near the Guinea frontier).[3] The family was descended from al-Ḥājj ʻUṯẖmān

1 The dates are taken from the *Ta'rīkh al-Madaniyyu* (IASAR/451).

2 The *Dukhūl al-Islām* gives 1190 A.H. The Muftī of Bobo-Dioulasso, al-Ḥājj Muḥammad Saghanughu, showed me a work from his library which gave the date 1168. The Muftī drew on this work in his recent *Ta'rīkh 'Ilm*, but has corrected 1168 to 1108. This seems a quite unacceptable revision.

3 See the *Ta'rīkh al-Islām fī Būbū*, ch. VII. The *Dukhūl al-Islām* seems in error on this point.

Saghanughu, who is said to have left 'Mande Kaba', i.e. the ancient Malinke centre of Kangaba on the Upper Niger, because of pagan practices there, and to have resettled at Mafarru, a town which has now vanished but which seems to have been in the mountainous region south-east of Kankan in Guinea.[1] The *Ta'rīkh al-Islām fī Būbū* gives the date of al-Ḥājj 'Uthmān's pilgrimage as 1009 A.H., 1600/1 A.D., but the authority for this seems doubtful.

Communities using the salutation-name Saghanughu (Sakanughu, Sakanuwu, etc.) are to be found in many parts of the Western Sudan. To the west, one group is localized near Tambacounda in Senegal;[2] to the east, another in Wagadugu in Mossi country (see Levtzion 1968: 164–5). In Malian tradition as narrated by the griots, the Saghanughu are classed among the five original Muslim lineages of the Mande world (Dieterlen 1957: 125). The group under consideration in this paper appears to have moved, in the course of the seventeenth and eighteenth centuries, out of metropolitan Mali and across the network of southerly Muslim trading towns: Samatiguila, Koro, Kani,[3] Boron (see Fig. 1). Muḥammad al-Muṣṭafā Saghanughu himself is reported to have taught at Samatiguila, at the invitation of the Kasamba and Jabi *'ulamā'* there, before retiring to Boron.[4] His family continued the dispersion. The eldest son al-'Abbās settled in Kong at the request of its Watara rulers, became *imām*, and died there in 1215 A.H., 1801 A.D.[5] Another son, Sa'īd, became *imām* in Bobo-Dioulasso where he had settled in 1177 A.H., 1746 A.D.;[6] he was joined by his brother Ibrāhīm, who became *imām* in turn and died there in 1241 A.H., 1825/6 A.D.[7] Two brothers of Muḥammad al-Muṣṭafā, 'Uthmān and Aḥmad Saghanughu, appear to have established a further branch of the family in the Dafin country, around Safane near the northern bend of the Black Volta.[8] Wherever they settled, the Saghanughu *karamokos*

[1] Field-notes, Bobo-Dioulasso, 8 May 1966. Many Dyula groups preserve stories of having left Kangaba—always called Mande-Kaba—because of its paganism. The *Ta'rīkh Ahl Tarawiri min Mandi*, which I was shown in Wa, has a similar account of the emigration of Tarawiri groups from Kangaba (see field-notes, Wa, 3 August 1964).

[2] Professor P. Curtin has recently found a history of the Saghanughu of Soudouta, near Tambacounda; see *Fonds Curtin*, IFAN, Dakar.

[3] Kani was an important kola mart: see Caillié (1830), I, pp. 331, 339, 345.

[4] Field-notes, Bobo-Dioulasso, 10 May 1966.

[5] On Tuesday, 8 Dhū 'l-hijjat, after afternoon prayer, according to an obituary note by his son 'Umar penned on the cover of a work on syntax in the library of the Muftī of Bobo-Dioulasso, al-Ḥājj Muḥammad Saghanughu.

[6] According to both the *Ta'rīkh 'Ilm* and the *Ta'rīkh al-Islām fī Būbū*, apparently following a note by al-'Abbās, brother of Sa'īd, on Tuesday, 9 Rajab. Another MS seen in Bobo-Dioulasso, however, offers the alternative dates 1168 and 1188 A.H. (see field-notes, Bobo-Dioulasso, 12 May 1966).

[7] Field-notes, Bobo-Dioulasso, 8 May 1966. The *Dukhūl al-Islām* gives the date 1224 A.H., but this seems incompatible with, for example, Ibrāhīm's apparent association with al-Ḥājj 'Umar al-Fūtī mentioned in the same work.

[8] *Ta'rīkh 'Ilm*; field-notes, Wahabu, 14 May 1966.

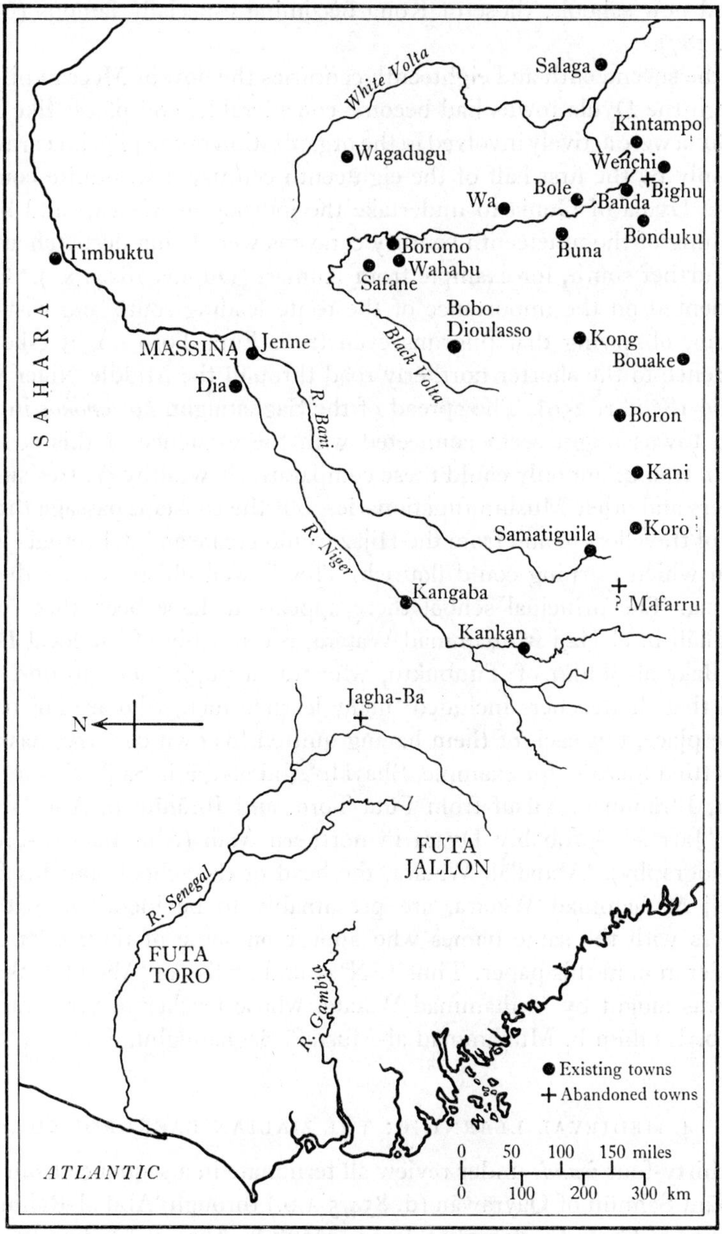

Salaga
White Volta
Kintampo
Wagadugu
Wenchi
Bole
Bighu
Wa
Banda
Bonduku
Boromo
Buna
Timbuktu
Wahabu
Safane
SAHARA
Bobo-
Dioulasso
MASSINA
Jenne
Kong
Black Volta
Bouake
Dia
R. Bani
Boron
Kani
Koro
Samatiguila
R. Niger
? Mafarru
Kangaba
Kankan
Jagha-Ba
N
FUTA
JALLON
R. Senegal
FUTA
TORO
R. Gambia
Existing towns
Abandoned towns
0 50 100 150 miles
0 100 200 300 km
ATLANTIC

Fig. 1.

opened new schools, those of Kong becoming especially famous (Marty, 1922: 187).

In the seventeenth and eighteenth centuries the flow of Meccan pilgrims through the Dyula towns had become considerable, and places like Kong and Buna were actively involved in the organization of the pilgrim caravans.[1] Certainly by the first half of the eighteenth century it was quite common for the Dyula of Gonja to undertake the journey to Mecca,[2] and by the beginning of the nineteenth century caravans were being despatched from even further south, for example from Kumasi (Dupuis 1824: xv).[3] Caillié commented on the importance of the route leading south and east from Kankan, observing that pilgrims even from Futa Toro might take it in preference to the shorter northerly road through the Middle Niger valley (Caillié 1830: I, 259). The spread of the Saghanughu *karamokos* into the Dyula towns might seem connected with the existence of this southern pilgrim traffic: not only could these comparatively wealthy centres support teachers and other Muslim functionaries, but the constant passage through them of travellers to and from the Hijaz would create an intellectual climate within which learning could flourish. This is well illustrated by the case of Buna. The principal school there appears to have been that run by ʻAbdallāh b. al-Ḥājj Muḥammad Watara, presumably of the local Dyula. Abū Bakr al-Ṣiddīq of Timbuktu, who was a pupil there around 1800, noted that the teachers included 'many learned men, who are not natives of one place, but each of them having quitted his own country, has come and settled there'—for example, Shaykh ʻAbd al-Qādir Sankari from Futa Jallon, Ibrāhīm b. Yūsuf from Futa Toro, and Ibrāhīm b. Abī 'l-Ḥasan from 'Jarrah'—probably Dyara in northern Mali (Abū Bakr al-Ṣiddīq: autobiography). ʻAbdallāh Watara, the head of the school, and his father al-Ḥājj Muḥammad Watara, are presumably to be identified with the teachers with the same names who appear on some of the *isnāds* under consideration in this paper. Thus ISN/25 and 27 list an ʻAbdallāh Watara, who was taught by Muḥammad Watara, whose teacher in turn was Abū Bakr b. Ibrāhīm b. Muḥammad al-Muṣṭafā Saghanughu.

4. MEDIEVAL LEARNING: THE MALIAN BACKGROUND

The thirty-four *isnāds* under review all terminate in a sequence from ʻAbd al-Salām Saḥnūn of Qayrawān (d. 854/5 A.D.) through ʻAbd al-Raḥmān b. al-Qāsim of Cairo (d. 806/7) to Imām Mālik b. Anas of Madina (d. 795),

[1] For Kong, see Caillié (1830), I, p. 418. For Buna, see Abū Bakr al-Ṣiddīq, autobiography.

[2] See *Kitāb Ghunjā*, entries for A.H. 1136; 1138; 1140; 1145; 1146; 1148; 1149; 1158.

[3] Dupuis also obtained in Kumasi a number of route-books for the use of the intending pilgrim, see pp. cxxiv–cxxxv.

Nāfi' (d. *c.* 735), 'Abdallāh b. 'Umar b. al-Khaṭṭāb (d. 693) and the Prophet. This is a well-known chain (Schacht 1950), usually considered the principal line of transmission of Mālikī teachings into North Africa and the Maghrib. Its popularity in West Africa may be due to the fact that Ibn Abī Zayd al-Qayrawānī (d. 996), whose *Risāla* is so widely read there, attached himself to it (Russell and Suhrawardy 1963: xx).

The first readily identifiable West African figure in the chains is al-Ḥājj Sālim Sūwarī. Between Saḥnūn of Qayrawān and al-Ḥājj Sālim four names are interposed: Ibn Isḥāq, Sīssī Kūri, Tūrī Kūri, and, most recent, al-'Abbās al-Mandawiyu.[1] Ibn Isḥāq is probably another North African figure, though I have been unable to identify him. The other three figures are considered by the Dyula scholars to be West African, and indeed 'Sīssī' and 'Tūrī' are presumably the Soninke names Sissay and Turay, while *al-Mandawiyu* means 'from Mande', i.e. the Malian. Since, as we shall see, al-Ḥājj Sālim Sūwarī probably belongs to the fifteenth century, there is clearly a large gap in the chain between the ninth-century North African teachers and the earliest of the West African ones. I incline to the view that written *isnāds* of the kind found in the Dyula towns were first awarded in West Africa by al-Ḥājj Sālim, who gave them form by adding to his own name and that of his teacher al-'Abbās the Malian two further conventionalized names in token of earlier groups of Soninke Sissay and Turay teachers, and then linked this rudimentary chain to the established North African one of Saḥnūn.[2]

In several works, though not ones independent of each other, the death of al-Ḥājj Sālim Sūwarī is placed in 542 A.H., 1147/8 A.D. (*Dukhūl al-Islām*; *Ta'rīkh 'Ilm*; etc.). I do not know the authority for this date, but it is almost certainly too early. Al-Ḥājj Sālim appears to belong to the period of the hegemony not of medieval Ghana but of the later Mali. He is successor rather than predecessor to those Mālikī jurisconsults who, as we know from al-'Umarī, were encouraged to settle in Mali by the ruler Mansa Sulaymān in the mid-fourteenth century (*Masālik al-Abṣār*, ch. x). For example, Kasamba Diakhanke genealogies list an al-Ḥājj Yūsuf Kasamba as a student of al-Ḥājj Sālim Sūwarī, and place him in the twelfth ascendant generation from Karamoko Qutubu Kasamba, who died in 1905 (*Ta'rīkh al-Madaniyya*; also Marty 1921: ch. III). Allowing between thirty and forty years for a generation, a fifteenth-century *floruit* for al-Ḥājj Sālim would seem indicated. His position in the *isnāds* is consistent with this

[1] This last name has become curiously corrupted in the *isnāds*, which have forms ranging from Fatiki al-Mandawiyu to Fatiki Mandighu, Manka, etc. The form I have preferred is from the *Ta'rīkh 'Ilm*.

[2] The problem of Tūrī Kūri exercised one Dyula writer, who noted on ISN/15 that he is said to be Sa'īd b. Murkula, otherwise Muḥammad al-abyaḍ.

view. The thirty-four chains have on average twenty-two transmissions from al-Ḥājj Sālim to living *karamokos*, in the range twenty to twenty-five but with a low deviation from the mean. If 1500 is taken as a notional date for the death of al-Ḥājj Sālim, then the average age-gap between a teacher and his pupils (a 'teaching generation') is a little over twenty years; if on the other hand we accept 1147/8 as correct, then an average teaching generation of about forty years is indicated. In the light of what has been said about the comparatively advanced age at which students commence higher studies, the former date seems eminently reasonable, the latter quite unlikely.

Al-Ḥājj Sālim Sūwarī is associated with the important early Western Sudanese Muslim centre of Jagha (Diakha)—also known as Jagha-Ba, 'big Jagha' (*Ta'rīkh al Madaniyya*; IASAR/164). According to Muslim tradition he moved to Jagha from Dia in Massina (apparently the Zāgharī of Ibn Baṭṭūṭa) at the time of an extensive migration of Soninke Muslims out of the Middle Niger valley and into the region between the headwaters of the Senegal and Niger rivers.[1] Jagha itself lay on the Bafing, the main tributary of the Senegal,[2] only about 150 miles from the old Malian centres such as Kangaba on the Upper Niger. Indeed, Valentim Fernandes writing at the beginning of the sixteenth century refers to 'Jaga' as the residence of the Mali kings (Fernandes, 1951 ed.: 37). In this he was presumably in error, though Jagha does appear to have been for a time one of the foremost Muslim towns in Mali. The *Ta'rīkh al-Madaniyyu* refers to the big city (*madīnat kabīr*) of Jagha in Bambuk as a major centre of Islamic teaching. The Malinke griots remember 'Diaghan, la ville des marabouts' (Niane 1960: 129). But the most interesting description of it is that given in the sixteenth-century *Ta'rīkh al-fattāsh*:

There was at the time of the supremacy of the kings of Mali a town of jurisconsults (*balad al-fuqahā'*) called Jagha-Ba (*Ja'ba*) situated in the interior of Malian territory. The king of Mali never entered it, and no one exercised authority there over and above the *qāḍī*. Whoever entered the town was safe from violence and molestation by the king. Even if he had slain one of the children of the king, the king could not claim compensation from him. It was known as the city of God.[3]

Al-Ḥājj Sālim is said to have been nicknamed Sūwarī—Soninke, 'red horse'—from the colour of the animal on which he made the pilgrimage to Mecca, his true *nasab* or salutation-name being the Soninke one of

[1] *Ta'rīkh al-Madaniyyu*. See also Monteil (1932), pp. 31–3; De Mézières (1949), pp. 20–4; Monteil (1953), pp. 361 ff.

[2] It is shown (as Diaka) on the map in Gallieni (1885), though presumably nothing of the old town survived at that date.

[3] Edition of 1913, Arabic text, p. 179; French text, p. 314.

Sissay (De Mézières 1949: 23). In the Soninke cosmologies he is listed among the sons of the founding ancestor Dinga: so bringing the Soninke maraboutic groups within the general schema (Monteil 1953: 372). The *Ta'rīkh al-Madaniyya* refers to him as '*shaykh* above all *shaykhs* of Jagha'. I have several times heard him described as having been 'Muftī for Mande', i.e. Mali. He must certainly have been one of the leading jurisconsults of that kingdom in the late medieval period. A number of his *fatwās*—rulings on points of law—are still referred to by the Dyula '*ulamā*', for example that on the marriage contract (*Dukhūl al-Islām*). He is also reported to have ruled on issues affecting Muslim communities in *bilād al-kufr*, pagan territory: a matter of particular concern to the far-ranging Malian traders. A full study of opinions regarded by the Dyula as based upon the legal authority of al-Ḥājj Sālim is needed.[1] In the absence of such, I would suggest very tentatively that two features broadly characteristic of Dyula thought may be derived from him: first, the tendency to reject *jihād*, battle, as an instrument of social and political change,[2] and second, subscription to the ideal of withdrawal from secular political activity.[3] Whatever his doctrinal positions, however, al-Ḥājj Sālim's main claims to innovation lie in the pedagogical field. Over a large part of West Africa the institutional framework within which teaching has been organized seems largely his work, and the high esteem in which learning is held—see the numerous works in its praise (for example IASAR/96; 106; 393)—must be attributed in no small part to the existence of regulations which militate against charlatanism and venality. The special place in the system held by the three works *Tafsīr al-Jalālayn*, *Muwaṭṭā'* and *al-Shifā'* may possibly date from al-Ḥājj Sālim's time,[4] and indeed if we are right about his *floruit* then the first of these may have been brought back to West Africa by him from Cairo, where it was completed in 1485. The award of the turban to those completing the study of the three works, and of the staff and *burnūs* to those qualifying in more advanced jurisprudence, are, as we have noted,

[1] I have often been assured that works by al-Ḥājj Sālim Sūwarī survive. Those which I have been shown, however, have turned out to be by the later al-Ḥājj Sālim Kasamba of Touba in Guinea, died 1836/7.

[2] The Dyula played little part in the West African *jihāds* of the nineteenth century. The Saghanughu '*ulamā*' of Bobo-Dioulasso are said to have advised al-Ḥājj 'Umar al-Fūtī against his *jihād*: field-notes, Bobo-Dioulasso, 8 May 1966.

[3] The special status of Jagha, as described in the *Ta'rīkh al-fattāsh*, exemplifies this. Although many Dyula do of course become involved in political activity, the older men still tend to deplore this. An interesting comment is to be found in *Répertoire de populations de l'A.O.F.*, Cercle de Kédougou (IFAN, Dakar): al-Ḥājj Sālim 'ayant à tout jamais condamné les ambitions politiques'.

[4] These three works were certainly taught in Timbuktu in the seventeenth century, as Maḥmūd Kāti and al-Sa'di show. For the state of learning in that town, and for the importance there of the Baghayughu Dyula teachers, see Hunwick (1964 and 1966).

regarded as his introductions,[1] and the practice of keeping written *isnāds* may also be attributable to him.

Three main lines for the transmission of learning are regarded by the Dyula as stemming from al-Ḥājj Sālim, namely, those through his three students Muḥammad Duguri, al-Ḥājj Yūsuf Kasamba, and Muḥammad Būni.[2] Of the first of these lines I know little: Muḥammad Duguri appears to have been associated with Koro in the western Ivory Coast and the *isnāds* of many of the Fufana teachers are said to pass through him. The second, al-Ḥājj Yūsuf, was responsible for the organization of learning among the western Diakhanke *'ulamā'* of the upper Gambia towns, Futa Jallon and elsewhere; the *Ta'rīkh al-Madaniyya* and other works deal with this chain.[3] The third student, Muḥammad Būni, is the one who appears on the thirty-four chains collected from the Dyula towns. He lived in the now vanished Mafarru, already mentioned (IASAR/164). Those three lines, however, do not account for all the groups having an original association with al-Ḥājj Sālim Sūwarī.[4] An interesting link between the Malian and Fulani *'ulamā'* is suggested in the Fulani work *Taariixa Almaaniibe Fuuta-Jaloo*, History of the Almamis of Futa Jallon, which reports that the ancestors of the *almamis* (i.e. *imāms*) settled there at the behest of al-Ḥājj Sālim of 'Jaakaabe' (Sow 1966: 210–11).

The *isnāds* list two teachers, an unidentified *faqīh* al-Mandawiyu and his pupil 'Umar Fufana (of Kankan), between Muḥammad Būni and the first of the Saghanughu, al-Ḥājj 'Uthmān, who, as we have seen, supposedly made the pilgrimage in 1600/1. The connection of the Saghanughu with learning, however, dates back much further: that is, al-Ḥājj Sālim is to be seen not as originating a tradition of learning in the Western Sudan, but as re-invigorating and restructuring an already existent one. Thus the *Ta'rīkh al-Sūdān* refers to a jurisconsult Muḥammad Saghanughu al-Wangara who settled in Jenne at the end of the fifteenth century.[5] The earliest reference to the Saghanughu, however, would seem to be that by Ibn Baṭṭūṭa, who visited the easterly Malian town of Zāgharī (usually presumed to be Dia in Massina) in 1352. Of it he noted: 'It is large and inhabited by black traders called Wanjarāta. With them are a certain number of white men who

1 *Ta'rīkh al-Islām fī Būbū*; *Dukhūl al-Islām*.

2 Field-notes, Bobo-Dioulasso, 10 May 1966.

3 The *Fonds Curtin*, IFAN, Dakar, contains three versions (nos. 1, 27, 29) of an MS which also deals with the Diakhanke *'ulamā'*. See also Marty (1921), ch. III. For the Diakhanke in general, see Smith (1965).

4 The work *Al-asmā' al-'ulamā' Zāghā* (*Fonds Curtin*, three versions, nos. 3, 23, 26) lists the names of twelve students of al-Ḥājj Sālim. These appear to be quite other than those named in Dyula sources.

5 Edition of 1900, Arabic text, pp. 16–19; French text, pp. 31–4. Corrections by Monteil (1965), p. 490. Muḥammad Saghanughu is said to have moved to Jenne from Biṭu, which may be the southern Dyula centre of Bighu, also sometimes referred to as Bitu.

belong to the schismatic and heretical sect known as the Ibāḍīs; they are called Ṣaghanaghu' (1922 edition: IV, 394–5). He adds that the 'Wanjarāta', that is, the Wangara or Dyula, used the Soninke name Turay. This fourteenth-century association between Ṣaghanaghu Ibāḍīs and Wangara traders looks structurally similar to the later position in towns such as Kong, where Saghanughu *'ulamā'* likewise lived within a Dyula trading community. If, as seems very likely, Ibn Baṭṭūṭa's Ṣaghanaghu and the later Saghanughu are one and the same, then it appears that by the middle of the fourteenth century they were not yet fully 'Sudanized' nor had their Ibāḍī affiliations withered away under the pressure of the dominant West African tradition of Sunni Māliki Islam. It may further reinforce the hypothesis of the connection of the Saghanughu with the Ibāḍīs of Ibn Baṭṭūṭa, who must certainly have been of Maghribi background, that in at least one extant line of Saghanughu tradition their genealogies are attached to Andalusian Ummayad ones (*Dukhūl al-Islām*; *Ta'rīkh 'Ilm*).

5. THE MODERN PERIOD: AL-'ABBĀS SAGHANUGHU TO THE PRESENT

Muḥammad al-Muṣṭafā Saghanughu died, as we have noted, at Boron probably in 1776/7. He is said to have married four free wives (all from prominent Western Sudanese *'ulamā'* families—Baghayughu of Timbuktu; Duguri of Koro; Fufana of Kankan; Saghanughu of Séguéla), and one slave wife from Casamanse.[1] By them he fathered twelve sons and nine daughters.[2] In each of the thirty-four *isnāds* considered in this paper the line of teachers passes through one or more of five of the sons of Muḥammad al-Muṣṭafā: al-'Abbās, Yaḥya, Sa'īd, Ibrāhīm and Muḥammad Fudimuru (also known as al-Muṣṭafā). All five removed from Boron to Kong,[3] where the eldest, al-'Abbās, started teaching and later became imām. The *isnāds* suggest that only al-'Abbās had been taught personally by his father, and that the younger sons received instruction through their elder brothers. The cohesion of the set of sons in this period is expressed strongly in some *isnāds* which show a chain passing through several of the brothers in succession; thus, for example, ISN/5 lists al-'Abbās as teacher of Yaḥya, Yaḥya as teacher of Ibrāhīm, and Ibrāhīm as teacher of Muḥammad Fudimuru. Subsequently the main Saghanughu school in Kong came under the direction of Muḥammad Fudimuru, youngest of all the twelve sons of Muḥammad al-Muṣṭafā. Of the elder brothers, al-'Abbās and Yaḥya remained in Kong, and Sa'īd and Ibrāhīm (as already

[1] Field-notes, Bobo-Dioulasso, 9 May 1966.
[2] *Ibid.* For a prayer made in the names of the twelve sons, see IASAR/446.
[3] Field-notes, Bobo-Dioulasso, 9 May 1966; Sunyani, 21 June 1966.

noted) moved to Bobo-Dioulasso where they established another school (see, for example, ISN/9; 40). Others of the twelve sons settled further afield, in Timbuktu, Casamanse and elsewhere, and no *isnāds* passing through them have been obtained from the region of the Dyula towns. I shall call the school maintained by Muḥammad Fudimuru the Karankara school, from the name of the quarter in which it was situated. Features of its early structure are shown in Table 1.

TABLE 1. *The Karankara school, Kong, in the nineteenth century (based on ISN/1; 5; 14; 20; 25)*

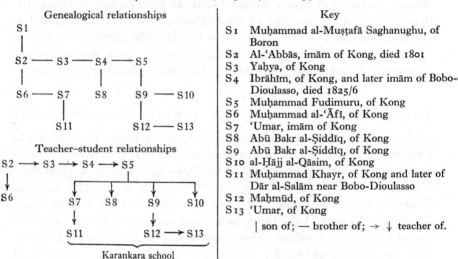

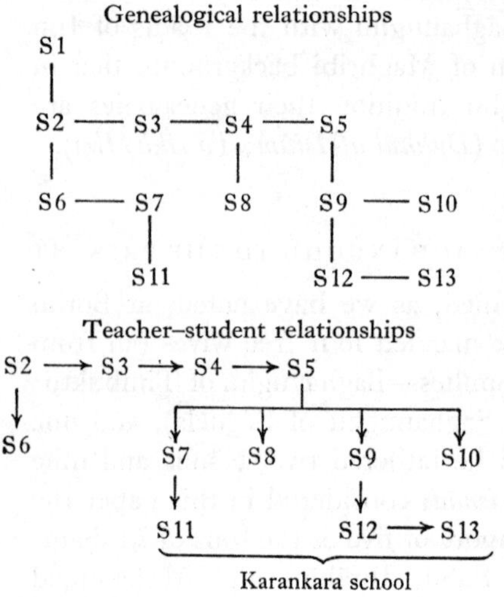

Key

S1	Muḥammad al-Muṣṭafā Saghanughu, of Boron
S2	Al-'Abbās, imām of Kong, died 1801
S3	Yaḥya, of Kong
S4	Ibrāhīm, of Kong, and later imām of Bobo-Dioulasso, died 1825/6
S5	Muḥammad Fudimuru, of Kong
S6	Muḥammad al-'Āfī, of Kong
S7	'Umar, imām of Kong
S8	Abū Bakr al-Ṣiddīq, of Kong
S9	Abū Bakr al-Ṣiddīq, of Kong
S10	al-Ḥājj al-Qāsim, of Kong
S11	Muḥammad Khayr, of Kong and later of Dār al-Salām near Bobo-Dioulasso
S12	Maḥmūd, of Kong
S13	'Umar, of Kong

| son of; — brother of; → ↓ teacher of.

The founding of a school, with the usual range of studies extending from elementary instruction in the reading and writing of Arabic to advanced work in the Islamic sciences, requires a heavy outlay in terms of human capital: primarily teachers; of physical capital: buildings, books, writing materials;[1] and of social capital: a fund of knowledge and skills on which rest the reputation and 'goodwill' of the institution. The organization of resources for such an enterprise is just the sort of corporate activity to which the Dyula *lu*—as with commerce—is highly adapted, and the foundation of schools appears always to have been accomplished within the *lu*

[1] The traditional Dyula flat-roofed buildings of sun-baked mud, using local materials, presented problems of manpower rather than of cash outlay. The modern and regrettable penchant for cement and corrugated iron, however, has reversed the position. Similarly libraries were formerly built up by the industry of young students working as copyists, the price of manuscripts putting them in general beyond the means of scholars. This too is changing with the increasing availability of printed texts from Middle Eastern and North African publishing houses.

framework, that is, within the agnatic group of a two- or three-generational span, the composition of which has been described above (pp. 170–1). Reference to Table 1 shows how the Karankara school developed around four teachers—further *isnāds* might reveal others—all trained by Muḥammad Fudimuru (S 5), namely, two of his sons (S 9, S 10) and two of his brothers' sons (S 7, S 8): a typical *lu* formation. Table 2 shows comparable features in the development of the Saghadughu (not to be confused with Saghanughu) school in Kong, over which Karamoko Alimuru Saghadughu presided in the early years of this century. It was described later by Marty when, under Alimuru's two brothers Ismā'īl and 'Abdallāh, it was in a state of decay, with only ten pupils (Marty 1922: 191–2).

TABLE 2. *The Saghadughu teachers of Kong (based on ISN/24; 37 (i) and (ii))*

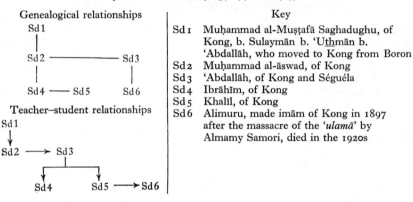

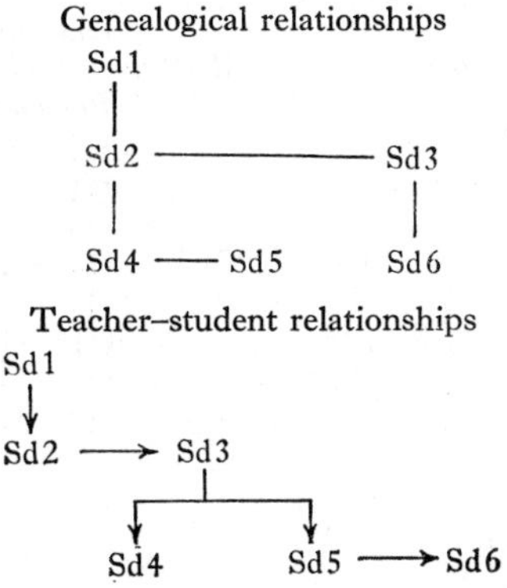

Key

Sd 1	Muḥammad al-Muṣṭafā Saghadughu, of Kong, b. Sulaymān b. 'Uthmān b. 'Abdallāh, who moved to Kong from Boron
Sd 2	Muḥammad al-āswad, of Kong
Sd 3	'Abdallāh, of Kong and Séguéla
Sd 4	Ibrāhīm, of Kong
Sd 5	Khalīl, of Kong
Sd 6	Alimuru, made imām of Kong in 1897 after the massacre of the *'ulamā'* by Almamy Samori, died in the 1920s

It is the case that most *isnāds* indicate not only teacher–student relationships but also bonds of close agnatic kinship: father, father's brother, and brother.[1] It is unusual, on the other hand, for an *isnād* to give the domicile of the teachers it names, and these data have to be obtained independently: usually from the testimony of living descendants of the persons in question. It will be apparent, however, from the examples already given, of the Saghanughu and Saghadughu teachers of Kong, that when a close correspondence is found in the chains between the pattern of genealogical relationships and that of teacher–student relationships, then this is *prima facie* evidence of the foundation of a school by corporate *lu* enterprise. But the existence of such a school has to be verified by its identification in the field. This procedure is illustrated further by Table 3, which shows the

[1] Patrilateral parallel cousins are described as 'brothers' but may be distinguished from real brothers by the filiation given: thus A son of X and B son of Y are classificatory brothers when X and Y are real brothers. Very occasionally the *isnāds* indicate matrilateral relationship, usually mother's brother, e.g. ISN/8.

antecedents, as revealed in the *isnāds*, of three twentieth-century schools, namely, those of the Kunatay *'ulamā'* of Kong and of the Timitay and Qunbala (or Gbani) of Bonduku. According to Marty's survey of Muslim communities in the Ivory Coast, in the 1910s, the Kunatay school, then under Karamoko Wiḍi (Oulé), was (like everything else in Kong after the massacre of its *'ulamā'* in 1897) in a state of decline, with only five pupils. The parent Timitay school in Bonduku, under Imām Sa'īd Kunandi, had about twenty pupils in the elementary Qur'ānic classes and also ran advanced courses, while a second Timitay school under Karamoko Timitay —probably Abū Bakr (T 13)—was of similar size. Finally the Qunbala school, then under 'Abdallāh (Q 5), had about fifty pupils (Marty 1922: 197, 223–6).

TABLE 3. *Three twentieth-century Dyula schools, showing their interconnection (based on ISN/16; 18; 20; 21; 23)*

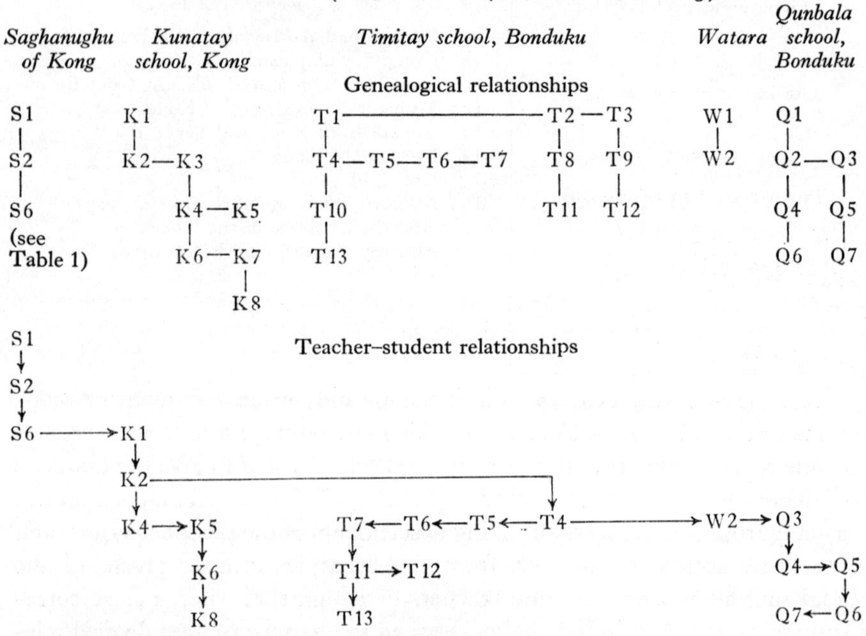

Key

Saghanughu	See Table 1.
Kunatay	K1: al -Ḥasan; K2: 'Umar, alias Alimuru; K3: name not known; K4: al-Ḥasan; K5: Alfa 'Umar; K6: Karamoko Wiḍi; K7: 'Abd al-Qādir; K8: al-Ḥājj al-Ḥasan (of Kong and later of Wenchi).
Timitay	T1: Muḥammad; T2: Sa'īd; T3: 'Abd al-Raḥmān; T4: 'Abd al-Qādir; T5: Sa'īd; T6: Ibrāhīm; T7: Ismā'īl; T8: Mālik; T9: Ibrāhīm; T10: al-Ḥasan; T11: Sa'īd Kunandi; T12: al-Ḥājj Muḥammad; T13: Abū Bakr.
Watara	W1: 'Umar Kunandi; W2: Ibrāhīm.
Qunbala	Q1: 'Abdallāh; Q2: al-Ḥājj 'Abd al-Raḥmān; Q3: 'Ali; Q4: Muḥammad; Q5: 'Abdallāh; Q6: 'Abdallāh; Q7: al-Ḥājj Dāwūd.

It must be stressed that the economic activity of *lu* members is diversified, and that teaching—even in a lineage with a strong tradition of learning—does not exclude a continuing participation in commerce and agriculture. But the foundation of a school, as will be apparent from the examples considered, places a heavy burden upon the resources of the *lu* by involving most or many of its adult male members for much of their time in a venture which, however rewarding socially, does not yield economic returns commensurate with those from, for instance, trade. Involvement at this level, therefore, ceases once the school is fully established. The changes that occur are 'age-specific': the description of them will vary according to whether the senior or junior age-set in the *lu* is taken as the point of reference. In the first case, at the level of the senior set of brothers, responsibility for direction of an established school is assumed by one brother and indeed frequently by a younger one—as exemplified in the Kong Saghanughu teachers S2–5 in Table 1 and the Bonduku Timitay teachers T4–7 in Table 3. In this phase of development an elder brother may choose to secede from the group, that is, to settle elsewhere and start trading, farming or teaching in his own right—as Ibrāhīm Saghanughu (S4 in Table 1) and his brother Sa'īd (not shown) left Kong for Bobo-Dioulasso. In such cases the secessionary brother or brothers become dissociated from the corporate activities of the parent body, though the high degree of collaboration which often obtains between them helps to sustain those extensive networks of mercantile and scholarly enterprise so characteristic of the Dyula. Other brothers may remain but, withdrawing from involvement in the activities of the school, will devote themselves to trading, farming or, perhaps, the discharge of official functions as imāms, *qāḍīs*, and the like. The reorganization of tasks involved in this phase of development is usually accompanied by fission of the *lu*, that is, the elder brothers with wives, sons and other dependants establish their own households, and in this way new *lus* are formed of which only the one remains (residually) involved with the school. The several *lus*, however, continue as parts of a more extended group, known in Dyula as the *so*, and a measure of corporate activity may survive at this level, particularly in the commercial sphere, since an established business involved in long-distance trade (unlike an established school) frequently requires more agents than the individual *lu* is able to provide.[1]

If these same processes are looked at with the junior generation within

[1] A still more inclusive unit is known in Dyula as the *kabula*, from the Arabic *qabīla*, 'tribe'. The *kabula* often forms a distinct quarter within a town. Common social and political interests, rather than corporate economic enterprises, bind together the various *sos* that comprise it. For this and more extended groupings, see Tauxier (1921), part IV, ch. II.

the parent *lu* as the point of reference, then the changes that occur once a school is fully established appear differently. First, there will be a tendency to educate fewer members of the generation to the high level of the *karamoko*, but only sufficient to provide replacements for older teachers lost through death or retirement (and these often the younger members, see above, p. 170). Educated persons surplus to establishment, as it were, may leave the *lu*, for example in response to an invitation from a community elsewhere in need of a *karamoko*, and may or may not return. Thus Muḥammad Khayr (Table 1: S 11) left Kong for Dār al-Salām (near Bobo-Dioulasso), where his descendants remain, at a time when the latter town suffered an acute shortage of scholars.[1] Secondly, while the number of students drawn from the *lu* itself falls, in so far as the school has established a reputation (has teachers with strong *isnāds*, good library resources, and the like) it will attract an increasing number of candidates from other communities who may spend several years studying there and, by their payments of *ṣadaqa*, will contribute materially to its economic viability.

The development cycle of the Dyula *lu* is extremely complex, partly as a result of the varied nature of the economic determinants of the processes of fission and secession briefly described above. The point is, however, that an understanding of these very processes is crucial to the whole question of the survival and multiplication of teaching institutions, and so to the wider issue of the spread of literacy and learning in the Dyula region. When the Saghanughu say that the Muslims of Banda, Bonduku, and Buna, for instance, or of Wa, Wahabu and Wenchi, are their *ṭalaba*, their students, they are drawing attention to the fact that in each of these places there are cadres of scholars responsible for the furtherance of learning and the preservation of Islamic values whose *isnāds* all stem, directly or indirectly, from those of the early Saghanughu teachers in Kong. In this section I have attempted to show the adaptability of Dyula forms of social organization to this general process. In a final example, that of the Timitay of Bonduku considered in greater detail, one cadre will be looked at in a somewhat less abstract setting.

Timitay settlement in Bonduku followed the dispersion of the Dyula from Bighu after the collapse of that southerly trading centre in the early eighteenth century.[2] In the second half of the century they obtained the imāmate of Bonduku, apparently from the Kamaghatay '*ulamā*' there,[3] and

[1] Field-notes, Dār al-Salām, 11 May 1966. Muḥammad Khayr is therefore described locally as a *mujaddid*, a renewer.

[2] Field-notes, Bonduku, 20 Dec. 1959; Bofie, 31 Dec. 1965 and 22 June 1966. The Timitay also make claims to ultimate Arab origins: see field-notes, Bonduku, 15 September 1964.

[3] Field-notes, Legon, 17 June 1966. For a list of (apparently) the earlier Kamaghatay *imāms*, see IASAR/81.

continue to hold it to the present time. The first Timitay *imām*, and probably one of the original settlers, was Shehu 'Abd al-Qādir. The genealogy in Table 3 shows the relationship to him of the Timitay *karamokos* who figure in the thirty-four *isnāds* considered, Muḥammad, Sa'īd and 'Abd al-Raḥmān (T 1–3) being his sons. He is always spoken of by the Timitay as a man of great learning,[1] but nothing is known of his education since no *isnād* through him has so far been found. More is known, however, of that of his eldest son Muḥammad, the second *imām* (Table 3: T 1); he was taught by Isḥāq b. Sulaymān Saghanughu, though whether in Kong, Bobo-Dioulasso or elsewhere is not clear.[2] He had as students—no doubt among others—his son 'Abd al-Qādir (Table 3: T 4), who became fourth *imām* of Bonduku, and 'U<u>th</u>mān b. Imām Sa'īd Tarawiri of Wa, whose descendants still preside over the Tamarimuni school there.[3] In this school the *isnād* through Muḥammad Timitay and Isḥāq Saghanughu is still issued to students (see ISN/40), but in Bonduku itself it appears now unknown, having been superseded by two later *isnāds* acquired by 'Abd al-Qādir b. Muḥammad Timitay. The first of these, for *Tafsīr*, passes through 'Umar b. al-Ḥasan Kunatay (Table 3: K 2), under whom 'Abd al-Qādir Timitay studied in Kong; this is the line shown in Table 3 and occurs in ISN/18 and 23. The second, for Imām Mālik's *Muwaṭṭā'*, passes through Muḥammad b. Ibrāhīm Watara, who was himself a student of Abū Bakr b. Ibrāhīm Saghanughu (Table 3: S 8) and taught probably in Buna;[4] this line is to be found in ISN/19, 25 and 33. The reinvigoration of learning that takes place when a *karamoko* resumes teaching after an absence spent in studying or restudying various books under a scholar of particular renown is the process described by the Dyula by the Arabic term *tajdīd*, renewal (see above, p. 165). They regard it as critical for the maintenance of contact between the dispersed cadres of scholars and the wider world of Muslim learning, and see in it one of their main safeguards against syncretism and heterodoxy, backsliding and possible apostasy. The fact of *tajdīd* in this sense, however, does mean that the *isnāds* cannot give a complete picture of the lines of transmission of knowledge of the Islamic sciences, since earlier chains become extinguished by later ones—as the

[1] See, for example, field-notes, Bonduku, 15 Sept. 1964.

[2] Isḥāq Saghanughu appears only in ISN/40 of those I have examined. My Saghanughu informants have been unable to identify him. His chain, however, reaches back in the usual manner to al-'Abbās of Kong and his father Muḥammad al-Muṣṭafā of Boron.

[3] 'U<u>th</u>mān Tarawiri's father, Imām Sa'īd of Wa, the effective founder of this school, was himself educated in Kong under al-'Abbās b. Muḥammad al-Muṣṭafā Saghanughu, see Wilks, *Research Review*, II, 2 (1966), pp. 65–6. Sa'īd probably returned to Wa on the death of his teacher in 1801.

[4] He is probably the al-Ḥājj Muḥammad Watara whose son 'Abdallāh presided over a school in Buna around 1800: see above, p. 176.

Timitay chain through Isḥāq Saghanughu was superseded by those through the Kunatay and Watara teachers and thus extinguished in Bonduku though, as it happens, surviving in Wa.

In the early years of this century the leading representative of the Timitay *'ulamā'* was Sa'īd Kunandi (Table 3: T 11). Born about 1858 and appointed ninth imām of Bonduku in 1894, Delafosse met him there in 1902 and has left a favourable and detailed appraisal of his erudition in Arabic.[1] Almost two decades later, when Marty described Bonduku, he remained the leading personality in the district: 'un marabout intélligent et lettré, qui lit et écrit assez correctement l'arabe littéraire, et n'est pas sans connaissances théologiques sur la religion' (to quote Marty's condescending description). With his duties as *imām*, teacher and Qādiriyya *muqaddam* he combined an active interest in the kola and cattle trades (Marty 1922: 221–4). The text survives of a circular addressed by him to 'the Muslims of the Bonduku region and particularly the Timitay', in which support is expressed for the Allied cause and regret for the Turkish position (Marty 1922: 488–9).[2]

The Timitay *isnāds* through the Kunatay and Watara continued to be issued by the schools in Bonduku run by two of Sa'īd Kunandi's pupils, Abū Bakr b. al-Ḥasan Timitay (Table 3: T 13) and al-Ḥājj Muḥammad b. Ibrāhīm (Table 3: T 12). The former, better known as Karamoko Sabruni, died in 1957. His great renown as a teacher attracted to him students from many of the Dyula towns. He is author of numerous poems on ethical, devotional and topical themes (IASAR/153; 224; 229; 230; 247). His mantle has now fallen on his pupil and nephew Muḥammad Timitay (Sabruni Muḥammad) of Barabo. The second of Sa'īd's students, al-Ḥājj Muḥammad, is the present and eleventh Timitay *imām* of Bonduku, and one of the most famous of modern Dyula scholars. He studied for two years at the Al-Azhar University in Cairo in the early 1950s, and is author of a collection of *fatwās*—legal rulings—published there.[3]

6. THE ROLE OF THE 'ULAMĀ'

The Dyula accept the ideal of universal literacy (in Arabic, though interest in both French and English is growing) as a highly desirable one, and in the nineteenth century many communities, as we have seen (p. 167), could

[1] See Delafosse (1910), pp. 188–90 (where he is mistakenly named Muḥammad Timitay).

[2] Sa'īd Kunandi's attitude to the French administration was equivocal, however, and in 1914 he spent some months in the then Gold Coast exploring the possibilities of re-settling the old Bighu site.

[3] Muḥammad Ibrāhīm al-Tīmī al-Qādirī al-Azharī, Muftī Bundūkū, *Al-jawāb al-shāfī 'an al-tanāzu' al-munāfī*, Cairo, 1374/1955.

count a high proportion of literates among their members. But while there was no evident barrier to the development, through the agency of the Qur'ānic schools, of general literacy, the growth of higher education was in contrast limited by basic economic factors, and the *'ulamā'* class consequently remained a small one. In 1919, for example, according to Marty, Kong and its neighbourhood had only thirty-nine teachers, Bonduku and neighbourhood thirty-eight, and Buna and neighbourhood twenty-two (Marty 1922: 490). While in such relatively prosperous towns a number of persons not actively engaged in teaching would have completed higher studies, the total number of *karamokos* could not greatly have exceeded that of teachers: the *'ulamā'* formed a small section of the urban population, and a numerically insignificant fraction of the total population of a region.

A detailed examination of the supply-and-demand mechanism in respect of the training of *karamokos* is beyond the scope of this paper. Basic economic growth, however, appears to create a steady rise in demand for men of learning. For example, a community previously existing at a subsistence level, but producing for the first time marketable surpluses, may decide to invite a *karamoko* to join it, and a delegation is sent to the nearest town to request the *imām* to find a suitable person. This process is important not only for the growth of literacy, but also for the spread of Islam as such, since it is not only Muslim communities but also sometimes pagan ones that see advantages in the acquisition of a *karamoko*. I was able to observe such a case over several years at the Isala village of Karipre in north-western Ghana, whose non-Muslim inhabitants sent requests for a *karamoko* to the authorities in Walembele some twenty-five miles away. They were fortunate in obtaining the services of Karamoko Sawatay Sissay, who was teaching there, and who had studied from about 1928 to 1934 in Kong under al-Ḥājj al-Qāsim Saghanughu (ISN/1; 2). Karamoko Sawatay built a small grass-roofed mosque in Karipre, the first there, and opened a Qur'ānic school. Today some of the elders of the village have begun to pray, and observe the fast of Ramaḍān, and many of their children attend the school regularly except at those times in the year when their assistance is necessary on the farms. Karamoko Sawatay has taught his elder brother *Tafsīr*, though he does not stay in the village, and a younger brother is being sent to Kong; both may in time settle in Karipre if a demand for more advanced instruction, or for further Qur'ānic classes, develops there.[1] A much earlier description of a similar situation is given by Mungo Park, who resided for six months in 1796–7 at Kamalia—a pagan Malinke village near Kangaba, on the outskirts of which a few Muslim traders and *'ulamā'* had settled. Park lodged in the house of the schoolmaster, Funkuma, whose

[1] Field-notes, Karipre, 7 March 1963.

library seems to have been a considerable one, and who taught the Qur'ān and Arabic to seventeen boys and two girls, mostly the children of pagan parents whose aim, as Park remarks, 'was their children's improvement' (Park 1799: 313–21). In the late nineteenth century Binger gave a most interesting account of the manner in which the *'ulamā'* of Kong were in process of establishing their influence, by the creation of schools, over the non-Muslim rural people:

They have established, from place to place, Kong families in all the villages on the roads from Kong, to Bobo-Dioulasso first, to Jenne next. They have taken fifty years to endow each pagan village with one or two Mande families. Each of these immigrants has organized a school, asking some of the inhabitants to send to it their children; then little by little, through their relations with Kong on the one hand, and with other commercial centres on the other, they have been able to render various services to the pagan chief of the district, winning his confidence and imperceptibly involving themselves in his affairs [Binger 1892: I, 327].

In recent years there has been discernible a reluctance on the part of the *karamokos* to leave the towns and settle in more remote places lacking such amenities as piped water and well-stocked stores. I have several times been asked by village elders to intercede on their behalf with the authorities in nearby towns, in an attempt to find a *karamoko* willing to settle with them.[1] Sometimes in such circumstances a pagan community will send one of its members to a town for education, wishing as Marty observes 'de posséder parmi elles un karamorho, qui "rachète leur fétichisme"' (Marty 1922: 268).

In contrast to the 'Malthusian' situation in some parts of North Africa, in the Dyula region of West Africa no considerable surplus of *karamokos* exists, and hence mendicant 'holy men', unless strangers, are uncommon. Indeed, an excess of demand over supply has been more usual, and an acute shortage of *karamokos* has occurred in two quite different contexts. The first arose when widespread conversions to Islam—as a result of *jihād* or of movements of Mahdist type—gave rise to a sudden demand for numerous *karamokos* to open new mosques, schools and courts; and it was the failure adequately to meet that demand that led in part to the loss of revolutionary drive in many such movements in West Africa, and to the re-emergence of older institutional forms under the new leadership. In this century, however, a similar rapid growth in the demand for *karamokos* has resulted from the urban explosion: the large mining and commercial centres particularly of the Ivory Coast and Ghana attract many immigrants from the Dyula towns, and each community, once established, turns to

[1] See, for example, field-notes, Sati, 17 May 1967.

its home town to provide it with an *imām* and with teachers. Some of the *'ulamā'* have responded to this challenge by greatly expanding their programmes of higher studies. Thus, for example, the Mufti al-Ḥājj Muḥammad Saghanughu of Bobo-Dioulasso had, by 1966, 'graduated' 214 students in *Tafsīr*, many of whom had become teachers in the large urban centres. Of fifty-six known students of al-Ḥājj 'Umar b. Abī Bakr of Salaga and Kete Krakye (d. 1934), a Hausa teacher with close connections with the Dyula *'ulamā'*, twenty-two later settled in towns with between 2,500 and 12,000 people, ten in ones with between 12,000 and 40,000, and eighteen in ones of over 40,000.[1]

Characteristic of Western Sudanese society is the presence within it of what are often described as castes: briefly, of groups highly specialized in function (blacksmiths, leather-workers, etc.), their social boundaries delimited in terms of, for example, marriage patterns, and their social cohesion expressed through sets of ritual observances, obligations and prohibitions.[2] As the jurisdiction of a land-owning group is exercised over a territorial 'parish', so that of a skilled craft group is exercised over an area of technological competence, for example, the blacksmiths in a locality over its high-temperature forced-draught fires; and as the ritual observances of the former are regulated by the custodian of its land-shrines, so those of the latter are regulated by, to take an example from the smiths, the custodian of the anvil and tools of the founder of the group. The *'ulamā'*, that is, the cadres of scholars in various localities, may be seen similarly as exercising control over a field of technological enterprise—writing: the alphabet, pens, ink, paper, etc.—and as organized under the ritual authority of their *imāms*. Indeed, in traditional Western Sudanese modes of thought the *'ulamā'* are regarded in just this way, and are usually ranked in status below the nobles of the ruling groups (who exercise managerial skills) but above such artisan groups as the smiths or leather-workers (Boyer 1953: 72–3). In virtue of their technological resources the *'ulamā'* assumed important functions in the Islamized courts of the early Sudanese kingdoms, Mali, Songhai, Bornu and the rest, and, conducting correspondence and keeping records, by their closeness to the throne attained positions of considerable political influence and sometimes authority. By the early nineteenth century their standing was high even in the great non-Muslim kingdoms such as that of the Bambara of Segu, where, as Park observed in 1805, the 'prime minister' was a Muslim (Park 1815: 145). A study of the influence of the

[1] Field-notes, Kete Krache, 15 June 1963.

[2] Many such groups are referred to in the *Ta'rīkh al-Sūdān* and *Ta'rīkh al-fattāsh*. Modern studies of them are surprisingly few, but see, for example, Boyer (1953), pp. 72–3; Paques (1954), pp. 63–4; Sidibé (1959), pp. 13–17. As Paques points out, the term 'caste' is misleading.

'ulamā' of Dyula and other origins in the Ashanti court at the same period has been published elsewhere (Wilks 1966: 318–41). The Western Sudanese *'ulamā'*, however, have seldom regarded their resources as primarily at the disposal of the ruling classes but rather at that of the communities of the Muslim faithful: the Dyula disinclination for secular political activity has been commented on above (p. 179). They have distinguished themselves from all other groups within Western Sudanese society, whether of higher or lower status, by their persisting efforts to obtain and maintain conformity (conversion and orthodoxy) between the local ritual observances, obligations and prohibitions and those of the universal Muslim community. To the Dyula, dispersed within a numerically preponderant non-Muslim population, this function has been seen as crucial to their very survival as distinct societies.

The Dyula *karamokos* describe themselves as the guardians of the *sunna* or way of life of their community, and seek to model this upon the Sunna of the Prophet Muḥammad. Their role within society is one of leadership, and they see their main concern as being with *mau'iẓa*, social and moral guidance. Hence recruitment to the *'ulamā'* class takes place on the basis of knowledge of the three works, the *Tafsīr al-Jalālayn* in explication of the Qur'ān, the *Muwaṭṭā'* of Imām Mālik in elucidation of legal matters, and *al-Shifā'* of 'Iyāḍ b. Mūsā in illustration of the example of the life of the Prophet. Guidance is exercised through various institutions such as the arbitration courts where *fatwās*, legal rulings, are issued on the basis of *ijmā'*, the consensus of learned opinion, but especially through the educational structure which has been the subject of this paper. Surely rightly, the Dyula *karamokos* have seen that the presence within society of an educated élite, the *'ulamā'*, is a necessary but not a sufficient condition of the preservation of Islamic values, but that the sufficient condition is realized in the juxtaposition of a scholarly élite and a broadly literate majority capable of responding to their leadership. The point was nicely made by Mungo Park over a century and a half ago:

> By establishing small schools in the different towns, where many of the Pagan as well as Mahomedan children are taught to read the Koran, and instructed in the tenets of the Prophet, the Mahomedan priests fix a bias on the minds, and form the character of their young disciples, which no accidents of life can ever afterwards remove or alter [Park 1799: 60].

The Dyula measure failure in leadership in terms of a regression through *ihmāl*, non-observance or 'backsliding', to ultimate *kufr*, unbelief. The symptoms are unmistakable. The field of application of Muslim law, particularly on marriage, divorce and inheritance, shrinks, and local customary procedures take its place (Anderson 1954: 266–7). The written word increasingly becomes valued not as a medium of communication but for its magical qualities, and the art of writing, if it is not lost completely, becomes an esoteric possession of a clique which is feared rather than respected. A Qur'ān may become regarded as a sacred object in its own right, no longer read but worshipped and perhaps, as among the Kamara of Larabanga in northern Ghana, only exposed to public view once in a year,[1] or an *imām's* staff of office may be enshrined and periodically purified and sacrificed to, as among the Sanu of Bobo-Dioulasso.[2] The fast of Ramaḍān may continue for a time to be observed, but as an expression of the group's ritual solidarity rather than as an obligation of Islam. Such trends the Dyula regard as the results of isolation, and attempt to prevent them by *tajdīd*, the reinvigoration of learning through continuing contact with scholars in other Muslim communities, and by the performance of the pilgrimage to Mecca by young and old alike, and by women as well as men.[3]

While such regressions from Islam have ended in some cases in ultimate apostasy and assimilation to non-Dyula cultures (see above, p. 165), in general the communities of the Dyula dispersion have not only preserved intact the Islamic content of their culture but have increasingly asserted their leadership over their non-Muslim neighbours. This phenomenon has impressed many observers. Thus Marty, in the earlier years of this century, noted how Imām Sa'īd Kunandi Timitay 'possessed great influence, not only in the Mande-Dyula Muslim community of Bonduku and the region, English as well as French, but also among the pagan population of the region, Abron and Kulango, chiefs and subjects, who came to him to ask advice' (Marty 1922: 222). Marty surmised that the situation resulted from French colonial policies towards Islam, but earlier Binger, for example, in 1888 had noted that in the states of Kong (whose ruler was a regular attendant at the *imām*'s classes for adults) even the chiefs of pagan villages would take no decisions without first consulting the nearest *karamoko* (Binger 1892: I, 326–7).

I wish in conclusion to express my deep indebtedness to the Mufti al-Ḥājj Muḥammad Saghanughu of Bobo-Dioulasso, who personifies today the intellectual vigour and charismatic leadership that for many centuries

[1] Field-notes, Larabanga, 19 June 1962; 9 March 1963; 2 May 1966. Over these few years the Kamara have achieved the return to a considerable measure of orthodoxy.

[2] Field-notes, Bobo-Dioulasso, 9 May 1966. The Sanu, who are Bobo-Dyula, began a return to orthodoxy in the later nineteenth century, and in this century have taken over from the Saghanughu the imāmate of the central mosque.

[3] The prevalence of the pilgrimage is of course closely linked with the economic circumstances of the community. In the later nineteenth century its performance seems to have been less common than in earlier times. In this century many Dyula make it, and a town such as Wa with a total population of about 15,000 probably has of the order of 200 *ḥājjis*.

have been typical of the Dyula *'ulamā'*. From his many writings, and at his feet, I have acquired much of the insight that has made this paper possible.

APPENDIX I

List of 'isnāds' examined

ISN/1 (M) 'Abbās Sawatay b. 'Abdallāh Sissay, of Karipre, studied in Kong. n.d. (IASAR/49)

ISN/2 (T) 'Abbās Sawatay b. 'Abdallāh Sissay, of Karipre, studied in Kong. n.d. (IASAR/50)

ISN/3 (M) Ṣiddīq b. Sa'īd b. Aḥmad b. al-'Abbās al-Subāṭi b. Imām Sa'īd Tarawiri, of Wa and Obuasi, studied in Kong. n.d.

ISN/4 (Sh) Ṣiddīq b. Sa'īd b. Aḥmad etc., of Wa and Obuasi, studied in Kong. n.d.

ISN/5 (Q) Ṣiddīq b. Sa'īd b. Aḥmad, etc., of Wa and Obuasi, studied in Kong. n.d.

ISN/6 (Q) Idrīs b. Ya'qūb Kunatay, of Sunyani, studied in Sunyani. n.d. (IASAR/141)

ISN/7 (T) al-Ḥājj 'Abd al-Raḥmān b. Imām Mālik b. 'Abd al-Raḥmān Bamba, of Wenchi, studied in Wenchi. n.d.

ISN/8 (T) al-Ḥājj Sa'īd b. 'Abd al-Raḥmān Bamba, of Wenchi, studied in Wenchi and Banda. n.d.

ISN/9 (T) al-Ḥājj Ḥusayn b. al-Ḥājj Isḥāq Bamba, of Menji (Kiyisi), studied in Menji. n.d.

ISN/10 (T) al-Ḥājj Adam b. Ṣāliḥ, of Wenchi, studied in Wenchi. n.d. (IASAR/439)

ISN/11 (T) Muḥammad Bamba, of Wenchi, studied in Wenchi. n.d. (IASAR/338)

ISN/12 (T) al-Ḥājj 'Abd al-Raḥmān b. Mukhtār Sienu, of Shukr li-'llāhi, studied in Loropeni. n.d.

ISN/13 (T) Muḥammad Fudimuru b. Muḥammad Saghanughu, of Dar al-Salām, studied in Kong. n.d.

ISN/14 (Q) Ibrāhīm b. Dāwūd Jani of Dār al-Salām, studied in Dār al-Salām. n.d. (IASAR/295)

ISN/15 (i), (ii) (M) Ibrāhīm b. Mu'ru Sanbi Kamaghatay, of Bonduku, studied in Bonduku. n.d. (IASAR/175)

ISN/16 (i), (ii), (iii) (Q) Ibrāhīm b. Mu'ru Sanbi Kamaghatay, of Bonduku, studied in Bonduku. dd. A.H. 1338. (IASAR/175)

ISN/17 (i), (ii) (Q) Ibrāhīm b. Mu'ru Sanbi Kamaghatay, of Bonduku, studied in Bonduku. n.d. (IASAR/175)

ISN/18 (Q) Harūn b. Bābā Watara, of Kintampo, studied in Bonduku. dd. 1360/1941.

ISN/19 (M) Harūn b. Bābā Watara, of Kintampo, studied in Bonduku. dd. 1360/1941.

ISN/20 (Q) 'Abd al-Raḥmān b. Hamīd Tarawiri, of Wa and Kumasi, studied in Bonduku. dd. 1370.

ISN/21 (T; M; Sh) al-Ḥājj Muḥammad b. Isḥāq Sūwāri, of Wenchi, studied in Wenchi. n.d.

ISN/22 (T; M; Sh) al-Ḥājj Aḥmad Bābā b. Sulaymān Bamba, of Wenchi, studied in Wenchi. dd. 1355.

ISN/23 (i), (ii) (T) al-Ḥājj 'Uthmān b. Isḥāq of Kintampo, studied in Bonduku. dd. 1961. (IASAR/162; 427)

ISN/24 (T) Sa'īd Fufana, of Wa, studied in Bole. n.d.

ISN/25 (Q) al-Ḥājj 'Abd al-Mū'min b. Sa'īd Tarawiri, of Wa, studied in Wa. dd. 1373.

ISN/26 (M) 'Abd al-Mū'min b. 'Umar Mādī, of Wa, studied in Kintampo. n.d.

ISN/27 (Q) Ya'qūb b. al-Ḥājj Sa'īd Tarawiri, of Wa, studied in Wa. n.d.

ISN/28 (T) Sulaymān b. al-Ḥājj 'Uthmān Tarawiri, of Wenchi, studied in Wenchi. n.d. (IASAR/438)

ISN/29 (T) al-Ḥājj Ibrāhīm b. al-Ḥājj Muḥammad Sa'īd, of Sunyani, studied in Wenchi. n.d. (IASAR/232)

ISN/30 (T) Muḥammad b. Harūn Tarawiri, of Wa, studied in Wenchi. n.d.

ISN/31 (Q) Ibrāhīm b. Mū'min b. Jibrīl, of Boromo, studied in Boromo. n.d.

ISN/32 (T) al-Ḥājj Ya'qūb, of Wenchi, studied in Wa. dd. 1375. (IASAR/339)

ISN/33 (M) al-Ḥājj 'Uthmān b. Isḥāq, of Kintampo, studied in Bonduku dd. 1961. (IASAR/163)

ISN/34 (Q) al-Ḥājj Mū'min Sanaf, of Ozani, studied in Boromo. n.d.

ISN/35 (Q) al-Ḥājj Khālid b. 'Umar b. Ibrāhīm Saghanughu, of Boromo, studied in Wahabu. n.d.

ISN/36 (Q) Adam b. Isḥāq Jayr, of Boromo, studied in Boromo. n.d.

ISN/37 (i), (ii) (Q) Imām Ibrāhīm, of Bonduku (?) n.d. (IASAR/162; 427)

ISN/38 (T) Aḥmād b. Ṣiddīq Saghanughu, of Wahabu, studied in Wa. n.d.

ISN/39 (T) 'Abd al-Mū'min b. Abī Bakr, of Kumasi, studied in Banda. n.d.

ISN/40 (Q) Abū Bakr al-Ṣiddīq b. 'Abd al-Mū'min Tarawiri, of Wa, studied in Wa. n.d.

Abbreviations: Q: *isnād* for the Qur'ān. T: *isnād* for *Tafsīr*. M: *isnād* for *Muwaṭṭā'*. Sh: *isnād* for *Al-Shifā'*— The documents described as *isnāds* for the Qur'ān seem in fact always to be for *Tafsīr al-Qur'ān*. The preponderance of *isnāds* for *Tafsīr* reflects various circumstances: (i) it is regarded as the most basic of the three works, and some discontinue studies, temporarily or permanently, after completing it; (ii) a student reading all three works from one teacher may be awarded only the one *isnād*, usually that for *Tafsīr*; and (iii) a *karamoko* frequently keeps his *isnād* for *Tafsīr* within the covers of his Qur'ān, and, since this is always at his side, is most likely to produce this *isnād* when approached.

APPENDIX II

The early chain to Muḥammad al-Muṣṭafā Saghanughu of Boron (preferred readings from collated 'isnāds')

Muḥammad al-Muṣṭafā b. al-'Abbās Saghanughu, from
Muḥammad al-'Āfi (al-Ḥāfiẓ) Saghanughu, from
Al-Ḥājj Muḥammad Saghanughu, from
Imām 'Uthmān Saghanughu, from
Al-Ḥājj Muḥammad Saghanughu, from
Abū Bakr Saghanughu, from
Muḥammad Tarawiri, from
Al-Ḥājj 'Uthmān Saghanughu, from
'Umar Fūfāna, from
Mandi Kūri (al-Mandawiyu), from
Muḥammad al-Būni, from
Al-Ḥājj Sālim Sūwarī, from
Fatiki al-Mandawiyu, from
Tūrī Kūri, from
Sīssī Kūri, from
Ibn Isḥāq, from
'Abd al-Salām Saḥnūn, from
'Abd al-Raḥmān b. al-Qāsim, from
Imām Mālik b. Anas, from
Nafi', from
'Abdallāh b. 'Umar, from
The Prophet

Translations of first sections of four 'isnāds', showing convergence upon Muḥammad al-Muṣṭafā Saghanughu of Boron

ISN/9: 'Isnād' through the Bamba teachers of Menji and Banda

'...al-Ḥājj al-Ḥusayn b. al-Ḥājj Isḥāq Ba'ba [Bamba] of the town of Kiyisi [Menji] learned (*akhadha 'an*) *Tafsīr al-Qur'ān* from the very learned al-Ḥājj Yaḥya b. Muḥammad Ba'ba of Kiyisi, and he learned *Tafsīr al-Qur'ān* from the very learned al-Ḥājj Mahama, and he learned it from his father Imām Sa'īd al-Bābi [Bamba] of Fughulā [Banda], and he from the great *shaykh* 'Umar al-Bābi of the town of Fughulā, and he from al-Ḥājj al-Sanūsi al-Ṭūri, and he from his father the learned Sa'īd al-Ṭūri in the town of Ḍukuṣū [Lokoso], and he from the teacher Mukhtār Shaykh Sa'īd al-Sakanughu [Saghanughu] in the town of Julāṣū [Bobo-Dioulasso], and he from his brother Sayyid Yaḥya al-Sakanughu in the town of Qū [Kong], and he from his brother al-'Abbās al-Sakanughu, and he from his father the *shakyh* Muḥammad al-Muṣṭafā al-Sakanughu...'

(In all Bamba *isnāds* the teacher Ibrāhīm b. Muḥammad al-Muṣṭafā has become displaced into an earlier part of the chain, but should probably appear between Sa'īd Ṭūri and Sa'īd Saghanughu.)

ISN/15 (i): 'Isnād' through the Qunbala teachers of Bonduku

'Here follows the *isnād* for *Muwaṭṭā'* for Ibrāhīm b. Mu'ru known as Ṣanbi Kamaghati who learned from 'Abdallāh b. 'Ali, Qunbala by descent (*nisba*), and he learned from Muḥammad b. al-Ḥājj 'Abd al-Raḥmān, Qunbala by descent, and he learned from 'Ali b. 'Abdallāh, Qunbala by descent, and he learned from Muḥammad b. Yūsuf Kamaghati, and he learned from Ibrāhīm b. al-Muṣṭafā Ṣaghaḍughu, and he learned from his brother Muḥammad Fi b. al-Muṣṭafā Ṣaghaḍughu, and he learned from Yaḥya b. al-'Abbās Sakanuqu [Saghanughu], and he learned from his father al-'Abbās b. Muḥammad Sakanuqu, and he learned from Sa'īd b. Muḥammad al-'Āfi Sakanuqu, and he learned from 'Umar b. al-'Abbās Sakanuqu, and he learned from Muḥammad b. al-Muṣṭafā Sakanuqu, and he learned from his brother Ibrāhīm b. al-Muṣṭafā Sakanuqu, and he learned from his brother Sa'īd [margin: Yaḥya] b. al-Muṣṭafā Sakanuqu, and he learned from his brother al-'Abbās b. al-Muṣṭafā Sakanuqu, and he learned from his father Muḥammad al-Muṣṭafā Sakanuqu...'

ISN/18: 'Isnād' through the Timitay teachers of Bonduku

'Here follows the *isnād* for the study of the noble Qur'ān for Harūn b. Bābā Watara, who learned from Abū Bakr Karamoko b. al-Ḥasan al-Timiṭi, who learned from Imām Kunadi [Kunandi] b. Mālik al-Timiṭi, who learned from Imām Ismā'īl b. Imām Muḥammad al-Timiṭi, who learned from his brother Imām Ibrāhīm b. Imām Muḥammad al-Timiṭi, who learned from his brother Imām Sa'īd b. Imām Muḥammad al-Timiṭi, who learned from his brother 'Abd al-Qādir al-Timiṭi, who learned from Aḍimuru Qunāti, who learned from his father al-Ḥasan Qunāti, who learned from Muḥammad al-'Āfi b. al-'Abbās Sakanughu, who learned from his father al-'Abbās b. al-Muṣṭafā Sakanughu, who learned from his father Muḥammad al-Muṣṭafā Sakanughu...'

ISN/20: 'Isnād' through the Qunbala teachers of Bonduku

'Here follows the *isnād* for the noble Qur'ān for 'Abd al-Raḥmān b. Shaykh Hamīd, Tarawiri by descent. He learned from al-Ḥājj Dāwūd b. 'Abdallāh, and he learned from his senior brother 'Abdallāh b. Muḥammad b. al-Ḥājj 'Abd al-Raḥmān Qunbala, and he learned from 'Abdallāh b. 'Ali Qunbala, and he learned from Muḥammad b. al-Ḥājj 'Abd al-Raḥmān Qunbala, and he learned from 'Ali b. 'Abdallāh Qunbala, and he learned from Ibrāhīm b. Muru Kunadi Watara, and he learned from 'Abd al-Qādir Timiṭi, and he learned from Aḍimuru Qunāti, and he learned from his father al-Ḥasan Qunāti, and he learned from Muḥammad al-'Āfi Sakanuqu, and he learned from his father al-'Abbās Sakanughu, and he learned from his father Muḥammad al-Muṣṭafā Sakanughu...'

RESTRICTED LITERACY IN NORTHERN GHANA

The second of the contributions relating to Islamic literacy is also on West Africa. I take one part of the area discussed in Wilks' essay, that is, northern Ghana, and attempt to treat this as a single social field in terms of the impact of writing on non-literate 'tribes' and partially literate states; for this I use as examples the LoDagaa and Gonja respectively. An attempt is also made to determine some of the factors making for restricted literacy, that is, literacy restricted by factors other than the technique of writing itself.

RESTRICTED LITERACY IN NORTHERN GHANA

by JACK GOODY

To treat the units they study as self-contained, ahistorical isolates, as many sociologists have done, is to neglect important areas of social action. Non-European societies have often become frozen by the time outside observers come to study them, through the imposition of colonial over-rule. But the reality of social relationships (except in a few isolated parts of the world) demands that each 'society', each tribe, each settlement, be treated as part of a field of interaction that takes account of neighbouring peoples, the mutual influence of town and village, the nature of long-distance trade and wider religious affiliations.

If we look at northern Ghana as such a field we find an area where states and acephalous tribes interact in a number of contexts. From the military point of view, the states (Gonja, Mamprusi, Dagomba, Wa and Nanumba) dominated the stage. Through their command of cavalry, the ruling groups of these kingdoms could raid deep into the 'uncontrolled' territory in order to seize slaves either for use of for export.

In these kingdoms there were four main estates of the realm, the rulers, the commoners (i.e. conquered 'tribal' peoples), the slaves (who were gradually incorporated), and the Muslims.

In addition to the Muslim estate, which consisted of a series of largely hereditary groups bearing patronymics derived from the Mande in the north-west or the Hausa in the north-east,[1] there were converts from other estates, especially the slaves and the rulers. A few chiefs even became Muslims, though such an exclusive allegiance naturally embarrassed them in the performance of the 'pagan' parts of their official duties and was not encouraged by the masses. Unlike areas on the Saharan fringe, the same political/religious dichotomy existed throughout the area (Marty 1922: 309). As well as the local converts, special mention must be made of another group, namely the strangers, mainly Muslim traders, since it is upon the position of this group that the question of literacy often turns.

The Ashanti hinterland (as Rattray called it) was the site of a number of important trading 'towns'. Physically, these towns were little different from the villages in which they were set, except that they were larger in

[1] What Marty (1922), p. 92, calls 'les musulmans de caste et de traditions', though the term 'caste' is most inappropriate.

size and contained one or more mosques, often in the striking Sudanese style.[1] But these dusty mud-brick towns were the focal points for an extensive network of trade whereby the main products of the forest zone, gold and kola, together with European imports, were exchanged for the livestock, minerals (especially salt and natron) and manufactures of the north.[2]

The main figures involved in this long-distance trade that stretched right across the Sahara to the Barbary Coast, and thence to Europe and the Middle East, were all Muslims; indeed only as Muslims, with co-religionists scattered along the trade routes, with the production of 'passports' and the interchange of letters, were they able to engage in these activities. As a result, the western Sudan was dotted with Muslim communities of varying size, and the larger of these settlements were constantly in touch with North African as well as other Sudanese towns; so that Muslim learning, even if it sometimes fell into decay, was always capable of revival.

This widespread network of trade and Islam had important effects upon the pre-colonial societies of northern Ghana, apparent in Binger's account of his visit to the Gonja town of Salaga in 1888. The town was no longer the great commercial centre it had earlier been, for the Ashanti had shifted the outlet for their kola to Kintampo, following the slaughter of their representatives in 1874. Nevertheless, the kola traders from the north usually passed through the town, which was still a meeting-place of learned men and indeed was enjoying a period of considerable literary activity. Among Binger's visitors were Sharīf Ibrāhīm of Timbuktu, Al-Ḥājj Muḥammad Hatti from Bornu, and Al-Ḥājj Jābiri, who was of Hausa origin. All three had been to Mecca (a journey said to take seven years by foot) and had acquired a considerable knowledge of geography. 'They had heard of France, Marseille, and knew that we had vast Islamic possessions in the north and west of Africa; moreover, they often called us by the title "friends of the Sultan of Istanbul".' Al-Ḥājj Hatti had visited Tripolitania and Tunisia, while Al-Ḥājj Jābiri, after staying a while in Istanbul, had travelled as far as Baghdad and Iraq (1892: II, 86).[3]

[1] In northern Ghana, the eastern limit of the Sudanese style of mosque-building is roughly the White Volta; broadly speaking, the line of the river also represents the boundary of the flat-roofed compound, the 'secret society' and the xylophone, all Mande 'traits'.

[2] For the network of trade routes see P. C. Meyer (1897) and R. Mauny (1961). In addition to the items mentioned, slaves, ivory, cloth, metals, beads and weapons were major items of trade. The manufactures of the north consisted mainly of cloth, beads and work in metals and leather, most of which had strong North African links.

[3] In 1817 Hutchinson encountered in Kumasi a Muslim from Jenne on the Niger who had apparently been an eyewitness at Nelson's victory over the French fleet in 1798; this occurred off the Egyptian coast. He also met with Sharīf Ibrāhīm from Bussa (northern Nigeria) who had made the pilgrimage to Mecca. While the Sharīf may not have compromised with local cults to the same extent as other local Muslims, he certainly dealt in Muslim charms (Bowdich 1819: 397, 407; Levtzion 1966: 114).

All these movements of Muslim pilgrims, of royal raiders, and of long-distance traders meant that even the simplest societies in northern Ghana could not be totally unaware of the existence of writing, and even of literate (or partially literate) societies. The attitudes of the stateless communities towards these societies were often extremely hostile, for it was their chiefs and traders who raided them for slaves or sought to dominate them politically. In return they raided the caravans that passed their villages, paying off their debt in murder and pillage.

How did these contacts affect the cultures of northern Ghana? The account that follows is based upon my fieldwork among the LoDagaa and the Gonja, and I begin by considering the first, an acephalous community. In an earlier account of the funerals of these 'pagan' farmers, I noted how the Muslim costume worn by chiefs in centralized societies was used to 'dress up' the corpse at funerals (1962: 70); even for these egalitarian enemies of state systems, chiefs had high prestige, being associated with wealth and display, with trading and raiding. What about writing itself? Among the LoDagaa, the influence of the written word was largely 'magical'. From the rafters of Meb's house in Birifu hung a shrine consisting of an oblong gourd from which various blackened fragments of paper were suspended on threads. These scraps, inscribed with Arabic characters, had been acquired from an itinerant mallam, or from the nearby trading settlement of Babile. Like believers in Islam, Meb associated these writings with the power of God, that is, of *Naangmin*, identified, it is important to note, with the Allah of Muslims and the Jehovah of Christians. But he did not claim to be a follower of the prophet, certainly not if such a commitment meant the rejection of traditional beliefs. It was rather that he saw in the Muslim's capacity to write a more effective means of supernatural communication as well as of human intercourse: the very fact that writing enables man to communicate over space and time makes it more effective as a way of getting in touch with distant deities.

When Bowdich, an employee of the Africa Company, visited Kumasi in 1817, he noted the widespread use of 'saphies', leather sachets containing a piece of paper on which had been written some Arabic characters, often a verse from the Qur'ān. Paper was consequently in great demand by Muslims. The contemporary correspondence between Muslims in Kumasi and Gonja recorded in the Copenhagen manuscripts is concerned not only with 'charms' and 'formulas' but also with the supply of paper on which to write them (Levtzion 1966: 119).

Saphy (or safi) is the Mandingo word for the kind of written charm known to the Arabs as *ḥirz*. Talismans of similar kind were found in Mesopotamia and throughout the Middle East—the Greek phylactery, the Latin amulet, and the Jewish *kemi'a*, the small leathern box containing Hebrew texts on vellum which is worn during the morning prayer as a reminder, it is said, of the obligation to keep the law. This phylactery also had value as an amulet or charm, encapsulating the word of God.[1] Very similar uses of the holy scriptures are found throughout the written world, in Mandaean society (Drower 1943: 149–81) as in Buddhist Tibet.

Thus the value of writing as a means of communication with the supernatural powers appears to have been recognized throughout northern Ghana, in acephalous communities as well as states, among pagans as well as Muslims, among the non-literate as well as the partially literate. Added to this, the eclecticism of African religions allowed room for the entry of new practices and beliefs seen to have pragmatic merits in solving man's diverse problems. It is therefore not surprising to find that most chiefs and headmen in northern Ghana, of whatever persuasion, purchase hats with leather saphies or silvered amulets stitched upon them, and these garments are seen as offering protection as well as prestige to the office-holder. The great war-coats of the Ashanti,[2] deemed capable of warding off the bullets of the enemy, were made in the same way and probably formed the most costly item in a chief's wardrobe—certainly this was one of the most valued services provided by the literate for the non-literate.[3]

The extent of the demand for these services is well illustrated in Bowdich's account of his expedition to Kumasi in 1817. He writes of Ashanti religion:

The most surprising superstition of the Ashantees, is their confidence in the fetishes or saphies they purchase so extravagantly from the Moors, believing firmly that they make them invulnerable and invincible in war, paralyse the hand of the enemy, shiver their weapons, divert the course of balls, render both sexes prolific, and avert all evils but sickness, (which they can only assuage,) and natural death [1819: 271].

The war coats on which these charms were sewn were both expensive and cumbrous. Of similar dresses among the Mandingo of the Senegal region, Jannequin, who visited the country in 1637, wrote that 'their bodies are so encumbered with these defences, that they are often unable to mount on horseback without assistance' (Bowdich 1819: 272).[4] The comfort, spiritual and bodily, was great, if not well founded, for 'several of the

1 The verses are Deut. vi. 4–9, xi. 13–21; Ex. xiii. 1–10, 11–16.

2 See the photograph of the *batakarikɛsɛɛ* smock in Dr A. A. Y. Kyerematen's book, *Panoply of Ghana* (London, 1964), p. 69

3 When I was staying in the Gonja town of Bole in 1966, the *imām* was engaged in sewing such a coat, which he offered me for £100; the price was high because of his high status, both as an *imām* and as a learned man.

4 Wilks points out that these heavy coats also had a practical effect in stopping missiles.

Ashantee captains offered to let us fire at them', and it was this confidence, Bowdich suggests, that enabled them to undertake their daring military enterprises.[1] 'The Ashantees believe that the constant prayers of the Moors, who have persuaded them that they converse with the Deity, invigorate themselves, and gradually waste the spirit and strength of their enemies' (Bowdich 1819: 272). And it would appear that these convictions about converse with the Deity (for again the Ashanti *Nyame* is not seen as distinct from the Muslim Allah or the Christian Jehovah) were stimulated by their actual control of a superior technique of human communication, namely, that of writing.[2]

Services of this high order were not given for nothing. 'A sheet of paper', Bowdich remarks, 'would support an inferior Moor in Coomassie for a month.' Baba, the Mamprusi Muslim from Gambaga, charged six ackies (about half an ounce of gold) for 'a small fetish of about six lines, sewn in a case of red cloth.' As for the military attire, the Ashanti ruler gave the king of Dagomba 'for the fetish or war coat of Apokoo, the value of thirty slaves'; for others (one of which he illustrates), less.

The ability to provide these exports gave the northern kingdoms, who were militarily dominated by the Ashanti, a certain countervailing strength. In 1744, the Ashanti armies invaded the north-west and thenceforth Dagomba and eastern Gonja were under an obligation to pay an annual tribute to the Ashanti king. Bowdich (1819: 235) regards the agreement reached as a triumph for the Dagomba: 'At the expense of an inconsiderable tribute, he established a commercial intercourse, which, his markets being regularly supplied from the interior, was both an advantage and security to him, from the great convenience to his warlike neighbours, whose superstition assenting to his great reputation for making saphies, and for augury, would not only augment his revenue, but insure him superior respect as a tributary.' In other words, the position as tributary gave these kingdoms an increase in trade, which included exports of a magico-religious kind.

The nature of this demand for literary magic in the region is discussed in Marty's study of Islam in the Ivory Coast (1922). The author remarks that, among the forest peoples, 'the only local traces...[of Islam]...are the amulets which the Agni buy at a high price from passing "marabouts" and which they carry along with fetishistic [i.e. pagan] charms and talismans. Thus on certain days Boa Kouassi [Kwesi], king of Indénié, appears crowned with a diadem of six triangular containers in gold and silver, which enclose Arabic amulets' (1922: 52).

[1] I have reported a similar case of battle confidence among the LoDagaa (Goody, 1957, p. 359).

[2] For a valuable discussion of Islam in Ashanti at this time, see Wilks (1966*b*).

This religious intermingling is in part a reflection of the patterns of external exchange that exist throughout the area. In the savannah region, the main purchasers, the seekers after goods to buy, were Muslims, whether Moors from North Africa, Hausas from the central Sudan, or 'Mande' from the west. Those who have most to sell are the southern pagans, because they control the scarce natural resources of the forest, kola and gold, as well as access to the European trading stations on the coast. The nature of the exchange relationships between these groups, in particular the desire of the northern trader to penetrate closer to the sources of wealth where prices are lower, has meant a constant interaction between the Muslim and pagan worlds and a continual modification of the cultures concerned. The first way in which the pagan scene is modified is through the absorption of Islamic magic (the element of Islam most easily absorbed), a process that may eventually lead to complete conversion; while the effect on Muslims is that traditional practices are incorporated or retained, possibly leading to apostasy, to a return to eclecticism, to a 'burying of the Koran' (Marty 1922: 150, 151, 165, 171). The wide dispersal of Muslims means that Islam is subjected to a 'dégradation perpétuelle' (Marty 1922: 343); moreover, in these southern savannahs they rarely held political power, even in some situations where they clearly possessed the capability in terms of firearms, though the position was different in the short-lived governments set up by Samory and Babatu.

This interpenetration over space produces, over time, a state of dynamic disequilibrium in which the balance of force generally lies with Islam, since it possesses both a superior communications technology and a wider network of commercial contacts. It is, moreover, the religion of the towns; indeed in the rural areas, where there is little extra-religious pay-off in being a Muslim, apostasy is always likely to take place; '"islamisme" est synonyme de commerce et "animisme" de vie agricole' (Marty 1922: 395).

At any particular time, the interpenetration takes the form of a 'mix', where the exchange of services is not only commercial, but political and religious as well. In the nineteenth century, in both the Ivory Coast (Marty 1922: 309) and in Ghana (e.g. Gonja, Goody 1967: 186–7), the rulers were mainly pagan, though they accepted many services from their spiritual advisers, who included Muslims and pagans alike. In religious terms, one aspect of the mix was the provision of Muslim talismans for pagan consumption. According to Marty, services of this kind were rendered by all Muslims in the Ivory Coast, whatever their status, though the form in which they did so varied. The more learned Muslims disapproved of their co-religionists who moved like commercial travellers among the pagan communities, using the hard-sell to dispose of their wares (Marty 1922:

437). For some Muslims, this was their principal occupation and one renowned mallam, Sidiki Koné, was considered by Marty to be 'un marabout au service des fétichistes, sans plus' (1922: 63).

Wherein lies the strength of Islam's appeal to the pagan? There are undoubted attractions: superior commerce, greater doctrinal certainty, but, above all, a superior technology in the intellectual domain, the technology of writing; 'et surtout', writes Marty, 'et plus que tout le reste le prestige du science, de l'instruction, de l'école, du livre, de l'écriture' (1922: 96), and he quotes René Caillié's account of his journey to Timbuktu (1827) to the effect that the pagan Bambara had plenty of respect both for the followers of Muḥammad and for their writing, which they looked upon as 'a kind of magic'. But, as we have seen, the magical uses arise out of the 'rational' advantages of a literate technology, and the great demand for Islamic magic (and other literate systems) reflects a recognition of this superiority in the sphere of communications.

I came across a second use of the written word by non-literates during my stay in Birifu in the early 1950s. Coming back to the village after an absence of several months, I paid a visit to a diviner called Oyie who had himself returned from Kumasi not long before. Oyie's technique differed considerably from that of other diviners among the LoDagaa and their neighbours, and indeed it may have drawn some of its power from known Islamic practices, since it involved the use of a book. He had in front of him some of the customary gear of the traditional diviner, assorted stones, the bark of the *kakaala* tree, and the L-shaped stick which the client grasps in order to be shown the truth. These objects are associated with the beings of the wild; the stones are from hill and river, the bark and stick from a special tree, and it is these three places, hill, river and tree, that are the main abodes of the *kontome*, these beings of the wild who trouble mankind but also assist him to understand the supernatural world, and who in the present instance were said to have taught their protégé how to read. For, in addition to the usual paraphernalia, Oyie had in front of him a small flat stool of alien shape and on this rested a school exercise-book which had been filled with sums of pounds, shillings and pence. Oyie held the book sideways with one hand and in the other grasped a pencil which hovered momentarily over the page, then darted from one figure to the next, as if he were adding up the horizontal rows rather than the vertical columns. Suddenly, while pointing to something in the figures, he says, 'See your cows' (or some similar phrase), rounds on his client, and barks out a question, his eyelids flickering rapidly as he does so. He proceeds to ask more questions. The pencil darts again, to be followed by another batch of questions. And then, to sum the situation up, he comes out with a succession of proverbs (*zukpaaro*) and witty sayings, while those sitting round mutter their approval of the rightness of these appeals to traditional wisdom.

Here again writing is used by the non-literate as a mode of communication with the supernatural powers. On the one hand, such practices have clear affinities with the use of graphic signs for magico-religious purposes, which is widespread in the western Sudan. The LoDagaa commonly employ the sign of the cross, rudely painted in medicinal water on a flattish stone, to guard their fields from danger of various kinds; the Dogon have a more elaborate repertory of signs (Griaule 1951). On the other hand, the specific features of the new technique result from the contact of an oral society with one that is making use (albeit in a limited way) of literate techniques.

Some glimpse of the immense impact writing can make on oral man may be gained from a passage in the eighteenth-century autobiography of an Ibo who was captured, sold to European traders, and transported to the Americas. The captive, Olaudah Equiano, was later brought to England, where he made his first close acquaintance with literacy in the shape of books that apparently 'talked'.

> I had often seen my master and Dick employed in reading, and I had a great curiosity to talk to the books as I thought they did, and so to learn how all things had a beginning: for that purpose I have often taken up a book and have talked to it and then put my ears to it, when alone, in hopes it would answer me: and I have been very much concerned when I found it remained silent [1967: 40].[1]

For non-literate cultures, in northern Ghana as throughout the world, the magic of the written word derived from its pragmatic value as a means of communication, from its association with a priesthood, and from the high prestige and technical achievements of the cultures of which it formed part.

But apart from the truly non-literate communities like the LoDagaa, where writing had only a very peripheral role in the religious life, northern Ghana (like the rest of the savannah country of the western Sudan) was the home of a number of kingdoms where literacy played a definite part.[2]

[1] This book was first published in London in 1789 under the title, *The Interesting Narrative of the Life of Olaudah Equiano, or Gustavus Vassa the African, written by himself*. But the incident is not 'original', for it appears in two other works written by Africans in the same period, in *A Narrative of the most remarkable particulars in the Life of James Albert Ukawsaw Gronniosaw* (Bath, 1770), and in Ottobah Cugoano's *Thoughts and Sentiments on the Evil and Wicked Traffic of Slavery* (1787), p. 80. As Equiano's editor, Paul Edwards, suggests, the story appears to have been a common one among Africans then resident in Britain (1967, p. 186).

[2] The distinction between non-literate 'tribes' and partially literate states is an over-simplification, for some small Muslim communities were also found scattered amongst

I turn now to describe the role of literacy in one such state (or former state), the kingdom of Gonja, and begin by recalling the distinction I made earlier between the older Gonja Muslims and the newer strangers, some of whom are settlers, others visitors.[1]

The older Muslims have unique access to the position of *imām* to the paramount and divisional chiefs, whose advisers they are. They are also the official representatives of the Islamic community *vis-à-vis* the ruling group. Apart from these political *imāms*, an office of the same name is found in the pre-Gonja settlements of Dokrupe and Larabanga. Only in the formerly important trading town of Salaga does the stranger community have its own *imām*, and there his role is largely an internal one.[2]

Today, the literacy rate among Gonja Muslims is low—on whatever basis it is calculated. At one time Gbuipe (Eng. Buipe) and its forerunner, the pre-Gonja town of Manwule, were important centres of Islam; Gbuipe is the burial-place of the legendary conqueror of Gonja, Ndewura Jakpa, and it is the Muslims of this town who supply the *imām* for the paramount chief; at the beginning of the nineteenth century its Muslim inhabitants had close connections with the Ashanti capital of Kumasi. But in the 1940s the Gonja paramount no longer appointed his *imām* from the town 'after the disgrace of the last Limam [*imām*] of Yabum who could not read the Arabic script' (Tomlinson 1954: MS. 30). In 1956 I knew only three men who could read at all: the population was small and the uses of literacy few. Formerly an important centre for the kola trade, it had now become a rural backwater with some 350 inhabitants.[3] Although one of the literate mallams took scholars (he had one boy living and farming with him), I saw no instruction take place during the many hours I spent in his house. Indeed the three

the Isala, the Dagarti (Dagaba) and similar peoples; indeed some pagan groups claim to have formerly adhered to Islam. There has clearly been a long history of intercourse and movement between the two kinds of society, in trading, raiding and the exchange of religious practice and belief. In certain respects the partially Islamic, partially literate, states constitute models of prestigious behaviour even for the 'tribal' peoples. But only in certain respects; in other ways, the 'tribal' groups organize their social actions in direct opposition to those of the worlds of chiefs and Muslims.

[1] A similar situation clearly obtained in Kumasi in 1817. When the king made a present of gold to the Muslims of the town 'for their services', they tried to exclude Sharīf Ibrāhīm because he was a stranger. Ibrāhīm demanded to be treated as equal in rank to Bābā, the leader of the local Muslims, since 'he was superior from his knowledge, and belonging to Mahomet's family'. Eventually he was given the same amount as Bābā, a sum of three periguins (Bowdich, 1819, p. 403).

[2] There is also an *imām* at the trading town of Ko on the road between Salaga and Tamale. For the distinction between the *imām* of the Friday prayer (*imām al-jum'a*) and the *imām* of the Chief (*imām al-bilād*), see Wilks (1966*b*, p. 336).

[3] In 1956 the position was undergoing further changes since a new north–south road was being constructed to run 7 miles east of the old town, and the administration were encouraging the inhabitants to move to the roadside; at this time, some 100 people were living in New Buipe, on the main road. At the time of the 1960 census, the population was: Old Buipe, 231; New Buipe, 426.

literates had all had their education elsewhere, at towns where stranger Muslims provided more adequate instruction (i.e. Salaga, Daboya and Prang). To acquire even the elements of literacy meant prolonged residence outside the local community. It should be added that the pattern of acquiring learning, here as elsewhere in the western Sudan, was peripatetic, and scholars moved from one learned man to the next in order to acquire greater knowledge. The movement of scholars from place to place is a notable feature of even the most advanced educational systems. But when the peripatetic system is so dominant and manifests itself at elementary levels of learning, this is a sign of the restricted nature of literacy; the movement of media has not yet effectively supplemented the movement of people essential to oral transmission.

One reason for the poverty of learning in Gbuipe lay in the changed economic situation. From being a large centre of trade, it now depended on subsistence farming and the sale of bush meat, and this was as true for Muslims as for commoners and chiefs. Though the divisional chief himself did not go to the farm, most other elders did so—in the rather spasmodic way that characterizes Gonja agriculture.

It is true that in more active centres of trade, the Gonja Muslims are more involved in farming than the strangers; for even when the former do engage in commerce (and some young men spend periods 'walking about' to peddle goods), they are largely dependent upon the long-distance traders, the strangers with their wider range of contacts, the *madugu* (Hausa, 'caravan leaders') who have settled down to act as local agents and landlords for their fellow countrymen. And since the localized Muslims are less dependent upon trade they also tend to have less use for literacy.

I do not wish to imply that writing was employed in any major way in commercial transactions; bargaining lay largely in the realm of oral intercourse, calculation in the sphere of mental arithmetic.[1] Indeed, one essential difference between the market-place in Europe and that in the Middle East or Africa is that the West has adopted the literate technique of displaying a fixed price, while the latter employs the oral mode of bargaining around a flexible offer; and those used to one type of transaction are often profoundly unhappy with the other, which they see as transgressing their basic economic ethic, their mode of monetary communication. But quite apart from actual selling, writing in Arabic is little used in Gonja even for accounting purposes, and this in turn limits the extent of the economic operations that can be undertaken.[2]

[1] A vivid picture of market transactions emerges from Binger's travels in the Voltaic area, especially from his stay in Salaga (II, pp. 85 ff.).

[2] Where so much trading is done on a credit basis, memory places severe limitations upon the number of debtors and transactions a trader can keep track of; this has been shown

More use may formerly have been made of writing for commercial enterprise. Certainly from early times the Saharan trade employed such techniques, for in A.D. 961 the geographer Ibn Hawkal writes of the use of debit notes for sums of 42,000 dinars—more than £100,000 in present-day values (Hunwick 1964: 25). A book of debts and contracts of a Tuwātī merchant of the early nineteenth century was also found in Katsina (Hunwick 1965: 36). And nearby, in the northern Ivory Coast, those who achieved literacy used it for keeping personal records. Many mallams keep a note of births in the family and of the amounts paid out in marriage transactions.

> Those engaged in commerce thus have the rudiments of accountancy [Marty 1922:267]...Some use wooden writing boards to keep a note of itineraries, profits and losses, credits and debits, the villages where they traded, stayed, and the loans made; information on the country they cross, the names of places, of chiefs, etc....Arabic writing is therefore constantly in use in everyday life. Today it also permits Mande traders to compare the prices of imported goods at different stores and to buy at the lowest price [1922: 400].

In Gonja, the only evidence of accounting I know of is in the very simple records of payments in the Kpandai papers (App. 1 Sect. F) and these refer to European-imposed taxation.

Somewhat farther north the French traveller, Binger, observed that writing was used on the bars of salt coming from the Saharan mines of Taodeni (I, 375); this consisted in various signs together with personal names which he thought were those of the first purchaser, or the producer himself (374). It is possible that these marks of identification indicated the existence of a credit system of the kind found today in the Ghanaian fish trade, but they may also have been there for magical purposes. Small pieces of rock salt are found even today in the markets of northern Ghana, where it is assigned a much higher ritual value than the powdered variety; part of this value may derive from the holy words inscribed upon the bars, words which may also serve as a protection against theft or destruction.

Other literary forms employed in the course of commerce were the itinerary and the 'passport'. All good Muslims should keep an itinerary of the road to Mecca,[1] in case they find themselves able to make the pilgrimage and thus fulfil one of the main religious duties; but they may also keep

in Keith Hart's work on 'Frafra' economic life and I am indebted for discussions with him on this point. The use of graphic techniques for recording commercial and bureaucratic transactions was an important feature of the protoliterate societies of the Fertile Crescent and of the Eastern Mediterranean.

[1] For an example of an itinerary from Salaga to Mecca, see Dupuis (1824), app. no. 6, written by 'Muhammad Kama'te known as Kantoma', possibly the son of the *imām* of the paramount chief of Gonja (Levtzion, 1966, p. 113).

itineraries of the routes on which they travel in the course of trade, and examples of these are provided by Dupuis, the leader of the British mission to Kumasi in 1820, where he found his knowledge of Arabic of great value.[1] A further instance is given by Abū Bakr al-Ṣiddīq, who was captured in an Abron ('Bonduku') attack upon Buna in the early years of the nineteenth century. Sold to European merchants, he was transported to the West Indies, where his ability to write came to the attention of R. R. Madden, who played a prominent part in the movement to stop the slave trade.[2]

The passport consisted of a letter of introduction written by one Muslim to an acquaintance in another town in order to introduce a third party. A safe-conduct of this kind was given to Binger as he passed through the present Ivory Coast on his way to the Mossi capital of Wagadugu. His host, Diarawary Wattara, gave him a letter whose standard opening emphasizes its proximity to the oral tradition: 'Praise be to God who gives us paper as a messenger and a reed as a tongue.' The letter then proceeds to recommend his Christian guest to the rulers of the various towns through which he must pass (I, 331–2).

Letters of a less formal kind were also used in the organization of caravans. The caravan trade was a large-scale enterprise in which a number of merchants banded together under an experienced leader and his staff, who acted as organizer, guide, agent and, above all, protector. The caravans were large, 150–200 on the north-western route (Marty 1922: 61) but from Hausaland they were often bigger. One of the main reasons for travelling in a company of this size was to prevent the depredations of the peoples through whom they had to pass, whether these were acephalous, centralized or free-booting.[3]

In long-distance trade on this scale writing played an important part in maintaining a link between the scattered trading communities. But it had a more specific function in enabling distant customers or agents to place orders for goods or services, as can be seen in the correspondence between Kumasi, Gbuipe and Salaga at the beginning of the nineteenth century (Appendix I, Sect. B). The same interchange provides evidence of more personal uses of letters as a means of giving news of death and of

[1] See Dupuis (1824), app. no. 4, for a route from Salaga to Hausaland written by Suma, a Gbuipe Muslim then living in Kumasi. See also Wilks (1961, 1966*b*) and Levtzion (1966).

[2] R. R. Madden, *Twelve Month's Residence in the West Indies* (London, 1837); G. C. Renouard, 'Routes in North Africa, by Abū Bekr es Siddik', *J. R. Geog. Soc.* VI, pp. 102–7. See I. Wilks, 'Abū Bakr al-Ṣiddīq of Timbuktu', in P. D. Curtin, *Africa Remembered* (Univ. Wisc. Press, 1967), pp. 152–69.

[3] See the letters between Caravan Leader Isa and the Chief of Dagomba, collected by the German traveller, G. A. Krause, and translated in J. Goody and T. M. Mustapha, 'The Caravan Trade from Kano to Salaga', *J. Hist. Soc. Nig.* III (1967), 4, pp. 611–16.

the hardships of the bereaved. Even today one major use of writing in the smaller townships is in the composition of telegrams to recall kinsfolk to funerals, a facility much in demand by the non-literate; a scribe may be found sitting outside the local post-office, waiting for custom. The corpus of Gonja writing listed in Appendix I includes two other sets of letters, but neither of these relates to commercial enterprise.

If commerce was not one, what were the main uses of literacy among the 'local' Muslims? The role of *imām* to the divisional chief included that of scribe as well as adviser. For the *imām* was responsible for the chancery correspondence that went on between the heads of sovereign powers.[1] 'Praise be to God,' wrote one Kumasi Muslim, 'who created the pen for use as speech, and who made paper that we may send it, in place of ambassadors, from country to country' (Wilks 1966*b*: 329). On the other hand, agreements and alliances were rarely if ever recorded in writing;[2] they were normally sworn verbally, but on the Qur'ān, in the manner described by Braimah in his account of the Salaga civil wars (1967: 6, 7, 38). Here the Qur'ān played a similar role to the use of the Christian Bible; the penalties for the breach of a 'rule' difficult for humans to apply are placed outside mortal hands.[3]

I should add here that in Gonja writing was not used for recording court cases (Krause gives a unique example). One reason was that, on the political level, Islamic law was not applied; the judicial body consisted of chiefs, not mallams. In disputes the role of the latter is that of mediators between the conflicting parties and, while their voices are listened to, in council and out, I have never myself come across a specific appeal to Muslim law in such assemblies, as distinct from general references to the will of God. In the larger trading communities like Salaga and within certain Muslim groups (e.g. in Bole), Islamic codes are an established source of law; this one can see from the library list given in Appendix II. But as far as the state as a whole was concerned, the situation differed radically

[1] Known examples of this correspondence are listed below in Appendix I; the surviving letters are mainly between chiefs and representatives of the colonial powers. On attempts to establish a chancery in Ashanti, see Wilks (1966*b*), p. 328.

[2] The use of written pacts of friendship between Bornu and Kanem in the late sixteenth century is recorded in Imām Ahmed ibn Fartua's account of the Kanem wars. 'Peace and friendship were established between our Sultan Ḥājj Idris and the Sultan of Kanem Abdul Lahi ibn Abdul Jalil, so that they even became related by marriage' (Palmer, 1928, p. 19). Literacy was more widely used in Hausaland and Bornu than in the Ashanti hinterland (see Hunwick, 1965). But Wilks notes that Reindorf speaks of treaties in Arabic between Ashanti and both Gyaman (Abron) and Dagomba.

[3] See Palmer (1928), I, pp. 75–6, for a comment on the use of 'hidden sacra' in Bornu and Hausaland. An example of the swearing of an oath on the Qur'ān, a typical combination of oral and written techniques, occurs on p. 28. But visitors to Ashanti were often tested in the same manner (Wilks, 1966*b*, p. 328), as was Harold during his enforced visit to the Duke of Normandy.

from the administration of Islamic law by alkalis (*qāḍīs*) found in northern Nigeria after the Fulani conquest in the early nineteenth century.

A further body of Gonja correspondence comes from the collection of Al-Ḥājj Baba of Kpandai (now Jawula Ababio, chief of Kpembe). It consists of letters written by his father, Mahama Karatu, later Jawula, chief of Kpembe (1931–6), mainly to learned Muslims in Salaga and elsewhere in northern Ghana, especially to Mallam Al-Ḥasan, compiler of the histories in Hausa of Mossi, Mamprusi, and Dagomba.[1] The administrative papers of which these letters form part (Appendix I, Section F) also include notes on people, villages and chiefdoms. Some of these are clearly written in response to the demands of colonial rule, which required an elaborate documentation of payments and other financial transactions, and was supported by a battery of inquisitive and mobile officials whose job was to institute a comprehensive series of record books for reference purposes. One of the most striking and immediate changes produced by the colonial conquest lay in the sphere of administrative techniques; there was constant recourse to writing, even in the midst of the initial campaign that established British rule, and the district officials had subsequently not only to keep detailed records of financial expenditure, record books giving information upon every village, a personal diary specifying their work, movements, etc., but also to produce a record of criminal and civil cases they heard and the moneys they collected from caravan, ferry and other taxes. In addition, they engaged in a voluminous correspondence, personal as well as official. The increase in scale of literate communication was enormous, and the advent of such an administration (dependent upon widespread secular literacy) appears to have stimulated the use of writing among those with a knowledge of Arabic script. But even so Jawula was an exceptional case; chiefs in Gonja were rarely literate because they were rarely Muslim, though they took part in Islamic festivals and adhered to certain Mohammedan practices. But Jawula's father had engaged in long-distance trade (a most unusual occupation for a Gonja prince) and as a consequence had become a committed Muslim; indeed it would be difficult to engage in the northern trade except as a follower of Islam. Because of his wealth, his Arabic schooling, his entrepreneurial skill and his capacity for forthright leadership, Mahama Karatu attracted the attention first of the German and then of the British administrators who became their successors in Togoland after 1914. By the usual series of steps, Mahama eventually became chief of Kpembe. But his attachment to Islam, combined with his authoritarian behaviour, led to his downfall and he was dismissed by his

[1] An account of the elevation and subsequent dismissal of this chief is given in J. A. Braimah and Jack Goody, *Salaga: the Struggle for Power* (London, 1967), pp. 70 ff.

fellow chiefs, partly on the ground that he had declared his intention of going on the pilgrimage to Mecca and leaving his son as deputy.

Jawula was an unusual chief in many ways; it is clear that his training made him more likely to make use of literate techniques than other rulers in northern Ghana, who delegated such work to their *imāms*.

It is difficult to assess the extent of letter-writing in pre-colonial Gonja (or in northern Ghana generally), partly because the condition of literacy that prevailed (which I call 'restricted literacy') makes for large variations over space and time. But while there is little apparent evidence of the same degree of chancery and other correspondence that existed in Bornu and Hausaland, the town of Salaga in fact produced a standard work on Islamic epistolography, written in 1877 and later published in Cairo. I refer to *Kitāb al-sarḥat al-warīqa*, the first-known work of Al-Ḥājj 'Umar b. Abī Bakr, the remarkable Kano-born scholar who settled in Gonja about 1870. But it would seem that this guide to letter-writing (which consists of a series of models together with advice to the secretary) owed more in terms of literary inspiration to the environment in which the author was educated (the Hausa towns of Kano, Kebbi and Gobir) rather than the place he found himself in, as a result of his father's activities as a trader in kola nuts, and where he was to stimulate a considerable revival of learning.

The other scribal function of the Gonja Muslims (the writing of letters being common both to strangers and to local men, though more widespread among the former) was to keep formal lists of past chiefs and their *imāms*. In Kpembe, the capital of eastern Gonja, the major festival of Damba, held on the anniversary of the prophet's birth, was the occasion on which the names of previous rulers of the division were read out before the assembled multitude.[1] While the function of these records is partly historical, there are also politico-religious overtones. Since both the chiefship and Imāmship are vested in specific patronymic groups, the reciting of the names of former office-holders substantiates their continuing claim as well as legitimizing the office itself in the eyes of the populace. But the recitation is also a prayer, for the well-being of the dead as well as of the living, for the past chiefs, as well as being pacified, are also called upon (implicitly rather than explicitly) to assist the present incumbent and his people. And for these and similar services, the Gonja Muslims expect alms and support from the ruler.

In one outstanding instance the local Muslims proved themselves custodians of tradition in a more fundamental respect. In 1752, Al-Ḥājj

[1] See Braimah and Goody (1967), p. 4. On the only occasion I attended Damba at Kpembe no such list was read out, either because of some dispute over the possession of the manuscript or because the Muslims claimed the chiefs had not given them sufficient presents. Both reasons were given to me at different times.

Muḥammad b. Muṣṭafā completed a history of the kingdom which recounted the legend of its origin and gave a yearly chronicle of events from the death of the king, ʿAbbās, on 25 May 1710; an addendum was written for the years 1763 to 1766 by Imām ʿUmar Kunandi b. ʿUmar. Both of these were learned men and their horizons took in part at least of the Mediterranean world. Muḥammad made the pilgrimage to Mecca.[1] In 1731/2, his father Muṣṭafā set out, but died the following year near the Hausa town of Katsina. In 1733/4, Muḥammad went on the pilgrimage and returned three years later, a rather quick journey as the time taken was usually some seven years.[2] These and other journeys emphasize that Gonja was in constant touch with the literate world outside. In 1724/5 Sulaymān and Abū Bakr set out for Mecca; the former at least returned, for his death is reported in 1746/7. In the previous year, Ṣāliḥ b. al-Amīn had returned from Mecca.[3]

The stimulus to chronicle the history of the kingdom (and this is at present the only record of its kind from northern Ghana) may have come direct from the Middle East, through the contacts of pilgrims and scholars. Or it may have come from the historical traditions of the western Sudan itself; Sulṭān Bello of Sokoto traces the beginning of historical writing in the Sudan to Mallam Yusiyu, probably of the sixteenth century, who wrote that 'whenever he met a person he asked him whence he came...Afterwards he wrote down any information he had gained which was worth recording. Before this, scholarship had been confined to traditional learning. From this time forward historical writing became common' (Hiskett 1957: 571). The birth of historical writing in northern Nigeria seems to have been stimulated by mallams from Timbuktu, which was already flourishing in the previous century and produced three outstanding scholars in the shape of Aḥmād Bābā, the chronicler, Maḥmūd Kāti (d. 1543), author of the *Ta'rīkh al-fattāsh*, and al-Saʿdi (*fl.* 1635), another historian.

Other historical documents have made their appearance in Gonja and these are listed in Appendix I. Particularly noteworthy are the writings about the Salaga civil war of 1892 and the series of histories of different states recorded by Mallam Al-Ḥasan. But it seems possible that some of

[1] The situation is a little confusing, since Al-Ḥājj can be used as a personal name if the individual concerned has become spiritually associated with an ancestor who made the journey. It could perhaps also be used if the attempt had begun but failed. And certainly a moneyed man could finance another who made a vicarious pilgrimage on his behalf; an example of this is given in the Chronicle (Goody, 1954, p. 37).

[2] Wilks (1963), p. 413. Is 'seven years' simply a set phrase for 'a long time'?

[3] The pilgrimage was no rarity at this time. The Fulani author of a series of magical books made the journey in about 1730 and remained in Egypt. Marty writes of a group of twelve mallams who left the northern Ivory Coast for Mecca in the mid-eighteenth century (1922, p. 130), but Wilks informs me that Marty misunderstood this manuscript.

these particular compositions may represent not so much a continuation of the indigenous literary traditions but a response to colonial over-rule, an answer to the historical questions so often directed at them by the alien administrators.[1]

However this may be, the main point that needs emphasizing here is that neither Salaga, Gonja, northern Ghana, nor yet the western Sudan can be considered as closed systems for the purposes of socio-cultural analysis. In their studies of non-European societies most sociologists have tended to over-emphasize internal as against external relationships.[2] Boundary problems, inter-tribal trade, marriage to outsiders, and war, these have received too little attention, partly as the result of the methods of study used and the 'theoretical' approaches superimposed.[3] Both functional and structural analyses (of whatever 'school') tend to place too much stress on social and cultural homogeneity, thereby ascribing a premature rigor mortis to a large field of human action and belief. Nowhere is this more clearly brought out than in some recent analyses of religious and mythological systems.[4]

Yet institutional systems of belief, since they depend so directly upon linguistic intercourse, are very open to changes in the network of communication which in turn is influenced by changes in the media themselves. The introduction of literacy, even in a restricted form, immediately expands the intellectual horizons of a community, bringing at least some of its members into active contact with the ideas of individuals of diverse cultures and of different centuries. The influence of such contact varies of course from place to place, within and between societies. But it cannot be unimportant to the intellectual life of any society that some of its most highly valued members are absorbing religious ideas, practising divinatory systems, and acquiring mental skills that have emerged in quite another context,

[1] Wilks considers the same point in discussing the manuscripts from the town of Wa in northern Ghana. He notes that the written histories 'are not chronicles, but rather compilations of oral tradition. Yet though historical in content, they are legalistic in intent. They form a corpus of constitutional documents, utilized in the determination of claims to office, rights in land, etc.' (1966*c*, p. 64). When the socio-political relationships are thrown into question by the presence of a colonial power dependent upon literate techniques, it is not surprising to see an increase in the number of such documents. But it should be pointed out that Wilks regards the Wa compilations as a continuation of an earlier written tradition (p. 65).

[2] On this subject see I. Potekhin's essay, 'Social and Economic System of the Southern Bantu at the beginning of the nineteenth Century', *23rd Int. Congress of Orientalists* (1954).

[3] For a fuller discussion of this point see my 'Inheritance, Social Change and the Boundary Problem', *Comparative Studies in Kinship* (London, 1969).

[4] See, for example, the discussion in *African Systems of Thought* (G. Dieterlen and M. Fortes; London, 1966), and the review article by Audrey Richards, 'African systems of thought: an Anglo–French dialogue', *Man*, II (1967), pp. 286–98. See also my review of M. Griaule, *Conversations with Ogotemmêli* (Fr. ed. 1948), in the *American Anthropologist* (1967), pp. 239–41.

at quite another time. These ideas always undergo a process of reinterpretation at the local level, but they can never be wholly absorbed into the particular culture to which they have been transmitted without at the same time modifying that culture in certain major respects. Moreover, ideas communicated by literary means can never be totally absorbed like those passed on orally, because the book always remains there as a check upon the transformations that have taken place. The check is generally ignored, but at critical moments the primordial version can always make an uncomfortable reappearance.

The situation, then, is this. Throughout northern Ghana, as in the rest of the western Sudan, small groups of people who could read and write Arabic, Hausa and other local languages are found scattered through a basically non-literate peasantry. Under such conditions, literacy in any one place is likely to be somewhat precarious; a small Muslim community may cease altogether to have any members who can read and write, a situation that can lead to a relapse into paganism of the kind recorded for a number of groups in the area.[1] But the potentiality for a revival of learning is also present while Islam retains even a token pull, since a man may send his son to some distant town to receive an education.[2] And the books, even if unread, remain stocked up on his shelves (though subject to the depredations of white ants, worms and the dry harmattan wind from the north). Because of this possibility too, no state like Gonja, Dagomba or the Mossi kingdoms, nor even any acephalous 'tribe' like the LoDagaa or Tallensi, can be exhaustively analysed without taking into account the intellectual links that bring the western Sudan into contact (or potential contact) with the Islamic world of North Africa and the Middle East and through this to the Graeco-Roman and Semitic civilizations of the Eastern Mediterranean.

The links in this system of intellectual communication are the books in which information is stored and the men who have been trained to interpret them. And such links exist not only in the major towns of the western

[1] Jack Goody, 'Marriage Policy and Incorporation in Northern Ghana', in *From Tribe to Nation in Africa* (ed. R. Cohen and J. Middleton), in press. On a dynastic level, see the Hausa history in R. S. Rattray, *Hausa Folk-lore* (Oxford, 1913). The group of Sakpare Muslims who formerly provided the Imām of the Kuli subdivision in eastern Gonja seem to have attained this condition and in Gbuipe in central Gonja I have encountered Mbontisua ('Ashanti Muslims') who are neither Ashanti nor Muslim, though apparently both in origin. The crucial factor here, as Marty also points out, is the failure of local Muslims to observe the prohibition on marrying pagan girls. Among the Gonja, pagan brides are 'converted' by the marriage ceremony; as a result, divorce often brings renunciation. Marty describes a very similar situation among the Dyula of the Ivory Coast: 'les femmes légitimes...sont prises parmi toutes les femmes du pays sans *distinction de religion*' (1922, pp. 310, 353).

[2] In the northern Ivory Coast, even pagans sometimes send one of their sons to a Qur'ānic school, taking out a supernatural insurance policy with Islam (Marty, 1922).

Sudan but in relatively small centres distributed along the multitude of trade routes that thread their way throughout the savannah country, places such as Salaga (pop. in 1960, 4,199) in Gonja, and further north, along the historic route to the Mossi capital of Wagadugu that skirts the Tong Hills on and around which the Tallensi reside, settlements such as Pong-Tamale (pop. 2,354) and Savelugu (pop. 5,949) in Dagomba.[1] These untidy clusters of huts, with only a mud-built mosque rising above the thatched roofs, attract little or no notice from contemporary travellers. Nevertheless they contained, and still do, libraries of books, some of local origin, but mostly emanating from North Africa and beyond. The library of al-Ḥājj Ḥusayn of Savelugu, for example, contains forty-three titles, which the author divided under four headings:[2]

(1) Jurisprudence (largely Mālikī)	15 'books'
(2) Syntax (*'ilm al-naḥw*)	18
(3) Morphology (*'ilm al-ṣarf*)	3
(4) Arabic language and dictionaries	7

A list of the library of another inhabitant of Savelugu, Mallam Abū Bakr b. Muḥammad, the teacher at an Arabic school (*makaranta*)[3] in Pong-Tamale, comprised twenty-one volumes, the authors of which included natives of Cordova, Bagdad and Kairouan (Tunisia) and were equally dispersed over time as over space (Appendix II). A recent survey of libraries in Salaga produced 495 titles in the libraries of fourteen men, an average holding of thirty-five books. These works are nearly all printed copies of relatively recent origin; in addition, most senior residents of Salaga have a number of manuscript copies acquired at an earlier period, either by travel, by local purchase, by inheritance, or by their own industry as scribes.[4]

These are by no means isolated examples. In the Ivory Coast of 1920, every mallam had a library, usually consisting of three to four volumes, but

[1] This was the route travelled by Binger in 1888, a decade before the forces of the European powers penetrated the area. His account provides evidence of the considerable trading activity between Salaga and Wagadugu. This trade had to be carried out by large caravans because of the danger of attack from pagan groups like the Tallensi, who clearly derived some benefit from the merchants that traversed their territory.

[2] This library list was kindly collected by Mrs C. Oppong of the Institute of African Studies, Legon, Ghana, and translated by N. Levtzion. For other lists, see Marty (1922), annexes III–IX.

[3] The word, used throughout Ghana, is derived from the Arabic *qara*, 'to read'; a similar word, *karanta*, is used in Mande, but the Gonja term is presumably a direct loan from Hausa. The Gonja word for Muslim, *kramo*, is however Mandingo though the root is again from the Arabic (Wilks, 1962). The Ashanti word *saphy*, which Mrs Lee (Bowdich's widow) described as 'scraps of the Koran, esteemed as charms' (*African Wanderer*, 1854, p. 290), is derived from the Mandingo *safaye*.

[4] These lists were collected by Aḥmād Adamu Wangara of Salaga and I am most grateful to him, to J. A. Braimah, and to the owners of libraries for their co-operation.

some had much larger collections of up to 200 works (Marty 1922: 274–5). Some idea of the extent of written works circulating in West Africa can be gained from recent catalogues of manuscript collections. In their catalogue of the Jos libraries, Arif and Hakima list over one thousand manuscripts. The range is extremely wide, the main subjects covered being History, Religion, Language (Arabic Grammar), Poetry, Astronomy, Astrology, Mathematics, Folk-lore, Prose, Geography, Education, Sociology, Logic and Jurisprudence (1965: vi). Libraries of this variety and size are most likely to be found in larger towns like Kano and Timbuktu. These were towns, which, then as now, drew men to travel from country to country in order to sit at the feet of more learned scholars and so increase their wisdom through the study of books. At such towns there existed permanent educational centres around the mosques, which were the counterparts, in origin as in function, of the medieval universities of Western Europe. The mosque of Al-Azhar in Cairo was by far the most outstanding example in Africa; and the French explorer Dubois, who visited Timbuktu soon after the conquest at the end of the nineteenth century, wrote glowingly of the achievements of its 'University' of Sankore.[1] At the beginning of the sixteenth century, this university 'was at the height of its prosperity, the fame of its professors being known not only in the black countries but throughout Arabian Africa itself. Learned strangers flocked hither from Morocco, Tunis, and Egypt. The civilization of Arabia clasped hands with the civilization of Egypt, and from their union resulted the apogee of Timbuktu (1494–1591)' (1897: 237–8).

That apogee occurred during the period when the Songhai occupation provided a measure of peace, and ended with the Moroccan invasion across the Sahara, carried out partly by Christian renegades, acting as gunmen, and supported by technical aid received from the Protestant Queen of England in return for the saltpetre she needed for gunpowder. Timbuktu rebelled and was repressed, the best of her scholars being exiled to Morocco. Among these was Aḥmād Bābā (1556–1627), a member of the Masūfa Tuareg family of Aqīt that provided a line of scholarly *qāḍīs*; he later became a famous teacher in Marrakesh, where he wrote: 'Of all my friends I had the fewest books, and yet when your soldiers despoiled me they took 1600 volumes' (quoted from *Bedzl el Mouasaha*, in Dubois 1897: 307).

Manuscripts in quantity were imported from North Africa. In the sixteenth century Leo Africanus, a Moor captured by Christians and working for the Vatican, wrote: 'Hither are brought divers manuscripts or written

[1] Hunwick regards this description of the mosque and quarter of Sankore as misleading, although 'there is abundant evidence of scholarly work and higher Islamic education' (1964, p. 29). But Marty even speaks of Kong as 'l'universitaire' (1922, p. 190).

books out of Barbarie, which are sold for more money than any other merchandize' (1600: 288). He complained at the same time that there were many doctors, judges and priests who were completely ignorant, but the tenor of this comment may have been governed by his situation as a Christian convert. Ever since Mansa Musa, king of Mali from 1307 to 1332, returned from the pilgrimage accompanied by learned men from the Middle East, scholarship and writing were given much support by the emperors of the Keita clan; books were imported, schools encouraged, copyists established, mosques constructed.

The literary culture that arose with the spread of Islam was not simply a receptive one. As well as reading books, men wrote them, some of their compositions being works of considerable merit. We know the names of forty of Aḥmād Bābā's compositions. Apart from an astronomical work in verse and some commentaries on the holy texts, his writings were chiefly elucidations of Mālikī law. While he was in exile he wrote *Al-Kashf wa 'l-bayān* (or *Miraz*), a dissertation upon the different peoples of the Sudan, which were Muslim and which pagan (and hence potential slaves). He also composed *Nail al-ibtihāj*, a biographical dictionary that forms the main source on Mālikī scholars of the period; by means of this volume it is possible 'to reconstruct the intellectual past of Timbuktu' (Dubois 1897: 309).[1] One of the most remarkable works from the Niger bend was written under the Moroccan domination, *Ta'rīkh al-Sūdān*, by 'Abd al-Raḥmān al-Sa'dī al-Tinbuktī, an invaluable source for the history of the western Sudan and one of a large number of manuscripts that dealt with local history, of which the Kano and Gonja chronicles are lesser examples. For it was these scholars from Timbuktu, some of whom had studied in Egypt under writers such as Al-Suyūṭī (d. 1505), who returned from the pilgrimage to write textbooks and commentaries for their students and to spread their knowledge to Hausaland and elsewhere (Hunwick 1964*a*: 30).

Although Timbuktu was of central importance in the diffusion of scholarship throughout West Africa, even creative writing was not confined to this or the other major centres of learning; in Gonja, on the very periphery of the Islamic world, we find not only the mid-eighteenth century Chronicle but, in the following century (the long gap, representing the period of Ashanti dominance, may well be of historical significance), the extraordinarily impressive list of writings by Al-Ḥājj 'Umar, which includes theological works, historical verses, poems of anti-Christian protest, a letter-writer's handbook and writings of a more ephemeral character (Appendix 1, Sect. C). These compositions, in Arabic and Hausa, are of

[1] See J. O. Hunwick, 'A new source for the biography of Aḥmād Bābā al-Tinbuktī (1556–1627)', *Bull. S.O.A.S.* XXVII (1964*b*), pp. 568–93.

some literary worth, especially his poem on the Coming of the Christians and certain of his translations from the Arabic into Hausa.

The achievements of Al-Ḥājj 'Umar were recorded by the administrator-anthropologist, R. S. Rattray, who was his pupil ('a very humble disciple') as District Commissioner at Kete-Krachi, a town to which 'Umar retired after the Salaga civil war. In 'Umar's library, inherited from his father, were the poems of the pre-Islamic Arabian poet, Imruil Kaisi ('Imru' al-Qays, A.D. 492–542) in an annotated copy said to have been made in Katsina in the latter part of the eighteenth century. 'Umar, wrote Rattray, had

> spent many years of his life wandering over Arabia...and...made a very special study, extending over many years, of the works of this Arabian poet, had collected and critically examined a considerable quantity of literature dealing with his subject and had finally translated the thirty-four odes written by Imruil Kaisi into Hausa [1934: 256].

Latin translations of the bulk of these odes were published by Baron de Slane in 1837, and one of the odes was later translated into English by a number of writers including Arnold, Lyall and Lady Anne Blunt. But Rattray considers 'Umar's the best and most scholarly of all these translations (now superseded by Arberry's, *The Seven Odes*).

> Among the MSS. which formed his library...was an old MS. copy of a work on Arabic prosody called Uryunul Gamirati written in A.H. 200 by one Shaihu Hazaraji. From this work Limam Umaru had worked out fully the forms and names of the different metres for each of the thirty-four odes in the original Arabic MS [257].

The extent of original writing in northern Ghana has recently been examined by Hodgkin (1966) and Wilks (1963) on the basis of the 400 manuscripts of the Institute of African Studies, Legon. Together with the library lists of printed and hand-copied books emanating from the Maghreb, the Middle East and other parts of West Africa (the latter mostly by members of the Dan Fodio family), these writings present a picture of northern Ghana very different from the usual conception of a 'simple' society.[1]

Looking at the societies of northern Ghana as an interacting field (and remembering the arbitrary nature of the boundary), the extent and functions of writing for both the non-literate and the partly literate peoples of the area become clearer. The very considerable achievements must make one shy away from applying the epithet 'simple' to such societies, and the success of this medium of communication in diffusing systems of belief that derived

[1] Although many of these manuscripts were collected in southern Ghana they were generally obtained from Muslims whose families had migrated from the north, mostly from Salaga after its occupation by Kabachewura Isifa and the Dagomba forces in December 1892.

from a very different social environment must make one wary of certain of the simplistic functional and structural approaches to intellectual processes of the Durkheimian school and its more mechanistic followers. Whatever merits such approaches may have for the analysis of oral cultures, those societies in which speech can be given a tangible form need to be treated with different considerations in mind (see above, pp. 55–67).

The advent of literacy had important consequences of a general kind for the area, since writing brought access to a 'world' religion and a universalistic legal code, some of the implications of which I discuss later. It also realized some of the potentialities that Watt and I saw as related to the Greek achievement. In an extremely patronising comment, Marty makes this very point about the Muslims of the forest fringe.

> Their intellectual worth, clearly feeble when compared with that of a European of middling education, is nevertheless truly remarkable in comparison with that of other blacks, because *writing has put* in their hands an incontestable means of perfectibility, of immense value, so they could reasonably lay claim to a certain evolution, while without us the animists were condemned to stagnation.
>
> The intellectual activity of Islam, however absurd its methods, has nevertheless developed, without a shadow of doubt, their intelligence and their critical capacity. The reading and explanation of texts has refined their minds and one is amazed to see certain mallams explain difficult texts with a real feeling for exegesis and grammar, which is even more remarkable considering the absurdity of the means employed to acquire this knowledge [1922: 450].

A means of intercultural communication, a critical intelligence, the impetus to question and explain, a concern with the structure of language, these Marty sees as related to the acquisition of writing. But despite these achievements, the introduction of writing did not have the same results as in the Mediterranean world, and it seems pertinent to try and see why. Such a discussion inevitably raises issues of greater scope, geographical and cultural, for we have to take into account the position of writing not only in western Africa but also in the Muslim world generally.

As with other Semitic scripts, some complications arise from the instrument itself; the absence of distinctive vowel signs at first created a measure of ambiguity for the reader. This difficulty was partly overcome with the introduction of vowel points by ad-Du'ali in Basra during the latter part of the seventh century.[1] Even so, Arabic scripts still present problems, and in the U.S.S.R. the extension of literacy was linked with

[1] The vowel points were introduced in order to facilitate the learning of the language by non-Arab converts, a process which also stimulated the teaching of grammar and vocabulary. Undoubtedly this change led to an increase in literacy. 'Before Islam', Hunwick writes, 'there were very few Arabs who could read and write their own language and the Arabic script was still primitive without *the dots and vowel markings which seem almost essential to the correct reading of any text not known by heart*' (1964*a*, p. 24; my italics).

the use of the roman alphabet. Latinization was demanded by Lenin; and in 1928 Kemal Pasha replaced the Arabic script used in Turkey with a roman system.

Of greater significance than the character of the medium is that of the educational system. Whether we examine the level of primary or of advanced education, the most noticeable feature of the education offered is its predominantly religious character.

In Gonja towns like Salaga and Bole a considerable number of children from Muslim families are today taken into the Islamic schools or taught by kinsmen.[1] Nevertheless, fluent literacy among Muslims is a rare accomplishment.

One major underlying reason lies in the identification of education with religious instruction. A pupil is primarily engaged in learning not the technique of reading and writing but the Holy Book itself; thus he has to learn not only the word of God but the language of God. For anyone other than an Arabic speaker, the learning of the literate skills is overlaid, indeed confounded, with the learning of another language.[2] Reading can never be what the alphabetic script permits, a matter of phonetic identification.

As so often where learning is linked to a religion of the Book, the preservation of the language in which it is written places an enormous hindrance on a realization of the full potentialities of writing. The use of Latin in Europe, Sanskrit in India, Pali in Thailand, all have made literacy more difficult to attain for those outside the 'priesthood'.

Secondly, in religious literacy it is more important to learn the Holy Word than to learn to read. In the better primary schools of Hausaland or of nineteenth-century Cairo (Lane 1871: I, 75–6), children were often taught to read by means of the alphabet. But in many other schools, including those I myself visited in northern Ghana, the elementary class is taught not to read but to recite, simply using the letters as mnemonics for what comes next. Thus learning tends to be 'by rote' rather than by recognition, though eventually the brightest and more persistent pupils are able to read.

Thirdly, there are certain features about the organization of these schools that diminish their effectiveness as educational institutions. Most Qur'ānic

1 There is a continuum between a father teaching his son and a man teaching a whole class of children which makes it difficult to give precise figures for school attendance. Marty (1922) presents detailed information on attendance at Muslim primary schools in the northern Ivory Coast and judges that 60 per cent of pupils were close kinsmen of the teacher, 20 per cent were distant kin, and a further 10–20 per cent were from other Muslim families in the area; occasionally a pagan family would send along a child as a kind of hostage to God; il 'rachète leur fétichisme' (Marty, 1922, p. 268). The average number of pupils per school (i.e. teacher) works out at only 4·5 (p. 490).

2 The use of Arabic script for writing local languages appears to have been a late development throughout the Sudan.

schools in Gonja are part-time and the students themselves often spend more hours on their teacher's farm than in study.[1] This situation is more marked in the smaller settlements where neither teachers nor parent can afford to do without the boy's productive labour. In Gbuipe, the only instruction that took place was given by Mallam Tahir to the children in his house and to one pupil who lived with him and worked on the farm, which he himself rarely visited; the fields were looked after by other members of his compound, principally by two adult sister's sons. The time spent on study was severely limited. In the larger towns like Salaga, where the schools are often attached to the local mosques of the different quarters of the town, instruction was more systematic. Nevertheless, even there a pupil usually farmed for his teacher and the period spent at school was often used less effectively than it might have been. Of the conduct of schools in the Ivory Coast Marty writes: 'Au sein de la classe, nulle discipline, nulle organisation; les élèves les moins ignares demeurent en contact avec les élèves débutants; il en résulte que les progrès sont d'une lenteur décourageante' (1922: 264). The strictures on the internal organization are certainly over-severe.[2] Nevertheless, progress is slow, partly because some boys go to school only in the dry season when there is no farming, partly because of the limited amount of teaching, partly because of its quality. According to Marty, boys attend school (in theory) from six to seven each morning and from five to six in the evening. Finally, there remains the fact that in communities of this kind, where the uses of literacy are relatively few, the demand is satisfied by a few literates and there is therefore little incentive (religion aside) for a person to put in the time and work needed to acquire the skill.

These factors help to explain the very sharp and narrow-based pyramid of literacy that is characteristic of such societies. Even among those who attend school the fall-out is very high and the attainments generally low; correspondingly, the number of technically efficient literates is small. Among certain sub-groups, like the Saghanughu described by Wilks (1966*a* and above p. 172), the rates are significantly higher, but the overall level is low. As Hiskett writes of northern Nigeria, 'the Fulani *'ulama'* were a small but cultured group in a society where standards were generally low.'[3]

[1] The tradition of 'working for the teacher' persists in many state schools in northern Ghana, where boys and girls are often expected to perform a whole variety of services for their masters.

[2] The largest school in Bole at present has its own uniform and a considerable *esprit de corps*. The Ahmadiyya school at Wa, established by missionaries in the 1930s, has a European-type timetable and has obtained government recognition.

[3] Hiskett sees the capacity of the Fulani to carry out the conquest of the Hausa kingdoms as being due 'to their sense of cohesion and intellectual superiority over the surrounding Hausas. This gave them a degree of organizing ability and political acumen above that of the Hausa aristocracy' (1957, pp. 575–6).

A small percentage of those who attend primary school go on to take further studies, which form a graded series of steps up the ladder of knowledge. The process of acquiring this knowledge has recently been outlined in a comment on the early life of the Fulani leader, Al-Ḥājj 'Umar Tall:

Al-Ḥājj thus seems to have been following the classical pattern of Islamic education, which at this time in the early nineteenth century was being given a great impetus throughout the Western Sudan. Piecing together biographical material from several prominent lives, and what we know of the state educational systems of Futa Toro, Futa Jalon, Masina and the Northern Nigerian emirates the following rough schedule emerges. From seven to about ten years the boy would learn elementary reading and writing of Arabic, possibly at home, as did al-Ḥājj with his father. Then at the age when, in the usual Fulani manner, he would stop sleeping with his mother, he would attach himself to a teacher and begin compulsory prayers and to seriously learn the Qur'ān by heart.[1] On average this would take about four years, though al-Ḥājj and Shehu Aḥmadu Bari are said to have been able to recite it at twelve, the age at which, incidentally, this recitation is now the entry requirement to several primary sections of Al-Azhar. The following four-year period was then spent in comprehension of the text, after which the student would graduate as a *ḥāfiẓ*.

If a higher level of learning were then sought the student would be expected to travel to seek the most renowned teachers, and in this quest al-Ḥājj, still in his teens, began to travel extensively in Mauretania, Futa Toro, Futa Bondu and Futa Jalon, in which country he probably received his initiation into the Tijaniyya.

Kong is the next place linked with his name...At Kong al-Ḥājj pursued an education which was already well advanced. In West Africa at this time Islamic higher education was divided into principal and auxiliary subjects which show little significant difference from the medieval classification of knowledge, as used for example at Al-Azhar till the later nineteenth century. In the former category are the Qur'ān itself, *tafsīr* (Qur'ānic exegesis), *ḥadīth* (the authenticated deeds and sayings of the Prophet), *tawḥīd* (knowledge of God and his attributes), *uṣūl al-fiqh* (principles of canon law) and *taṣṣawuf* (philosophy of mysticism). The second category, which were taught in far fewer schools, and for which the Saghanughu of Kong seemed appropriate, comprised *naḥw* (grammar), *ṣarf* (syntax), *ma'ani* (rhetoric), *bayān* (a related subject concerned with public speaking) and *manṭiq* (logic) [Holden 1966: 69–70].

Another example of scholastic progress is that of 'Abdullāh ibn Muḥammad (*c.* 1766/7–1829), younger brother of Shehu dan Fodio, leader of the seizure of power in the Hausa states. In his introduction to 'Abdullāh's account of the wars, *Tazyīn al-waraqāt*, Hiskett writes:

He came of a long line of scholars and commenced his religious education at an early age. Indeed the lives of the clerical Fulani centred around the practice of

[1] It was at the age of 13, when he had finished reading the Qur'ān, that 'Abdullāh dan Fodio was handed over by his father to the care of his elder brother, 'Uthmān (Hiskett, 1957, p. 561).

the Muslim religion, and the learning and teaching of religious sciences was of extreme significance. The system was that of 'master-seeking' and teaching was at times peripatetic, and at times took place in the mosques and schools. Among the clan to which 'Abdullāh belonged teachers were sought largely, though not exclusively, among kinsmen. 'Abdullāh has left us a detailed account of his teachers, and the curriculum which he followed. Like all Muslim boys his education commenced with the learning of the Qur'ān, which he acquired from his father. At the age of thirteen he was put in the hands of his brother the Shehu 'Uthmān, and under him he studied *al-'Ishrīnīyāt*, *al-Witrīyāt*, the Six Poets, *tawḥīd* from the works of the Sanūsi, and others. From the Shehu he also learnt syntax, and with him he studied *al-Ājurrūmīya*, *al-Mulḥa*, *al-Qaṭr*, and other works. With him he also studied Sufism, Law, Qur'ānic exegesis and *ḥadīth*.

He attributes his lasting interest in religious studies to the influence of Shehu 'Uthmān and he appears at this time to have conceived a deep devotion for his brother which remained a constant throughout his life. He must also have become a copyist during this early period, for he states 'it was rarely that a book on the science of the Unity reached our country and I knew of it, and did not copy it down from him'.

Among others who taught him were his uncles Muḥammad b. Rāj, 'Abdullāh b. Muḥammad Thanbu, and such famous pre-*jihād* scholars as al-Ḥājj Jibrīl, Muḥammad al-Firabrī, Muḥammad al-Buttugha, and Muḥammad al-Maghūrī. Later on he himself became tutor to his nephew Bello b. 'Uthmān. His education continued well into his adult life, for in the years immediately preceding the *jihād* we find him travelling with Shehu 'Uthmān, to sit at the feet of the learned, and he received the *ijāza*, or licence to teach, from scholars such as al-Ḥājj Jibrīl, 'Abd al-Raḥmān b. Muḥammad, al-Ḥājj Muḥammad b. Rāj, and others [Hiskett 1963: 6–7; also 1957].

Advanced education was influenced as much as primary instruction by its religious orientation. First, progress was relatively stereotyped. Secondly, higher learning was mainly peripatetic, and hence restricted and time-taking. This was due partly to the scatter of scholars and partly to the fact that the scholars were themselves on the move, sometimes on the road to Mecca.[1] Thirdly, teaching was largely expounding, another reason for slow progress. 'We were three years over the explanation of the Teshil of the Imam Malek before we acquired a thorough mastery of the subtleties of the Arabian language, says a writer of Timbuktu' (Dubois 1897: 293). Fourthly, even at this level, students were required to memorize the texts they read. As Hiskett remarks of Fulani learning in the early nineteenth century: 'It is hardly necessary to add that teaching and learning were by *lectio* and *memoriter*' (Hiskett 1957: 574). Of a certain scholar, 'Abdullāh, the Fulani leader, writes: 'He was learned, having memorized most of

[1] 'The peripatetic system was bound up with pilgrimage, for the teacher passed up and down the country on his way to and from the East; and with him went his students' (Hiskett, 1957, p. 574).

what he read, and it was he who read to them the commentary of al-Karāshī. If ['Uthmān] made a mistake, or let anything slip, this maternal uncle of ours would correct it for him without looking in a book...' (Hiskett 1957: 563). Fifthly, the syllabus was very limited in the direction of empirical knowledge, even by the standards of the corpus of Arabic writing. In his enthusiastic appreciation of Timbuktu, Dubois wrote:

The branches of instruction were many and various. The theologians commented upon and analysed the great sacred books, and taught rhetoric, logic, eloquence, and diction in order to prepare the student to spread abroad the word of God and maintain controversies. The jurist expounded the law according to the Malekite dogmas, and the stylists taught the art of writing 'in ornamental terms'. Others professed grammar, prosody, philology, astronomy, and ethnography; and others again were 'very versed in the traditions, biographies, annals, and histories of mankind'. Mathematics do not appear to have formed a special course; and as for medicine, the grossest empiricism was mingled with the hygenic principles of the therapeutic Arab [Dubois 1897: 292].

But with additional evidence at his disposal, Hiskett gives a rather more critical assessment of the position. 'An examination of the works which 'Abdullāh and his kinsmen studied makes it clear that they depended on the Qur'ān and on a few classical texts...and then on a fairly large collection of later semiclassical and mainly secondary texts of the seventh and eighth centuries of the Hijra...' (1963: 7). The gaps are very important. For there was apparently little knowledge of that great branch of Arabic literature, the work of the early geographers, and medical and scientific writings were virtually unknown, though 'Abdullāh dan Fodio was taught 'the science of arithmetic, the elementary (part) of it, the easy (part)'.[1]

This situation is connected with the fact that literacy was dominated not only by religion but by magic too.[2] For in Islam magic is legitimized by religion. I mean by this that the whole apparatus of cabalistic learning found in books such as Al-Būnī's *Shams al-ma'ārif*, the use of magic squares, numbers and names, is closely tied in with the Holy Book and constantly employs the names of God, his archangels and his caliphs (Doutté 1909).

[1] Hiskett (1957), p. 562. The author tells me that at a later date they were familiar with the writings of Ibn Khaldun, though these were largely historical. Wilks adds that the *Aṣl al-Wanghariyyīn*, written in Kano in 1650, shows quite clearly that al-Idrissi's 'Geography' was known there at that time. It is obvious that subsequent research may lead to a revision of any assessment of the state of learning in the western Sudan.

[2] In this paper I employ a distinction between magic and religion which is useful in discussing the world religions but of little help in non-literate societies. In speaking of magic, I refer to the use of material objects, such as charms, amulets and the written word, in order to advance one's well-being in this world. As Goode (1951, pp. 52 ff.) and others have pointed out, we need to think in terms of a continuum between the magical and religious poles rather than a hard and fast distinction.

Even in the more urbanized environment of nineteenth-century Egypt, the trade in *materia magica*, resting firmly on the twin pillars of religion and literacy, was extensive.

One of the most remarkable traits in modern Egyptian superstition is the belief in written charms. The composition of most of these amulets is founded upon magic; and occasionally employs the pen of almost every village schoolmaster in Egypt. A person of this profession, however, seldom pursues the study of magic further than to acquire the formulae of a few charms, most commonly consisting, for the greater part, of certain passages of the Kur-án, and names of God, together with those of angels, genii, prophets, preeminent saints, intermixed with combinations of numerals, and with diagrams, all of which are supposed to have great secret virtues [Lane 1871: 1, 312].

The most esteemed of all *ḥijā* or charms is the Book itself (*muṣḥaf*). The next in point of estimation is a book or scroll containing certain chapters of the Qur'ān, generally seven. Alternatively, the ninety-nine names, or epithets, of God, comprising all the divine attributes, may be written on paper (or simply repeated) in order to produce far-reaching effects; similar manipulations of the great (and often secret) names of God are found in Jewish, Christian and Mandaean magic.

The written charm is considered to be so effective because it gives speech a concrete embodiment; so can other material objects, and their handing over often acts as a kind of pledge or affirmation in supernatural and in human communion. But writing clearly has a special value because of its intimate relation with speech.

Because they materialize speech, it is easier to extract the full power, the full meaning, from written formulae than from oral incantations (Doutté 1909: 151). The Islamic *ḥirz* consists of two elements, a *da'wa* or spell and a *jadwal* or 'picture', the latter being some type of magical design,[1] and the advantages of these written forms consist in their portability, tangibility and divisibility, advantages which are quite apparent to the actors, as Doutté explains in an interesting passage:

We have earlier explained how the magic power (*vertu*) attributed to oral formulae was related to their meaning and ended by being attributed to the words themselves and to the sounds that made them up. Since the graphic signs which represented the words are much easier to handle than the sounds and are capable of enduring, as they have a material form, it is inevitable that magical force is seen as encapsulated in them; in other words, writing itself is reputed to have magical powers. Furthermore, one sees the advantages of a written incantation: since it is not oral, one can increase its value by repeating the magical names a thousand times. Since these are written, it is easier to extract from them all their

[1] Of the kind illustrated in Marty (1922).

power. In the first place, you can carry them around, put them wherever you wish, then divide them, write them in different ways, on the spot, backwards: a great number of amulets are written in boustrophedon (like a plough, moving in alternate directions), reputed to have a most magical character. Moreover, the words of a single formula can be separated, aligned in series, distributed according to various geometric designs; in this way words belonging to different classes of ideas could be mixed. For example, the names of God, the names of angels, the names of demons, verses of the Qur'ān, are scattered in geometric figures, laid out in squares, broken down into letters; these letters, corresponding to numbers, can be replaced by them. Lastly, as the incomprehensible figure had a special power, because of the magical character of anything mysterious and secret, they increased the unknown signs which were thought to represent names with marvellous properties. The designs formed in this way, mostly rectangular polygonal, are called *jadwal*, in Arabic 'picture' [150–2].

I reproduce this quotation from Doutté because it stresses that the advantages assigned to written as against oral forms of magic are precisely those that operate in a more 'rational' context. The ability to transcribe speech means the ability to dissect, rearrange and analyse the flow of language into distinct units; it is difficult to imagine the development of 'grammar' before the invention of writing, and it is significant that it was apparently not long after the introduction of the alphabetic script into India that the great Sanskrit grammarian, Pāṇini, composed his pioneering work.[1] It is this same ability of writing to dissect and reconstitute that led to the development of more complex schemes for organizing knowledge for magico-religious purposes, the kind of classification that Durkheim and Mauss regarded as specifically 'primitive' and that Lévi-Strauss sees as a product of *la pensée sauvage*. But far from being in the public domain, the social products of a particular culture, the key to its interpretation, they tended to be treated as secret formulae for the revelation of hidden truths, possessed and interpreted by a few book-owning scribes, and deriving power from their position in an international network of cultural communication. It was often the fact that book or practitioner filled the role of stranger that gave them authority in dealings with the esoteric.

Letters and numbers acquire a special magico-religious significance and are manipulated into different shapes and forms which are thought to assist man as 'medicines' or 'spells'.

1 While the Vēdic texts, the divine revelations of the Brahman tradition, do not seem to have been written down until the eighth or ninth century A.D., a corpus of works bearing on their correct interpretation appeared at an earlier date. These were the Vedāngas, the six branches of Vēdic science, which comprised Phonetics, Metre, Grammar, Etymology, Astronomy and Ceremonial; even these texts are mostly composed in a form (*sūtra*) 'consisting of strings of rules in the shape of tersely expressed aphorisms, intended to be committed to memory' (Eggeling, 1911, p. 160).

Schemas of this kind were not fixed, except in so far as they were put in writing, for authors produced many variations which could entail important changes in the system of representations or the structure of symbols. For example, the 3-volume work, *Occulta Philosophia* by Agrippa (1486–1535), published in Antwerp, set out a table of correspondences in which the seven planets were associated with 'magical squares' of increasing size, the 9-cell square being mystically linked with Saturn, the 81-cell square with the world. In 1539 Cardanus published his *Practica Arithmeticae* which reversed the whole system, linking the 9-cell square with the world (Ahrens 1917: 197 ff.); other writers had other correspondences. And the differences were of fundamental practical importance since it was these numbers that held the key to the universe.

Other societies have used numbers and letters in similar ways. The Brahmans had their spoken *mantras* with mystical letters or syllables and their *yantras* of mystical symbols inscribed on metal plates. The Mandaeans called their alphabet *abaga*, which when used as a verb means 'he read a spell'; each letter represents a power of life and light (Diringer 1948: 291). According to the Hebrew mystical text called the Book of Creation (*Sefer Yeẓirah*), God created the world by means of the alphabet, using especially the letters of his name in particular combinations; it is the discovery of these formulae that can make man the master of the created world.[1] The same doctrine appears in Christianity, for example in Arnold of Villanova's work on the *Tetragrammaton* or the ineffable name of Jehovah. At the close of the fifteenth century, the marvellous power of words, especially divine names, was much discussed by scholars, who interpreted the Scripture as allegory and interpreted the text as a cryptogram. Of such a kind were the doctrines of Pico della Mirandola (1463–94), John Reuchlin and Henry Agrippa, who owed much to works of Islamic origin and to the writings of the Jewish Cabala (Thorndike 1905: 20). One of the basic premises of the Cabala was, 'Jedes Wort ist eine Zahl, und jede Zahl ist ein Wort' (Ahrens 1917: 202). Given this linking of writing with magical formulae, it is not surprising to find that the Egyptian god, Theuth, the inventor of writing, was identified by the Greeks with Hermes Trismegistus, said to be the author of an important magical text (Thorndike 1905: 84).

Writing also permitted a much greater elaboration of divinatory techniques. The important institution of the horoscope, while based upon preliterate beliefs in the conjunction of events in the life of man and nature, was essentially an outcome of the rise of Babylonian mathematics and astronomy,

[1] Blau (1901), p. 548. The book *Raziel* proclaims a similar view. The idea that the right name (or combination) at the right time (astrologically calculated) held the secrets of the universe also appeared in Egyptian and Babylonian sources.

which depended ultimately upon developments in graphic techniques.[1] The systems of astrological calculation that spread throughout the Eurasian continent and then into large parts of Africa were a direct consequence of the invention of writing, preceding the coming of alphabetic literacy. In the present volume Maurice Bloch discusses the uses of Islamic astrology among the Merina of Madagascar, long after their separation from the Muslim world. Some of the divinatory practices of the Yoruba and Nupe of Nigeria clearly derive from Muslim forms (Nadel 1954: 59); and similar techniques, based upon the seven-day planetary week, are found throughout the Asian continent. The residue of such beliefs is found even today in the columns of the popular press of the Western world, and books of an astrological kind are a common import into the new nations, where some of the universal charisma of the book rubs off onto printed magic.

Writing does not, of course, expel magic. Indeed, the instruments of writing easily became invested with supernatural powers, particularly where writing is primarily a religious activity. Especially is this true of the ink and other colouring used in writing on paper, papyrus, slate or skins, for the material that actually gives concrete embodiment to speech is held to encapsulate the communicative power of the word. To wash the colour from off the writing surface and then swallow it down is to drink in, to internalize, a power which would otherwise remain external to the imbiber.

Hence in early pen-and-paper cultures, the 'drinking of the word' is often found in connection with curses, oaths and ordeals, since once again it intensifies oral communication (Bastian 1860: II, 211; for a Japanese example). As writing turns speech into a material object, words can be more readily manipulated.

An early example of the use of this technique is found in the Old Testament. In the Priestly code of Hebrew law (Numbers v. 11–28), it is laid down that a man who suspects his wife of adultery may bring her to a priest, along with an oblation of barley meal, so that she may undergo the ordeal of the bitter water (Frazer 1918: III, 304 ff.). 'And the priest shall write these curses in a book, and he shall blot them out into the water of bitterness that causeth the curse: and the water that causeth the curse shall enter into her and become bitter.'

The practice of 'drinking the word' is widespread today in those parts of West Africa that have been influenced by Islam. I have myself been offered the blackened water at ceremonies in Gonja, and from Senegal to

[1] F. Cumont, *The Oriental Religions in Roman Paganism* (Chicago, 1911); *Astrology and Religion among the Greeks and Romans* (New York, 1912); J. Goody, 'The Social Organisation of Time', *Int. Encyclopaedia of the Social Sciences* (New York, 1968).

Hausaland it is reported that the blessing of the Holy Word of the Qur'ān can be most fully absorbed in just this manner.[1] Such practices derive, as does literacy itself, from North Africa (and ultimately from the Eastern Mediterranean), where they have been recorded by many writers, among them Leared (1876: 272), Doutté (1909: 109) and Westermarck (1933). In Egypt Lane claimed that the most approved method of curing disease was to write certain pages of the Qur'ān on the inner surface of an earthenware bowl, then to pour in some water, stir it until the writing is quite washed off, and, finally, 'let the patient gulp down the water, to which the sacred words, with all their beneficent power, have been transferred...'[2] For the clients of these literate practioners, the desired effects are best ensured by the oral internalization of the written word. Very similar practices are reported among the descendants of Arab immigrants to Madagascar, among the Buddhists of Tibet, the Annamites of south-east Asia and in China itself, where spells 'are used as cures for sick persons, by being either written on leaves which are then infused in some liquid, or inscribed on paper, burned and the ashes thrown into drink, which the patient has to swallow'.[3] Indeed the same technique is used as a negative sanction in teaching, for recalcitrant scholars are sometimes made to swallow their mistakes. 'C'est une façon comme une autre,' remarks Marty, 'd'absorber sa leçon' (1922: 269).

Ink was also used as a divinatory medium. In his account of life in Cairo in the 1830s, Lane describes a series of seances with a certain 'Abd al-Qādir from the Maghreb (i.e. an outsider) who got individuals to see distant events or persons by peering into an inkblot. This he did by means of an intermediary, who had to be a virgin or a young boy below the age of puberty. At the seances which he attended, Lane received what he considered to be an accurate description of Shakespeare and of some distant friends, though later performances failed to live up to earlier achievements.

Kinglake's experience with the ink-diviners of Cairo was less successful. The same technique was used, a boy being asked to describe the image appearing in a blot of ink in his palm. But while the traveller had called for Keate, his old headmaster at Eton, a man with shaggy eye-brows and a short temper, the diviner reported the image of a fair girl, with golden hair, blue eyes and rosy lips (*Eothen*, 1844, ch. XVIII).

[1] See, for example, J. B. Bérenger-Feraud, *Les Peuplades de la Sénégambie* (Paris, 1879), p. 69; Binger gives an example from his enforced stay in the Mamprusi trading town of Walewale in northern Ghana (1892, II, p. 57).

[2] Frazer (1919), III, pp. 413–14; E. W. Lane, *Manners and Customs of the Modern Egyptians* (London, 1871), I, pp. 320–1.

[3] L. Waddell, *The Buddhism of Tibet* (London, 1895), p. 401. For this and other references, see Frazer (1919), III, p. 414. For examples from the classical world, see W. Robertson Smith, *The Religion of the Semites* (1889), p. 163.

Westermarck gives an account of a similar session in Morocco where an attempt was made to discover a thief.

At Fez the performance takes place on the spot where the theft was committed. The scribe washes the right hand of the boy ['who has not yet reached the age of puberty'], keeps it then over a fire-pot in which he is burning white and black benzoin, pours into the centre of the palm some Moorish ink, touches the boy's forehead with his own right hand, tells him to fix his eyes on the ink, and recites something from the Koran as an incantation. He asks the boy if he sees anything, and if the answer is no, goes on with his incantation until the boy says that he sees something. 'What do you see?', asks the scribe. 'I see people,' answers the youngster. The scribe tells him to say to them 'Make an army come out.'

The horsemen are then asked to bring the thief; and if the boy recognizes the man, he reports to the scribe; 'the latter tells him to pour the ink from his hand back into the inkstand, and when this is done the scribe licks up any ink that remains in the palm' (Westermarck 1933: 10–11).

This Moorish Rorschach test is carried out with the aid of an earthly scribe and a supernatural *jinn*, who can also be controlled by writing charms, usually passages from the Qur'ān arranged in special patterns.

Other divinatory systems involve the use of writing in a yet more direct manner. In parts of India, the names of suspects were sometimes inscribed on balls of wax which were then thrown into water. It was believed that the ball containing the name of the thief would float while the rest would sink to the bottom of the vessel. In the villages of Europe, Frazer notes, 'young people used to resort to many forms of divination on Midsummer Eve in order to ascertain their fortune in love. Thus in Dorsetshire a girl on going to bed would write the letters of the alphabet on scraps of paper and drop them in a basin of water with the letters downwards; and next morning she would expect to find the first letter of her future husband's name turned up...' (1918: II, 431–2).

In Egypt, as in the western Sudan, there are two features of this 'magic' which are especially relevant to the present discussion. First, except among some reformist groups (like the followers of 'Uthmān dan Fodio), it carries religious approval and is often practised by learned men. Secondly, it not only employs writing but is based upon works of reference, upon 'spell-books' and cabalistic texts. With regard to the first point, Lane writes that 'the more intelligent of the Muslims distinguish two kinds of magic, which they term "Er-Rooḥanee"...and "Es-Seemiyà": the former is *spiritual* magic, which is believed to effect its wonders by the agency of angels and genii, and by the mysterious virtues of certain names of God, and other supernatural means; the latter is *natural* and *deceptive* magic;

and its chief agents, the less credulous Muslims believe to be perfumes and drugs' (Lane 1871: I, 332).[1]

Spiritual magic consists of two sorts, high (or divine) and low (or satanic). The first 'is said to be a science founded on the agency of God...; to be always employed for good purposes and only attained and practised by men of probity, who, by tradition, and from books, learn the names of those superhuman agents, and invocations which ensure compliance with their desires. The writing of charms for good purposes belongs to this branch of magic, and to astrology, and to the science of the mysteries of numbers' (Lane 1871: I, 332–3). The highest attainment in this field also lies in knowing the name of God, the great name, *al-ism al-aʿẓam*, thought to be known only to prophets and apostles, and having the greatest power of all.[2] 'A person acquainted with it can, it is said, by merely uttering it, raise the dead to life, kill the living, transport himself instantly wherever he pleases, and perform any other miracle' (Lane 1871: I, 333).

In the Ashanti hinterland, texts of this kind are not only numerous, they are also widely distributed. In the town of Gbuipe in central Gonja, a work of this kind, containing magical squares for all purposes and a plethora of the type of cabalistic diagram often employed by anthropologists to present their formalizations of human thought and action, was the only book I saw in regular use during a stay of six months. Among the group of Gonja Muslims in Kpembe (also of the Sakpare, i.e. Kamagtay, group), a similar book of some 300 folios held a position of similar importance. Among the 'stranger' Muslims of Salaga, with their wider interests and alternative sources of income, such books did not assume such an important role; libraries were more diversified and volumes of this kind appear to have been consulted less frequently. Nevertheless, even a town like Salaga was a ferment of magical activity, alive with diviners and the prescribers of 'medicine'.

In West Africa, the demand for services of this kind is likely to be at least as great as under the conditions Lane was describing; for while the proportion of Muslims is less, the pagans form a considerable proportion of the clientele even of an Islamic mallam.

The demand for Muslim charms was an important element in the relations of Ashanti with the north of Ghana, and in the relations of the king and his court with the Muslims resident in Kumasi (Wilks 1966*b*). This much is clear not only from Ashanti accounts but also from the early

[1] A similar dichotomy existed in the early Christian view of charms and amulets: some forms were divine, others devilish (Von Dobschütz, 1910, III, p. 417).

[2] Similar use of the great name of God, often in acrostic form, occurs in Jewish, Christian and Mandaean magic. In Christianity the term 'word' itself was used as a mystical name for God.

nineteenth-century correspondence with the north; over 90 per cent of the 900 folios from Copenhagen consist of magical formulae and charms. Many of these depend on Mediterranean sources, e.g. Ibn Mughallatai al-Turkī, but they display some local variations. Levtzion describes the collection in the following words: 'Cabalistic formulas of all categories...are represented in this collection. Most of these are written on single slips of paper, but there are some treatises dealing at some length with various aspects of this craft.' Among these works are *The merits of Sûrat Yūsuf and its advantages* (the magical virtues of the *Sura* on Joseph in the Qur'ān), *The advantages of the month of Ramadan*, *Devices for a Holy War*, *The Mansions of Moon* (the use of the names of the moon for magical devices), and a list of good and bad days throughout the year Levtzion (1966: 101).

In Gonja such activities, rarely condemned by men of religion, were in much demand from political authorities and private persons alike. The Muslims are frequently consulted about auspicious times for action and the use of medicines for a variety of purposes. Their role as intermediaries with the supernatural goes back to the founding of the kingdom itself. In the Gonja Chronicle of 1752, we have an account of a tradition, still persisting throughout the country, that tells of the beginning of the relationship between the Sakpare Muslims and the Ngbanya ruling estate.

> [Muḥammed al-Abyaḍ] found [Mawura, the Gonja leader] at Kolo [Kawlaw], and that day, a Friday, he found him fighting fiercely...In his hand the Mallam carried a staff, the head of which was covered with leather. He planted it in the ground; he struck the ground and planted the staff in the earth between the combatants. So when he did this and the enemy saw, they fled. By the power of God did he do this [Goody 1954: 36–7].

And, the Chronicle continues, the Gonjas realized the power of these men and 'wished to enter Islam'.[1] A very similar tradition is found in western Gonja, but associated with a Timitay (*mobntisua*) group who are said to have assisted Ndewura Jakpa, the legendary conqueror of Gonja, in his struggle against the Mamprusi occupying the town of Mankuma (Goody, fieldnotes, 1965, 3221). For the more recent period we have many accounts of the mobilization of supernatural forces for mundane political purposes. A crucial moment in the events leading to the Salaga civil war of 1892 was the discovery by the Kabachewura, leader of the rebellious

[1] The sense in which they did so seems debatable if one uses other than Muslim evidence; certainly, in the recent past, the vast majority of chiefs and princes have not been Muslims, for they had to minister to men of all persuasions and carry out a variety of rites. Gonja Muslims often lament the reduced influence of religion; this seems likely to be a myth of the golden age. But other communities have indeed fallen away from Islam in just this manner and both possibilities are certainly on the cards. Whether or not they 'entered Islam', the major festivals of Gonja (as in neighbouring kingdoms of this mixed sort) centre upon Muslim ceremonies.

party, that the Chief of Kpembe, Napo, was consulting the same mallam as he himself (namely, the Imām of Salaga) in order to try and kill him. When the Kabachewura began his revolt, he obtained the assistance of Mallam Imoru from Miong in Dagomba, who provided him with the magical support necessary to defeat his enemies and enter Salaga (Braimah 1967: 24–7). Similar services continue to be rendered at the present day to the new generation of political leaders; one important Bole Muslim assisted the first president of Ghana in his magical affairs and on my recently taking leave of the Imām of Bole he kindly provided me with an unsolicited package (Gonja, *dugu*) to assist in warding off the dangers that can beset a traveller on the road south (fieldnotes, 3465).

Many of the services offered by Muslims are learnt from written sources and the texts they employ are undoubtedly similar to, and in many cases the same as, those in use in the Mediterranean region.[1] These works include the volume by al-Būnī (d. 1225, from Bone in Algeria) entitled *Shams al-ma'ārif* (GAL I, 655), the *Kitāb al-awfāq* (Book of Magic Squares) attributed to al-Ghazzālī (1058/9–1111), *Shūmūs al-anwār wa kunūz al asrār* by Muḥammad b. Muḥammad al-Tilimsānī (d. 1326; GAL II, 83), *Raḥ'mat al-Umma* by al-Suyūṭī (Doutté 1909: 58) on magical medicine, and al-Zanātī's *Kitāb al-Faṣl fi uṣūl 'ilm al-raml* on divination, and the writings of Abīr Ma'ashar al-Falakī.[2] Indeed an important contribution to this literature was made by a Fulani from central Sudan. Muḥammad b. Muḥammad al-Fulānī al-Kashināwī went on the pilgrimage in about 1730, at the same period as the father of the author of the Gonja Chronicle. He

[1] On the circulation of magical books in east Africa see C. H. Becker, 'Materialien zur Kenntnis des Islam in Deutsch-Ostafrika,' *Der Islam*, II (1911), pp. 31 ff. The books mentioned include Aḥmad al-Dayrabi's *K. al-Mujarrabāt* (d. 1738; GAL S II, 445), al-Kharūṣī's *K. al-Nawāmīs*, the work by al-Nāzilī (d. 1884), *Khazīnat al-āsrār* (GAL S II 746), al-Yamani's *K. al-fawā'id*, and al-Būnī's work, *Shams al-ma'ārif*. The last was printed in Bombay in 1880/1, whereas Doutté's copy of this popular and widespread work appeared in Cairo between 1900 and 1902; but in East Africa as elsewhere such texts gained additional efficacy when they were in manuscript. Becker also stresses the importance of secrecy.

On West African amulets, see Marty (1922), p. 419 and appendix. One earlier example is the talisman obtained by James Richardson from Timbuktu and discussed by Krehl, 'Der Talisman James Richardson's', *Dritter Jahresbericht des Vereins von Freunden der Erdkunde zu Leipzig, 1863* (Leipzig, 1864), pp. 52–63, with illustration. Dr B. G. Martin has referred me to illustrations by Ahrens (1915, p. 341; 1917, p. 227) of silver amulets from Sansanne Mango in northern Togoland, the kind that are found in chiefs' head-dresses throughout the western Sudan. The inscriptions on these charms are in fact 'magic squares' of the kind found throughout the Eurasian continent. For other references see Trimingham (1959).

[2] Doutté (1909), p. 58 and Dr B. G. Martin. Some of these works were subsequently printed in Cairo and elsewhere. Dr Martin also mentions *Manba' uṣul al-Ḥikma* by al-Būnī, *Kitāb al-Raḥma fi'l-Tibb wa'l-Hikma* by Jalāl al-Dīn 'Abd al-Raḥmān al-Suyūtī, and *'Ilm al-raml* by Aḥmad Efendī al-'Umarī, astrologer at the Ottoman court in A.H. 1292 (1875–6).

went to Cairo, where he was consulted by the father of the Egyptian historian al-Jabartī, in whose household he finally settled. He was the author of seven works 'primarily concerned with astrology, numerology, and similar subjects' (Bivar and Hiskett 1962: 137).

These writings themselves are based upon earlier Middle Eastern sources, in both oral tradition and the written works stemming originally from the Chaldeans, whose planetary system spread the seven-day week over such large areas of the world.[1]

In northern Ghana the actual identification of these texts is difficult since such literature belongs to a special category known as *asiri* (Gonja and Hausa, 'secrets'), derived from the Arabic, *siḥr*.[2] These books are rarely printed, since part of their potency lies in the manuscript (and hence archaic) form (Doutté 1909: 148). Consequently they rarely appear in library lists and are brought out only in the course of consultation. For the acquisition of these secrets often means laying out a considerable sum of money and their possession provides the owner with the possibility of a small but regular income.[3]

'Secrecy' invades other areas of learning not because of the specific content but because under restricted literacy all books tend to take on a special value through the scarcity of interpreters. The fate of the Gonja Chronicle illustrates the atmosphere that can develop around the written word in such conditions. The first part is a written account of oral tradition, from the Muslim standpoint. Then, from roughly fifty years from the beginning of the eighteenth century, the document provides an annual account of major events in the Gonja kingdom. In 1752, the record stops, though it starts again for three years between 1763 and 1766. Versions of this document spread to most Gonja divisions, where they form a historical source-book for educated Muslims. But at the same time the Chronicle acquired a 'ritual' value; it became a 'secret' kept away from public gaze and brought out only, if at all, on ceremonial occasions. In Gbuipe, for example, it had become part of the *imām's* regalia, an attribute of his office.

[1] The number 7 became the basis of main interpretative schemes throughout the Eurasian continent. In the Old Testament the Creation of the World was fitted into the seven days of the planetary week. In the Middle Ages, Alexander Neckam (1157–1217) finds evidence of celestial harmony and occult power in associating the 7 planets with the 7 liberal arts and the 7 gifts of the Holy Spirit (Thorndike, 1905, p. 15).

[2] For East Africa, too, C. H. Becker remarks, 'Kein Zweig der islamischen Wissenschaften ist für das Verständnis der grossen Rolle, die der Islam in Afrika spielt, so wichtig wie die Geheimwissenschaft, die Magie im weitesten Umfang des Wortes' (1911, p. 31).

[3] Such works were and are in circulation among the Fulani *'ulamā'* of the central Sudan, for in an account of his education 'Abdullāh [dan] Fodio, brother of the Fulani leader, records that he learned *Al-Tiryāq fī 'ilm al-awfāq*. Hiskett, the editor of his work (*'Īdā' al-nusūkh*), notes that this book on the mystical numerical values of Qur'ānic verses probably emanates from North Africa (1957, pp. 565–6).

The tendency to regard the book as not only 'magical' but also 'secret' clearly inhibits the main communicative function of writing. It spreads even to the Holy Book itself. In the Gonja town of Larabanga ('the town of the Arabs'), there rests a copy of the Qur'ān said to have descended from Heaven and to contain records of important dates in the history of the country. But inspection of this volume is forbidden to all, except on the 10th of Muharram when it is formally displayed to those present at the festival of Ashura, known locally as Jentige. The book has become a 'hidden sacrum'[1] and the advantages of literacy as a means of communication have been jettisoned in favour of the magic of the Book.[2]

The attraction of the secretive and magical aspects of Islamic learning did something to inhibit the development of widespread literacy; consequently the implications of this revolutionary new medium were limited in terms of both diffusion and content. But this was the case not only in black Africa (though the situation was aggravated on the fringes of the written world). For when literacy is primarily religious, the Book becomes less a means to further enquiry, a step in the accumulation of knowledge, than an end itself, the timeless depository of all knowledge.

It was for this reason, Doutté claimed, that in North Africa Islam reinforced 'ce caractère primitif de la religiosité des institutions'. Law is entirely religious and it is therefore unchanging. He quotes the official Egyptian representative at an international Congress of Orientalists in Algiers as proclaiming: 'The *sharīʿa* is applicable to every age' (Doutté 1909: 8). How can science flourish under these conditions? Though perhaps more favourable than Catholicism in the Middle Ages, because of its simplicity of dogma, Islam inhibited the potential development of critical thinking: the great effort towards rationalism by the Muʿtazilites was forcibly suppressed. The conservative element in Islam was partly institutionalized. 'Cette crainte de l'étranger,' wrote Doutté, 'et en général de toutes les innovations, prolongée dans la religion musulmane, s'y est

[1] For other examples in Bornu and Hausaland, see H. R. Palmer, *Sudanese Memoirs*, p. 75. The Kano Chronicle records an incident in the life of the last Hausa Sarki of Kano about the year 1800, when a famine occurred and he was asked to sacrifice to a shrine called Dirki: 'His chiefs said to him, "Sarkin Kano, why do you refuse to give cattle to Dirki?" The Sarki said, "I cannot give you forty cattle for Dirki." They said, "What prevents you? If any Sarkin Kano does not allow us cattle for Dirki, we fear that he will come to some ill." Alwali was very angry and sent young men to beat "Dirki" with axes until that which was inside the skins came out. They found a beautiful Koran inside Dirki. Alwali said, "Is this Dirki?" They said "Who does not know Dirki? Behold here is Dirki." Dirki is nothing but the Koran.' And the Chronicle continues by pointing the moral that it was during Alwali's time the Fulani conquered the seven Hausa states and the rule of the dynasty came to an end (H. R. Palmer, The Kano Chronicle, *J.R. Anthrop. Inst.* XXXVIII (1908), pp. 93–4, republished in *Sudanese Memoirs*).

[2] The Atharva Vēda of the Brahmins, the repository of much magical lore, is 'the Secret Work'.

épanouie dans la théorie de la *bid'a*: toute innovation est hérétique' (1909: 49).

Periods such as the 'Abbāsid caliphate of Baghdad saw a flowering of the arts and sciences. Nevertheless, there has been a constant tendency for Islamic culture to shy away from the free speculation that science and philosophy demand and which were such a notable aspect of life in the Greek world.

Religion was the prime aim of learning. As for science, it flourished, as O'Leary notes, mostly in the atmosphere of courts. 'Scientists usually depended upon wealthy and powerful patrons. They appealed little to the average man, and this chiefly because scientific and especially philosophical speculation was regarded as tending towards free-thinking in religion, and so "philosophers" were classed as a species of heretics.' It was those learned in jurisprudence, tradition and the Qur'ān who were universally respected, while scientists were only tolerated because they were under state protection; 'scientific and philosophical scholarship was confined to one privileged coterie' (O'Leary 1948: 5).

Even in theology, tradition was supreme. Of Mālikī communities generally Hiskett writes that 'theological speculation is regarded askance by the pious' (1963: 7). It was only under the Berber dynasty of *Murābiṭs* in the eleventh century that Muslim Spain began to be interested in philosophical speculation, as a result of Mu'tazilite influence from Baghdad, mediated by Jewish scholars who played a notable part in medical and scientific studies (O'Leary 1939: 237). The *Murābiṭs* were followed by another Berber dynasty, the *Muwaḥḥids*, who enforced orthodoxy among their subjects by means of persecution, but philosophers were nevertheless free to work provided that 'teaching was not spread abroad amongst the populace' (1939: 250). Ibn Rushd (1126–98), the greatest of the Arabic philosophers, known to the West as Averroës, elaborated this stratification of mankind into a specific doctrine when he distinguished between that class of men whose religious belief is based on demonstration, the result of reasoning from syllogisms, and the lowest stratum whose faith is based on the authority of the teacher; to them reason only causes doubt and difficulty (O'Leary 1939: 255). The first category, allowed to make use of Aristotelian logic, were of course the literates; the second, the followers, were the illiterate. And these categories were not simply conceptual, but born of experience, for he had himself been accused of heretical opinions, stripped of his honours and banished to a place near Cordova, because of the deep dislike with which the multitude viewed speculative studies.

I have attempted three lines of argument in this essay; all are related to the importance of literacy. First, I have tried to show that in northern Ghana, as in large regions of Africa, virtually the whole of the Eurasian continent and parts, too, of the Pacific, we rarely find societies that were not influenced in some way by the techniques and products of alphabetic literacy, even before the coming of the Europeans. A full recognition of this fact casts serious doubts upon the suitability of an all-embracing functional or structural analysis of such societies. For the presence of writing means that the analytical model must necessarily be more complex than that appropriate for oral societies since it must take into account the fact that the cultural data embodied in graphic signs include materials accumulated from diverse societies, distant in both time and space. When systems of magic squares stretch from China, India, the Middle East to medieval Europe (Ahrens 1917) and span an incredible variety of human societies, religions, 'codes', we cannot readily understand them as holding the key to any one of these cultures. As with other cultural phenomena transmitted in the same way, the degree of *entailment* in any one culture is necessarily limited. In some major respects they are free-floating, like other literary products; indeed these magical squares are born of writing itself and have spread with it.[1]

Secondly, I have tried to show the effects of literate techniques on the social systems of the area. While these effects lay mainly in the magico-religious field, other areas were also influenced. Writing impressed the illiterate as a means of communication, for supernatural as well as natural purposes; indeed these aspects of human intercourse are unlikely to be distinguished in oral cultures (Goody 1961: 155 ff.). Acceptance of the 'magical' quality of writing was in itself a move towards acceptance of the religious systems associated with it. Magic could therefore lead to conversion and hence, in turn, to a fuller literacy.[2] But the very fact that it was the attraction of writing that led to Islam increased the likelihood of apostasy, as did the dispersion of Muslims and their close affinal contacts with pagans. For the uses of literacy were few and, outside the trading community, could be carried out by a small number of practitioners.

The writing that Islam brought did not create the initial possibility of long-distance trade, but the man who could keep elementary accounts and communicate at a distance certainly had many advantages. Added to this,

[1] The history of magic squares is closely bound up with developments in mathematics (e.g. among the Pythagoreans); indeed the techniques of multiplication and division, as distinct from addition and subtraction, seem essentially graphic procedures. Of course, once invented, and memorized in tables, mental multiplication is possible; otherwise it is serial addition, just as division is serial subtraction.

[2] See also Hunwick (1964*a*), p. 34, and Wilks (1966*b*), p. 331.

membership of a universalistic religion formed a bond between traders from different groups, as well as providing the umbrella of a fixed legal code. Belonging to Islam was, Marty remarks, like belonging to a touring-club, and it is therefore hardly surprising to find that the most successful traders, the Dyula and the Hausa, were the most ardent Muslims. I knew only two Muslims from the LoDagaa villages in which I worked; both were traders and had moved off to a multi-ethnic settlement along the main road. The conversion of a trader is more firmly based than that of the peasant because of the economic and social pay-off.

As far as Gonja was concerned, the political benefits of literacy were few, but it did permit chiefs and Muslims to deal with one another at a distance and it enabled individuals to make some record of oral tradition and to chronicle the passing years. For the Muslims at any rate, history had emerged from 'myth' and was something more than the reflection of present concerns, just as lists of chiefs and *imāms* were no longer genealogical mirrors of social relationships, though the homeostatic processes of memory still controlled the transmission of the bulk of cultural forms.

Literacy also introduced another principle of stratification to set beside chiefship. The pyramid of learning, largely one of achieved status, supplemented the pyramid of chiefly power, largely ascribed.

What was the influence on the categories of the understanding, particularly upon concepts of time and space? In Gonja such concepts are stratified by social group. The horizons of the Muslims were greatly extended through the written word. Not only do they think in terms of an era and a succession of years, but the precise calculation of days and months is an essential part of all festivals; so too is the reckoning of the hours for prayer, though this is more crudely done. Concepts of space were similarly extended by trade, pilgrimage and books. While the works of the Arab geographers were little known, the Muslim community was inevitably more concerned with distant lands and the means of getting there. But their 'map-making' took a linear form, since it was expressed in one-dimensional itineraries rather than two dimensional charts.[1]

The influence of writing clearly lay not only in the medium but also in the message, that is, in the content of the books imported into the area, especially those concerned with magic, religion and law. The existence of a legal code which was so closely linked with the word of God (it was

[1] The problem that faced European map-makers of West Africa was to translate these itineraries into cartographic form, as for example in the maps of the Gonja region by de l'Isle (1714) and Rennell (1790); see Goody (1964), p. 203. Wilks calls my attention to Bello's map in Denham and Clapperton, *Travels and Discoveries in Northern and Central Africa* (1826), facing p. 109; this relatively sophisticated map still shows its direct dependence upon the itineraries of halting places, but it is a move away from purely linear schemes.

as if the only law was canon law) meant there were strong pressures upon certain societies, or anyhow upon important groups within those societies, to adopt new forms of social action. The influence of these law books—Mālikī law from the Maghreb—upon Sudanese societies has been touched upon by various authors and it cannot be doubted that changes of considerable significance have occurred and are continually occurring, in the system of kinship and marriage as well as in the organization of kin groups, in the position of the chief, etc. But what is of central importance here is not so much the diffusion of Islam but the fact that Islam is a religion of the book.

This point leads to the final aspect of my discussion. Given that alphabetic literacy has such explosive potentialities, why were its consequences in the western Sudan less radical than elsewhere? Literacy was restricted in its diffusion, its content and its implications largely because it was a religious literacy, dominated by the study of the Holy Book. Indeed learning to read at all meant learning a foreign language, Arabic, and the actual techniques of teaching were often more appropriate to oral rather than written cultures. But the main factor in restricting the developments in the cognitive sphere was the association of the book with magic and religion, an exclusive, all-embracing cult that claimed it had the single road to truth. It is above all the predominantly religious character of literacy that, here as elsewhere, prevented the medium from fulfilling its promise.[1]

APPENDIX I WRITING IN GONJA

by JACK GOODY AND IVOR WILKS

ARABIC SCRIPT

The following lists contain primarily works of local Gonja authorship, that is, works either by native Gonja or by persons domiciled there. The many works of Middle Eastern, North African and western and central Sudanese origins which circulate in Gonja are therefore omitted. Furthermore, no attempt has been made to list the numerous written prayers and magical formulae which most Gonja Muslims possess and which may be, in some sense, of local authorship. While the lists are not exhaustive, an attempt has been made to include most of the material to be found in public collections as of 1967. The principal source has been the Arabic Collection at the Institute of African Studies, University of Ghana. Abbreviations used in the lists are cited fully at the end.

[1] I am most grateful to Mervyn Hiskett, B. G. Martin and Esther Goody for their help in various ways, and I owe a special debt to Ivor Wilks for his learned comments over a number of years. It will be quite clear to any specialist the extent to which I have depended upon the work of colleagues like Hodgkin, Braimah, Levtzion and others, though their conclusions would certainly differ from mine.

Many of the items listed here have yet to be fully examined: their descriptions must therefore be taken as provisional. They are classed, for convenience, under seven heads.

A *General historical material*

The items in this section are all broadly historical in character, and include chronicles, office-lists (of chiefs and *imāms*), and recensions of oral tradition. The earliest item seems to date from the beginning of the eighteenth century; it is not clear how far beyond this the local tradition of authorship extends. The most important item in the section is the mid-eighteenth-century *Kitāb Ghunjā*. Its author, al-Ḥājj Muḥammad b. al-Muṣṭafā, was a member of a Dyula Kamaghatay group which, since the early seventeenth century, had provided the Gonja rulers with *imāms* and other Muslim functionaries. Other works of a historical kind will be found in special categories below, see particularly D and F.

B *Early nineteenth-century correspondence*

This section contains a series of letters, all apparently from the first quarter of the nineteenth century, between various *imāms* in Gonja and Gonja residents in Kumasi. Some were written for, or were addressed to, the Asantehene Osei Bonsu (d. 1824). Gonja had come under the influence of Ashanti power in the second quarter of the eighteenth century, though the effects were felt much more strongly in eastern Gonja than in western. The Ashanti king's letters were addressed to *imāms* in both regions. The first letter is of particular importance in signalizing the change in Osei Bonsu's attitude towards the Muslims in his territory: as Dupuis (1824: 98) noted, this king had commenced his reign 'an avowed enemy to the religion of Islam', but the letter confirms what is otherwise apparent from the accounts of early nineteenth-century visitors to Kumasi, that Osei Bonsu soon saw in the extension of his patronage to Muslims a means of strengthening his own position in relationship to that of his subordinate chiefs. Two route-books, compiled by the writers of some of the letters, have also been included. With this exception, all items are to be found in the Cod. Arab. CCCII collection in the Royal Library, Copenhagen (and photographic reproductions in the Institute of African Studies, University of Ghana). The Copenhagen collection also contains several copies of Middle Eastern works of *madīḥ* and sufism produced by scribes from Salaga, among them 'Umar Kunandi b. 'Umar al-Amīn, author of the later eighteenth-century addendum to the *Kitāb Ghunjā* and father of Mālik, *imām* of Buipe and later of Gonja in the early nineteenth century.

C *Writings of al-Ḥājj 'Umar b. Abī Bakr*

A renaissance of writing took place in Gonja with the arrival in Salaga of this Hausa scholar from Kano around 1874, just after the Ashanti had been forced to withdraw. Al-Ḥājj 'Umar's father, Abū Bakr b. 'Uthmān, had been engaged in the kola trade between Salaga, Kebbi and Kano: with the expansion of European influence in North Africa and in the hinterland of the Guinea Coast, the kola trade was one of the few remaining outlets for Hausa commercial enterprise and was of great importance at this time. Al-Ḥājj 'Umar was born in Kano about 1854. He went to school first in Kano, then in Kebbi, and then in Gobir. As a boy he seems to have accompanied his father on several trading expeditions to Salaga, and settled there when about twenty years of age. He produced his first work in Salaga in 1877—a volume on epistolary styles which was later published in Cairo. His later works in both Arabic and Hausa exhibit a range of topics, and a quality, which mark him off as one of the major literary figures in West Africa. Perhaps the most interesting of his writings are those concerned with the Salaga civil war of 1892 and with the subsequent European penetration into the area. The civil war led to a dispersal of the people of Salaga, many, like al-Ḥājj 'Umar himself, to Kete-Krachi, and later to *zongos* all over southern Ghana. Many of the schools and libraries scattered in different parts of the country have their origins in the dispersal of the *malams* or *karamokos* from Salaga after 1892. Al-Ḥājj 'Umar, or Alhajji Imoru Krachi as he is known colloquially, died in 1934 and was buried in the Krachi mosque, now beneath the waters of the Volta Lake. Al-Ḥājj 'Umar's writings appear to have enjoyed popularity not only in Ghana but also in Nigeria. Five of his works, for example, are listed from the National Archives of Kaduna (Last, *Bull. CAD*, 1967, 3, 1, p. 14). Two of these appear identical with IASAR/313 and IASAR/16 (iv) listed below, but the other three, *Kitāb al-tarsīl fī'l lughāt*, *Maḥmalat ṭanbūl*, and *Takhmīs bānat Su'ād*, cannot readily be identified with any of the MSS listed here without further examination.

D *The school of Salaga*

The teachings and example of al-Ḥājj 'Umar b. Abī Bakr would seem to have stimulated literary activity in eastern Gonja, especially in Salaga and Kpandai in the Kpembe division, but also over a much wider area. One Salaga writer of the immediate pre-colonial period was Maḥmūd, son of the chief of Lampor whose *Qiṣṣat Salgha Ta'rīkh Ghunjā* contains *inter alia* an account of the growth of Salaga and of the civil war there; a Hausa version of this work was produced by Malam al-Ḥasan, and subsequently English translations have been published from both Arabic and Hausa texts. Malam al-Ḥasan himself was an extremely active figure in Salaga literary circles, and was in later life *imām* of the Salaga Friday mosque (from which period many of his letters survive, see Section F) until his death in 1933/4. Malam al-Ḥasan was son of 'Umar al-Faqīh of Salaga, himself a man of considerable learning descended on his father's side from Shaykh Alfa Sabi, who left Djougou to settle in Salaga probably in the early nineteenth century, and on his mother's side from Alfa Hamma, a Massina Fulani whose son 'U<u>th</u>mān established a school at Kpabia—the old Muslim town between Salaga and Yendi (see Dupuis 1824: xcvii; Binger 1892: II, 72–3). It was probably whilst at this school that Malam al-Ḥasan produced his editions of the histories of Dagomba, Mamprusi, Wagadugu, Gonja and the Grunshi, since in one of these he describes himself as of 'Kobiya', i.e. Kpabia. Malam al-Ḥasan should be regarded as a colleague, rather than a disciple, of al-Ḥājj 'Umar; the School of Salaga may be seen as drawing its strength in the late nineteenth and early twentieth centuries principally from these two scholars. The descendants of Malam al-Ḥasan, however, say that he had a marked reluctance to make his writings public, and certainly few of them are yet known. Al-Ḥājj 'Umar, too, appears to have attracted far more students, and of these both 'Ali b. Muḥammad Baraw and Yūsuf Abin-Nema produced works on Salaga affairs written in the general style of their teacher. Other of his students became active in the literary field in their own towns, such as Imām Khālid b. Ya'qūb of Yendi, who recorded in Arabic parts of the Dagomba drum histories (IASAR/241). In general it may be observed that many of the manuscripts found in southern Ghana today are to be regarded as of Gonja origin, for when Salaga lost its importance as a commercial centre many of its inhabitants, like al-Ḥājj 'Umar himself, moved to such other centres as Kete-Krachi, Yeji, Attebubu and Kumasi. They took with them many of their books, and, as we have noted, sometimes continued to produce new works that are therefore essentially part of the Gonja tradition. In this category must almost certainly be placed the Hausa folk-lore material collected by Rattray (1913) when he was District Commissioner of Yeji. There, where the Kumasi-Salaga route crossed the Volta, and where 'each month thousands of Hausas from all parts of Nigeria' crossed the river taking cattle south and returning with kola, Rattray commenced his study of Hausa under the guidance of one Malam Shaihu, a scholar who had collected 'many hundreds of sheets of manuscripts (1907–11)' and had himself written down the texts or translated them from Hausa. One of the translations was that of a work on Hausa history up to the time of 'Uthmān dan Fodio. Most of the texts obtained from Malam Shaihu, however, appear to have been taken down from oral narratives, and consist of 'stories about people' (21 texts), about animals (9), accounts of customs (9), of various arts (3), and of proverbs, some 133. Earlier, during the period of the German occupation of Togo, Mischlich had collected from al-Ḥājj 'Umar, then resident in Kete-Krachi, accounts of early Hausa history, of the *jihād* of 1804, and of post-*jihād* history, the latter apparently the work of al-Ḥājj 'Umar himself (Mischlich 1903).

E *The Krause manuscripts from Salaga*

Gottlob Adolf Krause was in Salaga for several lengthy periods between 1886 and 1894, working as explorer, trader and scholar. His interest in the Hausa language, which he spoke fluently, led him to compile, whilst in Salaga, a series of texts in that language which were published, in Arabic script, in *Mitteilungen des Seminars für Orientalische Sprachen* (XXXI, 1928). They were republished, with Russian translations, in D. A. Olderogge, *Zapadnyi Sudan* (Moscow–Leningrad 1960). The character of these texts is varied. Some, for example, are translations into Hausa, made by Krause perhaps with the assistance of local scholars, of Arabic works by 'Uthmān dan Fodio and his brother 'Abdullāh' and others by Si'itu Bakatine and Yūsuf Baidafu. Others are animal fables almost certainly recorded by Krause from the narratives of informants. In this section we have listed all those texts which have a bearing upon Salaga affairs. Some, such as the letters between Madugu Isa and Ya Na Andani, are clearly copies (and probably translations from the Arabic) of written originals. Others, such as the account of the expulsion of the Ashanti from Salaga were probably dictated to Krause by witnesses of the events in question. His account of the Zabarima campaigns against the Grunshi contained in 30.S. 49–56, might turn out to be related to the history of the Grunshi compiled by Malam al-Ḥasan of Salaga (see Section D) which has not yet been recovered.

F *Administrative papers from the Kpembe division*

In 1964 a bundle of MSS was obtained from Kpandai which are concerned mainly with the administrative affairs of the area in the earlier part of this century. They include various lists, called *bābs*, 'chapters', presumably drawn up for taxation and census purposes, and many letters between the Kanunkulaiwura and local *imāms* and *malams*. A few items of a similar character from Salaga have been added. It is not yet known whether Arabic was used for general administrative purposes in Gonja in pre-colonial times. Unlike religious texts, such papers are not continually copied and recopied, and hence their survival value is low. It is interesting to note that the Moroccan Al-Ḥājj 'Abd al-Salām Shabīnī, who visited western Hausaland *c.* 1787 (whence Salaga received many of its immigrants), reported that written records were kept there of all land transactions, including notes of the areas of farms and of their boundaries (*An Account of Timbuctoo and Housa*, ed. J. G. Jackson, London, 1820).

G *Miscellaneous*

A residual category which includes one work written in Arabic script but in Gonja language, the only other example in public collections being the historical fragment from Kafaba listed in Section A. There are also biographical papers recommending the examples of al-Ḥājj 'Umar b. Abī Bakr and Malam al-Ḥasan; two letters sent to Salaga by a nephew of al-Ḥājj 'Umar then visiting Adamawa (one of which contains the text of a communication from 'Uthmān dan Fodio to Malam Adam); and miscellaneous twentieth-century correspondence between various northern chiefs and British administrative officials.

Abbreviations, References, etc.

Braimah (1967) J. A. Braimah, *The Two Isanwurfos*. London, 1967.

Braimah and Goody (1967) J. A. Braimah and J. Goody, *Salaga: the Struggle for Power*. London, 1967.

Bull. C.A.D. *Research Bulletin*, Centre for Arabic Documentation, Institute of African Studies, University of Ibadan, Nigeria.

Cod. Arab. Arabic Collection, Royal Library, Copenhagen.

Dupuis (1824) J. Dupuis, *Journal of a Residence in Ashantee*. London, 1824.

GAL C. Brockelmann, *Geschichte der Arabischen Litteratur*. Second ed. 1943–9, two vols. Supplement, 1937–42, three vols.

Goody (1954) J. Goody, *The Ethnography of the Northern Territories of the Gold Coast West of the Black Volta*. London, 1954.

IASAR Arabic Collection, Institute of African Studies, University of Ghana.

Jackson (1820) J. G. Jackson (ed.), *An Account of Timbuctoo and Housa*. London, 1820.

Mischlich and Lippert (1903) A. Mischlich and J. Lippert, Beiträge zur Geschichte der Haussastaaten, *Mitt. Sem. Or. Sprache*, VI, 3, pp. 137–242.

MSOS *Mitt. Sem. Or. Sprache*. Berlin.

Rattray (1913) R. S. Rattray, *Hausa Folk-lore*, 2 vols. Oxford, 1913.

Rattray (1934) R. S. Rattray, Hausa poetry, in *Essays Presented to C. G. Seligman* (ed. E. E. Evans-Pritchard *et al.*), pp. 255–66. London, 1934.

Research Review Bulletin of the Institute of African Studies, University of Ghana.

Zech (1896) Graf Zech, Aus dem Schutzgebiete Togo, in *Mitteilungen aus den Deutschen Schutzgebieten* (1896), XI, ii, pp. 89 *et seq.*

Note

Dr Martin has pointed out that the work of Arabic prosody with which Al-Ḥājj 'Umar worked (see p. 220) was presumably: 'Badr al-Dīn Muḥammad... Al-Makhzūmī al-Iskandarānī, known as al-Damamīnī (1362–1424), *Al-'Uyūn al-Ghāmiza 'Alā l-Khabāyā'al-Rāmiza*, a commentary on 'Alī al-Khazrajī (d. 1229), *Al-Rāmiza al-Shāfīya fī 'Ilmay al-Arūḍ wa'l-Qāfiya*, see R. Basset, *La Khazradjyah*, Algiers, 1902, pp. VII–IX.

He also informs us that the magical work of the early eighteenth century Fulani scholar (p. 235) is still one of the most widely-read texts in East Africa; it is entitled: *Al-Durr al-Manẓūm fi'l-Siḥr wa'l-Ṭilasm wa'l-Nujūm*, Cairo, Muṣṭafā al-Bābī al-Ḥalabī, n.d.

A *General historical material*

Date	Language	Reference	Title	Author	Description	Length	Notes
Early 18th century	Arabic	Cod. Arab. CCCII, iii, ff. 236–7, Royal Library, Copenhagen	—	—	Chs. I and II: circumstances of the conversion to Islam of the Gonja kings. Ch. III: list of the early Gonja kings with length of reign	2 ff.	Probably written *c.* 1712. Used by the author of the mid-18th century *Kitāb Ghunjā*, see below
1751/2	Arabic	IASAR/62	*Kitāb Ghunjā* (The Book of Gonja)	Al-Ḥājj Muḥammad b. al-Muṣṭafā	Compilation of early Gonja traditions, with dated king list, with a chronicle of events from early to mid-18th century	7 ff.	Other copies: IASAR/10; 11; 12; 13; 14; 248 (i); 272. Some of these have an addendum to the chronicle, from 1763–6, by Imām 'Umar Kunandi b. 'Umar. For a translation, see J. Goody, *Ethnography* (1954), app. IV
	Arabic	IASAR/263	*Amr Ajdādinā Jighi Jara* (concerning our ancestor Jighi Jara)	—	An account of the Malian origins of the Gonja ruling dynasty, and of the creation of the kingdom	4 ff.	For other versions in translation, see Goody (1954), app. VI
	Hausa	IASAR/254	—	—	Account of relations between the Gonja ruler Jakpa and the Asantehene Osei Tutu, with a section on the pagans of Krachi	3 ff.	IASAR/255 is an Arabic version of the same work. For a translation, see Goody (1954), app. V
	Arabic	IASAR/268	*Ta'rīkh Ghazw Ghunjāwi* (History of a Gonja Raid)	—	Fragmentary notes on a Gonja campaign, etc.	1 f.	—
	Arabic	IASAR/271	—	—	Miscellaneous notes on various Gonja figures, the Yagbumwura al-Ḥājj Amua; al-Ḥājj al-Muṣṭafā who died in Katsina, etc.	1 f.	Apparently extracts from the *Kitāb Ghunjā*

Date	Language	Reference	Title	Author	Description	Length	Notes
1751/2	Arabic	IASAR/265	—	—	List of Yagbumwuras from Naba'a to Muḥammad al-Abyaḍ, and of Kpembewuras starting with Muḥammad al-Abyaḍ b. al-Latā (Jakpa)	1 f.	The first list apparently derivative from the Cod. Arab. CCCII, iii, 236–7 MS, see above
	Arabic	IASAR/266	(i) *'Asmā' amīr Kunbi* (ii) *'Asmā' amīr Sanghunghu*	—	List of Kpembe chiefs, commencing with Ṣāliḥ, and of Sungbung chiefs, with 'Abd al-Raḥmān	1 f.	—
c. 1915	Arabic	IASAR/269	*'Asmā' al-mulūk Layfu* (Names of the Kings of Layfu)	—	List of the chiefs of Lepo: Bagha, Kali, 'Uthmān, etc.	1 f.	—
	Arabic	IASAR/448	—	—	List of early Gonja kings, with *ajami* and Muslim names	1 f.	—
	Arabic	IASAR/259	*'Asmā' Sulṭān Kūbi*	—	List of Kpembewuras, from Mawura to Banbanga	1 f.	Zech (1896), p. 96, has a similar list from an Arabic MS
	Arabic	IASAR/262	*Al-'Asmā' al-umarā' Kafaba*	—	List of the chiefs of Kafaba	1 f.	—
	Arabic	IASAR/41	—	—	List of twenty-three chiefs of Daboya	1 f.	—
	Arabic	IASAR/42	—	—	List of the chiefs of Daboya	2 ff.	—
	Arabic	IASAR/40	—	—	List of the Ashanti kings, with length of reign	1 f.	Said by its owner, al-Ḥājj Qāsim of Bole, to be extracted from a longer work by his father 'Abdullāh
	Arabic	IASAR/341	—	—	List of eleven *imāms* of Dokrupe	1 f.	—
	Arabic	IASAR/500 (i)	—	—	List of twelve chiefs of Kafaba	1 f.	—
	Arabic	IASAR/500 (ii)	—	—	List of ten *imāms* of Kafaba	1 f.	—
	Gonja	IASAR/501	—	—	Concerning Kafaba, Kpembe and Kolo	1 f.	—

B *Early nineteenth-century correspondence*

(Cod. Arab. CCCII, Royal Library, Copenhagen)

Date	Language	Reference	Writer	Description	Length	Notes
1810 or shortly before	Arabic	Cod. Arab. CCCII, iii, f. 5	Bābā, son of the Imām of Gambaga, from Kumasi	Letter to Mālik, the Imām of Buipe, and to the Imām of Daboya, informing them of a decision of the Ashanti Council to free all Muslim slaves, with an account of ill-advice offered the Asantehene by one Karamo Ṣālī and his son	1 f.	—
	Arabic	i, f. 106	Idrīs b. Malam Karfā, Imām of Kpembe	Letter to Muḥammad, son of the Imām of Buipe, notifying him of the death of Imām Karfā and of the poverty of his surviving dependents	1 f.	—
	Arabic	i, f. 4	Muḥammad b. Abi Bakr, Imām of Kpembe	Letter to a resident in Kumasi, containing instructions for averting evil from the town by prayer and magic, with details of *ṣadaqa* to be paid	1 f.	Probably written in reply to requests made by the Asantehene
	Arabic	i, f. 126	'U<u>th</u>mān, son of the Imām of Buipe	Letter to the Asantehene, 'friend to the Muslims', wishing him victory; also conveying greetings to Muḥammad and Ṣūmā, Gonja residents in Kumasi	1 f.	Probably with reference to the Gyaman (Abron) campaign of 1818–19
1817 or 1818	Arabic	i, f. 146	—	Letter to the Asantehene, 'Sultan of the Muslims', *inter alia* predicting a successful outcome of the Gyaman war	1 f.	In the handwriting of the Imām of Buipe (or of his scribe)
	Arabic	i, f. 188	Imām of Buipe	Letter to the Asantehene containing advice about a woman he wished to marry	1 f.	—
Between 1818 and 1824	Arabic	ii, f. 1	Asantehene (scribe Muḥammad, son of the Imām of Gonja)	Letter to Mālik, Imām of Gonja, and to the Imām of Buipe, requesting prayers to avert sickness	1 f.	—
Between 1818 and 1824	Arabic	i, f. 169	Mālik, Imām of Gonja	Letter to Muḥammad and Ṣūmā, Gonja residents in Kumasi, asking them to read certain prayers before the Asantehene, and listing the *ṣadaqa*. Also asking for paper to be sent to them in Gonja	1 f.	Another copy, ii, f. 1

B *Early nineteenth-century correspondence (cont.)*

Date	Language	Reference	Writer	Description	Length	Notes
Between 1818 and 1824	Arabic	i, f. 73	Mālik, Imām of Gonja	Letter to the Asantehene, informing him that prayers are being made on his behalf and asking for *ṣadaqa* (including two slaves, twelve *mithqāls*, and a gun)	1 f.	—
	Arabic	iii, f. 6	Four *faqīhs*	Letter to, *inter alia*, Muḥammad and Ṣūmā, Gonja residents in Kumasi, sending medicine for the Asantehene, and complaining of famine	1 f.	The four authors of this letter are Ṣāliḥ, Sirifi, Kība, and Aljuma. There is no indication of their place of residence
	Arabic	Dupuis (1824), p. cxxv	Ṣūmā, a Gonja resident in Kumasi	Description of the route from Salaga to Hausaland, the Fezzan, Egypt and Mecca		For the use of pilgrims
	Arabic	Dupuis (1824), p. cxxviii	Muḥammad Kamaghatay, a Gonja resident in Kumasi	Description of the route from Salaga to Hausaland, the Fezzan, Egypt and Mecca		This route follows a more northerly road between Salaga and Katsina than the above

C *Writings of al-Ḥājj 'Umar b. Abī Bakr of Kano, Salaga and Kete-Krachi*

Date	Language	Reference	Title	Description	Length	Notes
1877	Arabic	IASAR/313	*Kitāb al-sarḥat al-warīqa fī 'ilm al-wathīqa*	Guide to epistolography, *inshā'*: collection of model letters with advice to the secretary	17 ff.	Published in the collection *Majmū'a taḥtawi 'ala al-qaṣā'id*, Cairo: Issa al-Babi al-Halabi. See also GAL S.I. 483. Also IASAR/378; 381
	Arabic	IASAR/16 (iv)	*Tarbi' al-zuhd wa'l waṣīya* (On abstemiousness, and admonition)	Treatment in *tarbi'* form of the *Kitāb al-zuhd wa'l waṣīya* of 'Alī Zayn al-'Ābidīn	16 ff.	Published in the collection *Al-qaṣā'id al-'asharīyāt*, Cairo, 1947/8. See GAL SI 76; 483
	Arabic	IASAR/24	*Tarbi' al-Burda*	Treatment in *tarbi'* form of the well-known poem of al-Būsīrī (The Prophet's Mantle)	13 ff.	Other copies: IASAR/122; 217. See GAL I, 264; SI, 467
	Arabic	IASAR/27	*Tanbīḥ fil-ikhwān fī dhikr al-aḥzān*	Poem on the decline of religion and morality in Salaga, and on the failings of its rulers, with an account of the civil war of 1892	9 ff.	Translation by B. Martin in Braimah and Goody (1967)
	Arabic	IASAR/16 (ii)	*Ṭal' al-munāfa'a fī dhikr al-munāza'a*	Account of the Salaga civil war	5 ff.	Translation by B. Martin in Braimah and Goody (1967)
1899/1900	Arabic	IASAR/3	*Naẓm al-la'ālī bi akhbār wa tanbīḥ al-kirām*	Poem lamenting the arrival of the Europeans and listing the towns and countries overrun by them	8 ff.	Other copies: IASAR/8; 139
1899/1900	Arabic	IASAR/4	*Mashra' mā al-khabar li-wārid wāriduhā bi'l naẓar*	Poem of the arrival of the Europeans; the author says that he will not return from Krachi to Salaga	4 ff.	Other copy: IASAR/417. Similar in theme to IASAR/3; 370; 43
Before 1903	Hausa	—	—	An account of Hausa history since the Jihad	—	Mischlich and Lippert (1903), with German translation
1903	Hausa	IASAR/43	*Labarin Nasara*	Poem on the arrival of the Europeans, with references to the defeat of Samori, the Zabarimas, Sokoto, etc.	8 ff.	Other copies: IASAR/302; 370

C *Writings of al-Ḥājj ʻUmar b. Abī Bakr of Kano, Salaga and Kete-Krachi (cont.)*

Date	Language	Reference	Title	Description	Length	Notes
1904/1905	Arabic	IASAR/109 (ii)	*Yā khalīlayya fa-ʻajabā idh raʼayta al-ʻajāʼib*	Poem criticizing the activities of Musa and his companions, who had arrived in Salaga and claimed to be a Mahdi	5 ff.	Other copy: IASAR/135. Translation by B. G. Martin in press
1908/1909	Arabic	IASAR/117	—	Poem on the author's residence in Gambaga, his quarrel with the Imām and his decision to make the pilgrimage	4 ff.	—
1916/1917	Arabic	IASAR/93	*Suʻād aw asmāʼ aw Daʻd aw Hawwā*	Two poems in praise of Yendi and its people	5 ff.	Other copy: IASAR/181. Work verbally attributed to al-Ḥājj ʻUmar
	Hausa	IASAR/292	—	Poem in praise of ʻUthmān, the ʻlion of Kumasi', with an exposition on the divine basis of kingship	16 ff.	Presumably in praise of ʻUthmān, Sarkin Zongo in Kumasi, died *c.* 1919. Attributed verbally to al-Ḥājj ʻUmar, by his grandson, owner of the MS
c. 1918	Arabic	IASAR/23	*Tunkuyawā* (Influenza)	Poem on the symptoms and treatment of influenza	3 ff.	Other copies: IASAR/131; 305. Probably written at the time of the 1918 epidemic
	Arabic	IASAR/76	*Sūl al-Rāthī*	Elegy for Muḥammad, father of al-Ḥājj Ṣāliḥ (of Jenene)	2 ff.	—
1921	Arabic	IASAR/113	—	Ijāza—permission granted to Muḥammad al-thānī b. ʻUthmān Ṣalagha to use the Tijāni *wird*	2 ff.	For other *ijāzas* issued by al-Ḥājj ʻUmar, see IASAR/147; 237. See also IASAR/126
1923	Arabic	IASAR/127	*Bushrā atāka bashīr*	Poem in praise of Ḥusayn al-Kashnawī, known as Salaw, Sarkin Zongo of Kumasi	8 ff.	Other copies: IASAR/16 (xiii); 168; 239 (i)
	Arabic	IASAR/9	—	Poem to thank those contributing to the repair of a mosque (Kete-Krachi?), with special praise for Salaw, Sarkin Zongo of Kumasi	4 ff.	Other copy: IASAR/161

Date	Language	Reference	Title	Description	Length	Notes
	Arabic	IASAR/133	*Ghādarat Salmā Diyāran*	Poem in praise of Ḥusayn al-Kashnawī b. Ya'qūb, Sarkin Zongo of Kumasi, with reference to the shortcomings of the *wazirs* of Kumasi	4 ff.	Other copy: IASAR/239 (ii)
	Arabic	IASAR/239 (iii)	*Fatabaraka al-khallāq*	Poem in praise of Amir Salaw, Ghaḍanfar ('the lion')	3 ff.	—
	Arabic	IASAR/16 (v)	*Mā bālu hind na'at 'annā bi-ghayr qilā*	Elegy for al-Ḥājj Labbu, son of the poet, with an account of the funeral	5 ff.	Other copies: IASAR/109 (iv); 138; 159; (239 (iv)
	Arabic	IASAR/16 (vi)	*Hal li-laylā min marām am li-hindi min kalām*	Poem in praise of the hospitality offered the author by the people of Tetemu (Kpone) Zongo	3 ff.	—
	Hausa	IASAR/171	*Talauci* (Poverty)	Poem on the social evils of poverty	7 ff.	Other copy: IASAR/371
	Arabic	IASAR/121	—	Satirical poem on the pupil of a Hausa *malam* who criticized the author's pronunciation of *al-ḥamdu li-'llāh*	3 ff.	Other copies: IASAR/137; 421
	Hausa	—	*Kundin wākōkin Imruil Kaisi, dan Hujuru*	One page of the translation of the first of thirty-four odes by the pre-Islamic poet 'Imru' al-Qays	—	Rattray, 'Hausa Poetry', with English translation
1932/1933	Arabic	IASAR/132	*Bārr al-Ḥaqq*	Poem addressed to the author's son, Abū Bakr, urging Muslims to be united whatever their differences of tribe	3 ff.	—
	Arabic	IASAR/219	—	Formulae, with prayers, to be used when visiting a grave	1 f.	Said to have been taken down from al-Ḥājj 'Umar
	Arabic	—	*Ta'rīkh iqlīm Ashantī*	Account of the beginnings of Muslim settlement in Kumasi	—	Published in Aḥmad Bābā al-Wa'iẓ: *Kanz al-mufīd li'l murīd al-ṣadīq* (Cairo, 1950), pp. 84–6. Translation by B. G. Martin in *Research Review*, II, 2 (1965), pp. 76–7

D *The school of Salaga*

Date	Language	Reference	Title	Author	Description	Length	Notes
c. 1900	Arabic	IASAR/1	*Qiṣṣat Ṣalgha Ta'rīkh Ghunjā* (Story of Salaga, History of Gonja)	Maḥmūd b. 'Abdullāh	Account of the campaigns of Jakpa, king of Gonja; of the growth of the trading town of Salaga; and of the civil war of 1892	54 ff.	Other copies: IASAR/6; 15; 261. Translation by Mahmud al-Waqqad in *Ghana Notes and Queries*, 3 (1961) and 4 (1962). Translation of a Hausa version of the same work by J. Withers-Gill, *A Short History of Salaga* (Accra, 1924). See also Braimah and Goody (1967)
	Hausa	—	—	Malam al-Ḥasan	History of Dagomba, recorded from the narrative of Malam Muhaman Kundungunda, grandson of Ya Na Ya'qūb	?	These three works, together with the Hausa version of the *Qiṣṣat Ṣalgha Ta'rīkh Ghunjā*, also by Mallam al-Ḥasan, were in the library of SOAS, London, but cannot at present be traced. English translations by Withers-Gill are to be found in *A Short History of the Dagomba Tribe* (Accra, n.d.) and *The Moshi Tribe* (Accra, 1924). Mallam al-Ḥasan also refers to a history of the Grunshi. This might be related to the history of the Zabarima campaigns among the Grunshi collected by Krause, 30. S. 49 *et seq.*
	Hausa	—	—	Malam al-Ḥasan	History of Gambaga, from Malam Salifu, a Mamprusi	?	
	Hausa	—	—	Malam al-Ḥasan	History of the Mossi, from Sharīf Mijinyawa b. Sharīf Ibrāhīm, who heard it from the Mogho Naba Wobogo when in exile in Gambaga (1897–1904)	?	

Date	Language	Reference	Title	Author	Description	Length	Notes
1921/2	Arabic	IASAR/7	*Fī najm dhī dhanab* (The Salaga comet)	'Alī b. Muḥammad Baraw al-Salghawī	Poem in two parts, dating the appearance of a comet in Salaga 21 Shawwal 1298 (16 Sept. 1881), and an earthquake to 1309 (1891/2), with praise for his shaykh, al-Ḥājj 'Umar	2 ff.	See Martin in Braimah and Goody (1967). Other copies IASAR/16 (xi); 408
1921	Arabic	IASAR/26	*Munā'ya madīḥ shaykhī dhi al-Sanā'i*	'Alī b. Muḥammad Baraw al-Salghawī	Acrostic poem in praise of Shaykh Maḥmūd b. Sa'īd Jalya, a Tijāni *muqqadam*, with additional verses also in his praise	2 ff.	Other copy IASAR/78 (with one additional verse)
1922	Arabic	IASAR/112	—	'Alī b. Muḥammad Baraw al-Salghawī	Acrostic poem in praise of Aḥmad al-Tijānī	2 ff.	Other copy: IASAR/16 (ix)
	Hausa	IASAR/169	—	Yūsuf Abin-Nema	Topical poem dealing with events in northern Ghana at the time of European penetration, with references to the Salaga civil war, etc.	2 ff.	—
	Arabic	IASAR/241	*Ta'rīkh Daghabāwī*	Imām Khālid b. Ya'qūb of Yendi (pupil of al-Ḥājj 'Umar of Salaga)	History of Dagomba, with references to Gonja and extracts from the *Kitāb Ghunjā*. Many obituaries added, including various Salaga figures	3 ff.	Other copy: IASAR/250

E *The Krause manuscripts from Salaga in Hausa*

Date	Reference	Description	Notes
	24. S. 35–6	Account of the expulsion of the Ashanti from Salaga in 1874	English translation by T. M. Mustapha in *Research Review*, II, 2 (1966)
1893	15. S. 25	Letter from Madugu (caravan-leader) Isa in Salaga to King Andani in Yendi, requesting his help, all the animals having died	Translation by T. M. Mustapha in Mustapha and Goody, The Caravan Trade from Kano to Salaga, *J. Nig. Hist. Soc.* (1967), 611–16
1893	16. S. 26	Letter from King Andani in Yendi, to Madugu Isa, expressing regrets about his difficulty, and ordering people not to molest the travellers	Translation as 15. S. 25
1893	17. S. 26	Message from the Dagomba soldiers in Salaga, that they will not harm Madugu Isa	Translation as 15. S. 25
1893	18. S. 27	Dispute about a slave girl	Translation in Goody and Mustapha, The Seduction of a Slave Girl (forthcoming)
1893	19. S. 28	Account of the death of Napo, the Kpembewura defeated in the Salaga civil war	Translation by T. M. Mustapha in Braimah and Goody (1967)
1893	20. S. 29.	Statement by the new Kpembewura about the death of his predecessor Napo, from information from Napo's relatives	Translation by T. M. Mustapha in Braimah and Goody (1967)
21 July 1893	25. S. 37–8	Statement by the new Kpembewura on the occasion of his accession, *inter alia* justifying his part in the civil war, with a report of speeches in reply	Translation by T. M. Mustapha in Braimah and Goody (1967)
	26. S. 39–40	Account of the composition of a caravan leaving Salaga, with a description of incidents on the road to Hausaland	
	27. S. 41–2	General account of organisation of a Hausa caravan	Translation as 15. S. 25
	30. S. 49–56	Account of the arrival of Alfa Gazari and other Zabarima in Dagomba; of their meeting with Alfa Hanno (? in Salaga); of the quarrels between the Dagomba and the Zabarima and of the Gonja involvement; of the campaigns against the Grunshi; etc.	—
1894	37. S. 76	Message from Ya Na Andani of Dagomba to the Kpembewura Isanwurfo, advising him not to embark on further war	Translation as 25. S. 37–8
1894	39. S. 77–8	Account of the coming of Salaga under English protection, 2 Sept. 1894	These two documents are not printed in the MSOS collection, but are apparently the ones enclosed in Krause's letters to the *Kreuz-Zeitung*, 520, Berlin, 6 Nov. 1894. See Goody, Salaga in 1892, *Research Review*, II, 3 (1966)
	40. S. 79	The same, from another source, in Hausa and Arabic, 19 Sept. 1894	

F *Administrative papers from the Kpembe division, including correspondence (mainly twentieth-century)*

Language	Reference	Length	Description
Arabic	IASAR/270	1 f.	List of names of persons, Kanunkulaiwura Muḥammad, Muḥammad Juwura (Jawula), etc., purpose unspecified
Arabic	IASAR/273	1 f.	Names of four places, Kunday, Balay, Balajay (?) and Bunkan (?), with names of 23, 49, 21 and 21 persons in them, respectively; possibly for taxation purposes
Arabic	IASAR/274	1 f.	*Asmā' al-nās fībalad Kpaday:* 'names of people in Kpandai town', also refs. to Kababura, etc.
Arabic	IASAR/275	1 f.	*Asmā' junū Sulṭān Alfay:* 'list of soldiers of the Sultan of Alfaire', with another list of twenty names of people from Kunthana (?), purpose unspecified
Arabic	IASAR/276	1 f.	*Zar' Tanghalantu:* list of farms, and names of occupants, in Tangelanto
Arabic	IASAR/277	1 f.	List of deaths in the town of Kunthana (?)
Arabic	IASAR/278	1 f.	*Al-ḥājj al-arḍ Ghunjā:* 'the pilgrim of the land of Gonja', that is, the chief of Kpandai
Arabic	IASAR/279	1 f.	*Amrā Bilād Alfay:* list of Alfaire villages
Arabic	IASAR/280	1 f.	List of villages
Arabic	IASAR/281	1 f.	*Amrā Bilād Alfay:* information about the Alfaire villages
Arabic	IASAR/282	1 f.	*Ḥisāb Almān:* on reckoning in German money
Arabic	IASAR/283	10 ff.	Correspondence: ten letters, mainly between Malam al-Ḥasan of Salaga and the chief of Alfaire
Arabic	IASAR/284	10 ff.	Correspondence: ten letters between Malam al-Ḥasan of Salaga and the chief of Alfaire
Arabic	IASAR/285	10 ff.	Correspondence: ten letters between the chief of Alfaire and various people including Malam Isḥāq, al-Ḥājj Muḥammad Jawula, Malam 'Abd al-Qādir, etc., some with reference to Wa, Yendi and elsewhere
Arabic	IASAR/286	10 ff.	Correspondence: eight letters (one dd. 1929, one 1932) between the chief of Alfaire, Malam Muḥammad b. Shaykh 'Abd al-Raḥmān, Imām Khālid of Yendi, Malam Ṣāliḥ of Wa, Malam al-Ḥasan b. 'Umar, Yaḥyā b. 'Abd al-Raḥmān, etc., with miscellaneous lists of places and chiefs
Arabic	IASAR/287	4 ff.	Correspondence: four letters between the Kpembewura, Malam al-Ḥasan, Malam Gambo, Bimbilla-Na (?), etc.
Arabic	IASAR/288	13 ff.	Thirteen miscellaneous documents, *inter alia*, on the descent of the chiefs of Lanfu (Lampor); on the skins of Kpembe and Kawose; on sanitation in towns; on pagan shrines in Kayeriso; on the Togo mandate
Arabic & Hausa	IASAR/289	4 ff.	Notes in Arabic on Kpembe affairs; itemized charges, in Hausa
Arabic	IASAR/290	2 ff.	Document, by al-Ḥājj Muḥammad, on Kpembe affairs
Arabic	IASAR/291	2 ff.	*Asmā' Bilād al-arḍ Sulṭān Kawāsi*, names of the Kawose villages, with notes on Kanyasi, Kawose, etc.
Arabic	IASAR/258	2 ff.	Miscellaneous notes on various chiefdoms of the Kpembe division
Arabic & Hausa	IASAR/257	4 ff.	Salaga affairs
Arabic & Hausa	IASAR/260	3 ff.	List of Kpembe villages, etc.

Recent printed works

Date	Language	Writer	Title	Description	Length
1934	Gonja & English	H. A. Blair	*Gonja Vocabulary and Notes*	Written by an English District Commissioner and printed by the Government Printer, Accra	—
1955	Gonja	S. S. Fuseini	*N'gbanyɛ miŋ karaŋ*	A Lauerbuch primer for teaching adults to read. Written by a headmaster and printed at the Vernacular Literature Bureau (Tamale. 2nd ed., 1957)	24 pp.
1956	Gonja	C. S. Kponkpogori	*Ngbanyɛ to ba asɛkpaŋ*	Gonja stories, proverbs, and synonyms. Written by a head-teacher and printed at the Vernacular Literature Bureau, Tamale	43 pp.
1956	Gonja	C. J. Natomah and O. Rytz	*Kabore doso, Yesu ba adua ne kase*	Christian catechism and hymns, published in Kumasi by O. Rytz	—
1957	Gonja & English	E. L. Rapp	*The Gonja Language*	Gonja English vocabulary. Guang-Studien II, Deutsche Akademie der Wissenschaften zu Berlin, Institut für Orient-forschung, vol. LII	—
1958	Gonja	S. S. Fuseini and O. Rytz	*Yesu benite awura k'lɛla*	Bible stories orginating from the Presbyterian (Basle) mission. Printed at the Vernacular Literature Bureau, Tamale; authors, a headmaster and a Swiss missionary	20 pp.
1961	Gonja	C. J. Natomah and O. Rytz	*Ebore be ashen lela ne nshe*	Published by the Presbyterian Church of Ghana (2nd ed.)	—
1966	Gonja & English	Rev. O. Rytz, C. S. Kponkpogori and Rev. C. J. Natomah	*Gonja Proverbs*	Miscellaneous publications, No. 1, Institute of African Studies, Legon; Gonja, with English translation	—
1967	English	J. A. Braimah	*The Two Isanwurfos* (with introduction and notes by Jack Goody)	The story of the Salaga civil war of 1892 and of the fortunes of the author's family to the present day. Longmans, London. Also included as Part 1 of Braimah and Goody (1967)	127 pp.
1967	Gonja	S. S. Fuseini and O. Rytz	*Yesu b'kasherkpan dzunpar so nama*	Bible stories; printed by the Vernacular Literature Bureau, Tamale	—
1967	Gonja	C. J. Natomah and O. Rytz	*Yesu b bushungipo b Ashen*	Acts of the Apostles, tentative edition, published by the Presbyterian Church of Ghana, Accra	—
1967	Gonja	C. J. Natomah, J. W. Y. Amankwah and O. Rytz	*Enyenpe Yesu b angasa na*	Some parables, published by Scripture Gift Mission, London	—

APPENDIX II: A LIBRARY IN NORTHERN GHANA

by I. WILKS AND J. GOODY

In the library of Mu'allim Abū Bakr Ibn Muḥammad in Savelugu are the following volumes:

1	Al-Azharī, Sāliḥ 'Abd al-samī'	*Hidāyat al-muta'abbid al-sālik* [Guide to the worshipper who follows the spiritual path]
2	'Abd al-Raḥmān al-Raqa'ī al-Fāsī	*Nazm muqaddimat ibn Rushd* Versification written in 1449 of the work of Abū 'l-Walīd Muḥammad b. Aḥmad b. Rushd (known as Averroës, born 1126): *al-muqaddima fī 'l-farā'id*, a work of Mālikī *fiqh* (GAL II, 176 and GAL S I, 662)
3	'Abd al-Raḥmān b. Muḥammad b. 'Abd al-Raḥmān al-Baghdādī al-Mālikī b. 'Askar	*Irshād al-sālik* Compendium of Mālikī law (GAL II, 163; GAL S II, 205)
4	Unidentified	*Kitab sabīl al-sa'ādah li ma'rifat aḥkām al-'ibādah* (Imām Mālik) [The path to happiness is knowing rules of worship]
5	Unidentified	*Kitāb manẓūmat al-Qurṭubī fī al-'ibādāt 'ala madhhab al-Imām Mālik* Teaching poem by Al-Qurṭubī on worship according to the Mālikī school. Almost certainly a work by Abū 'l-'Abbās Aḥmad b. 'Umar al-Anṣārī al-Qurṭubī (d. 1258), a scholar in Mālikī *fiqh*. The work is not recorded in Brockelmann, but for the author see GAL S I, 664
6	Al-Qayrawānī, Abū Muḥammad 'Ali b. Abī Zayd (d. A.D. 996)	*Kitāb*, ed. by 'Abd al-Samī', Saliḥ The *Risāla*, a well-known Mālikī law book in West Africa. The editor or commentator is presumably either a West African, educated in Cairo, or an Egyptian. GAL, S I, 301
7	Abū Zayd 'Abd al-Raḥmān b. Yakhlaftan b. Aḥmad al-Fāzāzī (d. 1230)	*Al-wasā'il al mutaqabbila fī madḥ al-nabī* Composed in 1204: a well-known devotional work in neo-classical poetic form (GAL S I, 482)
8	Unidentified	*Majma'ah tahtawī' alā al-Qaṣa'id al-'Aṣrīyyah fī al-naṣā'iḥ al-dīniyyah* [A collection containing ten poems of religious advice]

9	Unidentified	*Murshid al-'awamm li aḥkām al-ṣiyām 'alā al-madhāhib al-arba'ah* [Guide of the common people for the rules of fasting (month of Ramaḍān) according to the four schools (*madhāhib*)]
10	Burhān al-dīn al-Zarnūjī	*Ta'līm al-muta'allim* [Teaching the educated]. It contains the following chapters: 1. the science; 2. intention, purpose; 3. choice of knowledge; 4. teaching the science; 5. seriousness; 6. the beginning of race; 7. trust in God, etc. Written in 1203. The commentary is by Ibrāhīm b. Ismā'īl, and was produced in 1588 for the Ottoman Ṣultān Murād III (GAL I, 462; GAL S I, 837)
11	Unidentified	*Mawā'iz balīghah min zabūr Sayyidnā Dawūd* (and others) [Profound advice taken from our master David's psalms]
12	Zayn al-'Ābidīn b. Ibrāhīm b. Nujaym al-Miṣrī al-Ḥanafī (d. 1563)	*Al-Tuḥfat al-Marḍīyyah fī 'l-Araḍi 'l-Miṣrīyyah* A collection of *fatwās*, Ḥanafī *fiqh* (GAL II, 310–11)
13	Imām Muḥammad b. 'Abd al-Wahhāb (1703–91)	*Al-uṣūl al-thalātha wa adillatuhā wa yalīhā shurūt al-ṣalah wa wājibātuha* [The three fundamentals and their proofs followed by rules and conditions of prayer] Written by the founder of the Wahhābiyya (GAL S II, 530–31)
14	Unidentified	*Al-Hidāyah al-Islāmiyyah lilmadāris al-Ilzāmiyyah* The Islamic guide for primary schools
15	Unidentified	*Makārim al-Akhlāq* Noble characteristics (noble traits of character). There are various works of this title. This is most likely to be the one by Abū Bakr b. 'Abdallāh Abī 'l-Dunyā al-Qurashī, born 823, died 894 (GAL I, 153). General exhortation based upon the Traditions
16	Unidentified	*Waṣāyā al-Shaykh Ibrāhīm al-Kawālījī al-Tījanī* The commands of Shaykh Ibrāhīm al-Kawālījī al-Tījanī, possibly Shaykh Ibrāhīm of Kaolak; a Tijani manual
17	Muḥammad Amīn b. M. Ḥassan b. M. 'Ārif	*'Ilm al-Fara'iḍ* Law of descent and distribution, presumably a compilation of Mālikī rules

18	Unidentified	*Ḥujjat al-basmalah fī al-farīḍah sirran aw jahran* The argument on the utterance of the invocation *Bism al-Allāh al-Raḥmān al-Raḥīm*, 'In the name of God, the Beneficent, the Merciful' in the obligatory divine service, whether it is recited silently or aloud
19	Unidentified	*Thalāth majālis sunniyah* [Three Orthodox assemblies]
20	Unidentified	*al-Darajāt al-ūlā* [The high steps]
21	Unidentified	*al-Ḥujjah al-Bālighah* [The profound argument]

The following general comments are offered on this list. There is: (1) a strong emphasis upon Mālikī *fiqh*—items 2, 3, 4, 5, 6 and probably 17; one general work on law concerning fasting according to the four schools, item 9; one collection of Ḥanafī rulings, item 12; and a Wahhābī work, item 13, probably *fiqh*; (2) one *madḥ* or devotional poem, item 7; (3) one work of pedagogy, item 10. (4) one Tijanniyya manual, item 16; (5) a remainder comprising mostly works of general exhortation, *wa'iẓ*; probably a number of these are of West African authorship since many local figures commit to writing their favourite sermons given at the Friday prayer. There is, however, also a large amount of late sub-classical literature in circulation, much of it, as Hiskett observes,[1] produced by minor Sanhaja and North African scholars, which has never been recorded in bibliographical compilations, European or Arabic; these works are very important for West African Islam, but in the world of metropolitan Islam virtually unknown.

The following items may be dated by century: item 2, eleventh to twelfth, with commentary of fifteenth; 3, twelfth to thirteenth; 5, thirteenth; 6, tenth, with (probably) recent commentary; 7, thirteenth; 10, thirteenth, with commentary of sixteenth; 12, sixteenth; 13, probably eighteenth; 15, perhaps ninth. There is thus quite a strong emphasis upon the 'neo-classical period', with works of Maghribi and Spanish provenance just outnumbering those of Egyptian and Middle Eastern origin.

APPENDIX III: LITERACY IN NINETEENTH-CENTURY CAIRO

The kind of situation of restricted literacy that I have been describing for the western Sudan is partially the result of its position on the periphery of Islam, in an area where pagan and Muslim operate in overlapping fields of social relationships. In such a situation the demand for the religious and magical elements in Arabic learning is greater than for the natural sciences, the very elements

[1] Personal communication.

that owed so much to the Greek knowledge with which the Muslims came in contact when they occupied Damascus and Alexandria.[1]

But even at the centre of the Islamic world the position was at times not altogether different.

The lineal descendant of the great library of Alexandria was in one sense the 'Splendid Mosque' of Cairo, the Azhar, now more usually known as the University. But Lane's account of Cairo in the 1830s, before the reforms of Mohammed Ali had taken effect, indicate a literary condition somewhat more impoverished than in Ptolemaic times. 'There are, in Cairo, many large libraries; most of which are attached to mosques, and consist, for the greater part, of works on theology and jurisprudence, and philology: but these libraries are deplorably neglected, and their contents are rapidly perishing, in a great measure from the carelessness and dishonesty of their keepers and of those who make use of them' (1871: I, 263).

The whole emphasis of education was essentially theocratic. Lane describes the actual process of learning to read in the following way. 'The boys first learn the letters of the alphabet; next, the vowel-points and other syllabic signs; and then, the numerical value of each letter of the alphabet [for the Arabic letters are often used as numerals]...When he has become acquainted with the numerical values of the letters, the master writes for him some simple words, as the names of men; then, the ninety-nine names or epithets of God: next, the Fát'ḥah (or opening chapter of the Ḳur-án) is written upon his tablet, and he reads it repeatedly until he has perfectly committed it to memory. He then proceeds to learn the other chapters of the Ḳur-án: after the first chapter he learns the last; then the last but one; next the last but two, and so on, in inverted order, ending with the second...It is seldom the master of a school teaches writing; and few boys learn to write unless destined for some employment which absolutely requires that they should do so; in which latter case they are generally taught the art of writing, and likewise arithmetic, by a 'ḳabbánee', who is a person employed to weigh goods in a market or bázár, with the steelyard. Those who devote themselves to religion, or to any of the learned professions, mostly pursue a regular course of study in the great mosque El-Azhar' (1871: I, 75–6).

The alphabetic mode of instruction was used in Cairo at this time, whereas it rarely seems to form the basis of elementary learning in northern Ghana, mainly perhaps because a foreign language is being taught. But instruction was similar, first, in its emphasis on knowing the Book rather than understanding the medium, secondly, in its emphasis on reading rather than writing, and finally, in the largely religious content of knowledge. In these respects, the education of Christians in Cairo was no better. 'The Copts have numerous schools: but for boys only: very few females among them can read; and those have been instructed at home. The boys are taught the Psalms of David, the Gospels, and the Apostolical Epistles, in Arabic; then the Gospels and Epistles in Coptic. They do not learn the Coptic language grammatically...and...there are few persons

[1] For a general account of the Muslim absorption of Greek knowledge from Christian, Jewish, Buddhist, Indian and other sources, see De Lacy O'Leary, *How Greek Science Passed to the Arabs* (London, 1948).

who can do more than repeat what they have committed to memory, of the Scriptures and Liturgy' (Lane 1871: II, 281–2).

Anyone who wanted to know more than 'to read, and perhaps to write and to recite the Ḳurán' had to attend the Azhar, where he was instructed by learned men of his own sect and district. A man learned to become one of the '*ulamā*', those knowledgeable in religious law. But even if he became a professor at the Azhar an individual received no salary; he gained his livelihood through alms, inheritance, the gifts of relatives, copying manuscripts, tutoring students of wealthy households or reciting the Qur'ān in private houses, at tombs and other places. Professors had formerly been supported by the income from lands bequeathed to the mosque, but this property had been confiscated by Mohammed Ali. As the actions of Charlemagne, Henry VIII and Lenin testify, church properties are particularly vulnerable to seizure in periods of modernization.

Literary skills were therefore the attainment of professionals, who were at one and the same time religious specialists. 'The literary acquirements of those who do not belong to the classes who make literature their profession are of a very inferior kind. Many of the wealthy tradespeople are well instructed in the arts of reading and writing; but few of these devote much time to the pursuit of literature. Those who have committed to memory the whole, or considerable portions of the Ḳur-án, and can recite two or three celebrated 'ḳaṣeedehs' (or short poems), or introduce, now and then, an apposite quotation in conversation, are accomplished persons. Many of the tradesmen of Cairo can neither read nor write, or can only read; and are obliged to have recourse to a friend to write their accounts, letters, etc: but these persons generally cast accounts, and make intricate calculations, mentally, with surprising rapidity and correctness' (1871: I, 274).

What about the content of education? Lane, who was resident in Cairo for many years, was at pains to disprove the prevalent notion in Europe that 'the Muslims are enemies to almost every branch of knowledge' (1871: I, 274). But he had to admit that 'their studies, in the present age, are confined within very narrow limits. Very few of them study medicine, chymistry (for our first knowledge of which we are indebted to the Arabs), the mathematics, or astronomy. The Egyptian medical and surgical practitioners are mostly barbers, miserably ignorant of the sciences which they profess, and unskilful in their practice; partly in consequence of their being prohibited by their religion from availing themselves of the advantage of dissecting human bodies...Many of the Egyptians, in illness, neglect medical aid; placing their whole reliance on Providence or on charms. Alchymy is more studied in this country than pure chymistry; and astrology more than astronomy. The astrolabe and quadrant are almost the only astronomical instruments used in Egypt. Telescopes are rarely seen here; and the magnetic needle is seldom employed, except to discover the direction of Mekkeh' (I, 274–5). Many believed that the earth is flat: 'To say that the earth revolves round the sun, they consider absolute heresy. Pure astronomy they make chiefly subservient to their computations of the calendar' (I, 275). In other words, most of their scientific equipment and ideas were of the pre-Renaissance period; apart from the field of military technology, they had (before disturbed by Napoleon's incursion) learnt little from the West to whom they had earlier taught, or transmitted, so much.

The failure even to keep up with, let alone advance, contemporary knowledge was due largely to an educational system which was directed towards religious ends. This orientation comes out not only in Lane's remarks about the taboo on dissection and about the concern with liturgical time and with sacred direction, but also in what he says about the positive content of the education. In Azhar 'the regular subjects of study are grammatical inflexion and syntax, rhetoric, versification, logic, theology, the exposition of the Ḳur-án, the Traditions of the Prophet, the complete science of jurisprudence, or rather of religious, moral, civil, and criminal law, which is chiefly founded on the Ḳur-án and the Traditions; together with arithmetic, as far as it is useful in matters of law. Lectures are also given on algebra, and on the calculations of the Mohammadan calendar, the times of prayer, etc.' (Lane 1871: I, 266). From the European standpoint, the whole curriculum is literally medieval, and entirely oriented to religious ends.

LITERACY IN A NOMADIC SOCIETY: THE SOMALI CASE

Moving to the eastern side of the African continent, Dr Lewis looks at the role of writing among the Somali pastoralists of the Horn of Africa. In this uncentralized, nomadic society, the fully literate constitute 'a small religious élite', the role of which is in any case narrowly circumscribed. Nevertheless, they are in touch with Muslims of the coastal towns and by pilgrimage with Mecca itself. Learned in the Qur'ān, they advise the application of common Muslim norms in many cases of dispute, norms which run counter in some respects to local custom, thus producing an 'explicit tension' between the two.

Writing is primarily used for the contracts by which groups of agnatic kinsmen record the arrangements they have made for assistance in the payment of blood money. It is also used for recording the higher, more inclusive levels of the agnatic genealogies. The lower levels are stored only in the memory (indeed Somali culture is largely oral, despite their long-standing acquisition of religious literacy). The more immediate levels may therefore be subjected to the kind of manipulation and telescoping that has been noted in purely oral cultures, but since there are alternative ways of organizing inter-group relations by means of contractual alliances, the genealogies are not so sensitive to political realignment as they would otherwise be.

Lewis also observes that even written genealogies may be socially manipulated, a point that Freedman has recently made with regard to south-east China. In answering the question of whether the giant genealogies are statements of historical truth or retrospective constructions of the relations between lineages, he claims they are 'a mixture of historical accuracy and creative imagination' (Freedman 1966: 27). Lineages might make 'fraudulent claims' about their ancestry for political purposes and these often took a written form. But once written the genealogy acquired a partially independent existence of its own; 'once the general genealogy is given it may lead people to base their social relationships on it. Charter and grouping may interact' (1966: 28). As far as the local lineage was concerned (and he specifically excludes the higher-order lineage or clan, which among the Somali is the only one to be put in writing), Freedman maintains that the written genealogy 'was more or less immune to fudging', for the lineage 'is deprived of the means of rephrasing anomalies in the "true language" of patrilineal descent' (1966: 42).

LITERACY IN A NOMADIC SOCIETY: THE SOMALI CASE

by I. M. LEWIS

Separated as they are by only a narrow strip of sea from the centre of Islam on the Arabian peninsula, the Somalis have for over a thousand years participated at least in some degree in this universalistic literate culture. They have, however, reacted to this long exposure to Islam in ways which, as I have argued elsewhere (Lewis 1955–6, 1966), are broadly consistent with their own traditional social structure and culture. Thus amongst the northern nomads a popular form of Sufism laying stress on the veneration of saints, which fits nicely with the traditional lineage structure and cult of ancestors, is strongly developed. The Sufi brotherhoods (mainly Qadiriya, Ahmadiya, and Salihiya) are also well represented amongst the southern cultivating Somali. But here, where lineage ties vie with territorial connections in importance, agnatic ancestors figure less prominently, and less automatically, as saintly mediators between man and God. In both regions, until very recently, the most notable achievements of local literate culture have been those produced within this Sufistic tradition. Despite their long Islamic history, however, as far as is at present known most of this local religious literature is of comparatively recent origin; and little seems to have been produced, or if produced, to have survived from before the nineteenth century. Such Arabic manuscripts and a few published works written by Somali sheihks usually take the form of hagiologies, although there are also some legal works, Qur'ānic commentaries, and treatises on etiquette and Arabic grammar (Lewis 1955–6, 1958). Few chronologies or historical texts have so far been discovered.

This apparent dearth of any strong corpus of locally written literature reflects the fact that only a small proportion of religious men are in fact fully literate in Arabic. In general, knowledge of reading Arabic is more widely diffused than full literacy, competence in which has until recently been the monopoly of a small religious élite. In this generally uncentralized traditional society, the role of men of religion enjoying various degrees of literacy has in any case been rather narrowly circumscribed. Basically, these sheikhs or, as they are also known locally, *wadads*, are expected to act as mediators between man and man and between man and God. They do not normally hold political office and in the first capacity their competence is traditionally restricted to peace-making and arbitration, to the recommendation of Shariah awards of compensation for injuries and death, the administration of Muslim principles of inheritance (in certain cases), the solemnization of marriage, divorce, and all other matrimonial matters. In the second, they are regarded as ritual officiants possessing the appropriate liturgical lore for the conduct of all religious occasions, the treatment of sickness and misfortune with Qur'ānic remedies, and are similarly relied on as astrologers, diviners, soothsayers, etc. As we shall see presently, many of these traditional functions have been formalized and institutionalized in the colonial and post-colonial periods.

Men of God thus play essentially mediating roles and, in the absence in Somali history—at least since the sixteenth century—of stable large-scale centralized Islamic states, have not acquired a wider range of positions of authority: nor has literacy in Arabic traditionally overflowed much outside their ranks, despite the connection between trade and Islam. For, although a considerable proportion of these sheikhs have functioned as teachers, sometimes with peripatetic students wandering around the Somali bush and largely dependent on charity, they have not brought general literacy to the laity. The exigencies of the nomadic life allow few nomads to attend such schools regularly or over long periods, and teaching is in any case for the most part limited to learning the Qur'ān by heart and not directed towards teaching writing as such. Traditionally, then, the literacy rate for men is very low, and for women almost non-existent.

Another factor which seems of significance in contributing to the surprisingly slight extension of literate Arabic culture notwithstanding the Somalis' long exposure to Islam is the high development of oral communication. The Somali language is a particularly rich and versatile medium and its speakers are very conscious of its literary resources, which, it might be added, are closely geared to the circumstances of their society. Just, for example, as the society is highly acephalous and democratic, so the language is highly egalitarian: it is very difficult to express honorific titles in Somali, for almost none exist traditionally. At the same time skill in rhetoric and poetry is highly prized (Andrezejewski and Lewis 1964). Thus it is no accident that the majority of the most outstandingly successful leaders have been men who have won wide acclaim in these fields and whose poetry is often still remembered (e.g. Sheikh Muhammad Abdille Hassan[1]). More directly, Somalis appear to regard oral communication not merely as a refined art, but as a basic essential for successful survival. This may sound trite, but I wish to emphasize that there is

[1] Sheikh Muhammad led the Somali nationalist insurrection from 1900–1920 which was designed to free his people from alien Christian rule. His brilliant success as a leader was closely connected with his consumate powers as a poet. He made extensive use of poetry as a political weapon in campaigning for support against his enemies.

an explicit and articulate evaluation of the importance of oral Somali which in one important context can be illustrated by the following encounter. In an entirely spontaneous manner an illiterate nomad was once explaining to me the advantages of learning foreign languages, and more particularly of speaking the language of the country you happened to be in. If you did not speak the local language, he observed, how could you possibly know what people were saying about you? how could you know what their intentions towards you were? They might be plotting to kill you, and you would not have the defence of prior warning. This evaluation of oral communication is of course here directly related to the overwhelming Somali assumption that, unless there is very strong evidence to the contrary, the world is essentially hostile.

With this accent on the necessity for mutual intelligibility, oral Somali is used, particularly in the form of poetry, as an extremely important medium of mass communication. The power of the tongue and of the spoken word in spreading hostility and enmity, in countering it, or in broadcasting conciliatory messages, in ruining reputations or praising men to the skies, is very evident in Somali culture. Rapid and highly effective oral communication, and for that matter not merely the dissemination of news and gossip but also of cultural innovations, is, I think, facilitated by the strongly nomadic bias of Somali society. Despite the low density of the population, pastoral movements most effectively spread news and information whether it is encapsulated in memorable verse or merely relayed in prose. Each meeting of nomads functions as a relay station for the onward transmission of messages.

In fact the oral tradition is so strongly developed and so highly prized that there is also a certain, mainly religious, oral treasury of poetry in Arabic as well as Somali. But, of course, this is a two-way process. And although there is no record of when the process first occurred, the Arabic script has long been used as a medium for Somali as well as Arabic—or for a mixture of both. Various suitably modified scripts, better adapted to the special needs of Somali, have been developed locally as well as several quite independent non-Arabic scripts of which the phonetically most excellent and most widely known is that called Osmaniyya after its inventor, Isman Yusuf Kenadid (Lewis 1958). This alphabet and script, some of whose characters resemble Amharic, was invented about 1920 and initially enjoyed a limited currency amongst its inventor's close kinsmen and friends. Later its currency spread through its connection with modern Somali nationalism; and although its fortunes have waxed and waned in the interval, today it seems to be acquiring increased popularity (Lewis 1965: 115).

II

If one of the factors which seem traditionally to have hampered the spread of literacy in Arabic is the richness of the indigenous oral culture and its close adaptation to a predominantly nomadic setting, this is not to say that writing has had no significant impact in Somali society. In what follows I shall examine salient aspects of Somali social structure which do seem to me to have been affected by this literate presence. Although it is not always easy, in the nature of the case, to make the separation between Islam and the fact that it happens to be associated with Arabic, I shall try to indicate those effects which appear to depend upon writing as a factor rather than simply to inhere in Islam as such.

Let us begin by considering the range and character of dispute-settlement procedures among the Somali. Here the first thing to note is that all Somalis irrespective of their lineage affiliation recognize a common morality, and common procedures for the settlement of disputes. This is in fact one element which defines the boundaries of the Somali nation. Thus, although traditionally they were not united in a single political unit capable of acting concertedly, they did acknowledge uniform categories of wrong, and they possessed common means of settlement and restitution through the exchange of damages according to a common tariff. This tariff is based upon the law books of the Shafi' school of Islamic Law and is applied in specific cases by literate sheikhs. It details are in general so complicated, providing for the operation of so many different contingent factors, that I do not think such a corpus of damages could be effectively maintained except in writing. Prior to colonization such rulings on the amount of damages appropriate to a particular injury provided a basis for negotiations in disputes between lineages where arbitrators were called in. There was no formal machinery for enforcing such awards except that engendered by the desire of the parties to a dispute to make peace, and this, of course, was a function of their relative strengths and of the total political situation at any point in time. Ultimately force or its threat was the final sanction affecting settlement. In the colonial and post-colonial situation these awards became judgements enforceable by an official hierachy of courts operating with the full support of the state.

Today the procedure is as follows. The nature of an injury is first established by a doctor and then referred to a Kadi's court where the corresponding damages are assessed. A plea for payment is then filed in a court which may reduce the actual amount if it considers that it is unrealistically large or inconsistent with Somali custom. Similarly, even in a case of homicide when the murderer is caught and sentenced claims can be preferred for damages, particularly if the sentence awarded is light. And when, as frequently happens because of lack of evidence, a conviction is not obtained, a suit for blood-compensation will be filed and is often successfully sustained. This, it should be added, applies today even in the case of traffic fatalities in towns.

Here, then, we see the use of literacy as an important element facilitating dispute settlement on a national basis. This is equally evident in a parallel set of procedures which overlap with those just described. Here I refer to the fact that every Somali is by birth or choice the member of a particular blood-compensation paying group which provides for the security of his life and property. These insurance associations are basically composed of agnatic kin whose diffuse kinship obligations are given specific definition and content by a contractual treaty which stipulates the terms of their common indebtedness. Such treaties state the amounts of damages appropriate to particular categories of tort occurring within the group and also lay down the proportions in which outgoing damages claimed by external groups will be made up, and similarly how damages received from other groups will be disbursed internally. Such treaties mirror the structure of the groups to which they refer. And the actual amounts of compensation for injuries, which are usually set at a lower rate within the group than that obtaining between groups, are again ultimately derived from the Shariah law books of the written tradition. I hasten to add, however, that Islamic law here receives a peculiar Somali interpretation which is in fact contrary to the letter and spirit of the law. For while *Shafi'* law considers the culprit in deliberate homicide to be primarily responsible for making restitution without the support of his kin, Somalis regard the contractually defined kin group to be collectively involved, whatever the circumstances of a killing. Their practice thus runs counter to the Shariah, and their awareness of this is one of the components in the tension which exists in Somali culture between Islamic and customary morality, a point I shall return to later. This is another aspect of the existence of a written tradition here acting as a standard and immutable repository of ideal conduct.

Yet writing affects the position more fundamentally than this. These treaties based on consensual agreement normally amongst agnates have since colonial times been recorded in writing, whether in Arabic, English, or Italian. Thus recorded, they are lodged in the local District Office of the area regularly frequented by the groups concerned. Every District headquarters maintains a register of these 'dia-paying group' (from the Arabic *dia*, blood-money) arrangements, which have come to be accepted as defining the political and legal status of the individual members of the group concerned. They are consequently now a source of law since their existence is taken to define the legal status of any individual who is involved in a dispute. These, of course, are not immutable and unchanging documents any more than the placement of particular groups and the overall balance of power in the Somali segmentary system are fixed for all time. Thus, as groups change their segmentary alignment and unite or divide according to the context of disputes and as they see their interests, individual treaties are modified, abrogated, or rescinded and new ones submitted to the local representatives of the centralized government—now universally regarded as the final arbiter in disputes.

Although there is some indication that prior to colonization such treaties were sworn at the tombs of important saints and thus authenticated and solemnized, I find it difficult to be certain that such procedures could effectively uphold the validity of these treaties in the way and to the extent provided by the presence of a neutral third party—namely centralized government. But whatever may have been the situation in the past, what now seems clear is that the practice of recording these dia-paying group treaties in writing and lodging them with the government has had the effect of giving greater definition and rigidity to these units than they seem to have possessed in the past. If the level of agnatic grouping most frequently stabilized or 'frozen' in this way is in any case that order of segmentary grouping which most effectively answers the adaptive needs of the total Somali setting, its distinctiveness has nevertheless been increased in relation to other potential levels of association. Amongst the northern nomads where the dia-paying group thus defined is a low-level lineage, some five to eight generations in depth with a maximum population strength of a few thousand, this seems to have had the effect of reducing solidarity at wider and higher levels of grouping. Thus there is some indication that those much larger lineage units which because of their size (up to 100,000 strong) I call 'clans' have in the past greater rigidity as social units than they do today.

However, the primacy of social factors here and the true character of the complicated interplay between them and the use of written records are suggested by the contrasting situation amongst the southern cultivating Somali, who provide a convenient control in analysis. Here the comparable solidary groups representing the main axes of politico-legal action and affiliation, and possessing written treaties defining their unity, are in fact very large clans up to a population size of 100,000. This contrast, as I have argued elsewhere (Lewis 1968*a*), corresponds to the expansion of political solidarity in the south associated with the occupation of stable arable territories and the widespread adoption of clients. Thus, I am suggesting that in both cases writing here has further stabilized levels of group association which basically correspond to different adaptive needs.[1]

III

This discussion leads directly to a consideration of the influence, if any, of writing on the form and content of Somali genealogies. A marked feature of this society is the very long genealogies, sometimes consisting of more than thirty named ancestors, which are regularly and widely known. As in other segmentary lineage systems, these genealogies which children are taught to learn off pat at an early age are primarily concerned with establishing the identity of individuals and groups. Thus Somalis are fond of comparing their significance rather loosely with the use of street numbers and house addresses in Europe. Of course, among the Somali, genealogical identification carries immediate political and legal implications which are not normally conveyed by European addresses. When strangers meet, the normal procedure is for them to ask each other their pedigrees and for these to be traced until a point of reference which is mutually significant is reached. This can be done in two ways. One can ask a person's name and then that of his father and further ancestors until a significant referent is reached; or one can begin at the top and work down, simply asking the question: 'Of what group are you?', over and over again until the relevant point is reached. The relevant point varies to some extent with the circumstances, but it is unnecessary to go into that here. What is important is that the question 'Who are you?' is answered in genealogical terms and behaviour is, broadly speaking, adjusted accordingly.

The importance of this system of placement even in the modern urban setting can be gauged from the fact that when a few years ago it became fashionable to pretend that 'tribalism' had been replaced by the strength of nationalist fervour, one asked not a person's lineage, but his 'ex-lineage'. And indeed the English affix *ex* became adopted into the Somali language so that one could perfectly acceptably ask someone his 'ex', when one could not directly ask his lineage affiliation. More recently, this ingenious sophistry has been discarded in a climate of opinion which increasingly accepts that lineage divisions and hostility persist and cannot thus be suppressed but must simply be accepted as a basic, if unpalatable, fact of life.

With this background and given fluidity of Somali political groupings, the question which of course at once arises is: are these genealogies mere

[1] In this context the probable stabilizing effect of writing seems supported by the contrasting situation amongst the Baggara nomads, where each payment of compensation evokes a different pattern of solidarity and compensation-paying arrangements do not appear to be recorded in writing. See Cunnison (1966).

charters mirroring current political commitments and alignments and changing when they change? In the first place, the answer to this question depends upon whether one is concerned with the northern nomadic Somali or the southern cultivators.

Amongst the nomads one finds within the same lineage segments of very unequal strength and correspondingly disproportionate genealogies. Telescoping and foreshortening certainly seem to occur in what are known locally as 'short-branch' lineage genealogies. But 'long-branch' genealogies appear to conserve what is broadly a relatively true record of successive ancestors up to the level of clans, or those wider lineages which because of their extreme size I call 'clan-families'. Amongst the southern Somali, genealogies have a much more uniform character; they are generally much shorter and there are not usually such wide discrepancies between collateral segments. Here there is abundant evidence of genealogical manipulation and distortion, indeed of all those processes which, as amongst the Nuer and Tiv and elsewhere, maintain a close correspondence between the genealogical model and actual structural relations. These differences can be referred to the fact that among the southern cultivators the adoption and full genealogical assimilation of clients is a constant and regularly recurring process. In fact, the southern clans are vast federations composed of persons of every possible genealogical origin. Among the nomads, in contrast, adoption and genealogical client assimilation are rare. With them the constant process of political alliance and realignment is validated by the explicit contractual treaties we have discussed, rather than by genealogical manipulation. There are in practice two ideologies or models, the genealogical and the contractual; and in general the genealogical idiom provides the guide lines for action rather than defining or circumscribing this completely. Now this is also true of the southern cultivators, but the range and effectiveness of these two ideologies differ between the two groups. The political units of the cultivators are larger, less fluid and fleeting, and ultimately stabilized by land interests. Contract, broadly speaking, operates significantly only at an inter-clan level. Among the nomads it operates at all levels as occasion requires and is a more pervasive instrument of group definition. Thus for the southerners there is a wider social range of interaction, where relationships are defined genealogically rather than by contract, and genealogies are more subject to manipulative processes. In each case, consequently, the situation is that where social relations are ultimately defined by contractual treaties rather than by agnation alone, genealogies are less open to adjustment.

How is all this related, if at all, to writing? If northern genealogies are less distorted than southern pedigrees it might be supposed that the northerners are more literate. This, however, is not the case: indeed, if anything, the reverse is probably true. Moreover, the genealogies of which I am speaking are seldom in fact conserved in writing. Lineage genealogical lore is part of the oral tradition, taught, conserved, and transmitted mainly by word of mouth. I say 'mainly' because there is one area of genealogical lore which does tend to be conserved in writing. This is typically that part of the genealogies which reaches outside Somali society and postulates Arabian connections validating the Somali profession of Islam (Lewis 1962). In fact, standard Arabic genealogical handbooks have a certain limited circulation and knowledge of them is by no means rare among literate sheikhs. Moreover, the local hagiologies which celebrate clan and clan-family ancestors as saints of power and pedigree invariably contain appropriately exalted genealogies tracing connection to the family of the Prophet Muhammad. Although they state historical truths in the manner of a parable, these genealogies which are written are probably the most spurious of all.[1]

This evidence seems fully in accord with the situation in other societies with a specialized and restricted literate tradition and written genealogies, such as the Chinese.[2] It suggests that with only a limited currency, writing in a society which does not abound in disinterested, disengaged positions which might promote genuine historicism does not necessarily serve to preserve the literal truth. In this culture where it is traditionally associated with holy writ and has magical significance, writing appropriately enough serves to validate the overall genealogical charter of the total society, and in this sense helps to conserve its genealogical shape at the highest levels of agnation.

IV

In the Somali case the examples we have considered serve to show how the influence of the slender literate strand has been heavily affected by the structure of the traditional illiterate society. This seems consistent with what might be called the lubricatory role of its main bearers, sheikhs and men of religion, oiling the wheels of social intercourse, rather than throwing spanners in the works. Yet, the situation is not as simple or as clear-cut

[1] These remarks, of course, do not apply to those specialized religious genealogies by which office-holders and prominent sheikhs in the religious orders record the names of their teachers and their celebrated predecessors in the spiritual hierarchy. These 'chains of blessing' (*silsilad al-baraka*), as they are often called, are almost invariably written and act as, in effect, diplomas of religious instruction and illumination. Such professional *tariqa* pedigrees are an important source for the local history of the orders in Somalia.

[2] See Freedman, 1958 and 1966. In this context Bohannan's assumption that illiteracy is a precondition for genealogical manipulation and that this could not be sustained in a literate society seems to me naive (Lewis, 1961).

as this. For the existence of an unchanging written corpus of Islamic morality to which constant reference and appeal are made, and which is regarded as the final source of truth and the ultimate guide to human conduct, means that actual behaviour as well as popular morality is constantly open to scrutiny in a way which would not obtain in the absence of writing. As in other societies, there are of course double standards and several layers of morally charged ideologies. Put at its simplest there is the Islamic model of conduct as set forth in the Qur'ān and law books; there is the popular morality, Somali 'custom', of which Somalis have a very explicit awareness; and finally there is actual practice. These are all interrelated, and ultimately the last two, according to local views, are referable to the first for their legitimacy.

Somalis are generally aware of those major respects in which their practice and customary assumptions part company with Islamic ideals. In certain important areas of life, as for example in the frequency of fighting and feud and its resolution according to uncanonical compensation arrangements, there is an explicit tension between the Islamic model and the local model and practice. In the traditional setting this has tended to provide pressures towards modernity in the sense of the growth of national solidarity and the suppression of lineage enmities and hostilities. Today, however, the Islamic ideal world-view stands in a somewhat ambivalent relation to modern social change. Here it is necessary to recall that although the Muslim cosmology emphasizes an eschatological doctrine which contrasts sharply with the closed traditions of tribal worlds, it also encompasses many aspects which are regarded as archaic and impractical in most modern secular Islamic states. Thus while, on the one hand, certain passages in the Qur'ān can be used to provide ammunition for a modern view of monogamy which is increasingly popular amongst the young Western-educated Somali élite, other elements oppose new ideas and social change, at least among the least sophisticated. When, for example, news of rival Russian and American space-flights was broadcast in Somalia, some traditionalists were saying that this was nothing but Communist and anti-Communist propaganda. The Qur'ān, it was said, revealed clearly that there were seven heavens and man could never penetrate these.

Thus, in effect, one literate tradition is now increasingly challenged by another and attempts to reconcile the two are only partially successful. At the same time, independently of this, the mass of the Somali population have been, as it were, jerked into the modern world of mass radio communication and pop songs very largely through the medium of their own unwritten language. Again, new items of a foreign literate tradition are being selectively adapted to traditional needs and interests, at the same time as contributing towards overall social change. And in the present scramble for education and literacy by all age-groups, and both sexes, despite their traditional religious affiliation, English is emerging as the preferred written language and successfully thrusting Arabic and Italian into second place. This development is helping to resolve the difficulties posed in government and business by the dual (Italian and English) colonial heritage.

Of the significance of writing in the present context of change and development much could no doubt be said. I would, however, only like to draw attention by way of conclusion to the unusual degree of democracy and freedom which today obtains in the Somali Republic. Here, unlike the situation to which Goody and Watt refer in the origins of European democracy,[1] literacy is not a significant factor. In the context of the ethnically homogeneous Somali Republic, more relevant is J. S. Mill's observation that 'it is in general a necessary condition of free institutions, that the boundaries of government should coincide in the main with those of nationalities'.[2] Here, as in so many other respects, the Somalis tend to run counter to generalities applicable elsewhere.[3]

[1] See above, pp. 27–68. J. Goody and I. Watt, 'The Consequences of Literacy', *Comparative Studies in Society and History*, v (1963), pp. 304–45.

[2] J. S. Mill, *Considerations on Representative Government* (London, 1861), pp. 291–2.

[3] For a more detailed discussion of the special political circumstances in the Somali Republic, see Lewis (1968*b*).

ASTROLOGY AND WRITING IN MADAGASCAR

The study by Dr Bloch is of a society farther south down the East African coast, in Madagascar. He examines the role of Islamic-derived writing in the Merina state. While such writing was formerly used for administrative purposes as well as mystical ones, its present significance lies in the sphere of astrology. Bloch notes that the complex systematizations of reality used by the diviners are esoteric in their derivation (from the Middle East) and fall in a category of secret, specialist knowledge: 'the astrological cosmology is not the cosmology of the ordinary Merina'. It is a deliberate mystification of everyday life.

This conclusion has, I believe, important theoretical implications for the study of 'myth', 'classifications' and divination in such societies; it certainly corresponds to the situation among the Gonja of northern Ghana and it is a point I have elaborated in the introduction.

ASTROLOGY AND WRITING IN MADAGASCAR[1]

by M. BLOCH

The Malagasy word for 'written thing' is *Sora*, a word which comes straight from the Arabic. This is in itself an indication of where writing in Madagascar first came from.

The history and the nature of the influence of Arabic culture, and more especially of Islam, in Madagascar help us to understand certain aspects of present-day Malagasy culture. At present two groups of people claim close contact with Islam. A number of tribes claiming to be *Silama* (Islam) live in the extreme north-west and another group of tribes in the south-east of the island. The former are acquainted with part of the Qur'ān and Arabic cabalistic and magical lore. They follow certain of the Muslim laws. The vocabulary of their language, though basically Malagasy, contains many Swahili and Arabic words. They owe their Arabic culture to a string of trading posts along the north and west coasts of the island, the ruins of which can still be seen. Contact with the Arabs on this coast probably goes back to the tenth century (Grandidier 1908: 4–7). These trading posts were linked, up to the seventeenth century, with the Comoro Islands, which to this day are peopled largely with Swahili speakers, dominated by an Arabic ruling class. In medieval times the Comoro Islands and the Malagasy ports were probably linked to the East African port of Kilwa (Freeman-Grenville 1962: 85). At all events, the Arabic trading posts in the Indian Ocean were in contact with one another, and have remained so, to varying extents, to this day. In fact the renewed contacts between the Comoro and Madagascar have recently caused a resurgence of Islamic culture in the area.

These remnants of Arabic civilizations in Madagascar are well known, but objects of Malagasy origin have been found all along the east coast of Africa, and also along the trade routes known to lead to the Arab ports, for example, along the route leading to Zimbabwe (personal communication from P. Verin).

In Madagascar, however, the power of the Arabs was broken by the Portuguese, especially by Tristan da Cunha and his sailors, who burnt Arab towns all along the coast and exterminated the Muslim trading

[1] I carried out field work in Madagascar in 1965–6. This was financed by the Nuffield Foundation of Great Britain, to whom I wish to express my thanks.

population with notorious brutality. The sixteenth-century sailor Ludovico Barthema wrote of Madagascar: 'I believe it belongs to the King of Portugal because the Portuguese have already pillaged two towns and

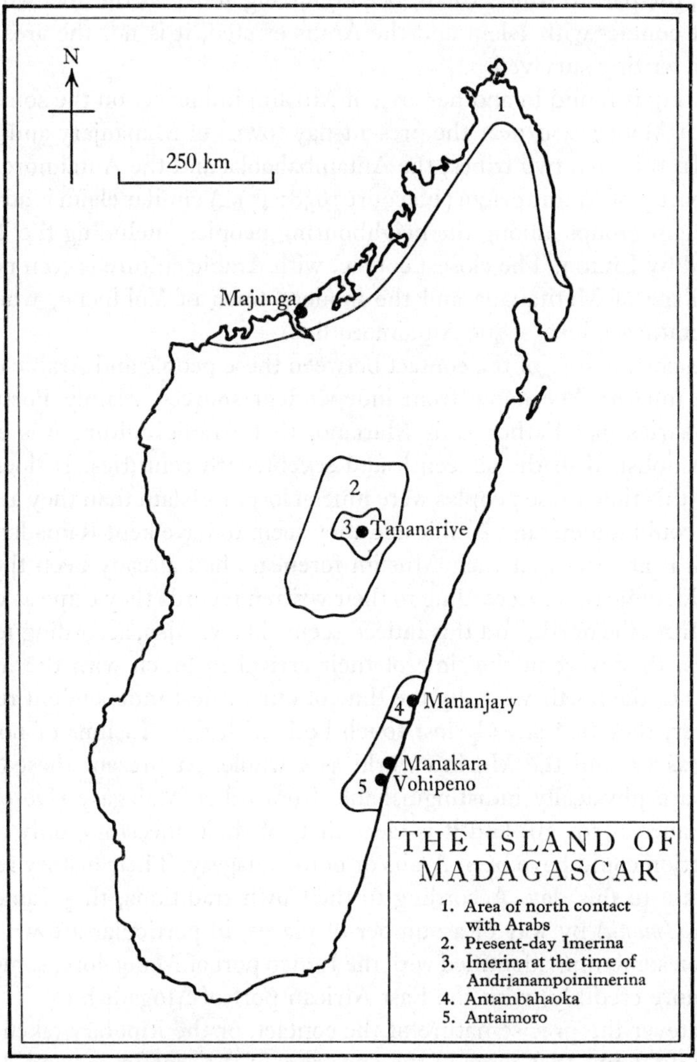

burnt them' (Ferrand 1891:52). Even more far-reaching than direct attacks was the fact that first the Portuguese, then other European nations, ruined the Arab trade in the Indian Ocean. Madagascar, one of the most remote outposts of the chain of Arab trading posts that existed in the Indian Ocean, became isolated from the rest of Muslim East Africa. It seems likely that the Arabs and Swahili themselves left Madagascar or were killed, and that the present *Silama* are descendants of converts made among the Malagasy.

This may explain the surprising fact that although the north-west of the island, the part to which I have been referring above, is the area where the closest contact with Islam and the Arabs existed, it is not the area where Arabic writing survived.

Writing is found in another area of Muslim influence, on the south-west coast of Madagascar near the present-day towns of Mananjary and Manakara. In this area two tribes, the Antambahaoka and the Antaimoro, claim to be partly of Arabic origin (Flacourt 1658: 47). A similar claim is advanced by certain groups among the neighbouring peoples, including the Tanala studied by Linton. The closest contact with Arabic culture is seen near the old village of Matitanana and the modern town of Vohipeno, where the aristocratic sections of the Antaimoro live.

The exact nature of the contact between these people and Arabic culture is still unclear. We know from independent sources, mainly Portuguese missionaries like Father Luis Mariano, that Arabic culture was already well established in the sixteenth and seventeenth centuries. It does seem that at this time these peoples were much closer to Islam than they are now. Some could understand Arabic and they seem to have kept Ramadan, even though it appears that their Muslim forebears had already been there for a considerable time. According to their written records they came at various times from the north, and this indeed seems likely. Also, according to these records, they were at the time of their arrival in touch with the Muslim centres of the north-west. By the time of our earliest independent records, however, they had already lost touch both with the Muslims of northern Madagascar, and the Muslim world as a whole. At present these 'Arab' tribes are physically indistinguishable from other Malagasy (Deschamps and Vianes 1959: 39) and it is clear that, of their ancestors, only a small proportion could have been Arabs or non-Malagasy. Their history remains uncertain to this day. According to their own traditions, they came from Mecca (*Imaka*) by way of a number of places, in particular a town which has been sometimes identified with the Indian port of Mangalore, sometimes (and more credibly) with the East African port of Mogadishu.

Whatever the precise nature of the contact, or the itinerary taken, there can be no doubt that some of the ancestors of the Antaimoro and Antambahaoka were bearers of an Arabic culture and are culturally and also possibly genetically linked with the Arabian peninsula. Archaeological evidence makes it clear that they must have originated in trading communities, probably governed by non-Malagasy but with a large non-Arabic element in their population (Deschamps and Vianes 1959: 10). This is a type of community with which we are familiar all along the east coast of Africa. Apart from archaeological evidence a certain amount of documentary evidence reveals the extensive nature of the Arabic colonization (Freeman-Grenville 1962: 133). Details of the Arabic contacts in the south-east are not known, however, and much of the speculation on this subject has only been made on the flimsiest evidence.

I am not qualified to judge which of the many theories concerning the origin of the Antaimoro and the Antambahaoka is the most acceptable, but one point is worth making: the geographical location of these groups makes them an even more remote outpost of the network of Arabic ports than the Islamized peoples of the north-west of Madagascar. This means that the cultural ancestors of the Antaimoro and the Antambahaoka would be even more affected by the breakdown of Arab trade which followed European intrusion into the Indian Ocean than their northern equivalents. This fact would explain the rather ambiguous (at the present day) relation to Islam of the Antaimoro and the Antambahaoka.

Even if they describe themselves as Muslims, the Antaimoro and Antambahaoka are only Muslims to a limited extent.[1] They perform hardly any of the Muslim rituals and have only the scantiest knowledge of Muslim theology. The Qur'ān is practically unknown, although some of the scribes remember odd, uncomprehended verses. Muslim prayers are not known, and feasts such as Ramadan are not kept. No Antaimoro or Antambahaoka makes the pilgrimage to Mecca. They have only a few practices of Arabic or Muslim origin: a special respect for Fridays, a taboo on pork (Deschamps and Vianes 1959: 70, 71), the occasional use of pious Arabic expressions (Ferrand 1905: 20), and, among the aristocratic group, the Anakara, certain short Muslim prayers, mostly in Malagasy (Ferrand 1905: 21). To this list must be added the use by a few ritual specialists of uncomprehended magical and astrological formulae, in what was once Arabic (Deschamps and Vianes 1959: 43). The Antaimoro and Antambahaoka combine with this incomplete version of Islam other beliefs which are in fact often incompatible with the theory of the Muslim religion. Nowadays, the majority consider themselves to be Christians, and a good many of them attend Protestant or Catholic churches regularly. They also all follow magico-religious practices common throughout Madagascar which are neither Christian nor Muslim in origin.

The most significant features in the heritage of Arabic culture possessed by the Antaimoro and the Antambahaoka, however, are the art of writing

[1] They have recently stressed their connection with Islam more strongly as a result of contact with immigrant Muslims such as the Comorians and the Indians who have settled in Madagascar.

in Arabic script and manuscripts. The effect of these manuscripts is that Arabic practices are not solely maintained by tradition, but can be continually reaffirmed by reference to written records.

The long-standing existence of writing in a particularly remote part of what was until the nineteenth century an othewise preliterate country has been the subject of much comment by European writers, from the earliest to those of the present day. So we are particularly well informed on this subject. We know that Arabic script was already in use in the sixteenth century. For example, at the very beginning of the seventeenth century a Portuguese sailor reports how he made a treaty with an Antaimoro ruler and how this treaty was written down in Arabic script in the Malagasy language (Grandidier 1908: 437–8).

The fullest early account of the place of writing in the Antaimoro country is given to us by the seventeenth-century French governor of a short-lived French colony sited around the town of Fort Dauphin. I give below a translation of what he says, including translations of the Malagasy words that he uses.

There are two kinds of witch doctors, the witch doctor writers and the witch doctor diviners. The witch doctor writers are highly skilled at writing in Arabic. They have several books which include a few chapters of the Qur'ān. For the most part they understand Arabic, which they learn to write in the same way as Latin and Greek are learnt in Europe...They heal the sick. They make *Hiridzi*, *Talizmans*, *Massarabes* and other writings which they sell to those in high positions and to the rich to protect them from a thousand possible accidents and diseases, from lightning, from fire, from their enemies and even from death, in spite of the fact that they cannot even protect themselves from it. In these ways these tricksters obtain cattle, gold, silver, cloth and a thousand other different commodities by means of their writings which they raise up unto heaven. These witch doctors are extremely feared, not only by the people, who believe them to be sorcerers, but also by their leaders who employed them against the French...These (sorcerers) sent to the fort of the French basketfuls of papers covered in writing, eggs laid on Fridays covered with figures and writing, unbaked mud jars covered in writing (etc.)...These witch doctors have been taught by those of Matitanana where there are schools which teach the young [Flacourt 1658: 171–2].

Flacourt then goes on to describe Antaimoro astrology, which he makes clear by implication is connected with the Arabic books which he lists. He gives the impression that the writers and astrologer diviners are two different sets of people, a division which, even if it did exist in the past, does not exist today. Having told us something of writers, he goes on to analyse in more detail their actual technique:

The script which the witch doctors use is like that used by the Arabs, written from right to left, but for some letters the pronunciation is different from what it would be in the Arabic language...The use of writing was brought to these parts two hundred years ago by certain Arabs who came from the Red Sea and who said they were sent to the island by the Caliph of Mecca. They appeared in their boats at Matitanana and married there. They taught and teach the Arabic language and the Qur'ān to those who wish to learn and run schools...[Flacourt 1658: 185–6].

This account is interesting from many points of view. It suggests that there existed then a much closer link with Arabic culture and language than at present, but it also makes clear that links with the Arabs had already been broken, and that the script had already been fully adapted to Malagasy. It emphasizes a feature which is still important today, that is, the power, religious, magical, astrological and medicinal, of the written word, both for those possessing the art and those without it, and it shows how the services of those who controlled writing were sought by neighbouring peoples.

This emphasis on the virtue and power of the writing of special texts is a common feature of Islamic cultures. In Madagascar, however, the emphasis is different in many ways from what we should expect to find in other, more orthodox Muslim countries.

The first point to notice is that the script has been separated from the actual Arabic language. It seems from Flacourt that Arabic was still used in his time, although already the script had been adapted for Malagasy. However, since the nineteenth century at least, Malagasy only has been written, and it seems that this must have been the case for a long time as no full-length Arabic texts written in Madagascar have been found, in spite of the fact that we possess quite a number of old manuscripts (Anon 1960: 113).

The adaptation of Arabic script for Malagasy has presented a certain number of problems which make it very difficult to read—in particular, the vowel signs sometimes added to the main line of the Arabic script have become attached to consonants, and often mislead Arabic scholars. Also, other signs have been introduced and the phonetic value of each is naturally different from what it is in Arabic. Because of these modifications, Arabic scholars have described the Antaimoro script as being a kind of picture puzzle. This is, in fact, completely unwarranted, and some people can read the script with little difficulty if they are acquainted with Malagasy, and with the few dialectical variants which are commonly found in that part of Madagascar. The task of adapting a foreign script to a previously unwritten language is formidable but we do not know when or by whom this was achieved.

The second most significant difference between the south-east of

Madagascar and any orthodox Muslim country, from the point of view of literacy, is that in Madagascar the Qur'ān is not of great significance. This point is related to the absence of the Arabic language. Since one cannot have Islam without the Qur'ān, and one should not have the Qur'ān without Arabic, an orthodox community cannot divorce the language from the Book. The lack of importance attached by the Malagasy to the Qur'ān removes the link between writing and Arabic. The Qur'ān is replaced by a series of sacred manuscripts called *Sorabe*, or 'great writings'. This is a series of books kept and copied by the scribe aristocracy of the Antaimoro and Antambahaoka. These books have often been described (Julien 1929 and 1933; Deschamps and Vianes 1959). Some are old, although their precise date is uncertain; others are more recent. There are two kinds of works. First are contemporary chronicles and historical works dealing with the mythical origins of 'Arabic' peoples of the south-east. It is these *Sorabe* which have been studied most often (e.g. Ferrand 1891; Julien 1929 and 1933). Second, and equally common, are works on the related subjects of medicine, geomancy, divination and astrology. These latter are of particular significance here because these sciences are what gave the possessors of writing such prestige in all pre-colonial Madagascar. I intend to discuss the nature of this knowledge later, but I shall just mention here that these works are (like most *Sorabe*), translations or adaptations of earlier Arabic works on these subjects.[1] A study of one of these astrological manuscripts by the orientalist G. Ferrand (1905) has shown quite conclusively the Arabic origin of Malagasy astrology, and links it up with some of the early Muslim writers (Ferrand 1936). Also of great interest are certain manuscripts manufactured in Egypt and Syria which had been kept in the Bibliothèque Nationale with Malagasy manuscripts. Closer examination revealed that they were not Malagasy, but this does not prove that they did not come from Madagascar. It seems probable that these are manuscripts which were in the hands of the Antaimoro, as they correspond with the *Sorabe* in many points, and that they were placed with Malagasy books because they had been brought back with such books from Madagascar. If this is true, they would complete the chain between Malagasy and Middle Eastern astrology, a chain which we know must have existed (Grandidier 1908: 636).[2]

The existence of a scribe aristocracy among the Antaimoro and Antambahaoka is important not only for our understanding of the society and culture of these people, but for our understanding of the society and culture

[1] Some of these manuscripts contain short passages in Arabic and, in one case, Persian (Faublée 1967: 2).

[2] Many of the books listed in the bibliography discuss the *Sorabe* in detail.

of the whole of Madagascar. The prestige and power of writing, and the magico-religious information that goes with it, are spread throughout Madagascar. It is clear from the passage by Flacourt quoted above that Antaimoro scribes and medicine men were employed by other Malagasy peoples. Other evidence of this includes the testimony of an eighteenth-century French traveller who noted how Antaimoro were used near Tamatave to record transfers of land and genealogies. Scribes from the south-east travelled throughout Madagascar and sometimes settled among other tribes, practising the arts of medicine, magic and divination. Indirect evidence of this contact is provided by the fact that astrological and divinatory knowledge recorded throughout Madagascar accords closely with what we find in the *Sorabe*. A comparison of the account of Betsileo astrology given by Dubois (1938: 949) or of Merina astrology given for the early nineteenth century by Ellis (1838: 156) with the *Sorabe* translated by Ferrand (1905) shows this clearly.

We possess, however, direct evidence of the influence of Antaimoro astrologers on other tribes during the reign of the Merina king Andrianampoinimerina. This king, whose probable dates are 1787 to 1810, began his famous reign by uniting the many small chiefdoms of what was to become Imerina, and then went further still, incorporating non-Merina peoples in a very large kingdom. This kingdom was greatly enlarged by his son, Radama (as he is called by writers on Madagascar), or Lehidama (as the Malagasy themselves call him). He set up an elaborate centralized state employing specialized judges, local representatives of the central government, messengers and other full or part-time government officials. We are fortunate in that we have detailed knowledge about the administrative organization set up by Radama, an organization which was responsible for the subsequent stability of the kingdom (Julien 1908).

One of the first acts of Andrianampoinimerina when his state became an important power in central Madagascar was to send for a number of Antaimoro astrologer-diviners whom he asked to settle at his court, which they did. This shows that Antaimoro astrologers must have been in contact with the Merina before, since the king was clearly aware of their reputation.

We are particularly well informed about the Antaimoro who came to the court at this time, since one of them wrote an account of the activities of their delegation (Ferrand 1891: 101 ff.). It is clear that the role of these Antaimoro at the king's court was to advise on astrology and other magical matters. They accompanied the king on his campaigns, advising him of propitious times for attacks and other dangerous actions requiring a specific time. They supplied the king with charms, some of which became the objects of major cults (e.g. Rakelimalaza). These charms were later to be a major object of missionary hostility and were to end by being burnt at the time of the queen's conversion. These Antaimoro were also doctors, making use of the recipes for medicines that are found in the *Sorabe*, and they used the mode of divination called *Sikidy*, for which they were renowned. Indeed to this day Antaimoro astrologer-diviners are still employed by the Merina for the same purposes.

I shall return to the effect of these magico-religious activities, but first let us consider a rather lesser known aspect of these astrologers' influence, which is nevertheless of the greatest significance.

At the end of the reign of Andrianampoinimerina a number of Merina officials could write Arabic script, and it would seem that the astrologers had set up a school in Tananarive. There is much evidence to suggest that the Antaimoro at the court trained Merina astrologers and magicians, but they must also have taught writing so that it could be used for administrative purposes. James Hastie, a British diplomat sent from Mauritius in 1817, reports that in Imerina only the king, the eldest prince and three other men could write (Berthier 1953: 2). However, Berthier points out that, although 'it is likely that the number of natives who had learnt to write Arabico-Malagasy was fairly limited', it was 'certainly much less so than James Hastie states in his journal' (1953: 3). Berthier gives some evidence to support this statement and points out that many Arabico-Malagasy texts must have been burnt with other 'idols' when Radama's successor was converted to Christianity.

Our most direct evidence for the use of Arabic script in Imerina is the school book of the son and successor of Andrianampoinimerina, Radama. It is known that this king could write well and easily, and later wrote letters. The so-called 'school book' contains quite a variety of materials. A section was used by Radama for learning French words from a French envoy named Robin; there is also information on financial and military matters and even a section on astrology which serves to remind us who the teachers of Radama were.

There is sufficient evidence to say that before the coming of the British missionaries and the introduction of European script, a certain amount of the business of government was carried out in writing in Arabic script, either by administrators who were themselves literate, or by ones who used Antaimoro scribes. These scribes had the dual roles of diviner-astrologers and secretaries. The importance of these Antaimoros should not be ignored in understanding how the Merina were able to hold together and administer a kingdom considerably larger than the British Isles.[1]

[1] M. Faublée mentions the discovery by M. J. Valette of an inventory of weapons dating back to this period (Faublée 1967: 2).

Arabic script has only a fairly small place in the history of Imerina because, as soon as it started to spread, it was replaced by European script. If we may hazard a guess at the date of the establishment of the Antaimoro school in Tananarive, it would be probably around 1800; by 1820, however, two missionaries of the London Missionary Society, David Jones and David Griffiths, with the co-operation of a Frenchman called Robin, produced an adaptation of the Roman script for Malagasy. According to Deschamps (1961: 161), who unfortunately does not give us the source of his information, by 1827 there were more than 4,000 people who could read and write in Imerina and new laws and edicts were pinned up at the Palace gate. By 1868, a compendium of Merina law had actually been printed and it is quite clear that writing was very widespread. I do not wish to follow through the development of writing as such after this date, but its adoption and spread were fantastically rapid. It seems possible that the Antaimoro astrologers had prepared the way for this advance by familiarizing the Merina with the concept of writing, probably for centuries before the coming of the missionaries. It is worth noting that today Imerina is probably the area of the 'third world' with the highest literacy rate.

There is one point about which we can be more definite. From the details of the present-day orthography of Malagasy in Roman script it is certain that this adaptation followed the earlier adaptation to Arabic script in many technical respects (Berthier 1953: 2). In other words, it is probable that Griffiths, Jones, Robin and some of their informants were aware and made use of the devices of Arabico-Malagasy writing.

In this way these Antaimoro astrologers and magicians introduced into Imerina a tool that was also used for the secular administration of the kingdom. What, we may then ask, are the relevant factors which enabled this secularization of writing to take place? First of all, the form of writing that began to be adopted under Andrianampoinimerina and Radama had been available, in all probability, for at least four centuries. It was, however, a special kind of writing. Compared with pure Arabic script it was rather clumsy. In its favour, however, are two important facts. First, it was fully adapted to Malagasy (and here I should mention that the dialect spoken in the Antaimoro country is very close indeed to that of the Merina and so there was not yet another language barrier); secondly, it was not associated with Islam. In fact, these two points are linked, since it is the association of writing with the Qur'ān which maintains the association with Arabic. The Malagasy sacred books were concerned only with history, astrology, divination and medicine. Astrology, divination and medicine are all forms of supernatural knowledge, but they are undertaken with very immediate practical ends in mind. It seems quite possible that this is an important factor in facilitating the adoption of writing for purely practical purposes. On the other hand, all this does not explain why writing was taken up at the particular point in time at which it was. Here, however, the evidence seems fairly conclusive. Writing was taken up when a large, powerful, centralized state grew up. In such a state there is a great need for writing. Some of the uses to which writing can be put in such a situation can be seen from the example offered by Imerina, first with Arabic script, then with European. These uses are:

(1) credentials of government employees;
(2) messages from the central government to its more remote representatives; and
(3) written laws.

In this way the astrology and writing which the cultural ancestors of the Antaimoro had brought with them spread throughout the island and gave prestige to the initiates. In Imerina in the nineteenth century, however, the Antaimoro started to teach directly, bringing about two results. One was the use of writing for secular purposes, which was quickly superseded by European missionaries and their schools. This secular writing is undoubtedly the most important from the point of view of the sociology of the Merina but it belongs to a different tradition and raises such important questions that it cannot be followed up here. The other result of the Antaimoro teaching was the use of writing and astrology as a source of prestige to a few specialists. This, too, has stayed and astrologers, the heirs of Antaimoro astrology, are still important in the Merina countryside. I want now to turn to an examination of the astrologers, their knowledge and writing, and show how the historical background to their science helps us to understand some of its features today.

In spite of the secular uses to which writing was put, there is no doubt that the Antaimoro at the court were primarily ritual specialists and their influence in this field is clearly present in modern Merina.

Some aspects of astrology, as I found it in the field in 1964–6, can be explained, even today, by the close association with writing. Before considering this, however, I must describe another symbolical system which is closely associated with astrology but is of a different origin.

Malagasy notions of direction are in terms of the points of the compass rather than in terms of distance, right and left. The points of the compass are used because of their practical value, but they are also given moral value. It is, basically, a simple system. The north-east is considered particularly good and associated with the dead and with God, whilst the opposite direction, the south-west, is considered as lacking in all virtue. Intermediate directions are considered to have varying degrees of religious and moral value (Hébert 1965). This according of different degrees of value to different orientations is manifested in a variety of ways, the most noticeable of which is the orientation of houses and tombs. In the case of a house, it means that the living room is to the north of the kitchen, while the door is to the south-west; the bed of the head of the household and his spouse is at the north-east of the living room, and children and servants sleep to the south-west of the main bed. In the north-east corner first-fruits are kept from one year to the next and 'medicines' and other articles with good supernatural associations are stored. When a group of people are together in a house, they position themselves in order of status around the walls, the most important at the north-east and the least important at the south-west. This practice is particularly noticeable on ritual occasions, such as marriages, circumcisions, and funerals, when the directional symbolic system is used to express essential aspects of the proceedings (Bloch 1967: chs. V and VI). In all these ways and in many others, this sytem of orientation influences some of the aspects of Merina life. However, for nearly all actions, only this simple scheme of orientation is relevant. By contrast, the elaborations of this scheme (which are considered below), linked as they are with astrology, are not relevant to everyday life. It should also be noted that, although the orientation system is universally known and accepted, no very great importance is attached to it. Informants with whom I discussed this matter denied that punishment would follow if a house was not built with the right orientation. It seemed to be rather a matter of etiquette, which was strongly sanctioned on ritual occasions as it was then an intrinsic part of the right way of performing the ritual in question.

Merina astrology is linked to this orientation system. It is a system of beliefs still basically close to those of the Antaimoro *Sorabe*, and consequently of the medieval Arab astrologers and cabalistic writers. Astrological systems are probably the aspect of Malagasy culture which has been most thoroughly and accurately described, probably because it is fairly easy to obtain statements of Merina astrological beliefs. One of the clearest accounts is given by J. Ruud in *Taboo* (1960). Briefly, the astrological system centres on the belief that one's destiny (*vintana*), lucky or unlucky, good or bad, dangerous to others or not so dangerous, is determined by the time of one's birth. Thus, lunar months are strong or weak, and so are the days of the month, the days of the week, and the times of the day. Astrology not only concerns itself with the time of one's birth, but also the time when one performs actions. The right time for an action is not simply a fixed matter, but is related to one's personal *vintana*. Thus, at least two variables must be taken into account if astrology is to be used as a guide for action. This system is further complicated when the actions involve more than one person, as their respective destinies interact on one another. Thus, the time of a marriage is determined by finding out at what time, day, and month the destinies of the two spouses will accord. In other words, three variables are taken into account.

As such, the system is still not over-complicated, but in fact it is usually elaborated in a variety of ways. First, the basic scheme is capable of great elaboration by the simple device of dividing and subdividing the significant units of astrological time. Second, the astrology proper is often associated and merged with other information and types of knowledge. Thus, colours, various kinds of stones, etc., are said to correspond to particular astrological times. In a similar kind of way, social, ethnic and politico-geographical divisions (Danielli 1950) are associated in a single scheme of classification, reminiscent in many ways of those systems described by Durkheim and Mauss in their essay on primitive classification.

A particularly striking and well-known example is the association of the orientation system described above and the astrological system. This is done by identifying the various months and their destinies with directions, and hence with the various parts of the house (since Malagasy houses should all have the same orientation). In this way (Figure 1) we have the following joining of month and direction:

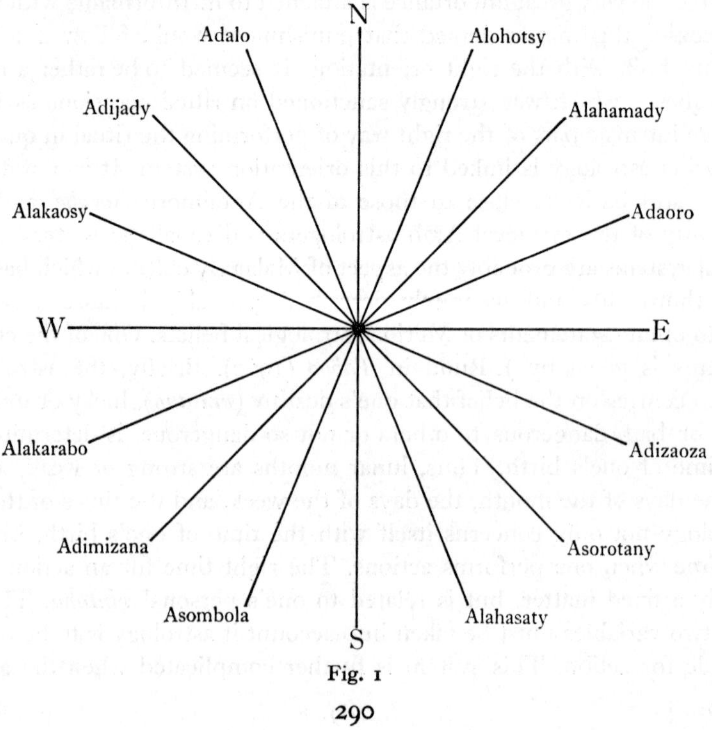

Fig. 1

The month and destinies are further joined to parts of the house, so that in a traditional Merina house facing west, the various parts of the walls are associated with lunar months. Thus, a normal house is divided in the way shown in Figure 2 and certain household articles normally stored in these parts of the house are also associated with the various destinies, as are the uses to which the articles are put.

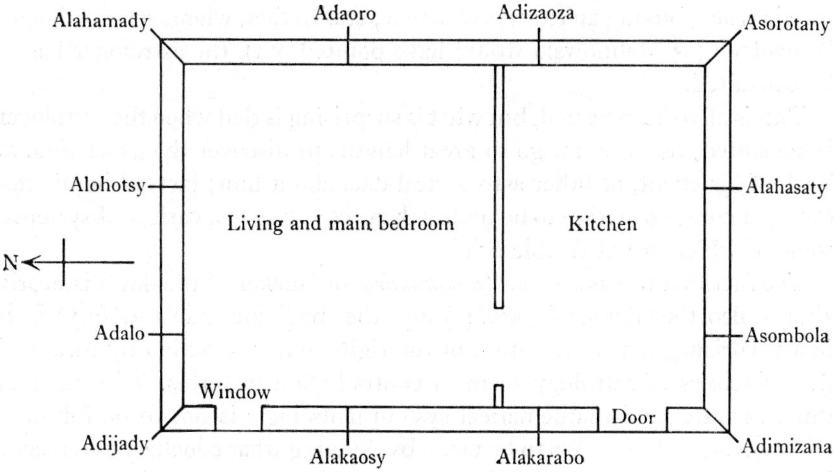

Fig. 2

Endless elaboration of the basically simple pattern of astrology in this way presents us with a system of classification which apparently takes in the entire universe. As such, this cosmological classification has fascinated many writers on Madagascar, in the same way as similar systems in other parts of the world have fascinated other writers. However, it is only when we see what this system is used for, and by whom, that we can evaluate its significance for the life of the Merina. I shall try to show that it would be mistaken to assume that such a complete organization of the world is necessarily the matrix which organizes the Merina's cognitive processes.

First of all, it is to be noted that astrology, to the Merina, is not only descriptive, but also predictive. The basic concept behind astrology is that it reveals a quality about people and things which, although apparently hidden, is more fundamental than the evident qualities, in that it determines these same evident qualities. In other words, *vintana*, if it were fully known, would explain everything about a person, past, present and future. The astrologer, owing to his capacity to know *vintanas*, knows the past, present and future, and of these three, the future is obviously the most interesting. The ordinary Merina, therefore, goes to the astrologer to discover what future actions he should take to fulfil his *vintana*, and to avoid the difficulties which will occur if he does not fulfil it. Thus, before a circumcision, the correct time for the operation must be discovered by the astrologer, taking into account the *vintana* of the boy concerned. In the same way, at a funeral, the time of the ceremony, and the colouring of the coats of the cattle to be eaten, are discovered by a consideration of the *vintana* of the dead, and of the mourners. The astrologer will be consulted before going on a journey, buying an expensive article, etc. In fact, whenever any danger is involved (as Malinowski would have pointed out), the astrologer has to be consulted.

This is all to be expected, but what is surprising is that when the astrologer is consulted, he does not go to great lengths to discover the exact time of birth of his client, or other astrological data about him; instead he divines the right course of action to be undertaken according to a variety of systems, some of which are of Arabic origin.

The fact that the astrologer (*mpanandro*, or 'maker of the day') is nearly always also the diviner (*mpiskidy*) and the medicine man (*ombiasy*) is at first surprising, since divination of the right course of action by means of the principles of astrology seems a contradiction in terms. Why refer to this elaborate semi-mathematical system if its logic is not to be followed anyway, and a short cut is to be taken by divining what conclusion to reach? The answer to this question is to be found when we examine the social position of the astrologer-diviner: this, in turn, helps us to evaluate his esoteric astrological knowledge.

A man or woman may become an astrologer-diviner in a number of different ways. He or she may, for example, be taught by a practitioner, and then perhaps introduced to a group of other astrologer-diviners who carry out certain regular rites to maintain their power. It is also possible to claim power as an astrologer-diviner through some mystical experience, or to do nothing more than claim the knowledge and power necessary. Being an astrologer-diviner is, like the subject matter of Merina astrology itself, a combination of the possession of complex knowledge and the possession of supernatural powers.

In practice, however, the lack of a clearly defined qualification for entry into the profession means that an extremely large number of people claim to be astrologer-diviners. What matters, therefore, is much more the ability to succeed in acquiring a large clientele than being a practitioner.

However, as soon as we look at it in this way, a very important fact begins to emerge. As regards social position, there are really two kinds of astrologer-diviners. One kind, which I shall call the professional, is extremely rare, and consists of people who make their living through divining, healing, and discovering destinies; to this day, these are often Antaimoro. The other much commoner kind are the amateurs, who practise the art for the sake of the prestige thereby acquired. These amateurs are numerous, and in the area where I worked nearly all the influential older men, apart from the *fonctionnaires*, were astrologer-diviners of one kind or another.

The reason for this is that there are now very few ascribed statuses in Merina society, and so a man who wishes to reach a position of importance or power, by, for example, being elected a *conseiller*, or by becoming the head of a family group or a village, must manoeuvre himself into that position. Naturally, there are many ways of gaining prestige, but, to be in the running at all, one must be a senior man (*raiamandreny*), which is achieved partly through age, partly through wealth, but also through the possession of knowledge, i.e. traditional knowledge, called *fomba*. The possession of this lore is demonstrated in a number of ways. Most important of all, a senior man must be a good orator, which means, apart from knowing how to express himself in the very complicated traditional speech form of the Merina, knowing also an immense number of proverbs and stories, either traditional or biblical. The more one knows of these the better, and so a suitably embellished speech may last two, three or more hours.

As well as knowing many proverbs and stories a man well versed in *fomba* is expected to have a large store of astrological knowledge and therefore, very probably, to practise divination and medicine. These important people are therefore those that one would expect to be astrologers, and this particular knowledge is thought of as part, a very important part, of their knowledge. The near identification of the roles of senior man and astrologer is demonstrated by the fact that many informants could never decide if the walking-stick made of power-giving wood (*mpanjaka be ny tany*, literally 'great king of the earth') was the symbol of office of a *raiamandreny* or of an astrologer. It seems clear that they sometimes said one thing and sometimes another, because they considered the two roles closely associated. An important man is a wise man, and a wise man is *par excellence* an astrologer.

Although the amateur astrologer is principally trying to gain political prestige, his skill is also a source of supplementary income. The family astrologer receives a small annual reward, consisting usually of a red cock and other minor commodities, and much more important major rewards when his services are required on special occasions. In the part of north Imerina where I worked, the usual payment for the services of an astrologer given in the case of a major ceremony was either a bull or the sum of about 5,000 FMG (i.e. £7. 10*s*.). However, receiving regular presents (which are really fees) is also part and parcel of the position of an important man, since all people of importance are regularly given presents by their inferiors, often quite substantial presents. The fact that the astrologer receives such fees is, to the ordinary Merina, yet another demonstration of his status.

Now this 'wisdom' possessed by the astrologer, if it is to be a sign which effectively marks off the *raiamandreny* élite from other more ordinary people, must be difficult to acquire. In addition, since acquiring status of this kind is very much a matter of competition, the more complicated the knowledge that a claimant has, the better. This element of competition was continually brought home to me during my field work. It was very quickly assumed that what I was trying to discover was this special esoteric knowledge in which the wisdom of the elders consists, since in many ways this is what seems to the Malagasy to be interesting in their society. As a result of this, people of importance were extremely offended when I tried to obtain information from ordinary people because, as I was told, 'they don't know'. Also, when I had been to one man of importance, and then went to another for information, the second would immediately ask me what the first had told me, and would then go on to explain and elaborate further, to the great admiration of all present. On one occasion I even witnessed a competition between two men of importance, rivals, before a wedding; they were arguing, obviously for the sake of prestige, on the nature and the ultimate significance of the rituals to be performed at the wedding. This was not for my benefit. Now, this argument, like the others I mentioned, was not to prove who was right and who wrong, but to show who knew the most elaborate version of what they were discussing. In such a situation, the occurrence of extreme elaborations of astrological theories is comprehensible. This competition for ever greater complication, not to say obscurity, seems to me to explain why the astrologer has to *divine* the solution to the problems presented to him. The astrologer, when first consulted, dazzles his client with all sorts of complicated and foreign facts about destinies, and other matters which are just as foreign and mysterious to him as to his client. Naturally, the astrologer cannot really *use* these facts for his solution, so he has to take a short cut, which is how I described divination.

One typical example of such an elaboration by a man of importance is the information reported by Mary Danielli (1950) in her article on the Merina state, information which she misleadingly presents as though it were generally known to the ordinary man. In fact, these rather fantastic schemes have often been recorded as a result of the techniques of most of the ethnographers who have worked in Madagascar and who have been satisfied with information obtained solely from the most renowned *raiamandreny*, who were most probably also astrologers.

If competition between learned men, especially in the field of astrology, explains the complexity and obscurity of some of the schemes which have been reported, this is not to say that the elaborations of these learned men are their own personal fantasies.

First, astrology is always based on the same rather simple pattern.[1] Secondly, the information which the astrologers incorporate into the astrological scheme comes from well defined sources. The astrologer uses information some of which is well known, such as the orientation of a traditional house, and shows that the orientation system is really the same scheme as the astrological one.

In the kind of scheme just described two kinds of material are juxtaposed. On the one hand, there is the strange foreign information which usually derives from written sources. As Goody and Watt have pointed out, it is no coincidence that the strange foreign information goes back to written works, for, if information in any amount keeps its foreign unexpected quality, it is likely to have been transmitted otherwise than by oral tradition since oral tradition is continually being moulded by the present conditions in which it is retold.

These written documents are available from two sources. First, the *raiamandreny* have usually at least one chap-book into which they have copied and preserved all kinds of information on many subjects, including astrology. These books are very precious, and are passed on from one head of a family to his successor. It is possible to record in them the most complicated information, long successions of proverbs, anecdotes and biblical quotations, which can then be produced at the right moment. In fact these men often look up several references before making a speech, and seem soon to remember effortlessly the most complex and esoteric information.

Not satisfied by these chap-books, however, most of these men now supplement them by small, cheaply printed books containing proverbs, anecdotes, model speeches and much astrological information or material associated with astrology. The few books (other than hymn books) normally read in remote areas are nearly all concerned with astrology. The contents of these books come from many varied sources. First, there are translations of *Sorabe*; second, missionary accounts of Merina beliefs, proverbs, etc.; third, foreign works, mainly on astrology and usually in French. Indeed, those few who can read French can supplement their astrological knowledge from the truly staggering number of French works on this subject on sale in Tananarive, and also from the columns of the

[1] J. C. Hébert points out how the basic simple structure of astrological information serves as a mnemonic device for the astrologer while his client, not knowing the basic scheme, is all the more baffled by the information.

many old French newspapers imported in bulk into Madagascar as wrapping paper.

The prestige of such works comes in part from their strangeness, in part from their being in written form. From the point of view of the villagers, these two qualities are really one, since they are things and statements which the villager has not made and which come to him, as it were, from an extraordinary, supernatural world, ready made. In fact, this power is thought to be present in all written things. During the period of my field work people would stare for hours at my books, especially at my dictionary. To the Merina villager, all written information was the same kind of thing, something which contributed to one's 'wisdom', the kind of knowledge of esoteric fact which marks out a *raiamandreny*.

Foreign written knowledge is particularly suited to marking out an élite since it is a scarce good, access to which is limited in four ways. First, one of the major sources of this knowledge is the chap-books which, as we saw, are passed on from one head of family to the next, unlike other property which is inherited bilaterally. Secondly, another source of foreign knowledge is books which are bought in bookshops in Tananarive and which are therefore restricted to those who are in contact with Tananarive. Thirdly, obtaining knowledge from written sources requires the ability to read with ease. Fourthly and most significantly, this 'knowledge' is so complex and difficult to acquire that it requires long study, practice, concentration and skill to master. In fact, as I suggested above, it is complicated and obscured for the sake of making it difficult to obtain—a scarce good.

The other kind of information incorporated into the astrological scheme is, by contrast, everyday. It is, as we saw, things such as the orientation of the traditional house, the moral qualities with which people are credited. In this case, the source of the prestige of the astrologer is different. It comes from the fact the he is able to reveal in his discourses and explanations connections where none were thought to exist before, and to show connections between the world of the obvious, which therefore pertains to oneself, and the strange world of foreign astrology. The astrologer is, to use Lévi-Strauss's analogy, a *bricoleur*, in that he uses materials intended for one purpose in another, completely different whole. But in this case, in contrast to the kind of scheme that Lévi-Strauss is referring to, the enhanced value of the elements comes from the fact that they are placed in *strange* relationships to one another. In other words, the order imposed by the astrological scheme is interesting to the actor because it runs counter to the classifications of everyday life: it is a scheme which appears to the actors, as it does to us, as nebulous, fantastic and supernatural, and it is because of these qualities that it is valued.

I have given this account of the nature of astrological knowledge to show the light in which the often reported descriptions of Merina astrological schemes should be viewed. There is a danger of our assuming, as Durkheim and Mauss do when discussing the Chinese 'classifications', that the astrological view of the world is a view which directs the actions of individuals. In the case I am considering here, these schemes are elaborations, even mystifications, by men competing for prestige. In confirmation, let me here quote Father Dubois, whose remarks on the astrology of the neighbouring Betsileo apply equally well to that of the Merina:

Let us note in this matter, that in the case of astrology, like that of divination, the professionals have gone out of their way to complicate their manoeuvres in order to increase the possibilities of associations, while retaining a certain uniformity of principles and method. The divisions, subdivisions and divisions of divisions of subdivisions are built up along the same pattern and in the same initial terms, but the scheme has been multiplied for the sake of it. All this gives greater freedom in the operations and impresses more those who are not initiates, who find themselves completely lost [Dubois 1938: 953].

Astrology is best seen as a work of art which makes use of the basic categories of Merina culture, not in the normal way but by 'playing' with them. This is not to say that this whole scheme is totally divorced from social action. The very fact that it is a credential of belonging to an élite and a system of competition between leaders gives it a social function. Secondly, it incorporates systems such as the orientation system, which, as we have seen, is a feature of everyday life. Nonetheless, the fact remains that the astrological cosmology is not the cosmology of the ordinary Merina; the reason for this can be explained when we take into account the origin, mode of transmission and formulation of the knowledge of the astrologers.

USES OF LITERACY IN NEW GUINEA AND MELANESIA

The next two chapters deal with literacy in the more modern sense. In the first, Professor Meggitt describes the impact of writing on a completely non-literate society. New Guinea lay beyond, but not far beyond, the part of the Pacific that was decisively influenced by writing at an early date—I refer to the Indonesian archipelago and the islands closest to the Asiatic mainland. Its encounter with writing was mainly through the Europeans, especially after the phase of active colonial penetration began in the latter part of the nineteenth century.

Meggitt contrasts the attitude to writing of the Melanesians on the coast and the Papuans of the highlands. The former placed a cultic reliance on the Word as a mystic sign, thinking that by manipulation of the *pas* or letter they could control the spirit world and hence secure access to material plenty. In the highlands, on the other hand, the attitude to writing was more pragmatic, a concomitant of European education, with its promise of worldly success. What Cargo cults occur are short-lived and their claims subjected to more empirical testing.

Meggitt sees this difference as related to outlooks which are also manifest in their religious activities. He then concludes by referring to the situation at the time of European contact and after. It is perhaps relevant to note that these coastal areas were subjected to European contact during the harshest phase of colonialism and by the harshest of European colonizers; under such conditions an emphasis on ritualization would seem a common reaction of the oppressed. But the highlands were effectively occupied only at a much later date, when the dominant attitudes of the colonialists had undergone significant changes; they were now more concerned with economic development than economic exploitation and there were effective means by which the indigenous peoples could advance. How far did this difference in the actions of the colonizers affect the reactions of the colonized?

It is noteworthy that the Cargo cults are not backward in their adoption of new communications techniques. They do not stop with writing. When wireless telegraphy is seen to be a key to European administration, imitation transmitters are erected. When airstrips become an essential feature of European transportation, they are also incorporated into the cults. The reason is clear. A large part of human life has to do with communication between men; a large part of magico-religious activity has to do with communication between men and gods.

There are two other points to make in connection with literacy in New Guinea. The uses of writing oscillate, like the aims of the new movements arising there, between the ritual and the pragmatic. The failure of the Book to bring the desired Cargo is sometimes attributed to its incompleteness, to the fact that the all-important pages have been torn out and hidden by their white masters who want to keep the secret knowledge to themselves (Worsley 1957: 137). The reverse of this story is found in West Africa, where courts frequently offer a witness the choice of taking an oath by the Bible, Qur'ān or some local shrine.

The pressure in favour of the literate alternatives in a literate court is enormous and I have noticed a strong tendency for educated pagans to opt for the Book. But to many the Book carries magical power as well as prestige and it is thought that such power can be reduced if the Book is incomplete. Anderson reports hearing of a court where a Qur'ān with a missing page was kept so that it could, on suitable occasions, be used with impunity (Anderson 1955: 265).

Another point which the letters in Pidgin raise is the considerable range of literate accomplishments that exists in societies in the process of modernization. I have known a number of intelligent but non-literate people who have taught themselves how to keep minimal records connected with their jobs. The efficiency of a lance-corporal is much increased by the ability to list and mark the names of his section; with a limited numerateness, a trader can keep a more effective record of his income and expenditure: and a cook is more valuable if he can work to a shopping list. Specialized literacy of this kind may be very limited in its scope, but it may have considerable utility in the everyday world.

USES OF LITERACY IN NEW GUINEA AND MELANESIA

by M. MEGGITT

I

In this essay I want to discuss briefly a characteristic feature of the millenarian movements or so-called 'Cargo cults' that have flourished intermittently in Melanesia during the last fifty years or so, that is, the way in which many followers of these cults have appeared to ritualize or, at least, to adopt a ritual attitude towards writing.

I do not pretend that such an observation is novel; some anthropologists who have studied particular cult situations have already commented on this phenomenon.[1] What I am more concerned to do here is, first, to treat this ritual view of writing as marking a stage in the development of such cults and, second, to note an interesting and somewhat puzzling difference in this respect between peoples of coastal and island Melanesia and those of the highlands of New Guinea. I shall not here try to deal exhaustively with the extensive literature on Cargo cults; rather, I shall merely refer to certain of those detailed accounts of specific movements that best exemplify the points I wish to make. There are, in any case, several surveys of the literature (and of attempts to explain these cults) to which I refer the reader.[2]

II

Anthropologists and missionaries have described various aspects of the indigenous (pre-European) religions of Melanesia, and, whatever their own interests, they have agreed substantially in referring to certain significant features of the religions.[3] In particular they have noted the relative simplicity (indeed, the naivety) of the epistemological and metaphysical assumptions made in these systems of belief, the way in which they combined and recombined a few conceptual elements in order to define what in general were practical ends in an essentially mundane existence. Native emphasis was primarily on the pragmatic manipulation of a limited number of ideas

[1] See for example, Lawrence (1954, 1965), Read (1958), Freeman (1959), Burridge (1960).
[2] See Berndt (1952), Inglis (1957), Worsley (1957), Thrupp (1962), Jarvie (1963), Valentine (1963) and Lanternari (1965).
[3] See Lawrence and Meggitt (1965) for general comments and bibliography, also Hogbin (1958), and Guiart (1962). My own views on Melanesian religions obviously owe much to those of Lawrence, and I thank him for his instruction.

and ritual expedients to acquire explicit socio-economic benefits for the practitioners. There was in this pervasive materialism little room (or incentive) for any deep concern with the spiritual *per se*; men did not, for instance, trouble themselves about the nature of the transcendental or try to assure themselves of personal salvation through attaining a state of grace. In effect, religion for the Melanesian was more like an alternative technology intended to deal with an anthropocentric, here-and-now cosmos, one that included both his 'natural' environment and his equally immediate 'non-natural' surroundings.

Thus, in substantive terms the native view of the universe commonly took it to include the physical, tangible world, the people in it, the spirits of dead people, and creative beings such as deities or culture heroes. Usually the last-mentioned were thought not only to have shaped the world (or at least its significant parts) and to have set man in it but also, at the same time, to have endowed man with culture—for instance, the arts of horticulture and animal husbandry, of hunting and fishing, of house-building and tool-making, of trading and ceremony. The myths related how the creators imparted this basic and esoteric knowledge to men through the medium of dreams and visions, together with certain secret information (such as the hidden names of tutelary deities, magical formulas, or rituals) whose private possession or employment was necessary to guarantee success to particular men or groups in the various social and technical activities of daily life.

The spirits of the dead, on the other hand, were not generally regarded as creative in this way but rather as protective of the everyday ongoing interests of their living kin, provided that the latter in turn behaved properly towards them by offering on appropriate occasions food, valuables, services, or simply public respect. The ghostly aid that men received might range from outright defence of their material property from encroachment by enemies to warnings in dreams of future events, whether feasts or fights.

Important in all these systems of belief, then, was the notion of communication with such 'supernatural' entities as gods and ghosts, especially to acquire certain esoteric knowledge whose possession ensured success or safety in doubtful situations. Equally important, however, in enabling the people to account for failures or for the unexpected was a characteristic feature of these traditional methods of communicating by means of dreams, visions, spirit mediums, namely, the attribute of inherent ambiguity in the techniques. That is, communications with the supernatural or non-empirical in Melanesia were essentially oracular, ritualized, and as susceptible of misinterpretation as ever they were at Delphi or at Cumae.

Given these tendencies in Melanesian religions, one can readily understand the initial reactions of many of the natives when Christian missionaries, Protestant or Roman Catholic, began work among them. Everywhere they quickly perceived that the missionaries had skills, wealth and power far in excess of their own, and they assumed reasonably enough that the newcomers had received these advantages from the omnipotent god whose message they strove to disseminate. At the same time the missionaries were assuring the people that, through attendance at church services and through conversion to the faith, they too could enter into communication with this deity and eventually attain a state of grace or achieve salvation.

Naturally, most of the audience equated these desired conditions with the observable power and wealth of the missionaries, and, as they were told that all were to be brothers in the kingdom of God, they saw themselves eventually occupying positions of equality in the plural society that was coming into being around the coasts of Melanesia. They were thus more than willing as a rule to join the missions and to share in these obvious benefits. Men were also keen to place their sons (although rarely their daughters) in the mission schools to learn the new arts of reading and writing and so penetrate more quickly the mystic secrets which missionaries alleged were contained in the Bibles and prayerbooks. With this esoteric knowledge in their grasp the natives could, so they thought, then directly command the help of the new deity just as they controlled their own gods.

Thus, from the beginning of their contacts with missions, many Melanesians displayed a curiously ritualized (yet practically understandable) attitude towards literacy. They took writing to be merely one more of those inherently ambiguous modes of communication with the supernatural with which they were already familiar. From this point of view, the virtue of writing lay in men's ability to manipulate it as an entity in a defined ritual fashion so that they could get a grip on the mission god and force from him his secrets. Indeed, writing soon came to be, in itself, an important symbol of the very goals of wealth and authority to which the people aspired. Many regarded words simply as aspects of the Word, a mark of the impending millennium and a 'Road to the Cargo'. (Cargo here meant not merely commodities but the combinations of wealth and power visible in the new socio-economic order.) At any rate, it seems that writing was rarely treated as a straightforward technique of secular action, one whose prime value is repeated and surrogate communication of unambiguous meanings in a variety of situations.

As we now know, the Melanesians were soon disappointed in most of the hopes they had placed in the mission forms of Christianity. No matter how conscientiously they participated in mission rituals, no matter how carefully they heeded the missionaries' moral exhortations, no matter how diligently their sons studied the school primers—the people remained materially poor and politically impotent. No amount of church-going bridged the social chasm that separated them from the Europeans, and in addition they found that they were acquiring new tastes that could be satisfied only by working hard for low wages in towns and on plantations. In short, there seemed to them to be no way through the missions of ritually achieving or controlling the Cargo they desired. Obviously, then, the missionaries were cheating and were somehow concealing from the people the true formulas that led to the mission god. For instance, according to some natives, the missionaries were not teaching all of the Bible but were keeping back the crucial few pages that listed the secret names of their god.[1]

The upshot of such widespread interpretations of the situation was a general withdrawal of the natives from mission churches and schools, followed by the emergence in many localities of men who claimed to have more effective ways of finding the Road to the Cargo. Usually the ideas and slogans promoted by these men urged the people to return to the old native religious beliefs and rituals while at the same time retaining in a kind of syncretism certain elements from the Christian teachings and practices. There is no need here to analyse these events in detail, but it should be noted that, following this retreat from the Europeans, the traditional modes of communicating with the supernatural once more became important. Seances, dream interpretation, vision inducement and similar equivocal techniques were again widely practised in endeavours to learn the whereabouts of the Cargo and how to bring it to the people; but in addition the ritualized manipulation of writing (for instance, in objectively irrelevant letters and books—*objets trouvés*, as it were) continued to be regarded as an equally potent device for understanding supernatural events and motives.[2]

This attitude towards the *pas* or letter in Melanesian cults has been noted in several anthropological studies but perhaps the most illuminating account is to be found in Burridge's book *Mambu* (1960, especially pages 193–4). His remarks deserve quotation at length:

> ...in everyday life, Tangu (people) associate the acquisition of European goods with a *pas*. Those who have served under Europeans have often been sent to the trade store with a *pas*, and on presentation of the *pas* goods are handed over

[1] Compare Pos (1951), p. 561, and Van der Kroef (1957), p. 432, on the Biak-Numfor people of West New Guinea, who held that a missing page of the Bible showed that Christ and their ancestral culture hero Manarmakeri were one. See also Lawrence (1965), pp. 88–90, for an account of similar beliefs in Australian New Guinea.

[2] Compare Williams (1923, p. 29, and 1928, pp. 75–6) for examples of such behaviour in Papua.

the counter. Administration officers, missionaries and planters or traders who require replenishment of stores send letters and in due course the cargo arrives. No money is seen to change hands, no apparent exchange seems to take place, no goods are returned to the store; the cargo comes, is distributed, consumed, and more comes...Each transaction is accompanied by a letter. Letters set the whole process in motion.

Tangu associate a *pas* with action, with trouble, with the triggering of a fresh series of events...Though all know what is written on a *pas* is normally merely a substitute for an oral communication, there is also a feeling that a *pas* has an efficacy *sui generis*, which words do not have...Whatever kind of origin cargo might have, the *pas* is part of a cluster of techniques required to obtain it.[1]

Now in many parts of Melanesia this state of affairs has continued to the present day. That is to say, people have remained ill disposed to Europeans who they believe have cheated them in one way or another of the wealth they desire. Variants of the typical Cargo cult constantly emerge, despite the attempts of the administration and the missions to combat them with force, jailing, counter-propaganda, or persuasion, and despite the belated offers of economic and political concessions to the natives. And, as long as this kind of chiliastic world view prevails in the village, European-sponsored education has little objective value for the majority of the people, and literacy has a different meaning from that held by the foreigners.

Not all of the cult situations, however, have persisted unchanged. In some localities there have appeared gifted men who have tried to divert the energies and interests of the cult members into channels of 'secular' political and economic action in order to reach the commonly accepted goals of wealth and power. Generally, it seems that such radicals are unable to sway the populace at large and must aim instead at recruiting that minority which has become disenchanted by the inevitable failure of the cult rituals to produce the Cargo.

It is significant that in these circumstances there is once again a demand, albeit limited, for education (though preferably in administration and not in mission schools). But a different attitude appears towards literacy; now writing is appreciated as an everyday technique of recording important decisions and events so that information will not be lost or distorted but can be more or less reliably communicated among scattered supporters or preserved for posterity. Such a change is well brought out in the detailed account that Schwartz (1962) gives of the Paliau Movement among the Manus of the Admiralty Islands. He shows how Paliau (who by any stan-

[1] Compare Read (1958), p. 283: The Ngarawapum 'who conceived of (Christian) God as the provider of wealth,...also said that the Missionaries had not "opened the right road" to God. To these people, learning to read and write in English seemed vitally important. Book learning assumed the characteristics of ritual knowledge...'

dards is an impressive figure) strove to ameliorate the social and political conditions of his countrymen through plans that stressed hard work and the rational exploitation of the limited economic resources of the islands. At the same time he had to engage in a protracted and bitter struggle with men who saw the local manifestation of Cargo cult as the only solution of the people's problems. Paliau said of the cult leaders, 'Whatever I say, they distort,' and it is significant that throughout this contest he and his lieutenants made the secular use of literacy one of their most effective weapons, especially in exposing and combating the inherently ambiguous traditional forms of communication and of rabble-rousing through seances and dream interpretation. Thus, some men of his party not only recorded the laws that Paliau had devised for social action but also wrote in exercise-books the history (as distinct from a mythology) of the Movement so that their sons 'would know what they had done in the Movement'. This is a far cry from treasuring a *pas* because of its putative inherent power.

Few of the published accounts of Melanesian Cargo cults are as clear and unequivocal in crucial instances as those of Burridge (1960), Lawrence (1954, 1965) and Schwartz (1962). Nevertheless, on the basis of these analyses, I am emboldened to summarize my argument by suggesting that the following developmental sequence is general for Melanesia:

(1) The Europeans arrive to find an indigenous religious system that stresses the acquisition of wealth and ritualized communication with the supernatural.

(2) There is an initial native acceptance of Christianity as another road to the Cargo and of writing as an additional form of ritualized communication.

(3) The failure of Christianity to deliver the Cargo is followed by its rejection in favour of some variety of Cargo cult in which writing continues to be but one of several ritualized modes of communication.

(4) The failure of the Cargo cult to produce the Cargo leads some far-seeing men to devise a political and economic movement for change, in which writing regains its typically European secular status as a means of communication.

III

Although I believe that a scheme of this kind should be generally valid in Melanesia, it certainly does not appear to apply to analogous events in the Papuan (that is, non-Melanesian) societies of the highlands of Australian New Guinea. It is therefore worth while seeing in what respects the two situations differ.

It is true the religious systems of the highlanders resemble those of the coastal peoples in that both are epistemologically and metaphysically naive and simple, and both place great emphasis on the importance, even the primacy, of material benefits. But whereas on the coast there exists the notion of acquiring secret knowledge to coerce in a relatively mechanical way the supernatural beings, especially deities, into conferring success, wealth and power on man, in the mountains the aim more often is to propitiate or to bargain with spirits of the dead (recent or ancestral) in the hope that these might choose to help man, or at least not obstruct him, in his efforts to achieve wealth, prestige and the like. Indeed, in a sense, many highland religions do not really offer a substitute for ordinary skills and hard work in attaining certain culturally valued ends. At best the rituals try to avert undesirable supernatural hindrance of men's actions, and their performers would, I think, generally echo Cervantes' maxim that 'diligence is the mother of good fortune, and sloth, her adversary, never accomplished a good wish'.

At the risk of over-simplifying, then, we might regard the coastal religions as a kind of quasi-technology whose proper employment almost automatically guarantees success in any situation, whereas the highland religions are a kind of quasi-sociology, whose predictions are always dubious but whose value for the believer lies in providing *post facto* explanations of important social events. Connected with this broad difference is the fact that, although in both systems seances, divining, dream interpretation and other modes of sooth-saying are used to communicate with the supernatural, these are as a rule treated differently in each. On the coast they have to be seen as essentially ambiguous, otherwise the belief in mechanical constraint of the deities would leave no place for an explanation of the many observed failures of prediction. In the mountains, on the other hand, such devices need not be regarded as deceptive *per se*; the equivocation inheres in the ghosts, who act as human beings do and deliberately mislead the living when it suits them to do so.

As might be expected, starting from their initial contacts with European (especially mission) culture, the reactions of the highlanders were generally different from those of the coastal peoples. Certainly, in a few localities, soon after particular groups first received European commodities, first suffered alien epidemic diseases, or first encountered coastal native policemen and catechists, sporadic small-scale chiliastic cults or movements developed.[1] Sometimes these appeared before there was any serious exposure to mission teaching or even before any Europeans settled in the area. Moreover, some of these cults did not primarily seek wealth or power but rather

[1] Compare Berndt (1952), Salisbury (1958), and Reay (1959).

promised their followers health or at least protection from new diseases.[1] However, what is most indicative of highland pragmatism is the short lives of such cults. Usually they would flourish only for a few months; then, as no benefits were forthcoming in the prescribed season, they would simply wither. Rarely did their followers try to revive them after the first failure or two; instead people were likely to say, as Enga men have said to me, 'We were stupid to think that we could really acquire healthy pigs that way; everyone knows you must work to get pigs.'[2]

This is, of course, a very different situation from that described for Melanesia where, in some districts, despite all kinds of European opposition for fifty years or more, Cargo cults have appeared over and over in many guises. Here the native view seems to have been that, if events do not follow as predicted by the cult leaders, it is not the rituals that are at fault; rather the followers are in some way morally lacking or culpable. That is, there is no recognition of an empirical test of cult claims, as occurred in the mountains, so that the coastal cults never die but are merely transformed.

It is not surprising, then, that the ritualization of writing, which we observed on the coast, has not occurred in the highlands, either as part of the millenarian cults or in the ordinary responses of the natives to the educative attempts of both the administration and the Christian missions. Instead, the people have generally regarded literacy with enthusiasm as yet another empirical tool to be added to hard work and the exercise of shrewdness in the struggle to get ahead in life. Thus in 1957 in the Wabaga region of the Western Highlands district, when administration officers announced that schools would be built in the next year or so, Enga men from outlying clans walked for days to bring their sons to the patrol station for registration as students. None of them, as far as I could tell, believed that this would enable his son to learn a 'secret' whose mere possession gave some kind of automatic control over the supernatural or over wealth. On the contrary, these men, some of them rustics indeed, regarded literacy simply as a means of securing employment with Europeans so that, by displaying due diligence, a young man could become relatively rich and powerful.

Moreover, even before this episode, during a period when the Enga had access to only a few inadequate mission schools, young lads (rarely girls) were already being encouraged to put their sketchy knowledge of reading and writing in Pidgin English to practical use for their elders. Thus, at the great inter-clan exchanges of wealth, instead of using the

[1] Meggitt, unpublished field notes from the Western Highlands District of Australian New Guinea.

[2] Compare Berndt (1952, pp. 58, 65, 143), Salisbury (1958, p. 74), and Reay (1959, p. 199).

traditional tally sticks to mark their allocations of pigs and pork, men began to rely on their sons to record these transactions in penny notebooks bought from the mission trade stores.[1] Also, since this time (1956), a few of the young bachelors have been visiting the coast to work on contract for two years at a time in European copra and cocoa plantations, while others have enlisted in the police force and the army and have gone to coastal depots for training. It has become an important duty of the schoolboys to spell out the letters from these men to their fathers and senior agnates and to answer them. For instance, a record of letters to and from one clan (about 300 people) kept during a sample period of six weeks in 1960 revealed the following pattern:

	Married men			Bachelors			
	At highland patrol posts		In army on coast	Labouring on coast		In highland school	
	A	B	C	D	E	F	Total
Wife:							
Letters received	2	—	2	—	—	—	4
Letters sent	—	—	1	—	—	—	1
Lineage 'father':							
Letters received	1	—	1	—	1	1	4
Letters sent	—	—	1	—	1	1	3
Lineage 'brother':							
Letters received	1	1	—	1	—	—	3
Letters sent	—	1	—	1	—	—	2
Total:							
Letters received	4	1	3	1	1	1	11
Letters sent	—	1	2	1	1	1	6

I have read a number of these letters and have found them to be characteristically Enga in content, style and sentiment; they are prosaic and effective communications of information, giving facts, asking questions and offering advice.[2]

[1] Read (1965, p. 203) indicates an analogous state of affairs among the Gahuku-Gama of the eastern highlands, where men expected him to keep written records of important public transactions in case the details were later disputed.

[2] To indicate this flavour, I quote a short letter in Pidgin English that a young hospital orderly sent to a father's brother's son in his natal clan:

Januari 12. Dia barata Tal, nau mi mekim liklik tok long yu. Bipor Kirisimas mi tok long dispela pauli. Em bihain mi ikam long Sari na mi no savi, sapos bihain mi ikam long Sari orait mitupela iken tok. Na mi no ikam long Sari, orait mi inap salim pas. Bipor mi tok pinis mi tok long dispela pauli mama, na yu tok ino laik. Na mi tinktink palanti. Mi mekim gutpela tok long yu, na yu tasol tok ino laik. Na mi lusim. Na tok liklik. Em tasol. Nem bilong mi Pirei. Mi stap long Mambisanda.

An English translation follows:

Dear brother Tal, Now I am about to talk to you. Earlier, at Christmas, I talked about this fowl. Thus (I said): I do not know if later I shall come to Sari but, if I do visit

Here then is no cultic reliance on the Word as a mystic sign, no preoccupation with ritual manipulation of the equivocal and supernaturally potent *pas* of the kind noted in the syncretic and millenarian movements in Melanesia. This is rather the mundane use of writing, of words as such, to communicate shared meanings clearly through time and across space; and it is all of a piece with that pervasive pragmatism of the New Guinea highlanders which, in the opinion of a number of observers, helps to distinguish the mountain people as a whole from the coastal peoples.

IV

Finally, I should remark that merely to contrast the presence of a pragmatic world view among one people with its absence among another obviously does not go very far in explaining their different attitudes towards, and uses of, literacy. Unfortunately, however, we still do not know enough about the nature of the native societies in each region at the moment of European contact, nor about the subsequent course of events there, to be able to account in a convincing fashion for the observed present-day variations. And simply to assert without producing relevant data that crucial differences in ecological, economic, or political factors must have been responsible for the differential reactions to contact is to do no more than proclaim one's faith in these kinds of explanations.

Sari later, we two can then talk. However, if I do not come to Sari, then I can send you a letter. At the time I spoke definitely about (keeping) this hen, but you said you did not agree. I have been annoyed (by this). I spoke sensibly, but you merely said that you did not agree, and that you disposed of it (the hen). Now explain. That is all. My name is Pirei. I live at Mambisanda.

THE MEASUREMENT OF LITERACY IN PRE-INDUSTRIAL ENGLAND

Dr Schofield's paper also bears upon literacy in a modernizing world, but the world is that of pre-industrial England. His paper arises out of the research in the history of English social structure carried out in association with Laslett and Wrigley. His problem bears upon one which has cropped up several times in the course of this book, the problem of measuring literacy—how literate was (or is) any particular society? For labels such as 'widespread' or 'restricted' literacy are for many purposes only a second best. Schofield's essay is an attempt to suggest a comparative measure.

But he also comments upon the nature of literacy in England, reminding us how closely the extension of its techniques was tied in with religious and moral indoctrination, and also of the necessity, also mentioned by Tambiah, of considering reading and writing as separate skills; in England, as in some other pre-industrial societies, the ability to read was given first priority.

THE MEASUREMENT OF LITERACY IN PRE-INDUSTRIAL ENGLAND

by R. S. SCHOFIELD

In history, as in anthropology, literacy is an important differentiating characteristic between individuals, groups and cultures.[1] The anthropologists' distinction between the intellectual frameworks of literate and illiterate, or oral, societies has far-reaching implications for the historian of English history.

> In oral societies the cultural tradition is transmitted almost entirely by face-to face communication; and changes in its content are accompanied by the homeostatic process of forgetting or transforming those parts of the tradition that cease to be either necessary or relevant. Literate societies, on the other hand, cannot discard, absorb, or transmute the past in the same way. Instead, their members are faced with permanently recorded versions of the past and its beliefs; and, because the past is thus set apart from the present, historical enquiry becomes possible. This in turn encourages scepticism; and scepticism, not only about the legendary past, but about received ideas about the universe as a whole [Goody and Watt 1963: 344: see also above, p. 67].

It is perhaps too easy for an historian to assume that England since the middle ages has been a literate society, without pausing to enquire whether there has not also been a second culture, an oral culture, substantially unknown to history, because history is derived from written records and written records are produced by literate men. But if this were indeed so, several interesting historical questions arise. If many of the activities recorded in history, for example in politics, religion and literature, in which the *normal* means of communication were literate, were experienced by some only indirectly through the agency of others, then the question of the proportion of the population in this dependent situation, and of the identity and interests of the intermediary agents, becomes an important one for many kinds of historian. Equally a movement of large groups in society from an oral to a literate form of communication impinges on a wide range of historical studies.

Historians of literature are perhaps most of all concerned with the extent of the diffusion of literary skills, for both the nature and extent of the reading public are relevant to most of their work. The extent of the interest

[1] I am grateful to Mr P. Laslett and Dr E. A. Wrigley for their comments on an earlier draft of this chapter.

which political historians have in literacy, however, depends on how far they feel literacy to be essential to the development of political awareness. Those who believe that it is only through reading that the illiterate mass becomes aware of the values and aspirations of the privileged literate minority and thus of its own relative deprivation of power will clearly wish to consider any evidence of changes in the social diffusion of literary skills.[1] In religious history too, literacy has seemed relevant to historians concerned with the communication of religious ideas. Whereas in an illiterate society it is the character of the priesthood which determines the quality and diffusion of religious ideas, in a literate society, where there is also direct access to religious ideas through the press, the issue is less simple: were books or the clergy the more important in the dissemination of religious ideas? Did the eighteenth-century masses, for example, have direct access to the New Testament independently of what they were told of it by the clergy and, if so, did they derive any revolutionary social or religious ideas from what they read there? Finally, in economic history literacy would appear to be a relevant, if little discussed, factor. Today literacy is considered to be a necessary pre-condition for economic development; but the historian might well ask himself whether this was so in England at the end of the eighteenth century.[2]

Despite its relevance to many kinds of historical study, literacy does not feature very often in historical discussion, and when it does appear a certain vagueness surrounds its meaning. This vagueness is in part forced upon historians by the facts of history. Historically the situation has been complicated by the fact that although England has long been neither a wholly literate nor a wholly illiterate society, at least from the sixteenth century literacy was no longer confined to a caste educated in a foreign tongue, as is the case in several of the developing countries today, and the existence of a vernacular literature made the whole population potentially members of the literate culture merely for the price of learning to read. In such a situation it only needs one or two members of normally illiterate groups, who have acquired an ability to read, to read aloud to their friends and neighbours, for a bridge to be thrown across any supposed divide

[1] For an example of conflicting views in this subject see P. Laslett, *The World We Have Lost* (London, 1965), pp. 194–5; K. W. Deutsch, 'Social Mobilization and Political Development, *American Political Science Review*, LV, no. 3 (1961), pp. 493–514, and C. Hill, *History and Theory*, VI, no. 1 (1967), p. 124.

[2] The necessity of literacy as a pre-condition for economic growth is a persistent theme running through many UNESCO publications. Correlations between measures of industrialization and literacy both in the past and in the present are established in UNESCO, *World illiteracy at mid-century* (Paris, 1957), pp. 177–89. These measures are very general and throw no light at all on the question of why literacy should be considered essential to economic growth.

between exclusively literate and illiterate groups within society. Historical evidence of bridging of this kind is necessarily anecdotal, so it is difficult to say how frequently it occurred. Perhaps the most that can be said at present is that the evidence would appear to relate to occasions on which interest in a subject was particularly strong. For example at the time of the Reformation, when the Bible was first made available in the vernacular, one eyewitness wrote, '...imedyately after diveres pore men in the towne of Chelmsford...bought the Newe Testament of Jesus Christ, and on sundays dyd set redinge in the lower ende of the church, and many wolde floke about them to heare theyr redinge'. Indeed it may have been just this kind of bridging rather than universal literacy as is sometimes supposed which prompted Henry VIII and his ministers to restrict the reading of the Bible to the higher social orders (Nichols 1859: 349).[1] Numerous other examples of public reading can be found in the early nineteenth century, when news and politics rather than theology comprised the subject of interest. Workmen would take on additional work so that they could release one of their number to read to them while they worked; public houses would employ professional news-readers (Webb 1955: 33–4). In the home, too, the barrier between literate and illiterate might be broken down: 'My learned friend would make the stirring events of the week known to his household, in reading aloud the *Reading Mercury*' (Cranfield 1962: 188).

On the other hand there were probably groups in the population, such as agricultural labourers in certain parts of the country, which were entirely cut off from any contact with the literate culture. But there seems to be little doubt that there was a large area in which there was effective participation in the literate culture by essentially illiterate people. And it is because it is so difficult to define the extent of this participation that historians have avoided making any dichotomy between literate and illiterate sections of society, and have been very properly tentative in their discussion of literacy in general cultural terms.

Unfortunately historians have also made the problem worse for themselves by being imprecise as to what they mean by literacy. This has meant that the level of literary skills considered appropriate in any historical context has rarely been adequately specified. This is perhaps not surprising as it is seldom easy to decide what this level should be. For example, in a discussion of the role of literacy in the history of politics, is the ability

[1] 34 & 35 Henry VIII c. 1, ss. 10–13 prohibited all women other than gentle and noblewomen, together with artificers, journeymen, husbandmen, labourers, and servingmen of and under the degree of yeomen, from reading the Bible in English either privately or to others. Anyone else could read the Bible privately, and gentlemen and noblemen could have the Bible read aloud to their households. Under s. 8 the Bible could not even be read aloud in church in English without royal or episcopal permission.

to write relevant? or is the ability to read sufficient, and if so to what level? enough to understand a simple handbill, or the works of Locke? For economic history the difficulties are even greater. For example, any assessment of the relationship between literacy and industrialization entails decisions as to the levels of literary skills necessary to the introduction of new techniques in agriculture and a wide variety of industries on the one hand, and to the replacement of traditional patterns of consumption and the generation of a mass market demand on the other. At least for the English industrial revolution it would seem that these necessary levels of literary skills varied widely in different sectors of the economy. The meaning of literacy therefore changes according to the context, and it is the responsibility of the historian to specify the appropriate level of literary skills consistent with his understanding of the context.

Another consequence of the vague use of the concept of literacy in history has been that research on the extent of literacy has been conducted on a wide, and at times ill-defined, front. This has been most marked in the case of studies which present evidence of a literary or anecdotal kind. Here some contemporary comment as to the proportion able to read is taken as an indication of literacy, without any examination either of the representativeness of the observation, for example, the sex, status, and residence of the people concerned, or of the level of reading ability in question.[1] Unfortunately, systematic contemporary evidence of the level of different skills attained in various kinds of communities is only available from the early nineteenth century, when a growing concern for the deleterious social and moral effects of an imperfect educational system produced a rash of educational and moral surveys.[2]

A further consequence of the traditional unspecific notion of literacy is the tendency to be found mainly amongst literary historians and bibliographers to assume that the appearance of some new form of publication, or an increase in the volume of production of existing forms, was associated with an increase in the level of literacy. The historian of the provincial press in the eighteenth century, for example, writes that the great increase in the number of provincial newspapers between 1700 and 1760 'played no

[1] Perhaps the most frequently quoted observation of this kind is that of Sir Thomas More for the early sixteenth century: 'farre more than fowre partes of all the whole [people] divided into tenne coulde never reade englishe yet' (Wm. Rastell (ed.), *The English Works of Sir Thomas More* (London, 1557) p. 850).

[2] These are to be found mainly in the *Journal of the Statistical Society of London* and amongst the *Parliamentary Papers*. The best guide to this material and to the whole question of literacy in the early nineteenth century is R. K. Webb, 'Working Class Readers in Early Victorian England', *English Historical Review*, LXV (1950), pp. 333–51, and the first chapter of his book, *The British Working Class Reader, 1790–1848* (London, 1955).

small part in that growth of literacy that was so noticeable a feature of the period' (Cranfield 1962: vi). Unfortunately, two difficulties prevent any inference being drawn from changes in either the volume or the nature of literary productions to changes in the level of literacy. The first is that there is no necessary relationship between the volume of production and the size of the readership, because the number of readers per copy cannot be assumed to be constant either over time or between publications. The second is that changes in the volume of production may be influenced by many factors other than changes in the level of literacy: technological innovations, such as the printing press in the fifteenth century and the steam press in the early nineteenth century, changes in legal status such as the ending in the second half of the seventeenth century of the restrictions on the number of printers and distributors and on the size of editions, and finally changes in fiscal policy such as the many different rates of stamp duty charged on newspapers in the eighteenth and nineteenth centuries.

The third general approach to literacy that has been adopted in English history is the study of the facilities available for formal instruction in literary skills. While this approach also fails itself to provide reliable estimates of the level of literary skills actually attained, it is an essential part of any study of literacy because the structure of education probably largely determines the nature of literary skills that can be acquired and this is a most important element in the interpretation of any direct measure of literacy that may be adopted. On the other hand it is possible that informal instruction, whether by parents, parish officers or friends, was as important as the formal structure of education in the diffusion of elementary literary skills.[1] At present there is no means of evaluating this possibility, but it is a real one and must be borne in mind throughout the following discussion of the formal structure of education.

At least from the later middle ages public education was provided by the grammar schools, which taught pupils to read and write Latin together with enough grammar to enable them to be admitted to the universities. This system was a vocational one; it was designed to produce priests, although it also produced bureaucrats. Already, by the fifteenth century, it had been invaded by the gentry, who had no intention of becoming priests, but gained a sufficient skill in Latin to enable them to go on to the Inns of Court, rather than to the universities, where they acquired a knowledge of the common law which fitted them for public service and private advantage. The gentry were followed by others lower down the social scale who also took advantage of the ecclesiastical system of education,

[1] Evidence of informal instruction outside the family can be found amongst ecclesiastical visitation records.

but left at a stage appropriate to their needs. Often these could be minimal and, during the sixteenth century, there are to be found a number of 'petty' schools which taught the basic skills of reading, and writing once the art of reading had been mastered. In the late sixteenth century reading began to be taught on English texts rather than on Latin, but higher education remained tied to the classical languages.

This public grammar school system of classical education endured substantially unchanged until well into the nineteenth century. From the seventeenth century the grammar schools were supplemented by a number of private schools which taught a wider range of subjects; but these schools were expensive and were attended almost exclusively by the sons and daughters of the rich. The dearth of educational facilities for the poor by the end of the seventeenth century provoked anxiety about the social and moral consequences of an absence of instruction in the articles of the Christian faith. The remedy adopted was the charity school founded by subscription. Here the emphasis was on moral and religious instruction; manuals for teachers in these schools dealt with this part of the syllabus in detail and paid little attention to the teaching of reading and writing. As in the 'petty' schools, writing was taught only to those who could read 'competently well', and figures were taught only after the art of writing had been mastered. From the 1780s Sunday schools were founded to increase the opportunities for the moral education of the poor. In these schools emphasis was placed even more heavily on moral and religious instruction, and the only literary skill that was taught was a little reading. In the early nineteenth century educational facilities were greatly expanded by the foundation of many schools by the two rival societies which used the monitorial system, the National and the British and Foreign. Here the syllabus was again of an elementary kind. In the British and Foreign schools, the whole emphasis was on the instruction of elementary literary and numerical skills, while the National schools, which were founded largely in anxious reaction to the potentially seditious and morally ruinous effects of godless education, retained a measure of moral and religious education.

In the monitorial schools the same hierarchy of skills applied: reading was taught before writing, which in turn was taught before arithmetic. In the nineteenth century schools were also attached to institutions: the workhouse schools and the industrial schools. Children were meant to be released by their employers to attend the latter, but unwillingness on the part of both employers and children made attendance at these schools irregular. Both the industrial schools and the workhouse schools probably did little more than impart a faulty instruction in reading.

At all times there were also the dame schools, many of which enjoyed very short lives. These schools on occasion provided elementary instruction but often, and this was especially the case in the towns, they were little more than day nurseries.[1]

There are two main characteristics of this group of educational facilities which should be emphasized. The first is that instruction in different skills was so phased that reading was taught first, then writing, and lastly arithmetic. Given the variable length of time spent by children in school and the irregularity of their attendance, this meant that the ability to read was probably much more widespread than the ability to write. For example, the master in charge of the Borough Road School in London, which was the model school of the Lancastrian, later the British and Foreign system, reckoned that it took twelve months to teach a child to read and between three and four years to teach it to write well together with some simple arithmetic. The average length of attendance at this school, which itself was well above the general average, was thirteen months, enough to acquire an ability to read, but not to write well.[2]

The second feature common to all schools, other than the Sunday schools and some of the institutional schools, was that fees had to be paid, ranging from the modest fees of the dame schools to the heavy charges of the private academies. Despite the large number of schools ostensibly free, very few genuinely free places were available. Consequently, as a survey of education in Westminster in 1837–8 by the London Statistical Society showed, the length of time that a child stayed at school depended on the economic circumstances of its parents. Economic circumstances also affected the regularity of a child's attendance, the child being removed when employment offered, or when the parents' income was so reduced that they were unable to pay the fees. The same survey of Westminster showed that only one third of the children enrolled at school were to be found in attendance at any one time. For this reason figures of enrolment, when they are available, not only give an optimistic estimate of the amount of instruction being received, but also mask important social differences in school attendance.

Thus in so far as the level of literacy was determined by formal education,

[1] There is a large bibliography on the history of education. The following works have been found particularly helpful: J. Simon, *Education and Society in Tudor England* (Cambridge, 1966); W. A. L. Vincent, *The State and School Education 1640–1660* (London, 1950); M. G. Jones, *The Charity School Movement* (Cambridge, 1935); R. Webb, *British Working Class Reader* (London, 1955); R. Altick, *English Common Reader* (Chicago, 1963). This last book gives the best summary of the traditional approach to literacy in English history, avoiding most of the pitfalls discussed. Further valuable material for the early nineteenth century occurs in the *Journal of the Statistical Society of London* and the *Parliamentary Papers*.

[2] R. K. Webb, *The British Working Class Reader* (London, 1955), p. 17.

it is probable that it varied between different social and economic groups, and therefore probably also between different kinds of communities and regions. This is not an unwelcome possibility for the historian, for most historical discussions turn less on the overall level of literacy than on the level of certain groups and above all on the differences between them. The economic historian, for example, may be interested to learn whether the general level of literacy rose during industrialization, but he would find information on differences in literacy between occupational groups, and especially between communities which experienced industrialization and those which did not, much more illuminating. The historian, therefore, not only requires a measure of literacy, he also needs to be able to make comparative judgements.

The traditional approaches to literacy in the past, while they have provided indispensable general indications of the overall educational and cultural context, have failed to give historians adequate information on the many different levels of literary skills for which they would like information, although in the early nineteenth century they have come near to achieving this. They have also failed to provide evidence which enables comparative judgements to be made. Since the number of levels of literary skills on which historians would like information is so large, and since evidence which would satisfy one historian's requirements is likely to be useless for another's, it would seem to be more sensible as a matter of strategy for further research to attempt rather to meet the historians' other need, the ability to make comparative judgements between people, between social and economic groups, between regions, and between historical periods.

From this it follows that the actual level of literacy that is measured is relatively unimportant compared with the suitability of that level as a comparative measure. If such a measure can be found, historical comparisons between rates of literacy become possible. These comparisons will only be valid for the level of literary skills being measured, to be sure, and this level may well not correspond to the requirements of the individual historian; but at least there will exist an agreed body of comparative evidence to which the individual historian may relate his requirements, instead of having to make do, as at present, with a disputable body of unevaluable evidence.

To enable historical comparisons to be made, any measure of the diffusion of literary skills that is adopted must meet two conditions. First, it must be applicable throughout the country to people of a wide range of ages and economic and social conditions and over a long period of time. Second, it must also be standard as a measure from one person to the next, from one group to the next, from one region to the next, and from one historical period to the next.

These requirements are stringent and eliminate almost every body of historical evidence, including the reports of the Statistical Societies. These reports, which are superior to other evidence in almost every respect, are unfortunately available only for a short period in the early nineteenth century. But even if similar evidence were available for earlier periods it is worth while remarking that, as with the Statistical Society reports, it would be based on answers to questions rather than on direct tests of literary abilities. Like most modern investigations of literacy, the figures in these reports are measurements of people's opinions of their literary abilities, as expressed to strangers, and not direct evidence of the existence of these abilities.[1] The dangers of misrepresentation in such cases, especially where status is involved with the possession of literary skills, hardly need stressing. A measure of literacy should therefore not only be universal and standard, it should also be direct.

There is one test of literary skill which satisfies almost all the requirements of a universal, standard and direct measure, and that is the ability to sign one's name. Casual collections of signatures are clearly of no use for this purpose; but there have been occasions in the past when large numbers, or whole classes, of people were required to attest their approval of a document by signing their names if they could, or if they could not sign by making a mark.

These could be situations, analogous to a census, in which virtually everyone was required to attest his approval of a document. The two occasions on which this occurred in pre-industrial England were the Protestation Oath of 1642, which had to be taken by all males over the age of eighteen to the effect that they would 'maintain and defend the true Reformed Religion expressed in the Doctrine of the Church of England against all Poperie and Popish Innovations', and the Test Oath of 1723, promising allegiance to George I and renouncing the jurisdiction of the Pope, which had to be sworn by everyone over the age of eighteen.[2]

One other documentary source nearly achieves the universality of these sources by virtue of its being produced on an occasion that most people

[1] Most of the measures of literacy published by UNESCO are based on answers to questions. Techniques of measurement are discussed in UNESCO, *Progress of literacy in various countries* (Paris, 1953), and *World illiteracy at mid-century* (Paris, 1957).

[2] The Protestation Oath was required by an order of both houses of Parliament. Returns are in the House of Lords Record Office. The returns for several counties have been printed, e.g. *Surrey Archaeological Collections*, LIX (1962), pp. 35–68, 97–104. The 1723 Test Oath was required by the acts of parliament I George I c. 13 and 9 George I c. 24. Returns are usually to be found amongst the Quarter Sessions records in County Record Offices.

experienced at some point in their lives. This is the Anglican marriage register, which from 1754 contains entries of all marriages other than those of Jews, Quakers and members of the royal family.[1] This is because of an act of Parliament of 1753 which, with the exceptions already noted, accorded legal validity only to marriages registered in Anglican registers and signed by the parties and two witnesses.[2] In 1837 other denominations were licensed to register marriages and a state system of registration was begun (6 & 7 William IV c. 86). All registrations, however, had to be certified to the Registrar General, who collated them and published them in his *Annual Report* (1839 *et seq.*).

Several other historical sources relate to other occasions on which signatures and marks were systematically recorded, but none of these attains the near universality of the marriage registers. When the signatures and marks of only a part of the population are recorded, the evidence is only of value if it provides sufficient information about who has been included and who has been excluded, so that the restricted population recorded can be specified in a meaningful way. Presentments of jurors to manorial courts, for example, record the signatures and marks of the jurors but fail to specify the age and status of the jurors. Research usually reveals that the jurors were substantial tenants, but knowledge of the proportion of 'substantial tenants' able to sign their names is too unspecific to be of much relevance to most historians. The three best sources of this type, however, wills, allegations and bonds for marriage licences, and the deposition of witnesses in ecclesiastical courts, although clearly deficient in signatures and marks of the lower social orders, nevertheless provide valuable evidence, because they describe in meticulous detail the names, age, sex, occupation, marital status and residence of those who signed or made their marks. While, therefore, these sources cannot directly yield an overall estimate of the proportion of the population able to sign, they can provide reasonably good estimates of the proportions able to sign in the groups recorded in them, and these groups are specified in such a way, for example by occupation, that they are of relevance to historians.

There is therefore a fair range of sources which should provide a reason-

[1] A rough idea of the proportion of the population never marrying and thus escaping observation in the marriage registers is given by the proportion of the age group 50–54 that was still unmarried. In 1851 11 per cent of men and 12 per cent of women were unmarried in this age group. These figures do not represent exactly the proportions of men and women never marrying because, although over 99 per cent of all first marriages took place before either partner had reached fifty years of age, it was probably not the case at this period that the mortality of single people below the age of fifty was equal to that of married people ('1851 Census of England and Wales', *Parliamentary Papers* (1852–3), LXXXVIII, pt I, p. ccj; Registrar General of England and Wales, *Annual Report of Births, Deaths and Marriages* (1851–2), p. viij).

[2] 26 George II c. 33, usually known as Lord Hardwicke's Marriage Act.

able estimate of the proportion of people able to sign their name in the past, but there are also certain drawbacks to their use. The census-type documents, the Protestation Oaths of 1642 and the Test Oaths of 1723, suffer both from an imperfect geographical survival distribution and from a severe under-registration of women.[1] The survival of sources which record part of the population, that is wills, allegations and bonds for marriage licences, and depositions of witnesses in ecclesiastical courts, is also uneven not only geographically but also over time. The marriage registers, although comprising an almost perfect series, suffer from other disadvantages. First, they are not available before 1754. Secondly, they refer only to the marrying population. They will therefore give a bad estimate of the ability to sign if this should be in any way correlated with propensity to marriage, although control over this possibility is possible from other sources which record signatures and marks both of the married and of the single. Thirdly, the registers record the signatures of people as they get married, thereby providing figures heavily biased towards the age group between 20 and 29 years.[2] This may be an advantage for some historians, but others may require an estimate of the ability to sign based on a wider age range. Theoretically, a general estimate for any year could be constructed by combining the figures for previous generations in the appropriate proportions, but it is possible that the level of ability to sign between the ages of 20 and 29 may itself represent a decline from school-leaving standards, and that considerable further deterioration occurred with advancing age. Here, too, some control over this possibility should be available from other sources in which the age of signatories is given.

There are serious drawbacks of a different type affecting the use of the marriage registers, especially the allegation that the registers do not adequately represent the ability of the brides and grooms to sign their names because the solemnity of the occasion was such that the more timid among them made marks when they would ordinarily have signed their names. In assessing the weight of this allegation it should be remembered that it originates largely from clergymen in the nineteenth century who in turn were seeking to discredit accusations of the appalling inefficiency of elementary education under Church and private control. These accusations

[1] Women were not required to take the Oath of 1642. They were required to take the Oath of 1723, but the numbers recorded are deficient.

[2] In 1851, the first year for which information of sufficient quality is available, 73 per cent of all bridegrooms and 70 per cent of all brides were between 20 and 29 years old. A further problem lies in the double-counting of further marriages of widows and widowers, especially if the risk of widowhood and the propensity to remarriage prove to have been social-class-specific. In 1851, 14 per cent of the bridegrooms and 9 per cent of the brides were widowers and widows respectively (Registrar General of England and Wales, *Annual Report of Births Deaths and Marriages* (1851–2), p. viij).

came mainly from advocates of a state system of education, who used the proportion of marks to be found in the marriage registers to support their case.[1] Towards the height of the educational controversy a member of the Statistical Society of London estimated that the consensus of clergymen objecting to this use of the marriage-register evidence was that between 10 and 25 per cent of those who made marks could have signed their names if they had been encouraged to do so. He found no evidence of regional differences in this respect, and concluded that it was probably only in crowded city churches where marriages were rushed that the proportion of those able to sign but who failed to do so was higher than elsewhere (Sargant 1867: 80–137). These estimates come from parties interested in discrediting the figures based on the marriage-register evidence and for this reason they should not be accepted at their face value. If indeed men and women who could sign were hustled or awed into making a mark, this should be apparent in the registers in the form of firm marks made by a hand accustomed to holding a pen. Examination of several thousand marks suggests that the proportion made with a firm hand is nearer 1 or 2 per cent than 10 per cent, which is the lowest figure claimed by the clergy in the nineteenth century. Another objection to the use of the marriage-register evidence has been that brides in particular were likely to have made marks when they could well have signed out of a feeling of delicacy for their husband if they saw that he had been unable to sign his name.[2] In this case too a fair proportion of firm marks would be expected; but the number of brides making firm marks when their husbands made marks has been found to be small, and certainly no larger than the number of brides who attempted incompetent signatures even though their husbands had been content to make their marks. While, therefore, it undoubtedly happened on occasion that a man or woman who could sign made a mark in the marriage register, the empirical evidence suggests that this is unlikely to have more than the most marginal effect on any figures based on the marriage registers.[3]

[1] The Registrar General of England and Wales used his *Annual Report* to campaign for educational improvement on the basis of figures supplied by his own department. Articles on education using the Registrar General's marriage register figures abound in the *Journal of the Statistical Society of London.*

[2] Baker, when analysing the registers of some parishes in the East Riding of Yorkshire, found an old lady who averred that the bride was supposed to be too 'overcome' to be able to sign her name (W. P. Baker, 'Parish Registers and Illiteracy in East Yorkshire', *East Yorkshire Local History Society*, no. 13 (1961), p. 7).

[3] Yet another variant of the 'feigned mark' argument is contributed by the Superintendent Registrar for Cornwall in 1903, who claimed that it was 'not uncommon' for all parties signing the marriage including the witnesses, to feign illiteracy to save an illiterate bride or groom from embarrassment (*Notes and Queries*, 9th series, XI (1903), p. 294). It is difficult to know how to evaluate this claim, because marks are rarely to be found in the registers at this date, only about 2 per cent of men and women being unable to sign.

The census-type documents of 1642 and 1723, the marriage registers from 1754, and the wills, the allegations and bonds for marriage licences, and the depositions of witnesses in Church courts, both before and after this date, should therefore provide a direct measure of one level of literary ability under standard conditions over a wide range of people and groups, and over a long period of time. The bulk of evidence available is so large that sampling is the only possible method of analysis. The marriage registers are available for about 85 years for about 10,500 parishes.[1] Sampling by individual is out of the question, so a fully random sample of about 300 parishes has been drawn. Unexpected regional variations in ability to sign evident in the Registrar General's figures, and some interesting differences amongst parishes already analysed, have suggested a number of hypotheses to explain variations in the ability to sign during the later eighteenth and early nineteenth centuries, and it is expected that the random sample will provide sufficient data to allow these hypotheses to be adequately tested.

The quantity of evidence available in the collections of wills, allegations and bonds for marriage licences, and depositions is even more daunting. Here sampling can be by individual, but the uneven survival both geographically and over time, together with the fact that these sources refer to a socially unrepresentative cross-section of the population, severely restricts both the descriptive and the analytical value of the data they provide. None the less, it is believed that they will yield reasonable estimates of the ability to sign amongst a large number of social and economic groups in several regions, and that, in conjunction with the marriage registers for the later period and the two census-type documents for the earlier period, they may provide a standard measure of one level of literacy which will allow comparisons to be made over a wide range of people and groups over a long period of time.

This may be valuable in itself to some historians, but many will be more interested in other levels of literacy, for example, the number and identity of people who could read John Locke, the New Testament, a political handbill, or an advertisement, or how many could write a diary, accounts, or a political pamphlet. It is very difficult to relate abilities at different levels of literary skill, but a comparison of the evidence from the surveys carried out by the statistical societies in the early nineteenth century with figures published by the Registrar General gives some general idea of the relation between ability to sign on the one hand and ability to read and ability to write on the other (see above, p. 314, n. 2, and p. 320). This evidence is particularly difficult to interpret because the standards of ability to read

[1] Marriage registers continued to record signatures and marks after 1838–9, but from this date they are collated by the Registrar General and printed in his *Annual Report*.

and write measured in the surveys are often not specified in sufficient detail. In general, however, it would appear from these surveys that so far as the ability to write is concerned, fewer people claimed to be able to 'write' than could sign their names. So far as the ability to read is concerned, about half as many again as could sign their names claimed that they could read. Now, in most of these surveys ability to read was taken to imply a very low standard indeed, often no more than spelling through words. If, therefore, a measure of a minimum standard of reading is required, then the measure based on ability to sign will be too low, and will need inflating by almost 50 per cent. But if a measure of ability to read fluently is required, the evidence of the surveys would seem to corroborate the opinion of an educational inspector of the time that since ability to sign was roughly equivalent to being able to read fluently, a measure of the former provides a good indication of the latter.[1]

For the early nineteenth century, therefore, a measure based on the ability to sign probably overestimates the number able to write, underestimates the number able to read at an elementary level, and gives a fair indication of the number able to read fluently. This result is comparable with what is known of the structure of education, for the phasing of the curriculum so that reading was taught before writing, together with the intermittent nature of school attendance, will have ensured that large numbers of children left school having acquired some ability to read but little or no ability to write. Although there are no comparable survey figures for the period before the nineteenth century, the structure of education was basically the same at least from the sixteenth century, and it is therefore probable that the relationships between ability to sign, ability to read, and ability to write remained the same throughout this period. This disparity of attainment between reading and writing tends to disappear both in conditions of universal compulsory education and also when there is so little education available that it is acquired only by those who stay to the end of the course. In both these extreme conditions the measure of ability to sign gives a closer indication of ability to read and ability to write than in the intermediate situation which prevailed in England between the sixteenth and mid-nineteenth centuries.

It is hoped that further analysis of the early nineteenth-century survey material together with research on school curricula will enable the relation between the ability to sign and other literary skills to be specified more completely. Even if this were to prove unforthcoming, the historian will at least have acquired an agreed body of consistent data which allows

[1] J. Fletcher, 'Moral and Educational Statistics of England & Wales, *Journal of the Statistical Society of London*, x, p. 212.

him to make comparative judgements at one level of literacy. In the context of some historical questions, especially those of a general social or cultural nature, difficulties of interpretation may well outweigh the value of a standard measure of literacy. But there are many fields of historical enquiry in which the possibility of comparative judgement will be welcome after the paralysis that semantic disagreements have inflicted on the study of literacy in pre-industrial England.

BIBLIOGRAPHY

NOTE: All ISAR references are copies of manuscripts in the Arabic Collection, Institute of African Studies, University of Ghana.

'Abd al-Raḥmān al-Sa'di. *Ta'rīkh al-Sūdān*. (edn. and French trans. by O. Houdas). 1900. Paris.

Ahrens, W. (1917). Studien über die 'magischen Quadrate' der Araber, *Der Islam*, VII.

Aiyappan, A. (1945). *Iravas and Culture Change*. Madras.

Allman, G. J. (1911). Pythagoras, art. *Encycl. Brit.* 11th ed. New York.

Altick, R. (1963). *English Common Reader*. Chicago.

Ames, M. M. (1963–4). Magical-animism and Buddhism: a structural analysis of the Sinhalese religious system, in Aspects of Religion in South Asia (ed. E. B. Harper), *J. Asian Stud.* XXIII.

Anderson, J. N. D. (1954). *Islamic Law in Africa*. London.

(1955). Tropical Africa: Infiltration, Expanding Horizons, in *Unity and Variety in Muslim Civilization* (ed. G. E. von Grunebaum). Chicago.

Andrezejewski, B. W. and Lewis, I. M. (1964). *Somali Poetry*. Oxford.

Anon. (1960). *Madagasikara. Regards vers le passé* (Etudes malgaches. Hors serié). Tananarive: Université de Madagascar.

Al-asmā' al-'ulamā' Zāghā. Fonds Curtin, IFAN, Dakar, nos. 3, 23, 26.

Untitled work on the Diakhanke. Fonds Curtin, IFAN, Dakar, nos. 1, 27, 29.

Apfel, H. V. (1938). Homeric Criticism in the Fourth Century B.C. *Transactions of the Amer. Philological Assoc.* CXIX.

Arif, A. F. Hakima, A. M. (1965) *Descriptive Catalogue of Arabic Manuscripts in Nigeria*. London.

Asante, D. (1880–1). A new route to the upper Niger (ed. Beck), in *Geographische Gesellschaft zu Bern*, III.

Ayyar, Krishna K. V. (1938). The Book of Duarte Barbose, and The Voyage of Pyrard de Laval, in *The Zamorins of Calicut*. Cambridge (Hakluyt Society).

Baker, W. P. (1961). Parish Registers and Illiteracy in East Yorkshire, *East Yorkshire Local History Society*, XIII.

Barnes, J. A. (1947). The Collection of Genealogies, *Rhodes-Livingstone Journal: Human Problems in British Central Africa*, V.

Bartlett, F. C. (1923). *Psychology and Primitive Culture*. Cambridge.

(1932). *Remembering*. Cambridge.

Basham, A. L. (1954). *The Wonder that was India*. London and New York.

Bastian, A. (1860). *Der Mensch in der Geschichte*. Leipzig.

Ibn Baṭṭūṭa. *Voyages* (edn. and French trans. by C. Defremery and B. R. Sanguinetti 1922). 4 vols. Paris.

Becker, C. H. (1911), Materialien zur Kenntnis des Islam in Deutsch-Ostafrika, *Der Islam*, II.

Bérenger-Féraud, L. J.-B. (1879). *Les Peuplades de la Sénégambie*. Paris.

BIBLIOGRAPHY

Berndt, R. M. (1952–3). A Cargo Movement in the Eastern Central Highlands of New Guinea, *Oceania*, XXIII.

Bernus, E. (1960). Kong et sa Région, in *Etudes Eburnéennes*, VIII.

Berreman, G. D. (1963–4). Brahmins and Shamans in Pahari religion, in Aspects of Religion in South Asia (ed. E. B. Harper), *J. Asian Stud.* XXIII.

Berthier, H. (1953). *De l'usage de l'arabico-malgache en Imerina au début du XIXe siècle: le cahier de Radama I.* Tananarive: Académie malgache (Mémoires 16).

Binger, L. G. (1892). *Du Niger au Golfe de Guinée.* 2 vols., Paris.

Bishop, J. L. (1955–6). Some limitations of Chinese fiction, *Far Eastern Quart.* XV.

Bivar, A. D. H. and Hiskett, M. (1962). The Arabic Literature of Nigeria to 1804: A Provisional Account, *Bull. S.O.A.S.* XXV.

Blanchard *et al.* (1958). *Thailand, its People, its Society, its Culture.* HRAF Press, New Haven.

Blau, L. (1901). Amulet, *The Jewish Encyclopaedia* (ed. I. Singer), I. New York.

Bloch, M. E. F. (1967). *The significance of tombs and ancestral villages for rural Merina social organisation.* Ph. D. thesis, Cambridge.

Bluck, R. S. (1949). *Plato's Life and Thought.* London.

Boas, F. (1904). The Folklore of the Eskimo, *J. Amer. Folklore*, LXIV.

Bohannan, L. (1952). A Genealogical Charter, *Africa*, XXII.

Bowdich, T. E. (1819). *Mission from Cape Coast Castle to Ashantee.* London.

Boyer, G. (1953). *Un Peuple de l'ouest soudanais: les Diawara.* Dakar.

Braimah, J. A. and Goody, J. (1967). *Salaga: the Struggle for Power.* London.

Brocklemann, C. (1943–9). *Geschichte der Arabischen Litteratur* (2nd ed.). Berlin.

Burnet, J. (1908). *Early Greek Philosophy.* (2nd ed.). London.

Burridge, K. O. L. (1960). *Mambu, a Melanesian millennium.* London.

Caillié, R. *Travels through Central Africa to Timbuctoo* (English edn. of 1830). 2 vols. London.

Carcopino, J. (1935). *L'Ostracisme athénien.* Paris.

Carey, J. W. (1967). Harold Adam Innis and Marshall McLuhan, *The Antioch Rev.* XXVII.

Cassirer, E. (1953). *An Essay on Man.* New York.

(1955). *The Philosophy of Symbolic Forms.* New Haven.

Chadwick, J. (1958). *The Decipherment of Linear B.* Cambridge.

(1959). A Prehistoric Bureaucracy, *Diogenes*, XXVI.

CHEAM. (1957). *Carte des Religions de l'Afrique Noire: République de la Côte d'Ivoire.* Paris.

Cherniss, H. F. (1935). *Aristotle's Criticism of Presocratic Philosophy.* Baltimore.

Childe, V. G. (1941). *Man Makes Himself.* London.

(1942). *What Happened in History.* London.

Cook, R. M. and Woodhead, A. G. (1959). The Diffusion of the Greek Alphabet, *Amer. J. Arch.* LXIII.

Cornford, F. M. (1923). *Greek Religious Thought from Homer to the Age of Alexander.* London.

(1952). *Principium Sapientiae: The Origins of Greek Philosophical Thought.* Cambridge.

Coss, J. J. ed. (1924). *Autobiography of John Stuart Mill*. New York.
Cranfield, G. A. (1962). *The Development of the Provincial Newspaper*. Oxford.
Cumont, F. (1911). *The Oriental Religions in Roman Paganism*. Chicago.
(1912). *Astrology and Religion among the Greeks and Romans*. New York.
Cunnison, I. G. (1959). *The Luapula Peoples of Northern Rhodesia*. Manchester.
(1966). *Baggara Arabs*. Oxford.
Czarnowski, S. (1925). Le morcellement de l'étendue et sa limitation dans la religion et la magie, *Actes du Congrès international d'histoire des religions*. Paris.
Danielli, M. (1950). The state concept of Imerina, compared with the theories found in certain Scandinavian and Chinese texts, *Folk-lore*, LXI.
David-Neel, A. and Yongden, L. (1959). *The Secret Oral Teachings in Tibetan Buddhist Sects*. Calcutta.
Delafosse, M. (1910). Le Clergé Musulman de l'Afrique Occidentale, *Revue du Monde Musulman*, XI. Paris.
Deschamps, H. (1961). *Histoire de Madagascar* (2nd ed.). Paris.
Deschamps, H. and Vianes, S. (1959). *Les Malgaches du sud-est* (Monographie d'ethnologie africaine). Paris.
Deutsch, K. W. (1961). Social Mobilization and Political Development, *American Political Science Review*, LV, no. 3.
Diels, H. (1951). *Die Fragmente der Vorsokratiker*. Berlin.
Dieterlen, G. (1957). The Mande Creation Myth, *Africa*, XXVII.
Dieterlen, G. and Fortes, M. eds. (1966). *African Systems of Thought*. London.
Diringer, D. (1948). *The Alphabet: A Key to the History of Mankind*. London and New York.
(1962). *Writing*. London.
Dodds, E. R. (1951). *The Greeks and the Irrational*. Calif. Univ. Press.
Doutté, E. (1909). *Magie et Religion dans l'Afrique du Nord*. Algiers.
Dow, S. (1954). Minoan Writing, *Amer. J. Arch.* LVIII.
Driver, G. R. (1954). *Semitic Writing*. London.
Drower, E. S. (1943). A Mandaean Book of Black Magic, *J. Asiatic Soc.*
Dubois, F. (1897). *Timbuctoo the Mysterious*. London.
Dubois, H. (1938). *Monographie des Betsiléo*. Paris: Institut d'Ethnologie (Travaux et Mémoires, XXXIV).
Dubois, J. A. (1947). *Hindu Manners, Customs and Ceremonies*. Oxford.
Dumont, L. and Pocock, D. (1957). Village studies, *Contributions to Indian Sociology*, I. Paris.
Dupuis, J. (1824). *Journal of a Residence in Ashantee*. London.
Durkheim, E. (1897). *Le Suicide*. Paris.
(1915). *The Elementary Forms of the Religious Life*. (Trans. J. W. Swain), London.
(1933). *The Division of Labor in Society*. (Trans. G. Simpson), New York.
Durkheim, E. and Mauss, M. (1903). De quelques formes primitives de classification, *L'Année sociologique* (1901–1902). Paris.
Eggeling, H. J. (1911). Sanskrit, *Encycl. Brit.* (11th ed.). New York.
Ekvall, R. B. (1964). *Religious Observance in Tibet*. Chicago.

Ellis, W. (1838). *History of Madagascar*, I. London.
Equiano, O. (1967). *Equiano's Travels* (1st ed., London, 1789). London.
Evans-Pritchard, E. E. (1934). Lévy-Bruhl's Theory of Primitive Mentality, *Bulletin of the Faculty of Arts, University of Egypt*, II.
(1937). *Witchcraft, Oracles and Magic Among the Azande*. Oxford.
(1940). *The Nuer*. Oxford.
(1948). *The Divine Kingship of the Shilluk of the Nilotic Sudan* (The Frazer Lecture). Cambridge.
Fallers, L. A. (1961). Are African Cultivators to be called 'Peasants'?, *Current Anthrop.* II.
Farrington, B. (1936). *Science in Antiquity*. London.
Faublée, J. (1967). Brève note sur les manuscrits malgaches en caractères arabes, *Bulletin de l'Académie Malgache*, XLII (1965).
Fernandes, V. (1951). *Description de la Côte Occidentale d'Afrique* (ed. Th. Mondo, A. Teixeira da Mota, R. Mauny). Bissau.
Ferrand, G. (1891). Les Musulmans à Madagascar et aux îles Comores. *Publication de l'école des lettres d'Alger, Bulletin de Correspondance Africaine*, IX.
(1905). Un chapitre d'astrologie arabico-malgache d'après le manuscrit 8 du fond arabico-malgache de la Bibliothèque Nationale de Paris, *Journal Asiatique*.
(1936). Madagascar, *Encyclopedia of Islam*. London.
Finley, M. I. (1954). *The World of Odysseus*. New York.
ed. (1959). *The Greek Historians*. New York.
Finot, L. (1959). Laotian Writings, *Kingdom of Laos* (ed. Berval). Limoges.
Flacourt, E. de (1658). *Histoire de la Grande isle de Madagascar*. Paris.
Fletcher, J. Moral and Educational Statistics of England and Wales, *Journal of the Statistical Society of London*, X.
Fortes, M. (1944). The Significance of Descent in Tale Social Structure, *Africa*, XIV.
(1945). *The Dynamics of Clanship among the Tallensi*. London.
Fortes, M. and Evans-Pritchard, E. E., eds. The Nuer of the Southern Sudan, in *African Political Systems*. London.
Francis, J. de (1950). *Nationalism and Language Reform in China*. Princeton.
Frazer, J. G. (1918–19). *Folklore in the Old Testament*. London.
Freedman, M. (1958). *Lineage Organization in South-east China*. London.
(1966). *Chinese Lineage and Society*. London.
Freeman, R. A. (1892). A journey to Bontuku, in the interior of West Africa, *Royal Geographical Society*, Suppl. papers, III, p. 2.
Freeman-Grenville, C. S. P. (1962). *The East African coast; select documents from the first to the earlier nineteenth century*. Oxford.
Froelich, J. C. (1962). *Les Musulmans d'Afrique Noire*. Paris.
(1966). Essai sur les causes et méthodes de l'Islamisation, in *Islam in Tropical Africa* (ed. I. M. Lewis). London.
Gallieni, J. S. (1885). *Voyage au Soudan Français*. Paris.
Gandz, S. (1935). Oral Tradition in the Bible, *Jewish Studies in Memory of George A. Kohut* (ed. Salo W. Baron and Alexander Marx). New York.
Gautier, E. P. (1902). Notes sur l'écriture Antaimoro, *Publication de l'école des lettres d'Alger, Bulletin de Correspondance Africaine*, XXV.

Gelb, I. J. (1952). *A Study of Writing*. Chicago.
Ghurye, K. G. (1950). *Preservation of Learned Tradition in India*. Bombay.
Gluckman, M. (1949–50). Social Beliefs and Individual Thinking in Primitive Society, *Memoirs and Proceedings of the Manchester Literary and Philosophical Society*, XCI.
(1954). *Rituals of Rebellion in South-East Africa* (The Frazer Lecture, 1952). Manchester.
Goode, W. J. (1951). *Religion among the Primitives*, Glencoe, Illinois.
Goody, J. (1954). *The Ethnography of the Northern Territories of the Gold Coast West of the White Volta* (mimeo). London.
(1957). Anomie in Ashanti?, *Africa*, XXVII.
(1961). Religion and Ritual: The Definitional Problem, *Brit. J. Soc.* XII.
(1962). *Death, Property and the Ancestors*. Stanford and London.
(1964). The Mande and the Akan Hinterland, *The Historian in Tropical Africa* (ed. J. Vansina *et al.*). London.
(1965). Introduction, Ashanti and the North-west, *Research Review* (I.A.S., Legon), Suppl. I.
(1967). The Over-kingdom of Gonja, *West African Kingdoms in the nineteenth century* (ed. D. Forde and P. Kaberry). London.
(1969). Marriage Policy and Incorporation in Northern Ghana, *From Tribe to Nation in Africa* (ed. R. Cohen and J. Middleton). San Francisco.
(1968). The Social Organisation of Time, *Int. Encyclopaedia of the Social Sciences*. New York.
Goody, J. and Mustapha, T. (1966). Salaga in 1874, *Research Review* (I.A.S., Legon), II, 2.
Goody, J. and Watt, I. (1963). The Consequences of Literacy, *Comparative Studies in Society and History*, V.
Gopalan, A. K. (1951). *Kērala, Past and Present*. London.
Gough, K. (1959). Cults of the Dead among the Nayars, *Traditional India: Structure and Change*. (ed. M. Singer) Amer. Folklore Soc., Philadelphia.
(1963). Indian Nationalism and Ethnic Freedom, *Concepts of Freedom in Anthropology* (ed. D. Bidney). Paris.
(forthcoming). Kerala Politics and the 1965 Elections, *The International J. Soc.*
Graham, A. (1912). *Siam: A Handbook of Practical, Commercial, and Political Information*. London.
Grandidier, A. and G. (1908). Ethnographie, in A. Grandidier, *Histoire physique naturelle et politique de Madagascar*. Paris.
Granet, M. (1934). *La Pensée chinoise*. Paris.
(1959). *Chinese Civilization*. New York.
Gray, W. S. (1956). *The Teaching of Reading and Writing: An International Survey, Unesco Monographs on Fundamental Education*, X. Paris.
Greene, W. C. (1951). The Spoken and the Written Word, *Harvard Stud. in Class. Phil.* LX.
Griaule, M. (1951). *Signes graphiques soudanais* (L'homme, cahiers d'ethnologie, de géographie et de linguistique, III). Paris.
Guiart, J. (1962). *Les Religions de l'Oceanie*. Paris.

Gurney, O. R. (1952). *The Hittites*. London.
Guthrie, W. K. C. (1962). *A History of Greek Philosophy*, I. Cambridge.
Al-Ḥājj Muḥammad b. al-Muṣṭafā. *Kitāb Ghunjā*. IASAR/10–13; 62; etc. Manuscript chronicle of Gonja affairs.
Al-Ḥājj Muḥammad Saghanughu. *Al-jawāhir wa'l-yawāqīt, fī dukhūl al-Islām fī'l-Maghārib ma'ā 'l-tawqīt*. MS in the author's library, Bobo-Dioulasso. English trans. by Ṣalāḥ Ibrāhīm, IASAR/246 (tr).
Ta'rīkh 'Ilm and *Ta'rīkh al-Islām fī Būbū*. Two MSS in the author's library, Bobo-Dioulasso.
Halbwachs, M. (1925). *Les Cadres sociaux de la mémoire*. Paris.
(1925). Mémoire et société, *L'Année sociologique* (3e série), I. Paris.
(1950). *La Mémoire collective*. Paris.
Hallowell, A. I. (1937). Temporal Orientations in Western Civilisation and in a Preliterate Society, *Amer. Anthrop.* XXXIX.
Hastings, J., ed. (1898–1904). *A Dictionary of the Bible*. New York.
Havelock, E. A. (1963). *Preface to Plato*. Cambridge, Mass.
Hébert, J. C. (1961). Analyse structurale des géomancies comoriennes, malgaches et africaines, *J. Soc. Afr.* XXXI.
(1965). La cosmographie malgache suivie de l'énumération des points cardinaux et l'importance du nord-est, *Taloha I. Annales de la faculté des lettres*, Université de Madagascar.
Henle, P. (1958). *Language, Thought and Culture*. Ann Arbor, Mich.
Hill, C. (1967). *History and Theory*. London.
Hiskett, M. (1957). Material relating to the state of learning among the Fulani before their Jihād, *Bull. S.O.A.S.* XIX.
ed. (1963). *Tazyīn Al-Waraqāt*. By 'Abdullāh b. Muḥammad, Ibadan.
Hodgkin, T. (1966). The Islamic Literary Tradition in Ghana, in *Islam in Tropical Africa* (ed. I. M. Lewis). London.
Hogbin, I. (1958). *Social Change*. London.
Holden, J. J. (1966). Note on the Education and Early Life of Al-Ḥājj 'Umar Tall, *Research Rev.* (I.A.S., Legon), II, 2.
Hone, J. (1942). *W. B. Yeats*. London.
Hulme, T. E. (1941). *Reflections on Violence*. New York.
Hunwick, J. O. (1964*a*). A new source for the biography of Aḥmad Bābā al-Tinbuktī, Bull. S.O.A.S., XXVII.
(1964*b*). The Influence of Arabic in West Africa, *Trans. Hist. Soc. Ghana*, VII.
(1966). Further light on Aḥmad Bābā al-Tinbuktī, *Research Bulletin*, Centre of Arabic Documentation, Ibadan, II, 2.
Ingalls, D. (1959). The Brahman Tradition, *Traditional India: Structure and Change* (ed. M. Singer). Amer. Folklore Soc., Philadelphia.
Inglis, Judy (1957). Cargo Cults: the Problem of Explanation, *Oceania*, XXVII.
Innes, C. A. (1908). *Malabar and Anjengo*. Madras.
Innis, H. A. (1950). *Empire and Communications*. Oxford.
(1951). Minerva's Owl, *The Bias of Communication*. Toronto.
International Institute of Intellectual Co-operation (1934). *L'Adoption universelle des caractères latins*. Paris.

Iyer, Ananthakrishna L. K. (1912). *Cochin Tribes and Castes.* Madras.
Jacoby, F. (1923). *Die Fragmente der Griechischen Historiker*, I, *Genealogie und Mythographie.* Berlin.
(1949). *Atthis.* Oxford.
Jaeger, W. (1939). *Paiedeia.* Oxford.
(1947). *The Theology of the Early Greek Philosophers.* Oxford.
Jarvie, I. C. (1963). Theories of Cargo Cults: a Critical Analysis, *Oceania*, XXXIV.
Jeffery, L. H. (1961). *The Local Scripts of Archaic Greece.* Oxford.
Jones, M. G. (1935). *The Charity School Movement.* Cambridge.
Julien, G. H. (1908). *Institutions politiques et sociales de Madagascar.* Paris.
(1929, 1933). *Pages arabico-madécasses. Histoire, légendes et mythes* (3rd series). Paris.
Kenyon, F. G. (1951, 2nd ed.). *Books and Readers in Ancient Greece and Rome.* Oxford.
Kirk, G. S. and Raven, J. E. (1957). *The Presocratic Philosophers.* Cambridge.
Klausner, J. (1964). Popular Buddhism in Northeast Thailand, *Cross-Cultural Understanding* (ed. Northrop and Livingston). New York.
Kosambi, D. D. (1966). *Ancient India.* New York.
Kramer, S. N. (1948). New Light on the Early History of the Ancient Near East, *Amer. J. Arch.* LII.
Krehl, H. W. (1864). Der Talisman James Richardson's, *Dritter Jahresbericht des Vereins von Freunden der Erdkunde zu Leipsig.* Leipsig.
Kyerematen, A. A. Y. (1964). *Panoply of Ghana.* London.
Lande, D. de (1959). *Relación de las cosas de Yucatán.* Mexico.
Lane, E. W. (1871). *An Account of the Manners and Customs of the Modern Egyptians* (5th ed.). London.
Lanternari, V. (1965). *The Religions of the Oppressed.* New York.
Laslett, P. (1965). *The World We Have Lost.* London.
Lawrence, P. (1954). Cargo Cult and Religious Belief among the Garia, *International Archives of Ethnography*, XLVII.
(1965). *Road Belong Cargo.* Manchester.
Lawrence, P. and Meggitt, M. J., eds. (1965). *Gods, Ghosts and Men in Melanesia.* Melbourne.
Leach, E. R. (1958). Primitive Time-Reckoning, *A History of Technology* (ed. C. Singer, E. J. Holmyard and A. R. Hall). Oxford.
Leared, Arthur (1876). *Morocco and the Moors.* London.
Lee, D. D. (1938). Conceptual Implications of an Indian Language, *Philosophy of Science*, V.
(1959). Codifications of Reality: Lineal and Non-lineal, *Freedom and Culture.* Englewood Cliffs, New Jersey.
Lee, Mrs S. R. (1854). *African Wanderer.* London.
Leo, John (Africanus) (1600). *A Geographical Historie of Africa* (trans. John Pory). London.
Lévi-Strauss, C. (1962). *La Pensée sauvage.* Paris.
Levtzion, N. (1966). Early nineteenth century Arabic manuscripts from Kumasi, *Trans. Hist. Soc. Ghana*, VIII (1965).
(1968). *Muslim and Chiefs in West Africa.* Oxford.

Lewis, I. M. (1955–6). Sufism in Somaliland: A study in Tribal Islam—I and II, *Bull. S.O.A.S.* XXVII; XXVIII.

(1958). The Gadaburse Somali Script, *Bull. S.O.A.S.* XXI.

(1961). Force and Fission in Northern Somali Lineage Structure, *Amer. Anthrop.* LXIII.

(1962). Historical Aspects of Genealogies in Northern Somali Social Structure, *J. African Hist.* III.

(1965). *The Modern History of Somaliland.* London.

(1966). Conformity and Contrast in Somali Islam, *Islam in Tropical Africa.* London.

(1968*a*). From Nomadism to Cultivation: the Expansion of Political Solidarity in Southern Somalia, *Man in Africa* (ed. P. Kaberry). London.

(1968*b*). Conflict and Cohesion in the Horn of Africa, *Tribalism and Transition in East Africa* (ed. P. Gulliver). London.

Lewis, O. (1955). Peasant Culture in India and Mexico: a Comparative Analysis, *Village India* (ed. M. Marriott). Chicago.

(1958). *Village Life in Northern India.* Urbana, Illinois.

Logan, W. (1951). *Malabar.* Madras.

Lord, A. B. (1960). *The Singer of Tales.* Cambridge, Mass.

McDiarmid, J. (1953). Theophrastus on the Presocratic Causes, *Harvard Stud. in Class. Phil.* LXI.

McDonald, E. E. (1965–6). English education and social reform in late nineteenth century Bombay, *J. Asian Stud.* XXV.

McLuhan, M. (1964). *Understanding Media.* New York.

McNeill, W. H. (1962). *The Rise of the West.* Chicago.

Madden, R. R. (1837). *Twelve Month's Residence in the West Indies.* London.

Maḥmūd Kāti, *Ta'rīkh al-fattāsh* (edn. and French trans. O. Houdas and M. Delafosse, 1913). Paris.

Malinowski, B. (1922). *Argonauts of the Western Pacific.* London

(1925). Magic, Science and Religion, in *Science, Religion and Reality* (ed. J. Needham). New York (Reprint ed. *Magic, Science and Religion*, 1954, New York).

(1926). *Myth in Primitive Psychology.* London.

(1936). The Problem of Meaning in Primitive Languages, *The Meaning of Meaning* (ed. C. K. Ogden and I. A. Richards). London.

Marriott, M., ed. (1955). *Village India: Studies in the Little Community.* Chicago.

Marrou H.-I. (1948). *Histoire de l'éducation dans l'antiquité.* Paris.

Martin, B. G. (1965). Summary of a Report on a Conference on Arabic Documents, University of Ghana, Feb., 1965, *Research Bulletin* (Centre of Arabic Documentation, Inst. of African Studies, University of Ibadan), I, 3.

Marty, P. (1921). *L'Islam en Guinée, Fouta-Diallon.* Paris.

(1922). *Études sur l'Islam en Côte d'Ivoire.* Paris.

Mauny, R. (1961). *Tableu géographique de l'ouest africain au moyen age.* Mém. de l'IFAN, no. 61. Dakar.

Mayne, J. D. (1892). *A Treatise on Hindu Law and Usage* (5th ed.). London.

Mead, M. (1943). Our Educational Emphases in Primitive Perspective, *Amer. J. Soc.* XLVIII.
Menon, Padmanabha K. P. (1929). *History of Kērala.* Ernakulam.
Menon, Sreedhara A. (1962). *Kērala District Gazetteers, Trivandrum.* Trivandrum.
Merton, R. K. (1957). Manifest and Latent Functions, *Social Theory and Social Structure* (rev. ed.). Glencoe, Illinois.
Meyer, P. C. (1897). *Erforschungsgeschichte und Staatenbildungen des Westsudan,* Supplement No. 121 to *Petermanns Mitteilungen.* Gotha.
de Mézières, A. Bonnel (1949). Les Diakanke de Banisiraila et du Bondou Meridional, *Notes Africaines,* 41.
Mill, J. S. (1861). *Considerations on Representative Government.* London.
Mills, H. C. (1955–56). Language reform in China, *Far Eastern Quart.* XV.
Miner, H. (1952). The Folk-Urban Continuum, *Amer. Soc. Rev.* XVII.
(1953). *The Primitive City of Timbuctu.* Princeton.
Moellendorff, W. *See* Wilamowitz-Moellendorff.
Mondain, G. (1910). *L'Histoire des tribus de l'Imoro au XVIIe siècle d'après un manuscrit historique Arabico-Malgache,* Publication de la Faculté des Lettres d'Alger, XLIII.
Monteil, Ch. (1932). *Une Cité Soudanaise, Djénné.* Paris.
(1953). La légende du Ouagadou et l'origine des Soninké, *Mélanges Ethnologiques.* Dakàr.
(1965). Notes sur le Tarikh es-Soudan, *Bull. de l'I.F.A.N.,* B, XXVII.
Moorhouse, A. C. (1953). *The Triumph of the Alphabet.* New York.
Morley, S. G. (1946). *The Ancient Maya.* Stanford.
Nadel, S. F. (1951). *The Foundation of Social Anthropology.* London.
(1954). *Nupe Religion.* London.
Nagel, E. (1961). *The Structure of Science.* London.
Namboodiripad, Sankaran E. M. (1967). *Kērala Yesterday, Today and Tomorrow.* Calcutta.
Needham, J., (1954). *Science and Civilization in China.* Cambridge.
Niane, D. T. (1960). *Soundjata ou l'épopée Mandingue.* Paris.
Nichols, J. G., ed. (1859). Narratives of the Days of the Reformation, *Camden Society.* London.
Nietzsche (1900). The Use and Abuse of History, in *Thoughts out of Season,* (trans. A. Collins). Edinburgh.
(1909). *Beyond Good and Evil.* Edinburgh.
Notopoulos, J. A. (1938). Mnemosyne in Oral Literature, *Transactions of the Amer. Philological Assoc.* LXIX.
(1949). Parataxis in Homer: a New Approach to Homeric Literary Criticism, *Transactions of the Amer. Philological Assoc.* LXXX.
Obeyesekere, G. (1962–3). The great tradition and the little in the perspective of Sinhalese Buddhism, *J. Asian Stud.* XXII.
O'Leary, de L. (1939). *Arabic Thought and its Place in History* (rev. ed.). London
(1948). *How Greek Science Passed to the Arabs.* London.

INDEX

22-2

Barthema, Ludovico, 279
Bartlett, F. C., 30, 30 n.
Basham, A. L., 73, 82
Bedouin, the, 31
Berbers, the, 238
Berreman, G. D., 15
Berthier, H., 286
Betsileo, the, 285, 297
Bible, the, 41, 137, 211, 298, 302, 303, 313 n.
New Testament, 312–13, 323
Old Testament, 31, 40, 230, 236 n.
Binger, L., 167, 190, 193, 200, 208 n., 209, 210, 217 n., 231 n.
blood-money, *see DIA*
Boas, Franz, 34
Bohannan, L. and P., 31 n., 32, 274 n.
Bole, 13
Bonduku, 166, 184, 186–7, 189, 193, 197, 210
books, 6, 6 n., 11–12, 12–13, 14, 15–16, 37, 40, 41, 52, 55, 135, 156, 205, 216–19, 229, 236 *et seq.*, 241, 262, 284, 295
the Book, 298–9
Book of God, 16, 19
Holy Book, 17, 222, 226
Magic Book, 17, 19
Malayālam books, 139
Religions of the Book, 2, 9, 132
see also literature, libraries, etc.
bookkeeping, *see* accounts
Bornu, *see* Hausa
Bowdich, T. E. 201, 202–3
Brahmans, the, 12, 15, 70, 74, 132, 139–45, 149, 154, 229
the Brahmi script, 89
see also Nambūdiri Brahmans, the
Braimah, J. A. 211
bricoleur, 296
British, the, 142, 210, 286
colonial administration, 32, 33, 135, 155, 167
rule, 133, 151, 212
and Foreign schools, 316–17
see also England and English
Bronze Age, 67
Buddhism, 5, 7–8, 15 *et seq.*, 24, 71, 74, 75, 78, 80, 85, 86–131 *passim*, 231
Buna, 162, 163, 164, 176, 189, 210
bureaucracy, 2, 21, 23, 37, 71, 74, 79, 80, 81, 84, 133, 208 n., 315
see also administration, centralization, etc.
Burma, 88, 90
burnūs, the, 169–70, 170 n., 179
Burridge, K. O. L. 303, 305

Cabala, the Jewish, 5, 229
cabalistic diagrams, 233
Cairo, 213, 218, 222, 231, 236, 261–4
Calicut, 132, 138, 147
Cambodia, 88, 90
capitalism, 69, 80, 83, 157
Cardanus, *Practica Arithmeticae*, 229
Cargo cults, 25, 298, 300–5, 307
cartography, *see* maps
Cassirer, Ernst, 43
castes, 12, 25, 70–1, 81, 191, 312
a caste of genealogists, 12
castes in Kērala, 132, 134–5, 139–41, 144–5, 148–51, 152, 154, 157
see Brahmans, Kshattriyas, etc.
categories of understanding, 52–4, 60
Catholic, Roman, 6, 136–9 *passim*, 148, 157, 237
Cervantes, 61, 306
census, 2, 321
centralization, 37, 41, 79, 285, 288
see states
ceremonies, 144–5, 150, 228 n., 230
see ritual, festivals, etc.
Ceylon, 7–8, 90
Chaldean, 18, 26, 236
Chan Kom, 6–7, *see* Redfield, R.
chants, 99, 105, 107, 118, 122, 130–1
charms, magical, 122, 129, 136, 149, 201–3, 227, 235 n., 282, 285
see spells, magic, etc.
Cheng Ch'iao, 24
Chēra, 133
see Kērala
Chicago school, the, 6–9
chiefs and chiefship, 33, 190, 199, 201, 202, 207, 211 *et seq.*, 234 n., 240
Ch'ien Hsüan-t'ung, 23
Ch'in, 21, 23, 71
China, 4, 8, 16, 19, 20–24, 45, 60, 70–84 *passim*, 132, 153, 231, 265, 274, 297
Chinese civilization, 8 n., 36
Chinese writing, 20–24, 35 n., 60, 69
Chōla, 71, 133
Christianity and Christians, 2–3, 18, 227, 229, 267 n., 286, 302–3, 305, 316
Christians, 17, 132, 136, 136 n., 152, 157, 218–19, 220, 262, 281, 307
see also missionaries
chronology and chronicles, 75, 143, 240
chronological, 34, 74, 86
chronicles, 132, 152, 214, 219, 242, 284
see also history
Ch'ü Ch'iu-pai, 23
cities, *see* urbanism
civilization
modern, 6, 55
Chinese, 8 n., 72
Greek, 42–3, 216

INDEX

Ong, W. J. (1965). Oral Residue in Tudor Prose Style, *P.M.L.A.* LXXX.

Oppenheim, A. L. (1964). *Ancient Mesopotamia.* Chicago.

Ortega y Gasset, J. (1959). The Difficulty of Reading, *Diogenes*, XXVIII.

Palmer, H. R. (1928). *Sudanese Memoirs*, I. Lagos.

Panikkar, K. (1960). *A History of Kērala, 1498–1801.* Annamalai University, Annamalainagar.

Pao, M. S. A. (1957). *Social Change in Malabar.* Bombay.

Paques, V. (1954). *Les Bambara.* Paris.

Park, M. (1799). *Travels in the interior districts of Africa.* London.

(1815). *Journal of a Mission to the interior of Africa.* London.

Park, R. (1938). Reflections on Communication and Culture. *Amer. J. Soc.* XLIV.

Parliamentary Papers, LXXXVIII (1852–3): 1851 Census of England and Wales.

Parry, M. (1930). Studies in the Epic Technique of Oral Verse-making, I: Homer and Homeric Style, *Harvard Stud. in Class. Phil.* XLI.

(1932). Studies in the Epic Technique of Oral Verse-making, II: The Homeric Language as the Language of an Oral Poetry, *Harvard Stud. in Class. Phil.* XLIII,

(1951). *Serbo-Croatian folk-song; texts and translations of seventy-five folk songs from the Milman Parry collection, and a morphology of Serbo-Croatian folk melodies*, by B. Bartok and A. Lord; with a foreword by G. Herzog (Col. Univ. Studies in Musicology, VII). New York.

(1953). *Serbo-Croatian heroic songs* (collected by M. Parry, ed. and trans. A. B. Lord), I. Cambridge, Mass.

Parsons, T. (1966). *Societies: Evolutionary and Comparative Perspectives.* New York.

Pearson, L. (1939). *Early Ionian Historians.* Oxford.

Peters, E. (1960). The Proliferation of Segments in the Lineage of the Bedouin of Cyrenaica, *J. Roy. Anthrop. Inst.* XC.

Phillpotts, B. (1931). *Edda and Saga.* London.

Piggott, S. (1959). Conditional literacy, *Approach to Archaeology.* London.

Plato, *Phaedrus* (trans. R. Hackforth, 1952). Cambridge.

Polanyi, K. (1957). Aristotle Discovers the Economy, in *Trade and Market in the Early Empires* (ed. K. Polanyi, C. M. Arensberg and H. W. Pearson). Glencoe, Illinois.

Pos, H. (1951). The Revolt of Manseren, *Amer. Anthrop.* LIII.

Pothan, S. G. (1963). *The Syrian Christians of Kērala.* London.

Powdermaker, H. (1933). *Life in Lesu.* New York.

Radin, P. (1926). *Crashing Thunder: the Autobiography of an American Indian.* New York.

(1927). *Primitive Man as Philosopher.* New York.

Rastell, W., ed. (1557). *The English Works of Sir Thomas More.* London.

Rattray, R. S. (1913). *Hausa Folk-lore.* Oxford.

(1932). *Tribes of the Ashanti Hinterland.* 2 vols. Oxford.

(1934). Hausa Poetry, *Essays Presented to C. G. Seligman* (ed. E. E. Evans-Pritchard). London.

Read, K. E. (1958). A 'Cargo' Situation in the Markham Valley, New Guinea, *Southwestern Journ. Anthrop.* XIV.

(1965). *The High Valley.* New York.

Reay, M. (1959). *The Kuma.* Melbourne.

Redfield, R. (1934). *Chan Kom, a Maya Village.* Washington, D.C.

(1941). *The Folk Culture of Yucatan.* Chicago.

(1950). *A Village that Chose Progress: Chan Kom Revisited.* Chicago.

(1953). *The Primitive World and its Transformations.* Ithaca, New York.

(1955). *The Little Community.* Chicago.

(1956). *Peasant Society and Culture.* Chicago.

Registrar General of England and Wales (1839 *et seq.*). *Annual Report of Births, Deaths and Marriages.*

(1851–2). *Annual Report of Births, Deaths and Marriages.*

(1903). Annual Report of Births, Deaths and Marriages in *Notes and Queries*, 9th ser. XI.

Reisman, D. (1956). The Oral and Written Traditions, *Explorations*, VI.

(1956). *The Oral Tradition, the Written Word and the Screen Image.* Yellow Springs, Ohio.

Rhys Davids, T. W. (1881). *Buddhist Suttas, The Sacred Books of the East* (ed. F. Max Muller), XI. Oxford.

Richards, A. (1967). African systems of thought: an Anglo-French dialogue, *Man*, II.

Richards, I. A. (1932). *Mencius on the Mind.* London.

Renouard, G. C. (1836). Routes in North Africa by Abu Bekr es Siddik, *J. R. Geog. Soc.* VI.

Russell, A. D. and 'Abdullāh Suhrawardy (1963). *First steps in Muslim Jurisprudence.* London.

Ruud, J. (1960). *Taboo: A study of Malagasy customs and beliefs.* London.

Salisbury, R. F. (1958). An 'Indigenous' New Guinea Cult, *Kroeber Anthropological Society Papers*, XVIII.

Sandys, J. E. (1921). *A History of Classical Scholarship.* Cambridge.

Sargant, W. L. (1867). On the Progress of Elementary Education, *Journ. Statistical Society of London.*

Sāstri, Nilakanta K. A. (1955). *A History of South India from Prehistoric Times to the Fall of Vijayanagar.* Oxford.

Schacht, J. (1950). *The Origins of Muhammadan Jurisprudence.* Oxford.

Schwartz, T. (1962). The Paliau Movement in the Admiralty Islands 1946–54, *Anthropological Papers, American Museum of Natural History*, XLIX.

Shih, H. (1922). *The Development of the Logical Method in Ancient China.* Shanghai.

Sidibé, M. (1959). Les gens de caste ou nyamakala au Soudan français, *Notes Africaines*, LXXXI.

Simon, J. (1966). *Education and Society in Tudor England.* Cambridge.

Singer, M. (1959). Preface to *Traditional India: Structure and Change* (ed. M. Singer). Amer. Folklore Soc. Philadelphia.

Skinner, G. W. (1964–5). Marketing and social structure in rural China, pts. I, II and III, *J. Asian Stud.* XXIV.

Smith, M. F. (1954). *Baba of Karo, a Woman of the Muslim Hausa.* London.
Smith, P. (1965). Les Diakhanke: Histoire d'une dispersion, *Bulletins et Mémoires de la Société d'Anthropologie de Paris*, XI sér., VIII.
Smith, W. Robertson, (1889). *The Religion of the Semites.* London.
Sow, Alfā Ibrāhīm (1966). *La Femme, La Vache, et la Foi.* Paris.
Spengler, O. *The Decline of the The West* (trans. C. F. Atkinson 1934). New York.
Srinivas, M. N. (1959). Foreword to A. M. Shah and R. G. Shroff, The Vahīvancā Bāroṭs of Gujerat: A Caste of Genealogists and Mythographers, *Traditional India: Structure and Change* (ed. M. Singer). Amer. Folklore Soc., Philadelphia.
(1966). *Social Change in Modern India.* California.
Staal, J. F. (1962–3). Sanskrit and Sanskritization, *J. Asian. Stud.* XXII.
Starr, C. G. (1961). *The Origins of Greek Civilization.* New York.
Surrey Archaeological Collections, LIX (1962).
Swift, J. *Gulliver's Travels* (ed. A. E. Case, 1938). New York.
Tait, D. (1961). *The Konkomba of Northern Ghana.* London.
Tauxier, L. (1921). *Le Noir de Bondoukou.* Paris.
Taylor, A. E. (1943). *Aristotle.* London.
Thompson, J. E. S. (1950). *Maya Hieroglyphic Writing.* Washington.
Thompson, J. W. (1940). *Ancient Libraries.* Berkeley.
Thorndike, L. (1905). *The Place of Magic in the Intellectual History of Europe.* New York.
Thrupp, Sylvia, ed. (1962). *Millennial Dreams in Action.* The Hague.
Tolstoy, L. *War and Peace* (trans. Louise and Aylmer Maude, 1942). New York.
Tomlinson, H. H. (1954). *The Languages and Peoples of Gonja.* MS.
Trimingham, J. S. (1959). *Islam in West Africa.* London.
Turner, R. E. (1941). *The Great Cultural Traditions.* New York.
al-'Umarī, *Masālik al-abṣār fī Mamālik al-Amṣār.* French trans. by Gaudefroy-Demombynes. 1927. Paris.
UNESCO (1953). *Progress of literacy in various countries.* Paris.
(1957). *World illiteracy at mid-century.* Paris.
Valentine, C. A. (1963). Social Status, Political Power and Native Responses to European Influence in Oceania, *Anthropological Forum*, I.
della Valle, Pietro. *The Travels of Pietro della Valle in India* (ed. E. Grey, 1942). New York.
Van der Kroef, J. M. (1957). Patterns of Cultural Change in Three Primitive Societies, *Social Research*, XXIV.
Vincent, W. A. L. (1950). *The State and School Education 1640–1660.* London.
Voegelin, C. F. and F. M. (1961). Typological Classification of Systems with Included, Excluded and Self-sufficient Alphabets, *Anthropological Linguistics*, III.
Von Dobschütz, E. (1910). Charms and amulets (Christian), art., *Encyclopaedia of Religion and Ethics* (ed. J. Hastings). London.
Waddell, L. (1895). *The Buddhism of Tibet.* London.
Warmington, E. H. (1934). *Greek Geography.* London.
Webb, R. K. (1950). Working Class Readers in Early Victorian England, *Engl. Hist. Rev.* LXV.

(1955). *The British Working Class Reader, 1790–1848*. London.

Weber, M. *Essays in Sociology* (trans. H. H. Gerth and C. Wright Mills 1946). New York.

The Protestant Ethic (trans. T. Parsons 1930). London.

The Theory of Social and Economic Organisation (trans. A. M. Henderson and T. Parsons 1947). New York.

Westermarck, E. (1933). *Pagan Survivals in Mohammedan Civilization*. London.

Whorf, B. L. (1941). Languages and Logic, *Technological Review*, XLIII, reprinted in *Language, Thought and Reality*, Selected Writings of Benjamin Lee Whorf (1956). New York.

(1941). The Relation of Habitual Thought and Behavior in *Language, Culture, and Personality, Essays in Memory of Edward Sapir*, Menasha, Wis., (ed. L. Spier), reprinted in Whorf, *Language, Thought and Reality*.

Wilamowitz-Moellendorff, U. von (1919). *Platon*. Berlin.

Wilhelm, R. and Baynes, C. F. (1951). *I Ching*, or *Book of Changes*, 2 vols. London.

Wilks, I. (1961). *The Northern Factor in Ashanti History*. Legon.

(1962). The Mande loan element in Twi, *Ghana Notes and Queries*, IV.

(1963). The Growth of Islamic Learning in Ghana, *J. Hist. Soc. Nigeria*, II.

(1966*a*). The Saghanughu and the Spread of Māliki Law: a provisional note, *Research Rev.* (I.A.S., Legon), II, 3.

(1966*b*). The position of Muslims in metropolitan Ashanti in the early nineteenth century, *Islam in Tropical Africa* (ed. I. M. Lewis). London.

(1966*c*). A Note on the Arabic MS IAR/298 and others from Wa, *Research Review* (I.A.S., Legon), II, 2.

(1967). Abū Bakr al-Ṣiddīq of Timbuktu, in P. D. Curtin, *Africa Remembered*, Univ. Wisc. Press.

The Mossi and Akan States, 1600–1800, in *A History of West Africa* (ed. J. F. A. Ajayi and M. Crowder). London, (in press).

Williams, F. E. (1923). *The Valaila Madness and the Destruction of Native Ceremonies in the Gulf Division*, Port Moresby: Territory of Papua Anthropology Report No. 4.

(1928). *Orokaiva Magic*. London.

Wilson, G. and Wilson, M. (1945). *The Analysis of Social Change*. Cambridge.

Wilson, J. A. (1949). Egypt, *Before Philosophy* (ed. H. Frankfort and others). London.

Winternitz, M. (1927). *A History of Indian Literature*. Univ. of Calcutta.

Woolley, L. (1953). *A Forgotten Kingdom*. London.

Worsley, P. (1957). *The Trumpet Shall Sound*. London.

Yeats, W. B. (1955). *Autobiographies*. London.

Yūsuf b. Imām Jābi Kasamba. Untitled MS known locally as *Ta'rīkh al-Madaniyyu*, IASAR/451.